TLC

2005 The Low Countries

ARTS AND SOCIETY IN FLANDERS AND THE NETHERLANDS

The Low Countries

8

ARTS AND SOCIETY IN FLANDERS AND THE NETHERLANDS

Flemish-Netherlands Foundation 'Stichting Ons Erfdeel'

ontents

Chronicle

Architecture

Cultural Policy

Society

Visual Arts

B orn
to Die

Simon de Passe, *Vanitas: Memento Mori*. 1612. Copper engraving, 27.4 x 33.7 cm.

Boymans-van Beuningen Museum, Rotterdam.

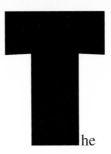he

Medieval Way of Death

It requires a considerable effort to grasp the fact that our drives and patterns of behaviour are subject to time and place; that even the most deeply-felt emotion is no given, but a component of the socio-historical process with a story of its own to be told. Quite literally, every aspect of everything is forever changing; and our outlook on mortality and our attitude towards the final hour is no exception.

In modern western society a certain display of resistance as a reaction to dying is almost taken for granted. Commoner still are anger and aggression at the apprehension, or certainty, of imminent death. Resignation in the face of mortality is now the prerogative of very few, and then only when they have reached extreme old age. Latterly television has also become crucial to the issue by leading and stage-managing a broad-based, emotion-charged media offensive in our own living-rooms. Increasingly the experience of death is moving into the secular, public arena, as often as not at the victim's own vociferous insistence that all the world should spiritually participate in his or her terminal throes.

It becomes less and less easy to comprehend that an actual yearning for death was quite widespread in the late Middle Ages. All the same, the origins of this spiritual orientation are not hard to identify. Christianity teaches that one's true life begins only after death. Hence death betokened no more than the culmination, even the fulfilment, of life. It offers the opportunity, to be grasped with thankfulness, to redeem the pressing burden of guilt called life; to cross the threshold into the solace of eternal rest. Above all, death heralded man's reunion with his Creator. For the nuns of the convents of the Modern Devotion, for example, this moment could scarcely come soon enough. In the *sisterbooks*, the biographies they have left us, they describe how they would all gather around the deathbed of a fellow-sister and engage the expiring woman in talk for as long as possible. They did this in the hope that she might in her last gasps share with them whatever she could glimpse of what lay on the other side of the door. *'Behold, it comes,'* cries out Alijt Comhaer with all her might when the end is upon her. Riveted, the sisters one and all hang on her lips. And as her final words, *'Father, into thy hands I commend my spirit,'* ring out, her companions are

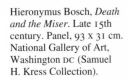

Hieronymus Bosch, *Death and the Miser*. Late 15th century. Panel, 93 x 31 cm. National Gallery of Art, Washington DC (Samuel H. Kress Collection).

11

reassured that it is He indeed on whom her eyes now rest. The invocation of the last words of Jesus was the customary formula with which the dying indicated their resolution to follow His path to God the Father.

The company of a coffin

It was not uncommon for people to go around in a perpetual transport of such anticipatory ecstasy over the rewards of the life to come that they lost

Pieter Bruegel the Elder, *The Triumph of Death* (detail). c.1562. Panel, 117 x 162 cm. Musea del Prado, Madrid.

Dirk Bouts, *The Fall of the
Damned.* 15th century.
Panel, 115 x 69.5 cm.
Musée des Beaux-Arts,
Lille.

all notion of propriety about keeping their impatience for greater glory to
themselves. Contempt for the world as a cesspool of sin and the devil's own
playground was, of course, as old as Christendom itself. Towards the end of
the Middle Ages, however, this defeatist approach to the bodily and the natural began to take on freakish proportions. This development was undoubtedly linked to the emergence of a counter-movement which grew rapidly
from the twelfth century on. This school took its inspiration from a (re)dis-
covery of the natural and the delight in living this entailed. Was not earth, it
argued, equally home to Eden? True enough, man had not had access to that
since the fall, but that did not alter the fact that the garden of delights remained the fount of the countless bounties which, borne upon the four par-
adisal streams, flowed ceaselessly over the earth. The backlash provoked by
the emergence of this challenge was an asceticism which was phenomenal
in its anathematisation of all earthly matter as the embodiment of the
world's everlasting perdition as a result of man's fall from grace.

Popular preachers roamed far and wide to bellow forth against the flesh-ly horror in which the soul resides. A fouler bag of corruption than the human body could scarcely be conceived; yet here – amid stench, slime, pus, urine, faeces, sperm and lustful blood – the soul languished in banishment on earth, thanks to man's sin. Verily the beauty our senses perceived was but an illusion; especially that of woman in all her outward semblance of seductive charm. Proof of this was that one had but to scratch the skin to discover that this fair exterior held nothing but swinish decay. And, we must not forget, man crawls into the world amidst excrement and other abominations. Clearly, this stinking, lascivious body was best brought to heel through mortification of the flesh by flagellation and starvation.

The female body, the devil's favourite instrument of beguilement, was of course the principal target that needed to be deconstructed into its true, intrinsic state of corruption. The *Biënboek*, a popular collection of exemplary anecdotes after an original Latin text by Thomas of Cantimpré, relates in graphic detail the revolting experiences of a certain Guido, a priest. A beautiful woman inflamed his lust for no less than three years, and then continued to do so even after her death. Perceiving that the devil would not cease to thus torment him, he '*surreptitiously one night disinterred the woman from her grave and then rubbed his nose and countenance in the filth of the half-decayed corpse for so long that he was well-nigh overcome by the unbearable stench*'. After this he proved to be completely cured of his fleshly desires.

Maximilian III of Austria, the first Habsburg ruler of the Low Countries and an unabashed exponent of the good life, towards the end reinvents himself as one who to the very last has sought to keep the blandishments of the flesh firmly in hand. Having throughout a fully-lived life committed said flesh to the service of every joy of God's creation, he determined, once he had had his fill of pleasure and the true life beckoned, that henceforth all memory of this disgusting rubbish dump of a body should be erased. In his testament he stipulates that his earthly remains should not be embalmed. In the interim, wherever he went he would be accompanied by a bare oaken coffin containing no more than a coarse-textured shroud and quicklime to be placed in his mouth, ears and eyes the moment he perished. For a full three years the Emperor travelled his domains thus equipped, his funerary paraphernalia '*always so disposed within his bedchamber as were it his dearest treasure*'.

By the end of the Middle Ages this kind of excoriation of the corporeal becomes almost grotesque. The *Ridderboek*, for example, an edificatory work for daily instruction published in the Brussels region in about 1400, proclaims the human body, constructed as it is of mire, to be nothing but '*foul, stench-ridden matter which originates as seed so loathsome that man is nauseous of it by nature, even in the telling of it. This seed is nourished within the stinking vat that is the body, so that the child, once born, is sorrowful and tearful. From then on the body is racked by worms, inside and out. Everything it touches is caused to stink: a mass of inner beastliness gushes from every orifice. To see this for oneself one need look no farther than what seeps out from ears, mouth, nose and other body parts*'.

The invention of purgatory

Contemporaneously an avalanche of works designed to guide the faithful towards a seemly end begins to appear. The *Artes Moriendi* were essentially step-by-step instructions on how to enter into heaven's rewards without mishap. Conservative forces were evidently so worried by the rival trend of extolling the joys of earthly life that they felt it could never be impressed enough on the flock that the earthly delights we see all around us derive without exception from the devil's deceitful machinations. But the burgeoning clarion call for life would not be quelled. Indeed, its protagonists now turned to an equally assertive tone of bellicosity; but directed against death, a death which was presented as mankind's most savage adversary. Most often he is personified as a fleshless skeleton clutching a scythe or other sharply-pointed weapon, with a nasty grin hovering about his cadaverous jaws.

Hatred of death reached a climax in 1482 when Mary of Burgundy, as athletic as she was beautiful, died after a fall from her horse. A collective hysteria, not unlike the world-wide horror at the death of Princess Diana, broke out. Public grief over the duchess' death finds expression in, among other things, a sorrow-laden street ditty in which Death himself is personally blamed for this harrowing tragedy. Out of simple callousness, or more likely plain envy of so much blossoming vitality, he has snapped this tender life's thread, just like that. The entire text is a passionate plaint over the inhumanity of Death, deliberate destroyer of felicity at its loveliest. Accordingly, the song opens by calling the malefactor to account: '*Oh Death, Death, Death, sparer of none, / What harm have you now done!*'

An image which became a favourite of the time exemplified the struggle against Death as a formal pitched battle. Man, of course, can never win.

Nonetheless, as long as he is armed with the proper virtues, he still has much to gain: he can prolong his allotted span on earth, and he can notch up credits for the life eternal. The often lavishly illustrated texts on this theme depict a frustrated Death frantically hopping in circles around an erstwhile frail and puny mankind transformed into a mighty warrior astride a prancing *destrier*, goading his adversary like a bullfighter taunting the bull. At the same time Death's irrevocability also increasingly becomes the subject of a more personal regret. Why-oh-why should we leave for another land? '*Ah, this life is so sweet! / Why must I die, I entreat/ When crafty Death creeps nigh/ Then must I to that other land hie!*'

In time the movement advocating joy in the earthly life, which despite its spoliation as a result of the fall was after all still God's creation by origin and nature, acquired theological justification in the construct of purgatory. Humankind's desire to delight in the world, it was argued, should not be hampered by fear of spending the true life to come in everlasting hell. It was to resolve this issue that the Paris theologians, in the twelfth century, dreamed up purgatory as heaven's antechamber.

Master of Spes Nostra, *Allegory of Mortality.* Early 16th century. Panel, 88 x 104.5 cm. Rijksmuseum, Amsterdam. The last line next to the grave reads: '*I am what you will be; what you are, I have been. I beg you: pray for me.*'

In fact, the concept was not entirely novel. Vague notions of some kind of waiting-room or prelude to the last judgement, a place which was neither heaven nor hell, had been around from the earliest days, though its exact function, name and location had never been established. Now that they had been, theology found itself with a satisfactory solution to long-simmering, disquieting problems such as: exactly how good did a soul have to be to be certain of heaven, or how bad to be certainly cast into hell? And what about those who were neither good nor bad – where did they go? The theologians worked out a perfect arrangement. A soul would spend a certain time in purgatory, where it would be punished by special, purpose-designed means until it was cleansed, the exact duration depending on the sins committed and on how much sin its surviving relatives could redeem by way of prayer, masses and the like. Once purified, the soul could then pass straight through the open gates of heaven. The really good thing about purgatory was that forward was the only way out.

Despite this, all late medieval mortality doctrine is particularly alert to the dangers of taking too much pleasure in life. If one hopes with excessive ardour for a prolonged earthly sojourn, then clearly this must be due to the devil's inveigling. And so we come full circle, with the advantages of death now couched in a new set of metaphors: '*Death is but an escape and release from the dungeon, an end to banishment, and liberation and deliverance from a heavy burden, that is the body.*' We must therefore meet Death, be he expected or not, with gratitude, '*or at the very least with equanimity, without any grumbling or protest, but under all circumstances with cheerfulness, even if it be that the flesh and earthly desire resist and shrink from him*'.

Around 1500 such dicta were common currency, not only through the countless editions and reprints of lay handbooks to mortality, but also through the influence of itinerant preachers. But what they really show is above all the extent to which the desire for death had been superseded by an inextinguishable joy in life espoused at all levels of the community. And it is this philosophy that we have inherited, however much our modern 'solutions' for acceptance of an inevitable demise might differ from theirs. Or could it be that the doctors of today have taken over from the medieval priests?

HERMAN PLEIJ
Translated by Sonja Prescod.

BIBLIOGRAPHY

ARIÈS, P., *The Hour of Our Death*. New York, 1981.
DUBY, G., *De middeleeuwse liefde en andere essays*. Amsterdam, 1990.
GUES, B. DE (ed.), *Een scone leeringe van salich te sterven*. Utrecht, 1985.
HUIZINGA, J., *The Autumn of the Middle Ages*. Chicago, 1996.
LE GOFF, J., *The Birth of Purgatory*. London, 1984.
PLEIJ, H., *Nederlandse literatuur van de late Middeleeuwen*. Utrecht, 1990.

rom

Midwife to Caesarean

Confinement and Beyond in Flanders

Since the beginning of time, the events surrounding childbirth have always
been women's work; and things were no different in Flanders. Sixty years
or so ago, giving birth at home with the help of a midwife was still the most
normal thing in the world. Only when there were serious complications was
it considered necessary to take the woman to hospital – no simple matter in
those car-less days. Bringing a child into the world, or helping to do so, was
the domain of women. And it was a mysterious domain, for men often
a frightening one. Births often took place at night, and mother and midwife
unleashed forces which in the eyes of many men appeared abnormal and
sometimes even supernatural. Because of the link with these mysterious
forces, women were in the past regarded as unclean after giving birth. This
delusion persisted for a very long time: right up until the middle of the twentieth century, new Flemish mothers underwent 'churching' to purify themselves again. This involved them going to church with their baby a few
weeks after the birth; after the Mass, the priest came for them and took them
to the altar of Our Lady. The young mother offered a burning candle and the
priest blessed mother and child. Only when this ritual had taken place did
women resume their place in public life.

Today, both Our Lady and the midwife have all but disappeared from the
scene during pregnancy and childbirth in Flanders. Childbirth has also lost
its supernatural aura, because science has laid bare practically all the secrets
of birth. Giving birth has become a medical event, for which the majority of
women go into hospital. Ensuring that everything goes well demands not so
much on blessings and rituals as on experienced doctors and gynaecologists,
sophisticated technical equipment and medicines.

A few figures: in 1998 62,222 children were born in Flanders – the lowest figure in absolute terms since the Second World War. A Flemish woman
has an average of 1.4 children, whereas an average of 2.1 is needed to keep
the population stable. Flemish women are having fewer and fewer children,
and are also having them increasingly late in life: at present the average age
for a woman to have her first child is around 27.3 years, but more and more
women are delaying having their first child until after their thirtieth birthday.
A great many women now devote their earlier years to their career: the per-

centage of women aged between 25 and 34 on the Flemish labour market has never been as high as it is today. Almost all women (94%) are supported during their pregnancy almost exclusively by a private gynaecologist; the GP is involved only occasionally (3.0%), whilst midwives have virtually disappeared from the scene (0.4%). Almost all Flemish children are born in a maternity unit: less than 1% of women choose to give birth at home. Flemish women spend an average of 6.3 days in the maternity ward – a very long time compared with the period of anything from a few hours to one day that a British woman spends in her maternity unit. Births are artificially induced in three out of ten Flemish women. Inducing labour is a very popular practice in Flanders and takes place in two-thirds of all cases, to suit the convenience of the parents or the gynaecologist. One child in six (15.2%) comes into the world via a Caesarean operation. The number of Caesarean sections has increased by 50% in the last ten years. One possible explanation for this could be that gynaecologists are afraid of the legal consequences if something goes wrong during a difficult birth. Rather than using forceps or suction cups, doctors tend instead to opt for a Caesarean. The Flemish medical journal *Artsenkrant* recently predicted that within a few years Caesarean sections will become the norm and vaginal birth the exception. Like the number of Caesarean sections, the number of painless births has also increased by 50% in the last ten years. In 1998 more than half of all women (55%) opted for a painless birth by means of an epidural anaesthetic. More and more women are justifying their decision by comparing it to a visit to the dentist, where anaesthetics are taken for granted.

In short, pregnancy and birth have become largely 'medicalised' in

Confinement in a birthing stool. Plate from Jacob Rueff's *De conceptu et generatione homini* (1587).

Flanders as in other countries during the last fifty years. Or, to quote a doctor: '*Women no longer* give *birth in a hospital; they are taken through the birthing process. Gynaecologists are mainly concerned with the technical aspects and less with the experience of the childbearing woman.*' A great many women are perfectly happy with this course of events and prefer the artificial to the natural. There is also no doubt that medical intervention and technological developments have saved a great many lives. And yet there are also women who do not feel comfortable with this approach and who see it as regrettable that a hospital delivery takes place more to the rhythm of the doctors and the technology than to that of mother and child. A small number of women are therefore trying to regain control of their pregnancy and the birth: they seek out a gynaecologist who shares their views and discuss their wishes with him in advance. The drawing up of a detailed birth plan is much less common in Flanders than in the UK; women who roll up with a 'shopping list' are quickly labelled 'difficult' by doctors and nurses. A small number of women opt to give birth at home, supervised by a midwife.

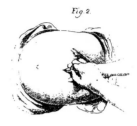

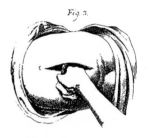

Breast is best

In contrast to the UK, where birth centres are an established phenomenon, Flanders has only a few such centres, run by midwives, where pregnant women can go with any questions they may have. In Flanders these centres are much more inclined to promote 'natural' birth. Midwife Leen Massy from the Bolle Buik Birth Centre in Brussels is one of the pioneers. She perceives a growing trend towards 'aware' birth: '*That doesn't only mean giving birth at home. We prefer to speak of natural birth, in accordance with the mother's wishes and without unnecessary medical intervention. It is not*

Henri-Vicor Wolvens,
Jean-Pierre in his Pram.
1931. Canvas, 80 x 100 cm.
Private collection /
© SABAM Belgium 2000.

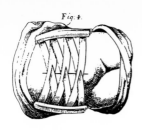

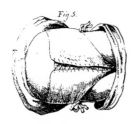

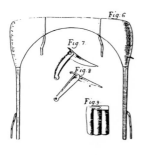

Plate xxii from the Ghent Professor Jacobs' *Obstetrical Training School* (Vroedkundige Oeffenschool, 1764), demonstrating the technical details for a Caesarean section.

only the location that is important, but also the way in which you give birth. and whether you are happy with it afterwards.' She calls it 'hands-off' medicine: being present with the woman as she is giving birth and helping where necessary, but only then. Leen Massy runs a team of midwives and is a strong campaigner for the reinstatement of a bigger role for midwives in the process of giving birth. In many Flemish hospitals midwives have been reduced to insignificant helpers, who have to make way at the moment of birth as the doctor sweeps in. For women who do not want to give birth either at home or in hospital, Leen Massy has set up a 'birthing suite'. It is a building with a normal living room, where everything is at hand that a woman might need when giving birth: pillows, a large ball, a birthing stool and materials necessary for caring for mother and child. The numbers are increasing at both ends of the scale, believes Massy: women who want everything to be more artificial and on the other hand women who want to go back to the natural way of doing things.

Like giving birth at home with the help of a midwife, breast-feeding has also gone completely out of fashion during the course of the twentieth century. Towards the second half of the 1960s, breast-feeding was absolutely 'not done'. Since then a number of projects have been launched aimed at promoting breast-feeding again, and during International Breast-Feeding Week in Flanders, the slogan 'Breast is Best' was launched. More than half of Flemish mothers try to breast feed, but often do not keep it up for very long. The promotion campaigns also ran into difficulties with the free products which are offered to women immediately after giving birth in a hospital, including a soother and adverts for milk products. On the other hand, a number of Flemish cities have recently taken the initiative of setting up 'breast-friendly' locations for breast-feeding mothers who are travelling with their babies. These locations are marked with a sticker and offer mothers a quiet, sheltered corner where they can feed their children.

Sugared almonds and 'wetting the baby's head'

Birth cards are the traditional way of announcing the birth of a child in Flanders. These postcards – with traditional, artistic or simply jolly drawings – state the name, date of birth and weight of the child. They also state who the godfather and godmother are and where and when the new baby can be admired. One of these cards is also pinned to the door of the hospital ward, so that visitors immediately know where to go. Flemings are very hospitable to these visitors, offering a drink and a pack of sugared almonds. Many years ago these were offered in a cotton nappy. Today sugared almonds are packed in imaginative or exclusive and expensive packaging. Some parents spend the entire pregnancy making mini-backpacks or mini-child chairs to serve as packaging.

In the second half of the nineteenth century children were baptised within three days of their birth, a practice born of fear of unexpected death. The baptism ceremony itself was very short, because the 'second baptism' in the bar was much more important. The soother was soaked in beer to stop the baby becoming 'dry and boring' in later life. Babies were dressed in a white christening gown, made from mother's communion dress or wedding dress.

There were fixed arrangements for the choice of godmother and godfather: for a first child, for example, the father's father was godfather and the mother's mother godmother. For a second child this situation was reversed. Today, baptising children is a much less common practice than in the past. Some people retain the ritual, but give it a different form, for example no longer requiring the godparents to promise to bring their child up as a Catholic, but rather to support the child throughout its life. Some also choose godparents from among their circle of friends. As an alternative to a church ceremony, some parents organise a 'birth party' or drinks reception at home. Sometimes they devise their own ritual to welcome the baby.

Today parents often choose their child's first name long before it is born. They are free to choose any name they want, and would not understand if someone tried to take away that freedom. Parents seek names for their children which they like the sound of or which are unusual. Sometimes they jump on the fashion bandwagon and name their offspring after film stars, pop idols or footballers. In earlier times, by contrast, originality in naming a child was thoroughly frowned upon. The first names of godfathers and godmothers, grandparents, aunts and uncles formed part of the family heritage and had to be passed down through the generations. Often they were saint's names such as Jan-Baptist, Josef or Maria. Today's names are more prosaic. This is the top five for 1998 from one of the birth centres in Flanders: Pieter, Ward, Ruben, Simon or Vincent for boys; Emma, Zoe, Elise, Hanna, Myrte and Stien for girls. Working-class babies are often given American or English names such as Kenny, Kevin or Kimberly. A hot tip for the coming months and years is the name Mathilde, after the new Belgian crown princess.

Flemish children are given the family name of their father. An unmarried parent can opt for the mother's name, but this is rare. Now and again voices are raised by women or couples who would like to see things done differently, for example continuing the mother's name or giving the child both parents' names as is customary in Spain. The majority of the Flemish population, MPS and government politicians are little troubled by this issue, however, so that Flemish men are still firmly in the saddle in this respect.

CARLA ROSSEELS
Translated by Julian Ross.

Flemish birth-cards.

A Catholic baptism ceremony in 1950s Flanders.

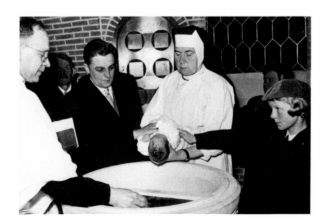

Rogier van der Weyden,
'Naming of St John'
(left panel of the *St John
Altarpiece*). c.1453-1455.
Panel, 77 x 48 cm.
Staatliche Museen zu
Berlin, Preussischer
Kulturbesitz.

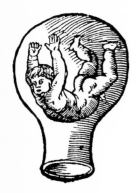

F

rom

Womb to Cradle

Born, Welcomed and Nurtured in the Netherlands

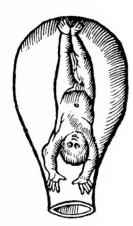

Embryo in a womb, which looks suspiciously like a light bulb. Plates from Eucharius Roesslin's *The Rose Garden of Impregnated Women* (Den Roseghaert van den bevruchten vrouwen, 1528).

Foreign visitors generally react with surprise when they visit a Dutch family and its new baby. After having duly admired the infant, they're sat down close to the childbed and given a piece of Dutch rusk with '*muisjes*' – multi-coloured aniseed comfits. The rusks are always buttered to keep the *muisjes* from falling off (so messy, after all). They also follow well-established colour codes: blue *muisjes* for the birth of a boy and pink for a girl. And that doesn't exhaust all the colour possibilities, for when a new branch sprouts from the royal tree – or the house of Orange – orange *muisjes* immediately go on sale. These are a special line produced by the Zaandam *muisjes* manufacturer De Ruijter, a name that each and every Dutch individual has identified with this product for more than a century.

The distribution of rusks with *muisjes* to celebrate the birth of a baby is not limited to the family circle. It's a custom that's repeated at work, at school, and frequently even at social clubs in the Netherlands. The tradition began during the second half of the nineteenth century. *Muisjes* are aniseeds covered with a hard casing of sugar icing. Anise is said to promote the production of milk, and an aniseed ends in a little tail, making it look something like a mouse – the very rodent that reproduces with such rapidity and has been a fertility symbol since time immemorial. Some folklorists believe the rusk with *muisjes* to be a distant echo of the sweet pastry offered by the ancient Teutons to the mythological Norns to thank those goddesses of fate for granting them a safe birth.

Initially there were only white *muisjes*: prickly ones for boys and smooth ones for girls. But around the turn of the twentieth century the pink variety was introduced, which the parents of new-born daughters would mix with white *muisjes*. The pink *muisjes* became more and more established in Dutch life, but they were thought to be too girlish for boys, so about twenty years ago blue *muisjes* made their appearance.

But there's more. Births in the countryside, like so many other festive events there, are celebrated with a wide variety of currant breads and loaves. And naturally there has to be something to drink. It's not for nothing that one of the most common gifts to the new mother is the 'birth glass', a handsomely decorated drinking glass, since maternity visitors are all expected to 'drown the baby'. Among all the other alcoholic pick-me-ups, '*boerenjongens*' (literally 'farmer's boys', a mixture of brandy and raisins) is one of the most traditional. And for the young mother herself there's the tried and true '*kandeel*', an old Dutch drink made by soaking cloves and stick cinnamon in two bottles of Rhenish, which is then steamed and enriched with the addition of ten egg yolks and sugar (lots of it). This hot drink, which is served in tall cups without handles (the so-called '*lange lijzen*', or beanpoles), apparently works quite well at getting both the new mother and the new father back in shape.

The living-room culture

On 1 January 2000, the population of the Netherlands was estimated at 15.8 million inhabitants. Each year, 11.9 live births are registered for every thousand inhabitants. Proportionately there are slightly more boys than girls being born: 1051 boys for every thousand girls. The infant mortality rate per thousand live births was 5.7 in 1998. The average number of children per family has been dropping for decades; in 1960 there were 722,000 childless families in the Netherlands as opposed to 723,000 families with three children or more. On 1 January 1997, this ratio had changed dramatically: 1,483,000 childless families as opposed to 394,000 families with three chil-

Cornelis Bega, *The Young Mother*. 17th century. Panel, 41 x 35.6 cm. Michaelis Collection, Cape Town.

dren or more. At the same time, the most common number of children per family was two, with 873,000 families falling into that category. Statistically speaking, the modern Dutch family has 2.3 children. (All figures from the Central Bureau of Statistics)

The number of home births is high in the Netherlands in comparison with other Western countries. At the end of the nineties, approximately 35 percent of all Dutch births took place at home. At that point there were about 7,200 practising general practitioners in the Netherlands, with 1,350 obstetricians (that is, midwives). Many Dutch women set great store by giving birth in familiar surroundings. A home birth almost always takes place in the presence of a midwife or a physician. In the event of medical complications, a woman giving birth at home is usually then rushed to the nearest hospital. If there are any medical indications early on in the pregnancy, a hospital birth is deemed necessary as a matter of course. Associated with the general preference for as 'natural' a birth as possible is that of most young mothers for breastfeeding over bottle-feeding.

Dutch culture is a living-room culture. Family, friends and acquaintances drop in and the whole group shut themselves off from the outside world. This homely atmosphere is the environment of choice when it comes to giving birth, and the lying-in period is regarded as another cosy fireside event. Within a few weeks, throngs of visitors descend on the young parents. During these visits, eating and drinking, as mentioned above, are of great importance; the party then takes care of itself.

Henk A. Henriët, *Infant in Cot*. 1936. Charcoal, 50.3 x 32.5 cm. Stedelijk Museum, Amsterdam.

The custom these days is to publicise the birth of a baby by way of sending out birth-cards and sometimes the placing of an announcement in the daily newspaper. The birth-card – successor to the 'birth letter' of the fifties – is often decorated with a cheery drawing, usually of young animals or happy babies, sometimes combined with the inevitable stork. The printed text generally includes the birth weight, the length and naturally the name of the baby. Often the card also mentions when mother and baby will be napping, that is, when visitors are less welcome. When it comes to naming the baby, many people in the country, especially those from more traditional families, follow a special naming system. Roughly speaking, this means naming children after family members such as grandparents or great-grandparents, uncles or aunts. In the past, the rules were sometimes so strict that a girl had to take the name of a male forebear, invariably resulting in male names that were 'feminised' by the addition of diminutive endings, such as Jannetje, Hendrikje, Josje, Geertje, Pietje or Klaasje. The same kind of thinking still goes into the naming of children today, but usually the models are pop singers, TV celebrities or sports heroes. After the Netherlands won the European Championship in 1988, Marco (after top scorer Van Basten) suddenly became an especially popular boys' name. And the recent success of the singer Anouk has provided her with scores of namesakes.

During the first half of this century, the idea of sending out written birth announcements was still unknown in most parts of the Netherlands. In the smaller villages everyone already knew who was pregnant, and the arrival of a doctor or midwife was information enough. The new father simply posted a notice so the curious of the town could keep abreast of the situation. Once the child was born, the man of the house would hang a festive ribbon on his front door: blue for a boy and pink for a girl. This ribbon was called a '*kraamkloppertje*' or a childbirth knocker, because it was usually fastened to the door knocker and at the same time helped to quiet the knocker's sound. Family members and friends who lived at a distance were informed by means of a member of the family, neighbour or servant who was sent round on horseback to announce the birth. People were expected to reward this 'announcer' with a fat tip and a substantial meal.

Baptism and the newer family celebrations

Old traditions are sometimes pushed aside by new ones. For centuries, baptism was something everyone took for granted. If a child was not purified in this way and received into the circle of believers, his little soul was lost for eternity. Today, however, Christianity – and its baptismal ritual – are by no means taken for granted. Yet the decline of baptism's popularity naturally means that non-Christian, lapsed Christian and even anti-Christian parents also lose their chance to turn the baptismal feast into another family celebration. No need to panic, though; this deficiency is being nicely rectified. Institutions such as the Humanist League provide booklets and other informative material that can be used for non-religious birth celebrations. These contain no religious texts but songs, fairy tales, poems and stories from a wide range of authors, from children's book writer Annie M.G. Schmidt to the Lebanese mystic Khalil Gibran.

Such multicultural influences are far from unusual in Dutch society, which is made up of large groups of people of foreign origin. In recent

Two Dutch women carrying babies to the church to be baptised. This picture dates from the 1930s

Post-card with rusk with '*muisjes*' on the occasion of a royal birth, 1909. Stichting Atlas Van Stolk, Rotterdam.

decades Dutch culture has been enriched in this way by elements from Turkey, Morocco, former Yugoslavia, Surinam, the Dutch Antilles, China, Ghana and countless other countries. At the moment, 4.5 percent of the Dutch population follows Islam and 0.5 percent is Hindu.

Naturally, this colourful influx has had its repercussions on the somewhat pale, interiorised Dutch character. Dutch women look on with astonishment as Surinamese mothers massage their babies with oil every day to 'shape' the skin and muscles. Pregnant Chinese women follow carefully outlined 'prenatal' and 'postnatal' diets which prescribe just the foods that are suitable for the various stages of foetal development (and for the care of the mother, too). And Turkish parents rub their babies with salt right after birth to combat unpleasant odours and to keep the baby from perspiring excessively later on.

All these influences leave their imprint. As cultural integration proceeds, more and more apparently successful customs from other cultures will be adopted. And new traditions will gradually take shape based on this acceptance. But the rusk with *muisjes* looks like it's here to stay, given that many non-native families in the Netherlands have already imported this custom into their own homes.

ED VAN EEDEN
Translated by Nancy Forest-Flier.

Death

Unveiled

Dead and Remembered in Flanders

James Ensor, *Skeletons Trying to Warm Themselves.* 1889. Canvas, 75 x 60 cm. Kimbell Art Museum, Fort Worth (TX) / © SABAM Belgium 2000.

The sight of dying and dead people is no longer part of everyday life in Flanders in 2000. Some fifty or sixty years ago, that was different. Then people generally died at home and were laid out there as well. On the day of the funeral the mourners went in procession to church. Sometimes, if decomposition was taking place too quickly and the smell of the corpse was becoming too penetrating, the actual burial took place before the church ceremony. The sight of a corpse in the early stages of decomposition was an everyday thing. Everyone knew what it looked like and it was talked about openly. Today even funeral directors hardly dare use words such as corpse or death when speaking to the surviving relatives. Most Flemings now die in the closed world of a hospital ward. Nurses and undertakers deal with things and have the dead body removed to a mortuary. If someone dies unexpectedly at home, the body is again removed quickly, odourlessly and efficiently, stored in a refrigerated room, laid in a chapel of rest and buried or cremated out of sight of the surviving relatives. After people have died, they disappear almost immediately from the stage of everyday life.

Many people feel comfortable with this modern, 'clean' approach: it saves a great deal of organising and effort and removes the sharp edges from the unpleasant confrontation with death. Ranged against this trend is a small but growing group of people who are seeking to bring death out into the open again; who want to allow terminally ill loved ones to die at home instead of in hospital; who want to keep a dead loved one at home; who want to help with the laying out – washing and clothing their dead loved one for one last time as an ultimate mark of respect – and who want to mark their exit from the world with an emotional, personal ceremony. Sometimes this is possible, sometimes not. For example, it costs a family much more money to care for a terminally ill patient at home rather than have them admitted to hospital. Compared with the UK, there are virtually no hospices in Flanders where terminally ill patients can spend their final months in a family-like atmosphere. Undertakers and priests are also not always entirely cooperative. A number of them prefer to do things the familiar way, despite the increasing demand for modernisation of customs and rituals.

The Church as a provider of rituals

Although the majority of Flemings rarely if ever go to church, many people nevertheless opt for a church burial when someone dies. Many Flemings have come to regard the Church as a provider of rites of passage, somewhere you can go to get married, to be baptised or to be buried. In small villages and towns, such a church ceremony often still takes place in accordance with traditional rituals: the bells are rung when the dead person arrives at the church, incense is wafted about the coffin and it is sprinkled with holy water, and there are readings from the Bible about Jesus' crucifixion and resurrection. Innovation is more likely in urban areas: next-of-kin have the coffin carried into church by friends or family members, choose the music themselves and express their feelings in personal texts. Some people no

Mass of the dead in the choir of a church. The margins show the exterior of the chapel and the crypt with the monumental tomb of the deceased. Flemish miniature from the Spinola Book of Hours, Master of James IV of Scotland, c.1515. J. Paul Getty Museum, Los Angeles (Ms. Ludwig IX.18, fol. 185; 23.2 x 16.6 cm).

longer want death to be hidden behind a veil. When Jan's mother died, for example, the undertaker wanted to drape a cloth over the coffin during the church ceremony. Jan refused: '*I'd much rather the reality was clearly visible. The churchyard is another example. Today, the coffin can be left standing near the door or in the chapel of rest, and is only buried after the mourners have gone home. In our village they use a mechanical crane for that. I had the crane removed and asked the undertaker to bury the coffin while we were there. A burial must be a burial.*'

Until a few decades ago, virtually everyone who died in Flanders was buried. Cremation was unheard-of for a long time. Even in the 1930s a certain Canon Janssen went into battle against this 'barbaric' practice, writing that it was the task of the Church to ensure that not one single corpse would ever be burned in Flanders. The reality turned out differently: the number of cremations has risen spectacularly in recent years, and in urban areas in particular the number of cremations already exceeds the number of burials. Crematoria originally offered little in the way of ceremony when bidding farewell to a dead person: a brief text was read out, a hymn was played and then the coffin rolled through two swing-doors into the furnace. Today, however, there are more and more non-believers who wish to bid farewell to their dead loved one in a dignified, authentic way without involving the Church. An illness such as AIDS, which affects young people particularly, is driving this trend in Flemish society. Chris Coenegrachts, director of a crematorium in the province of East Flanders, is a pioneer in this respect: '*When you're dealing with young people, especially those who have died of AIDS, you see more and more often that their family and friends want to organise the ceremony themselves. Often they are people from an artistic milieu who have the talent to do this. However, not everyone is so creative, and anyway, most people's lives give them little experience of organising funeral ceremonies,*' he says. '*Undertakers therefore face a new task. In the past, when the priest led the church ritual and people stood and watched, an undertaker was concerned almost exclusively with material and technical matters, such as ordering the coffin and organising transport for the body. Now that Catholicism is losing ground and fewer and fewer people are using the services of their parish priest, a gap has appeared. The step from the traditional church funeral to a new, individual ritual devised and shaped by the survivors themselves is usually too big. People need help with it.*' Undertakers have a duty to point out to people that they have options, believes Coenegrachts. Sometimes the choice they make can even be important for coming to terms with the event psychologically afterwards. '*The sprinkling of ashes is enormously popular in Flanders, for example,*' says Coenegrachts. '*But that's mainly because people devote little conscious thought to the different possibilities. And undertakers generally don't encourage them to do so, so people tend to stick to what is familiar. And yet sprinkling the ashes is not always suitable for everyone. If a person's ashes are scattered, the next-of-kin have nowhere to go to visit them afterwards; and for some people that's an essential part of the mourning process.*' Sometimes this need is partially accommodated by placing a monument next to the plot where the ashes have been scattered, to which the family can attach a nameplate. People who decide against scattering the ashes can have the urn containing the ashes placed in a columbarium. Some local authorities offer a third possibility, by creating a burial ground for urns with small tombstones; this has the advantage that flowers can be placed on the stone, something which cannot be done with a columbarium.

People regularly ask if they can take the ashes home with them. They perhaps know of a nice spot under a tree or near a lake where they want to scatter the ashes. Belgian legislation does not allow this yet: taking the ashes home is seen as more or less akin to desecration of the corpse. Another thing which is not permitted is that family or friends scatter the ashes on the crematorium plot themselves. Officially, this has to be done by a municipal official or an official staff member of the burial ground. And yet sometimes people need to do it themselves. Patrick's father, for example, had already indicated before his death that he wished to be cremated. Patrick decided together with his brothers and sisters that they wanted to scatter the ashes themselves. *'The undertaker didn't forbid us to do it, though it was difficult at first. He kept on asking if we could cope with it and if we wouldn't rather leave it to him. We stuck to our guns, however; my brother ultimately scattered the ashes. It wasn't easy, but we managed. For us it was a way of letting go of our father.'* One thing which has been permitted by law since 1991 is the sprinkling of ashes at sea, a ritual which gains more supporters every year in Flanders.

Funeral parlour in Sinaai, East Flanders. Design by Erik van Belleghem.

Mourning cards and commemorative cards

Flemish families generally announce a death by sending mourning cards and inviting friends and acquaintances personally to the funeral ceremony. If the deceased was an important or well-known figure, an announcement is also published in the newspaper. Depending on the age and lifestyle of the deceased, the tenor of these announcements may be formal and aloof or personal and informal. At the end of a funeral ceremony, those attending are usually given a commemorative card to take home, with a photo and a reflective text as a reminder of the deceased.

A new development in recent years is for the ritual to take place in a private, intimate circle, without any official advance announcement. In these cases the family prefers to keep the ceremony private and not to share its emotions with a larger group. When older people die, there are sometimes only a handful of family and friends remaining. In the case of the death of a young person, however, there will be a much wider circle of friends, colleagues and acquaintances who share the family's loss. If they are not invited to the funeral they are often left with feelings of mourning with which they are unable to come to terms.

In the past, Flemish men and women wore black clothing for some time after a funeral. This was partly a convention, a social obligation, but also gave their personal sadness a place within the community. The black clothes made it clear to other people that someone was still going through a difficult period. Today there is much less time for sadness, and in Flanders, too, people quickly take up the business of the day again and those around them expect people to be back on top of things within a couple of weeks. However, research has shown that after a major bereavement our emotions are dominated by feelings of mourning that last for at least a couple of years. Follow-

up rituals can help to ameliorate that slumbering suffering. In Flanders, however, we have retained few of these rituals. Catholic believers can request commemorative Masses and visit the graveyard on All Saints' Day and All Souls Day. Believers and non-believers often commemorate the birthday and date of death of the deceased.

In the past, removing the black clothing marked the end of the period of mourning. Today we are no longer supposed to wear mourning clothes, but this also means that we have lost the delineation of the mourning period. As a result, people continue mourning endlessly, for example young men or women who have lost a partner or young parents. If they stop mourning, they feel they have not been a good spouse or a good parent. If they continue mourning, they are unable to pick up the threads of their life again.

In short, the disappearance of the religious rituals means that Flemish society, like many others, now has few tangible guidelines to indicate how death and loss can or should be dealt with. This is not to say that we should look at the past with an exaggerated nostalgia: as in many other countries, many traditions have gradually lost their significance in recent decades, and where they were still observed this was primarily as a means of social control or for outer display.

Today, therefore, every Fleming faces the challenge of discovering for themselves what they need, and of learning to deal with death in a sensitive way in a society which does not always find it easy to deal with this harsh reality.

CARLA ROSSEELS
Translated by Julian Ross.

The new cemetery in
Kortrijk, by B. Secchi and
P. Viganó.
Photo by David Samyn

The grave of Flemish
painter Emile Claus, right
in the middle of his own
garden in Astene. The
sculpture is by George
Minne.

rom

Announcement to Cemetery

Deceased, Buried and Mourned in the Netherlands

For centuries, rites of passage have been used to try to deal with alarming changes. And nothing inspires as much anxiety as death, the big black hole waiting at the end of every life. As the old saying goes, there's no cure for death. Death has no almanac; he takes everybody – young or old, rich or poor – whenever it suits him. It's that terrible uncertainty about when the breaking of life's thread will occur that makes the finality and inevitability of death so horrifying – even to those who believe that after this life another, much better, life awaits.

Death will not be mocked – another admonition that still makes the rounds. This collective anxiety about death is what keeps countless old traditions concerning death and burial alive, especially in the countryside. Until well into the twentieth century, carrying a neighbour's coffin was regarded as an unquestionable funeral duty in rural communities, and to fulfil this obligation was to perform one of the works of mercy. The coffin of a man was taken up on the shoulders; that of a woman was carried 'by hand'.

Many of the customs that have come down to us have to do with exorcising the spirit of the deceased. According to popular beliefs, it's precisely during a period of great sorrow that people are most susceptible to evil influences from the realm of the spirits. That's why everything possible must be done to prevent the dear departed from dragging one or more of his kinfolk along with him, thereby proving the old saying, 'One funeral gives rise to another'. Whenever someone has died, it's always been the custom to wake up everyone in the house, since sleeping souls have less resistance against death.

Everywhere in the world – and that includes the Netherlands – those present at a death always shut the dead person's eyes, and keep them shut, if necessary, by laying coins on them. The reason for this, according to an old popular belief, is that if the unseeing eyes remain open, their staring alone can hasten the death of a beloved relative. In a house in which someone has died, it is still customary to turn all the mirrors to the wall or to cover them with cloths. This tradition can be traced back to the ancient fear that a spirit steals the reflection of the living, thereby dragging their souls irrevocably to their doom.

A dead person who has been laid out should be given peace and quiet so that nothing can disturb his sleep of death. That's why people whisper among themselves in the presence of the dead and any ruthlessly ticking clocks are brought to a stop – an attempt to keep the dead from realising that life is going on without them. The curtains in the house of the dead are always kept closed, but even in this semi-darkness the evil spirits should not be given the chance to approach the dear departed undisturbed. For this reason the bier is never left alone, and those in the house take turns keeping vigil over the corpse. And always there's the lamp left burning beside the body.

The only proper way to carry a corpse out is feet first. This keeps the irresistible gaze of the dead from compelling any family members to follow him. Usually all the windows and outer doors in the house of the dead are opened immediately after the death has occurred, to hasten the departure of the spirit. Then after a few hours have passed the house should be completely shut up to keep the spirit from being tempted to return. Once the dead person is carried out for burial the door should remain open until the procession returns. Otherwise it won't be long before the same door will have to be opened for another dead body. There are still farmhouses with separate 'corpse doors', to be used exclusively for carrying out the dead. For the same reason some village churches also have a 'corpse portal' that is opened only for funerals.

It's considered very bad luck for a moving funeral procession to be brought to a sudden stop. After all, everybody knows that the restless soul, respond-

A Protestant funeral in the Netherlands, with the hearse on its way to the church.
Photo by Marrie Bot.

ing to the lure of the grave, needs to be buried as soon as possible. This is why up until 1990 Dutch traffic laws gave right-of-way to funeral processions. During the funeral the death knell is rung in the local church to keep evil spirits and demons at a distance. In some Frisian villages the coffin is still carried three times around the church to keep the spirit of the dead from coming back.

In large sections of the country, families still observe a period of official mourning. Since ancient times, the house of the dead is identified with special wooden signs, closed shutters or curtains, death lamps and black crosses or bunting. The relatives themselves make sure their mourning is clearly visible by the clothes they wear. The mourning regulations for women contain degrees of mourning that are especially precise concerning the use of colours, jewellery and ribbons. Until well into the twentieth century, widows and widowers were expected to dress in black for the rest of their lives. Later on this period was reduced to seven years. According to an old bit of folk wisdom, any young couple who fall in love during their period of mourning don't stand a chance in the world of having a happy marriage.

There are even old regulations for the use of the dead person's wardrobe and bedding: if they're not washed quickly the spirit won't get any rest. But at least a month must pass after the death occurs before anyone else can use them; any earlier use will disturb the final rest of the previous owner.

Commercialisation

The modern way of informing friends and family of a death is by means of a death notice in the newspaper, a death announcement sent by post or possibly a distressing telephone call (or e-mail). Unlike the obituaries in the Anglo-Saxon world, death notices contain not only general information about the deceased (name, birth date and place, date and place of death, date and place of funeral), but usually also include a suitable quote from a poem or a somewhat more personal text. Often there's a sad reflection on the inevitability of death and the untimely demise of the deceased ('*Far too soon, God has called...*' or '*Bewildered and disconsolate, we announce the death of ... He / she leaves a great emptiness behind*').

In earlier years, these kinds of death announcements were brought round by a so-called 'announcer': a family member or neighbour whose job it was to publicise the death. In small rural communities, the announcer would go from house to house. An appropriate response to such an announcement was to offer the announcer (whose temporary function was recognisable by the feathered three-cornered hat he wore) a substantial amount of food and drink.

The Netherlands does not possess a lavish tomb culture. Most cemeteries feature simple tombstones or crosses. All graves are legally protected from disturbance for at least ten years to make sure that those who clear away the grave do not come upon a decomposing corpse. Even more prosaic are the crematoria. The first crematorium on Dutch soil was opened in Velzen in 1914. At that time cremations were merely tolerated, but in 1955 the law was adapted so that cremation was permitted if the deceased had requested it in writing beforehand. Since 1968 cremations and burials have been re-

Anonymous scattering of the ashes on the garden of rest of a Dutch crematorium. Photo by Marrie Bot.

A boy and his scooter on a grave in the Eindhoven cemetery.
Photo courtesy of Antoine Fonville / Uitvaartencyclopedie (www.uitvaart.org).

garded as equal before the law. Today there are more than forty crematoria in the Netherlands, and almost sixty percent of all deceased persons are cremated. The ashes of a cremated person can be scattered or kept in an urn in a columbarium or an existing grave. Since 1991 family members have also been permitted to take the urn home with them.

The standardised annual death rate in the Netherlands is now 7.8 per thousand inhabitants. Life expectancy is 72.3 years for men and 78.7 years for women. A great deal has changed in recent decades in the way the Dutch relate to their dead. Death has gradually become something untouchable, distinct from ordinary life. The aged and the sick who are approaching death are kept apart from everyday society and hidden away in hospitals and nursing homes. Funerals and all the associated fuss and bother have been placed safely in the hands of funeral parlours.

The efficient processing of the dead has been elevated to an art form, and nowhere is this more in evidence than in the crematoria. Cremations have degenerated into tightly organised, brief ceremonies in which the grieving are steered from one little room to another. There's time for receiving guests, signing the funeral register and listening to a few speeches and a bit of music, after which guests can watch the coffin disappear from sight. Then everyone is herded into a room for a brief, pleasant get-together. There the traditional funeral meal has been replaced by a cup of coffee (the 'cup of consolation') and a sandwich. Once everyone has paid their condolences to the family they're free to go home; the whole ceremony has taken less than an hour. No wonder the cynical term 'funeral factory' has become the generally accepted tag for crematoria.

Final resting-place of the Dutch poet / painter Lucebert (1924-1994) in Bergen, The Netherlands. Photo courtesy of Antoine Fonville / Uitvaartencyclopedie (www.uitvaart.org).

The *aarti* ritual of Dutch Surinam Sanaatan-Dharm Hindustani. In this sacrificial ceremony the next of kin are blessed with the *diyaa*. The *aarti* is the last step in each of the four ceremonies held during the twelve-month mourning period.
Photo by Marrie Bot.

The funeral laments, funeral poems and funeral songs of the past were replaced generations ago by the funeral oration. In his discourse to relatives and friends, the orator is usually guided more by flattery than by critical thinking. After all, you must speak only good of the dead. The mourning dress most commonly worn at funerals and cremations today is the mourning band. This black band, worn around the arm, replaces the traditional full suit of black clothing.

Since 1988, the National Mourning Centre has been open to serve anyone suffering from acute psychological need in the period after a death.

Back of the Dutch *Doodgewoon Magazine*. The ad sports lines such as '*Your wish, our options*' and '*More than just six wooden boards*'. Photo courtesy Anja Krabben & *Doodgewoon*.

Cover of the Dutch *Uitvaart* magazine, showing a more traditional means of transport for the deceased. Photo courtesy Jasper Enklaar & *Uitvaart* / cover design by José Troullioud.

Death with a bit more colour

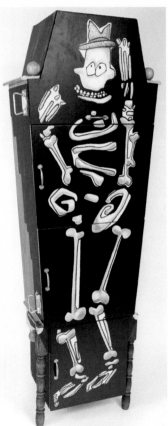

Useful in both life and after-life: 'Ga' CD-rack and coffin ('Picasso' Pim Feelen). Photo by Rob Mostert, courtesy of Jasper Enklaar.

But the old ways are not dead yet. Not everyone is content with the efficient, colourless affair that constitutes a burial or cremation ceremony. This is evident from the increasing number of church funerals, with the accompanying ritual, as well as from the newer phenomena: decorative urns, children's graves complete with toys, and playful happenings such as the inhumation of the flamboyant owner of the Amsterdam cult discotheque IT involving a canal cruise boat covered with flowers, several dance groups and all sorts of music. Also striking is the emergence of the general interest magazine *Doodgewoon* – from the common Dutch expression meaning 'dead ordinary' –, the increasingly popular quarterly journal completely devoted to all the phenomena surrounding death.

At the same time, death in the Netherlands is now subject to a vast array of multicultural influences: gypsies wear red to their funerals, the colour of life and energy, while Turks wear violet and Chinese purple as the mourning colour of choice. Religious Muslims, who are not allowed to be cremated, must be buried with their heads pointing towards Mecca. Indonesian families often fill in the graves of their dead by themselves. Chinese give large amounts of paper money to the deceased at the cremation so that the soul of the dead person can meet his financial obligations in the spirit world. The Surinamese sing and dance while carrying the bier of their dead to its final resting place. And large numbers of Moroccans commonly gather in cemeteries every Thursday, the day they believe the souls of the dead return to their graves.

With all these influences, the Dutch have started to think somewhat differently about death and mourning. And they've also begun more and more to appreciate their own traditions, which up until recently seemed doomed to extinction.

ED VAN EEDEN
Translated by Nancy Forest-Flier.

he

Low Countries Growing Old

The Second Demographic Transition

The term 'demographic transition' generally refers to the declines in mortality and fertility that occurred in western populations during the eighteenth and especially the nineteenth century as a result of improvements in health, sanitation and biomedical discoveries, and of deliberate fertility control through contraception. At the onset of this first demographic transition the average age of populations was still very young, but at the end of it a first ageing wave had taken place, mainly as a result of the shrinking proportion of younger persons (itself caused by reduced fertility). The outcome of this first transition should have been a stable population with a growth rate close to zero, life expectancy at birth of 70 years or more, and a fertility level of just over 2 children on average, i.e. the number needed to replace each generation. In addition, the dominant household type was expected to remain that of a married couple with children.

But things did not work out quite as expected. From the 1960s onward it became clear that this presumed stable equilibrium model was not emerging. In the Low Countries, the sequence of events from this decade onwards is typical of what has become known as the 'second demographic transition'.

Firstly, there was already a modest rise in the divorce rate, signalling that normative institutional structuring (via religion and law) in the domain of the family no longer went unchallenged. The expression '*a good divorce is better than a bad marriage*' clearly indicated that individuals aspired to a higher degree of control over their own lives and that a cost-benefit calculus could also be applied to the institution of marriage.

The next step was the onset of the decline in fertility. Around 1965, the 'baby boom' comes to an end, and from then onwards women at all stages of family formation curb their fertility. This is without doubt partly due to the considerable improvement in contraceptive technology (pill, intra-uterine device) and the gradual reduction in unplanned pregnancies. But later generations, who mainly start procreation in the 1970s, develop a new pattern altogether by postponing parenthood to a later age. This postponement effect is still going on, and it is one of the main reasons for sustained below-replacement fertility.

The third feature is the gradual replacement of legal marriage as a means of initiating a partnership by the spread of premarital cohabitation. Initially such cohabitants were to be found among the better-educated young adults, and particularly among the non-conformist segments of the population. But during the 1980s the pattern becomes widespread in all social strata and only persons with quite strong religious convictions resist it. In tandem with the drop in first marriage rates, there is also a decline in remarriage following divorce or widowhood. Post-marital cohabitation is to some extent replacing remarriage, and a variety of new household patterns emerges: there is a rise in lone parent households, in reconstituted households of cohabiting adults with children from earlier unions, in LAT-relationships ('Living Apart Together') etc.

Not only parenthood is being postponed; so also is the transition to a first partnership. Young people remain in the parental household for longer, or move out and start living on their own. The term 'the hotel family' has been coined to express the increased freedom of sons and daughters to go and come as they please, while parents are left with the laundry and are expected to be highly tolerant about other guests sharing bedrooms. The second type, i.e. single living, is not always associated with complete economic in-

1. Marital status & household composition	Flanders	Netherlands	Spain	France	Sweden
A. Without partner, no children	15%	23	35	24	18
B. With partner, no children					
B.1. single or previously married	7	21	4	13	14
B.2. currently married	22	20	17	13	6
C. Without partner, with children	3	3	3	6	10
D. With partner, with children					
D.1. single or previously married	4	3	2	10	17
D.2. currently married	50	29	40	34	35

2. Choice patterns	Flanders	Netherlands	Spain	France	Sweden
• Late home leaving & late partnership (row A)	15%	23	**35**	24	18
• Entry via cohabitation, premarital + postmarital (rows B1 + D1)	11	24	6	23	**31**
• Procreation within marriage (row D2)	**50**	29	40	34	35
• Procreation within cohabitation (row D1)	4	3	2	10	**17**
• Earlier parenthood (rows C + D1 + D2)	57	35	45	50	**62**
• Late parenthood (rows A + B1 + B2)	44	**64**	56	50	38

Most life cycle transitions occur in the age segment between 20 and 30 years. The distribution of women aged 25-29 according to the presence of a partner and of children and by marital status therefore highlights the differences in family forma-tion patterns. The data above, taken from the 'Fertility and Family Surveys' of the 1990s, document several diverse national patterns. The top half of the table shows the household data as they come; in the bottom half the rows are recombined to bring out differences in choices. Rounded percentages, may not add up to exactly 100%; Swedish data are for women aged 28 rather than 25-29; the FFS-survey for Belgium was conducted in Flanders and among Flemish speakers in Brussels only. (Source: FFS-surveys, national country reports, UN-Econ. Commission for Europe, various dates)

dependence either, but it is at least a clearer situation for all concerned. Furthermore, the growth in single living among young adults contributes to the number of one-person households, which are now the fastest growing household type.

From the 1980s onwards, increasing numbers of premarital cohabitants no longer convert their partnership into a legal marriage prior to parenthood. More and more of them start having children while cohabiting. The proportion of out-of-wedlock births starts rising to the current 18-20 percent in the Low Countries, which is still considerably short of the 40 to 50 percent of all births in the Scandinavian countries.

There is obviously no single factor that explains this demographic trans-

3. Total Fertility Rate	1970	1975	1980	1985	1990	1995	1997
A.'High' group TFRS							
* United Kingdom	2.45	1.81	1.89	1.80	1.83	1.71	1.71
* France	2.47	1.93	1.95	1.81	1.78	1.70	1.71
* Ireland	3.87	3.40	3.23	2.50	2.12	1.85	1.92
B.'Medium' group TFRS							
* Belgium	2.25	1.74	1.70	1.51	1.62	1.57	1.55
* Netherlands	2.57	1.66	1.60	1.51	1.62	1.53	1.54
C.'Low' group TFRS							
* Germany (former FRG)	2.02	1.45	1.44	1.28	1.45	1.34	1.39
* Italy	2.46	2.19	1.66	1.45	1.36	1.18	1.22
* Spain	2.82	2.80	2.22	1.64	1.36	1.17	1.15

The 'Total Fertility Rate' (TFR) is the typical period indicator of fertility in regions or countries. The TFR gives the average number of children that a fictitious (i.e. a statistical) generation of women would have by age 50 if they were subjected to all age-specific fertility rates (at ages 15, 16....49) as observed during a particular year in an actual population. The TFR therefore measures the fertility level of a particular period and not of a real generation which has its fertility over a period of 35 years. The replacement level TFR equals 2.08 children. In the table above, one can see that Belgium and the Netherlands have had a remarkably parallel evolution of their TFR-values, which hold the middle ground between those of a high group and of a low group within the EU. (Source: Council of Europe (1999): 59 (table T3-3)).

formation. Rather, it has been shaped by a series of other societal changes. In the social domain, the new pattern is linked to rising educational levels, particularly of women. In the economic area, a major driving force has been the rise in female employment, with both the development of female careers for those with higher education, and the increased need for an extra earner to sustain higher consumption aspirations in all social strata. In the cultural field, the second demographic transition is linked to secularisation, accentuation of individual freedom of choice, altered gender relations, greater stress on self-fulfilment, greater tolerance of other people's choices and lifestyles, etc. All of this means that further considerable growth in the non-conventional household types can be expected, and that the end of low fertility is not yet in sight. Moreover, below-replacement fertility is the major contributing factor to levels of ageing that will be much higher than would be expected on the basis of further rises in life expectancy alone.

Different countries, different patterns

One of the striking features of current developments in life courses and household types is that many countries are moving in the same general direction, but at different intensities and speeds. Hence, there is a remarkable heterogeneity in national and regional pattern developments; and the Low Countries are no exception. The Netherlands had a slow 'first demographic transition' compared to Belgium: in the 1950s the Dutch still had significantly higher fertility levels and population growth rates, and the proportion of employed women was among the lowest in industrialised countries. But the 1960s hit hard in the Netherlands, and from then onwards, this country overtakes Belgium in almost all aspects typical for 'the second demographic transition'. This is particularly evident in three features of the new Dutch pattern: (1) premarital cohabitation rises faster, (2) home-leaving occurs earlier in favour of much more single living, and (3) the transitions to marriage and particularly to parenthood are postponed to very late ages (see Table 1). Within the EU and even the OECD, the Netherlands stands out by virtue of its remarkable late age at motherhood, while Belgium still adheres to an earlier pattern. However, both countries remain conservative with respect to the arrival of the first child within legal marriage. The proportion of out-of-wedlock births increases rather slowly in comparison with other surrounding countries such as France or the UK. This also means that in this particular respect the Dutch are even more conservative than the Belgians since they have a proportionally greater number of young cohabitants, but only the same proportion of out-of-wedlock births. A correlate of this is that the proportion of lone parent households is still low in both countries.

Another similarity is the almost identical evolution of fertility levels in the two countries (see Table 2); in both, the total fertility rate (TFR) has been oscillating between 1.50 and 1.60 during the 1980s and 1990s. The Dutch have their children considerably later than the Belgians, but in the end they reach the same average. Projections of the proportions remaining childless among the generation currently aged 25-35, however, foresee a level for the Netherlands that could reach 25 percent or even more, whereas Belgian childlessness is likely to stay in the vicinity of 20 percent.

As usual, the Belgian figures are only an average of two distinct patterns for Flanders and Wallonia respectively. This has been a recurrent feature since 1880, i.e. the time of the initial fertility transition. Then, Wallonia was clearly the innovator with respect to fertility control and contraception. At present, Wallonia is playing an identical innovatory role, particularly by having a considerably higher incidence of cohabitation, procreation without marriage and non-conventional household types . But the timing of fertility is earlier than in Flanders and as a result, overall fertility levels are now higher in the South than the North. Flanders has a late home-leaving pattern, a relatively low incidence of single living among young adults, typically a strong adherence to marriage prior to parenthood and more like the Dutch, a later pattern of marriage and parenthood as well. It is as if Flemish material aspirations have been rising in tandem with disposable income, and there is a perception that stability and security need to be achieved (secure jobs, own house…) before children come on the scene. The Flemish pattern is quite conservative by European standards (see also Luxembourg or Switzerland), partly due to a history of slower secularisation as well.

The outcome is that Flemish fertility is now lower than Walloon fertility and life expectancy is higher in the former region than in the latter. Taken together, this means that Flanders is heading for a greater degree of population ageing. As a result of this reversal in regional demography, future per capita social expenditure in Flanders could become higher than in Wallonia; and that would introduce a new parameter into the delicate Belgian federal household, where social security costs are still being paid from the common purse.

The welfare state has been particularly kind to Belgians and Dutch alike; both have the lowest poverty rates in the EU and OECD. The ageing associated first with the arrival at age 60+ of the baby boom generation born in the 1960s, and then with the history of low fertility and rising life expectancy, will constitute a major challenge from 2015 onwards. Economically, the Dutch are in a better shape to meet this challenge, not least because they have pension fund reserves that are as large as the Belgian public debt (about 120% of GNP).

Consequently, policy responses to the ageing problem could be quite different in the two countries.

RON LESTHAEGHE

BIBLIOGRAPHY

COLEMAN, D. (ed.), *Europe's Population in the 1990s*. Oxford, 1996.

COUNCIL OF EUROPE, *Recent Demographic Developments in Europe – 1998*. Strasbourg, 1999.

KAA, D.J. VAN DE, 'Europe's Second Demographic Transition'. In: *Population Bulletin*, 41. Washington DC, 1987.

LATTEN, J. and A. DE GRAAF, *The Netherlands – Standard Country Report, Fertility and Family Surveys in Countries of the ECE Region*. New York / Geneva, 1997.

LESTHAEGHE, R. and G. VERLEYE, 'The Second Demographic Transition in Western Countries: An Interpretation'. In: Oppenheim Mason, K. and A.-M. Jensen (ed.), *Gender and Family Change in Industrialised Countries*. Oxford, 1995.

LESTHAEGHE, R., W. MEEUSEN and K. VANDEWALLE, *Eerst optellen, dan delen – Demografie, economie en sociale zekerheid*. Leuven / Apeldoorn, 1998.

LODEWIJCKX, E., *De 'Fertility & Family Surveys' in de landen van de Europese Gemeenschap –- Het rapport over België*. Brussels, 1998.

MÉRENNE, B., H. VAN DER HAEGEN and E. VAN HECKE, 'België ruimtelijk doorgelicht'. In: *Tijdschrift van het Gemeentekrediet / Bulletin du Crédit Communal*, 202, pp. 97-4. Brussels, 1998.

STATISTICS NETHERLANDS, *Compilation of Household Scenarios for the Countries of the European Union*, 1995-2025. Voorburg, 1998.

'Each

being too is pregnant with death'

Thirteen Poems about Birth and Death

Selected by Jozef Deleu

Jan Moritoen (?; 14th century)

Rondel	**Rondeel**
Egidius, where are you hiding?	Egidius, waer bestu bleven?
I long for you, companion mine.	Mi lanct na di, gheselle mijn.
You died, you left me here abiding.	Du coors die doot, du liets mi tleven.
How good was life when we were twain,	Dat was gheselscap goet ende fijn,
It seemed there could be no dividing.	Het sceen teen moeste ghestorven sijn.
Yet now you stand beside God's throne,	Nu bestu in den troon verheven
More radiant than the high sun riding,	Claerre dan der zonnen scijn,
All fruits, all riches now are thine,	Alle vruecht es di ghegheven.
Egidius, where are you hiding?	Egidius, waer bestu bleven?
I long for you, companion mine.	Mi lanct na di, gheselle mijn.
You died, you left me here abiding.	Du coors de doot, du liets mi tleven.
Now pray for me, who, here abiding,	Nu bidt vor mi: ic moet noch sneven
Must suffer still the world, its pain.	Ende in de weerelt liden pijn.
Keep me a place, a place beside you,	Verware mijn stede di beneven:
I've still to sing a brief refrain,	Ic moet noch zinghen een liedekijn.
Till Death shall make us one again.	Nochtan moet emmer ghestorven sijn.
Egidius, where are you hiding?	Egidius, waer bestu bleven?
I long for you, companion mine.	Mi lanct na di, gheselle mijn.
You died, you left me here abiding.	Du coors die door, du liets mi tleven.

From the Gruuthuse Manuscript (2nd half 14th century)

Translated by James Brockway.

Multatuli (1820-1887)
Saïjah's Song

Saïdjahs zang

I do not know where I shall die.
I have seen the great sea on the South Coast, when I was there making salt with my father;
If I die on the sea, and they throw my body into the deep water, sharks will come.
They will swim round about my corpse, and ask: 'Which of us shall devour this body, descending through the water?'

I shall not hear.

I do not know where I shall die.
I have seen the burning house of Pa-Ansu, which he had set on fire himself because he was demented.
If I die in a burning house, the flaming timbers will fall down on my corpse,
and outside the house there will be a hue and cry of people, throwing water to kill the fire.

I shall not hear.

I do not know where I shall die.
I have seen little Si-Unah fall from the klappa tree, when he was picking a klappa for his mother.
If I fall from a klappa tree I shall lie dead at its foot, in the bushes, like Si-Unah.
My mother will not cry out for me, for she is dead. But others will cry with loud voices: 'Lo, there lies Saïjah!'

I shall not hear.

I do not know where I shall die.
I have seen the dead body of Pa-Lisu, who had died of old age, for his hair was white.
If I die of old age, with white hair, the keening women will stand round my body.
And loudly they will lament, like the keening women round Pa-Lisu's body. And the grandchildren will also weep, very loudly.

I shall not hear.

Ik weet niet waar ik sterven zal.
Ik heb de grote zee gezien aan de Zuidkust, toen ik daar was met mijn vader, om zout te maken.
Als ik sterf op de zee, en men werpt mijn lichaam in het diepe water, zullen er haaien komen.
Ze zullen rondzwemmen om mijn lijk, en vragen: 'wie van ons zal het lichaam verslinden, dat daar daalt in het water?'

Ik zal 't niet horen.

Ik weet niet waar ik sterven zal.
Ik heb het huis zien branden van Pa-Ansoe, dat hijzelf had aangestoken omdat hij mata-glap was.
Als ik sterf in een brandend huis, zullen er gloeiende stukken hout neervallen op mijn lijk.
En buiten het huis zal een groot geroep zijn van mensen, die water werpen om het vuur te doden.

Ik zal 't niet horen.

Ik weet niet waar ik sterven zal.
Ik heb de kleine Si-Oenah zien vallen uit de klapaboom, toen hij een klapa plukte voor zijn moeder.
Als ik val uit een klapa-boom, zal ik dood neerliggen aan de voet, in de struiken, als Si-Oenah.
Dan zal mijn moeder niet schreien, want zij is dood. Maar anderen zullen roepen: 'zie, daar ligt Saïdjah!' met harde stem.

Ik zal 't niet horen.

Ik weet niet waar ik sterven zal.
Ik heb het lijk gezien van Pa-Lisoe, die gestorven was van hoge ouderdom, want zijn haren waren wit.
Als ik sterf van ouderdom, met witte haren, zullen de klaagvrouwen om mijn lijk staan.
En zij zullen misbaar maken als de klaagvrouwen bij Pa-Lisoe's lijk.
En ook de kleinkinderen zullen schreien, zeer luid.

Ik zal 't niet horen.

I do not know where I shall die.
I have seen many at Badur who had died. They were wrapped in
a white garment, and were buried in the earth.
If I die at Badur, and they bury me outside the village, eastward
against the hill, where the grass is high,
then will Adinda pass that way, and the hem of her sarong will
softly sweep the grass in passing...

And I shall hear.

From *Max Havelaar or the Coffee Auctions of the Dutch Trading Company*
(Max Havelaar of de koffieveilingen der Nederlandse Handelsmaatschappij, 1860).
Translated by Roy Edwards ((Harmondsworth: Penguin, 1987).

Ik weet niet waar ik sterven zal.
Ik heb velen gezien te Badoer, die gestorven waren. Men
   kleedde hen in een wit kleed, en begroef hen in de
   grond.
Als ik sterf te Badoer, en men begraaft mij buiten de
   desa, oostwaarts tegen de heuvel, waar het gras hoog
   is ...
Dan zal Adinda daar voorbijgaan, en de rand van haar
   sarong zal zachtkens voortschuiven langs het gras ...

Ik zal het horen.

Jan Hendrik Leopold (1865-1925)
That morning she'd been heavy, tired

Dien morgen was zij moe en zwaar

That morning she'd been heavy, tired,
and slow to leave her bed
and set about her daily chores
scarce knowing what she did.

She went forlornly round the room
heedless of where or why,
fiddled about with this and that,
shifting things aimlessly.

When suddenly she felt so strange
as something in her moved
and a new wondrous certainty
unfolded in her head,

and drawing in a deeper breath
she sank gently to the floor
and stayed a moment there until
she was herself once more.

–

and in pride and humility
her head she meekly bowed
and whispered through submissive lips
'behold thy handmaid, Lord.'

From *Collected Works I* (Verzameld werk I, 1967)
Translated by Tanis Guest.

Dien morgen was zij moe en zwaar
en talmende opgestaan
en had met achteloos besef
haar dagelijks doen gedaan.

Zij ging verloren door het vertrek
met ongevoelde schreden,
behaspelde dit en dat,
verschikkende zonder reden.

Als plotseling met een vreemd gevoel
zich iets in haar bewoog
en een nieuwe en wondere zekerheid
haar door de gedachten vloog,

en met een diepere ademtocht
was zij even neergezegen
en toefde een ogenblik totdat
zij zich zelve had herkregen.

–

en in trots en in deemoedig zijn
boog zij het hoofd ter neer
en fluisterde met toegevenden mond
'zie uwe dienstmaagd, Heer'.

Willem Elsschot (1882-1960)
At a Child's Deathbed

Bij het doodsbed van een kind

Earth's orbit goes the same way round
now your young heart beats no more,
the stars are shining as before,
the house is still quite safe and sound.

But strangled sobs and mournful sighs,
the coffee drunk to ease the pain
they cannot make you speak again
or put the light back in your eyes.

You'll never waken like you did:
you would not stir from where you lay
when loud creaks gave the man away
who crept upstairs to close the lid.

Good people, can't you see it's done?
What shall we do? Why don't we pray,
then for a little while I'll stay:
this night will be a sleepless one.

Can one of you, some learned sir,
most wisely and ingeniously
contend with plausibility
that worms will never feed on her?

From *Collected Works* (Verzameld werk, 1957).
Translated by Paul Vincent.

Bij het doodsbed van een kind

De aarde is niet uit haar baan gedreven
toen uw hartje stil bleef staan,
de sterren zijn niet uitgegaan
en 't huis is overeind gebleven.

Maar al 't geklaag en dof gesnik,
zelfs onder 't troostend koffiedrinken,
het kon uw stem niet op doen klinken,
noch licht ontsteken in uw blik.

Gij zult wel nimmermeer ontwaken,
want gij bleeft roerloos toen de trap
zo kraakte bij den stillen stap
des mans, die kwam om toe te maken.

Ziet, lieve mensen, 't is volbracht,
Wat gaan wij doen? Wij konden bidden,
dan blijf ik nog wat in uw midden,
gij krijgt toch wel geen slaap vannacht.

En heeft een uwer een ervaren
en hooggeleerd en vruchtbaar brein:
hij zeggen mij of 't waar kan zijn
dat haar de wormen zullen sparen.

The Raising of Lazarus in a Churchyard by a Chapel. Flemish miniature, 22.3 X 15.5 cm. Book of hours, Master of the Prayer Book, c.1500. Österreichische National-bibliothek, Vienna (Cod.1862, f.127v-128).

J.C. Bloem (1887-1966)

Insomnia

Thinking of death, I'm unable to sleep,
And sleepless, I think of death and the dead,
And life speeds on as it always sped,
And all that lives is doomed to the Deep.

How impotent the thin, weak noise
The life force makes it with its 'fight or die',
Compared with death's shrill clarion cry
That summons both greybeards and young boys.

Just as she who once lay down and gave
Must give birth to the child, if she will or no,
For the babe grows big inside her, so

Each being too is pregnant with death,
And the preordained goal of exchange of breath
Is no whit less than the cradle the grave.

From *Collected Poems* (Verzamelde gedichten, 1953)
Translated by James Brockway.

Insomnia

Denkend aan de dood kan ik niet slapen,
En niet slapend denk ik aan de dood,
En het leven vliet gelijk het vlood,
En elk zijn is tot niet zijn geschapen.

Hoe onmachtig klinkt het schriel 'te wapen',
Waar de levenswil ten strijd mee noodt,
Naast der doodsklaroenen schrille stoot,
Die de grijsaards oproept met de knapen.

Evenals een vrouw, die eens zich gaf,
Baren moet, of ze al dan niet wil baren,
Want het kind is groeiende in haar schoot,

Is elk wezen zwanger van de dood,
En het voorbestemde doel van 't paren
Is niet minder dan de wieg het graf.

Gerrit Achterberg (1905-1962)

Foetus

This is life's core, secure and satisfied;
inside a woman close together grow
two eyes and then two ears in turn and so
two cheeks are measured out and side by side

sustain a nose, and then a mouth's begun.
The blood, that dark and inbuilt firebrand,
keeps all its shooting tendrils close at hand
to occupy the regions newly won.

Small, deformed feet cannot find any ground,
hands, fingerless, reach out quite helplessly.
The frame is just a childish clump of tissues.

But mother's lymph and membrane slowly seal
the unfinished, and from this working round
an individual, quite complete, issues.

From Collected Poems (Verzamelde gedichten, 1964)
Translated by Judith Wilkinson.

Foetus

Dit is het leven, veilig en voldaan.
Binnen een vrouw ontstaan ze bij elkander:
twee ogen en twee oren om den ander
en tegelijkertijd, een neus komt staan

tussen de wangen en een mond vangt aan.
Het bloed, die donkre ingebouwde brander,
houdt overal zijn uitlopers voorhanden
om nieuw gebied te voegen aan lichaam.

Misvormde voetjes voelen nergens grond.
Stomphandjes steken hulpeloos naar buiten.
Het rompje is een klompje kindervlees.

Maar vocht en vliezen van de moeder sluiten
het onvoltooide toe, in deze geest,
dat er een mens langzaam wordt afgerond.

M. Vasalis (1909-1998)

Sotto Voce

So many varieties of pain –
I'll name them not.
Just one: the letting go, the parting;
and not the severing, but the state
of being severed, chills the heart.

Lovely still, the skeleton of a leaf,
light as a feather on the soil,
its only virtue now itself.
But between the arteries of grief
no joy left to grant relief:
meshes of your absence, framed,
held together now by pain,
and growing wider still with time.

Poor and, for being so poor, ashamed.

From Vistas and Visages (Vergezichten en gezichten, 1954).
Translated by James Brockway.

Sotto voce

Zoveel soorten van verdriet,
ik noem ze niet.
Maar één, het afstand doen en scheiden.
En niet het snijden doet zo'n pijn,
maar het afgesneden zijn.

Nog is het mooi, 't geraamte van een blad,
vlinderlicht rustend op de aarde,
alleen nog maar zijn wezen waard.
Maar tussen de aderen van het lijden
niets meer om u mee te verblijden:
mazen van uw afwezigheid,
bijeengehouden door wat pijn
en groter wordend met de tijd.

Arm en beschaamd zo arm te zijn.

Christine D'haen (1923-)
Birth of Anna-Livia

Geboorte van Anna-Livia

The light of birth broke through	't Geboortelicht brak aan
just when the morning sun	juist toen de morgenzon
its journey recommenced	haar reizen herbegon
for the child that crying, warm and damp from the womb	voor 't wicht dat schreiend, warm en vochtig van den schoot
put away to bed was and closed	werd weggebed en sloot
its eyes upon a tear.	zijn ogen op een traan.
She cried and would be hushed	Zij schreide en werd gestild
only by a deep draught	alleen door diepen dronk
of sweet milk and sank back	van zoete melk en zonk
into the slumber that prenatally she'd slept,	in 't slapen dat zij voorgeboortelijk, donker, diep
dark, deep and safe in the blood,	in 't bloed geborgen, sliep
from which she'd now been raised.	en nu werd uitgetild.
With eyes feeble and blind	Met ogen zwak en blind
she sought the light as does	zocht zij het licht gelijk
the new young leaf, released	het jonge blad, bevrijd
like her from the dark ground, this second month of the year;	uit duistren grond als zij, de tweede maand van 't jaar:
the green will grow with her	het groen groeit mee met haar
in warmer sun and wind.	in warmere zon en wind.
Oh see her gently unfold,	Ach hoe zij stil, zo stil
so gently; like the plant	ontplooit; gelijk de plant
that slowly opens wide	die langzaam openspant
its tight-furled flower, she wakes and on a sob	haar dichtgeloken bloem, ontwaakt ze en in een snik
she laughs with a sweet look	lacht zij met lieven blik
as though she wants to speak.	alsof zij spreken wil.
How bright and clear her face;	Hoe helder haar gezicht;
a mirror she, in which,	een spiegel is zij waar
bending, I plainly see	'k wanneer ik buig mij klaar
myself reflected, growing in life each hour,	weerkaatst zie, ieder uur aan leven toegenomen,
still swathed in dreams	versluierd nog in dromen
as is the early light.	gelijk het vroege licht.

From *Poems 1946-1958* (Gedichten 1946-1958, 1958).
Translated by Tanis Guest.

Gerrit Kouwenaar (1923-)

Genealogical

Genealogisch

One's born in a room
one dies in a room

Men wordt in een kamer geboren
men gaat in een kamer dood

in between breath, comprising the never-
ending wallpaper, which one first
learned to register with eyes, later
realised tore off cursed
with one's mouth, then thought lovely; then dire

daartussen de adem, beslaande het nooit
aflatend behang, dat men eerst
leerde registreren met ogen, later
waarmaakte afscheurde uitschold
met zijn mond, toen mooi vond, toen lelijk

that became a wood, a war, a town, a newspaper
with photos of maidens and murders, an inside, a child's
face, a very thick white darkness, and which one finally
forgot like everything

dat een bos werd, een oorlog, een stad, een krant
met foto's van meisjes en moorden, een binnen
kant, een kinder
gezicht, een heel dik wit donker, en dat men tenslotte
zoals alles vergat

jack begot a son
called jack
who begot a son
etcetera

piet gewon een zoon
die piet heette
die een zoon gewon
etcetera

this same tree was not
waving then, but an identical wind
although deceased years since
made another tree wave
although identical –

deze zelfde boom wuifde
toen niet, maar eenzelfde wind
hoewel sinds jaren ter ruste
deed een andere boom wuiven
hoewel eender –

From *Poems 1948-1978* (Gedichten 1948-1978, 1982)
Translated by Paul Vincent.

Hugo Claus (1929-)
Brother

Broer

'It's hard', he said, 'it's bloody hard.	'Het is hard', zei hij, 'godverdomme hard.
Unfair too, now at last I'm losing weight'.	En onrechtvaardig, voor het eerst word ik mager.'
Still autumn outside, maize reaching to the horizon.	Nog de herfst buiten, een maïsveld tot de einder,
The word falls, a horizon, finite.	het woord valt, einder, eindig.
Then no word more from him.	Dan geen woord meer van hem.
The plastic tube in his gullet.	In zijn slokdarm de plastic slang.
He hiccups for hours. Can't swallow.	Hij hikt uren lang. Kan niet slikken.
Still some movement in the right hand,	Nog beweging in de rechterhand
which supports the left like a plump lily.	die de linker draagt als een vette lelie.
The hand sticks up its thumb.	De hand steekt zijn duim omhoog.
He keeps signalling into his final decay.	Hij blijft seinen tot in zijn laatste verval.
His skin has turned white like a baby's.	Hij heeft wit kindervel gekregen.
He squeezes my fearful hand.	Hij knijpt in mijn angstige hand.
I'm just looking for a likeness, still, ours,	Ik zoek nog naar een gelijkenis, de onze,
her nerviness,	de onrust van haar.
his impatience (no time for time),	het ongeduld van hem (geen tijd voor tijd),
the mistrust and gullibility of them both	beider wantrouwen en goedgelovigheid
and I'm back in our earliest past,	en ik beland in ons eerste verleden,
in a world like a meadow with frogs in,	dat van een wereld als een weide met kikkers,
like a ditch full of eels	als een sloot met paling
and later bets, dares, table-tennis,	en later weddenschappen, tafeltennis,
the laws of the house, the 52 cards,	huishoudelijke wetten, de 52 kaarten,
the three dice	de drie dobbelstenen
and through it all the unquenchable hunger.	en aldoor de tomeloze honger.
(I'm getting old in your stead.	(Ik word oud in plaats van jou.
I eat pheasant and smell the woods.)	Ik eet fazant en ruik het bos.)
Now his accommodation is measured.	Nu is zijn behuizing afgemeten.
The machine does his breathing.	De machine ademt voor hem.
Mucus is sucked away.	Slijm wordt weggezogen.
A rattle out of his midriff,	Een ratel uit zijn middenrif,
and then his last movement, a lazy wink.	en dan zijn laatste beweging, een lome knipoog.

Transmigration. A disposition. A part cut away.
The body still dwindling
and then all at once in his face that was dead
a grimace, a spasm
and then a taut, savage gaze,
unbearably clear, the fury and terror
of a tyrant. What can he see? Me, a man
turning away, weakly surprised at his tears?
Then it's morning and they unfasten the straps.
And he then forever

From *Poems 1948-1993* (Gedichten, 1948-1993, 1994)
Translated by Tanis Guest.

Zielsverhuizing. Een ordening. Een portie afgesneden.
Het lijf nog verminderend
en dan plots in zijn gezicht dat dood was
een frons en een kramp
en dan een gesperde, woeste blik,
ondraaglijk helder, de woede en schrik
van een tiran. Wat ziet hij? Mij, een man
die zich afwendt, laf verbaasd over zijn tranen?
Dan is het morgen en maakt men de riemen los.
En hij dan voorgoed

Luuk Gruwez (1953-)
The Monks of Sénanque

De monniken van Sénanque

They died there quick and quiet
with no redundant death rattle hastened away
from death-place to death-place,
years older from years of longing.

Like singular lovers they lived in the landscape,
broken of desires of abundance,
benign as something not feared any more.
they would never move home again.

And we, who had come from the realms
of the recklessly rampant word,
knew that among dust and stone and silence
the sour ring of their steps was still preserved,

and were silent, as forever displaced,
in the instructiveness of rare lovers,
and from years of longing
we grew older, years and years.

From *Unrestrained Poems* (Bandeloze gedichten, 1996)
Translated by Tanis Guest.

Zij stierven er snel en stil
en zonder overtollige reutel spoedden zij zich heen
van sterfplaats naar sterfplaats,
jaren ouder van jaren verlangen.

Als zonderlinge geliefden woonden zij in het landschap,
aan alle wensen der weelde ontwend.
zachtmoedig als wat niet meer wordt gevreesd.
zij kenden geen verhuizen meer.

En wij, gekomen uit de oorden
van het roekeloos woekerend woord,
wisten tussen stof en steen en stilte
de ampere galm van hun stappen nog bewaard,

en zwegen, als voorgoed ontheemd,
in de leerzaamheid van zeldzame minnaars,
en van jaren verlangen
werden wij jaren en jaren ouder.

Esther Jansma (1958-)
Standing Empty

The manner of is always different, a fist
is clenched and falls, from water the cancer
of mould slowly leaks, but afterwards
the same thing's always gone: coherence,

the sheen of use. There is no wall here
signifying itself, no window plays
the mirror, no angle's yet right.
Uselessness is the beauty of decay and later

that's how I want to be, so naturally
overgrown with age as if with grass
sitting askew in my chair
and being superb at it.

From *Here is the Time* (Hier is de tijd, 1998).
Translated by Paul Vincent.

Menno Wigman (1966-)
To the Death

We didn't pity those who died.
    A solemn train, the parting pain:
it left us cold. We were young
    and scorned the clamour of flowers
and dressed-up sparrows, we walked away
    and lived our time to death.

The pleasures, not the pining, and the world
    a mattress. And in between all the kisses
a quiet sense that this was it: revelling,
    in the here and now, as beasts know how…
We didn't pity those who died.

And when we woke with a start in a white room
– far from the streets and the trains –
a malnourished man came to visit
    and pointed. We scarcely looked up,
remained calm and faded him out.

From *In the Summer All Cities Stink* (In de zomer stinken alle steden,
1997). *Translated by Paul Vincent.*

Leegstand

De manier is steeds anders, een vuist
balt zich en valt, uit water lekt langzaam
de kanker van schimmels, maar daarna
is altijd hetzelfde weg: samenhang.

de glans van gebruik. Hier staat geen wand
zichzelf te betekenen, geen raam speelt
voor spiegel, geen hoek is nog recht.
Nutteloosheid is de schoonheid van verval en later

wil ik ook zo zijn, zo vanzelf
door leeftijd als gras overgroeid
scheef zitten in mijn stoel
en daar heel goed in zijn.

Hard tegen hard

We waren niet begaan met wat er stierf
    Een trage stoet, een laatste groet:
het deed ons niets. We waren jong
    en hoonden het misbaar van bloemen
en verklede mussen, we liepen door
    en leefden onze tijd aan stukken.

De lusten, niet de lasten, en de wereld
    een matras. En tussen alle kussen door
een stil besef dat dit het was: het zwelgen,
    nu en hier, de wijsheid van het dier …
We waren niet begaan met wat er stierf.

En toen we wakker schrokken in een witte zaal
    – ver van de straten en de stoeten –
kwam ons een ondervoede man bezoeken
    en wees. We hebben amper opgekeken,
bleven kalm en deden hem verbleken.

A

Slice of Death

The Art of Dissection in the Low Countries

Huibrecht Sporckmans, *Anatomy Lesson in the Octogonal Theatre of the Antwerp Chamber of Surgeons*. 1660. Canvas. Museum voor Schone Kunsten, Antwerp.

Our bodies constantly remind us of our mortality. Show us images of surgery in action, and instantly we are flooded with a painful awareness of the frailty of the body. As for the sight, or just the idea, of dead bodies cut open, few of us have the stomach for it. On one level this is easily explained: our insides definitely are no feast for the eye. But beyond squeamishness lies a more deep-seated feeling that a person's remains are somehow sacrosanct. Thus it is the post-mortem that the families of murder victims often find

hardest to accept. Another illustration of this aversion to the idea of interfering with the dead is that leaving your body to science tends to be seen as a bit extravagant, or even pretentious.

This attitude is deeply ingrained in our culture and it took medical science a long time to come to terms with it. The founding fathers of Western medicine, the physicians of Periclean Athens, came out of a priestly tradition which perceived nature, and the human body in particular, as sacred, and a culture which was a priori predisposed against the idea of human dissection. For this reason, Hippocratic medicine, in spite of its many sound, still valid, technical achievements, remained quite rudimentary when it came to knowledge of anatomy and physiology. Whatever was known, or surmised, was almost entirely derived from studies of animals, which were closely observed and investigated. This remained the general situation until comparatively modern times. But, for at least one brief moment, the veil was temporarily lifted.

This moment occurred at the beginning of the third century BC in Alexandria, the great metropolis of the Nile delta, which under the Greek Ptolemaic pharaohs flourished for almost three centuries as antiquity's greatest centre of culture and learning. At the medical school, scientific anatomists worked without restriction, using the corpses – sometimes even the living bodies – of condemned criminals, which the state put at their disposal.

All this original research came to a halt with the Roman conquest of 30 BC. The Alexandrian anatomists had to revert to working on animals, while successive pagan and Christian Roman rulers destroyed the Ptolemaic public buildings, museum and great libraries.

Nonetheless, Graeco-Roman medicine produced antiquity's most celebrated anatomist: Claudius Galenus, known as Galen. Born of Greek parents in Pergamum in c.130, Galen was trained in Smyrna and Alexandria, and began his professional life as physician to the gladiatorial school at Pergamum. In c.160 he settled in Rome, where he became court physician to Marcus Aurelius. He died in c.200. Galen based his ideas on human anatomy and physiology, of which sixteen volumes of treatises are extant, on his studies of skeletons and his experimental surgery on gladiators, augmented by animal dissection and vivisection. His preferred *subjectum anatomicum* was the Barbary ape, the largest readily available primate which could last for a reasonable period of study before decomposing in the Mediterranean heat.

Because his findings about humans were extrapolated directly from animals, Galen's work was marred by invalid deductions and erroneous conclusions. Unfortunately for the development of medicine, Galen's status was such that for the next thousand years his ideas were to remain completely unquestioned. One explanation for this excessive respect for his authority may be that his credo of a single deity, and of the body as the soul's instrument, was acceptable to the prevailing orthodoxies, the Catholic Church as much as the Judaeo-Arab schools of learning, to both of which human dissection was anathema.

'Ecclessia abhorret a sanguine'

From about the sixth century onwards medical treatment passed mainly into the hands of the clergy. The great monastic institutions took in patients, and in towns hospitals staffed by priest-doctors provided both therapeutic care and surgery. We know that in Spain, for instance, Pablo, Bishop of Merida between 530 and 560, had no qualms about taking up the knife to perform Caesarean sections. The Church put an end to this sort of thing at the Council of Tours (1136), with the promulgation of '*ecclessia abhorret a sanguine*' ('the Church holds blood in abhorrence'), by which the clergy were explicitly banned from performing surgery. In the interim, secular medicine, which had not fallen entirely into abeyance, was undergoing a transformation that began in the medical school of Salerno in the tenth and eleventh centuries. Although Galen remained the yardstick, the focus of investigation at Salerno was on the pig, as the animal physiologically closest to man.

From Salerno the momentum spread. Existing universities, such as Bologna, established medical schools, while the new universities being set up – Montpelier, Paris, Oxford, Salamanca – included medical faculties for the training of professional medical practitioners. It was at Bologna that the first autopsy since classical times was carried out in 1303, and from 1314 Mondini di Luzzi pioneered the regular use of human cadavers to illustrate his anatomy lessons. Di Luzzi conducted his dissections on systematic lines, but his conclusions remained safely within the Galenic parameters. His *Anathomia*, a compilation of all anatomical theories to date, was a standard textbook for the next three centuries.

During the Black Death of the mid-fourteenth century the ban on autopsy was lifted by papal bull in order to facilitate inquiry into the pathology of the disease. But by this time sensibilities had in any case hardened somewhat – not least because during the crusades it had been fairly common for deceased warriors and pilgrims to be cut up and boiled, so that the heart and bones could be returned to Europe for burial. At the universities human dissection became less and less rare, but was still permitted only on the corpses of executed criminals, witches and other miscreants.

Medieval knowledge of the human anatomy remained sketchy in the extreme. Even so great an authority as the early fourteenth-century Flemish surgeon Jan Yperman in his treatises *Cyrurgie* and *Medicina* – which he wrote in the vernacular – describes the structure and inner workings of the body in only the most general terms. The few surviving anatomical prints of the period similarly testify to an astounding ignorance about the body's true construction. These depictions, though intended as teaching material to illustrate different types of wounds and diseases, make no attempt at verisimilitude, but aim to exemplify general principles; typically, the subject is projected frontally, in a squatting position with legs spread out. As the fourteenth century drew on, anatomy increasingly found a place in university curriculums, although 'practical' medical training continued to be mostly theoretical in character.

Not until the beginning of the sixteenth century did Pope Clement VII permit human dissection as an aid to the teaching of human anatomy. The first official anatomies were publicly staged events. Their object was not to learn, but to teach: occasions for eminent professors to exhibit their familiarity with Galen. Johannes de Ketham records one such scene in a print from his *Fasciculus medicinae* (1491). The professor, high on his rostrum, is reading from Galen, while an assistant points out the relevant organs on

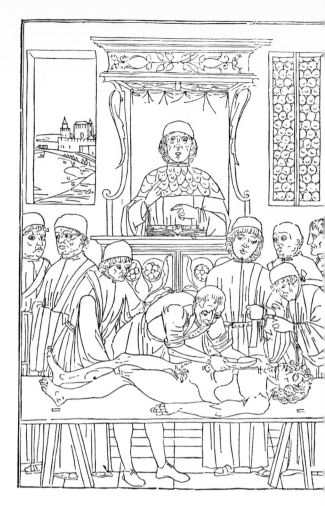

'Pre-Vesalius' anatomy, as shown in Johannes de Ketham's *Fasciculus medicinae* (Venice, 1491). The dignified professor is reading from Galen, while an assistant points out the relevant organs on the cadaver to the students. The actual cutting was done by barber-surgeons.

the cadaver. The dirty work – the actual cutting – was always relegated to barber-surgeons. Wherever the evidence diverged from Galen, this was attributed to chance aberration.

Thirst for knowledge

From the late fifteenth century onwards artists played a very special role in the new upsurge of interest in anatomy. Their concern was not with Galen, but with showing the human body as it really is – to rival antiquity in the representation of the *forma divina* as perfectly as possible. Leonardo da Vinci, as outstanding a scientist as he was an artist, was one of the first to approach the human anatomy without preconceptions, trusting only his own powers of observation. While in the service of the Borgia family he conducted dissections on over thirty corpses, working at night, in candlelit secrecy, in the mortuary of Santo Spiritu. This research produced more than a thousand drawings and voluminous notes, whose existence remained unknown until their discovery and publication in the eighteenth century.

The desire to understand the human body – so long obstructed by a

Church which held the soul's earthly shell in contempt – was just one dimension of a new thirst for knowledge. The Renaissance recast in a new mould the best elements of antiquity, discarding numerous ancient – and also more recent – misconceptions. Leonardo and Michelangelo took their inspiration from the Greeks, but absorbed their learning in a spirit of independence, testing it against the evidence of their own eyes.

With Andreas Vesalius (b. Andries de Wesel), anatomy was swept into the Renaissance. Vesalius was born in Brussels in 1514 of a prominent Brabantian family that had produced generations of medical men. He seems to have had an innate instinct for anatomical research for, by his own account, even as a child he had an insatiable appetite for taking apart moles and mice, with the occasional bonus of a stray cat or dog that had the misfortune to cross his path. In 1533, after preparatory studies in Leuven, he moved to Paris to study medicine. But to his disappointment the once-innovative medical school of the Sorbonne had become a bulwark of doctrinaire medical ideology. Anatomy, his special interest, was in a particularly sorry state as its leading lights thought hands-on work beneath their dignity, and left it entirely to their disdained underlings, the unlettered barber-surgeons. As a result, the faculty's acquaintance with human anatomy was lamentably slight, to compensate for which they clung like lice to Galen's mantle.

Even though Vesalius had had a traditional classical humanist education,

Portrait of Vesalius, from his *De humani corporis fabrica libri septem* (1543).

he was a passionate advocate of objective, scientific research. Paris offered no scope to the scientist in him. Among his professors, he recounts, there was one whose instruction consisted entirely of intoning Galenic treatises and of dissection of dogs. Of another he wrote that '*may this body of mine be cleft by the knife as oft as I observed him essay an incision upon the corpse of either man or beast, except it be at table*'. To alleviate his frustration at the paucity of study material to be obtained from a rare, official anatomy, he took to collecting bones from collapsed old tombs in the Paris graveyards. At other times, together with a few like-minded students, he would raid Montfaucon, that sinister hill crowned by '*the best gibbet in all the realm*'.

In 1536 he put Paris behind him and returned to Leuven, where he gained his baccalaureate in medicine the following year. His fascination with anatomy remained undiminished. Bit by bit he managed to cobble together his very first complete human skeleton – a treasure which he smoothly explained away to the authorities by saying it came from Paris. He even persuaded the mayor to allow him to conduct a public anatomy, an event that had not been witnessed in Leuven for eighteen years past.

'The book of the human body'

In 1537 Vesalius moved to the renowned medical school of Padua, in Italy, to complete his studies. In 1538, he was awarded his doctorate in clinical medicine in record time, and the day after was elevated to a chair in anatomical medicine. The new professor lost no time in making his debut: on the very day of his installation Vesalius, a crowd of avid students around him, was already bent over the dissection table investigating a good, fresh corpse. He combined the traditionally separate roles of surgeon, demonstrator and lecturer. Soon he developed an altogether new way of teaching anatomy, with the professor performing all the sawing, cutting and slicing himself, explaining his procedures on a skeleton hanging beside the dissection table. He used animal dissection – and sometimes vivisection – in his lectures, too, to show how organs function or to clarify points of comparative anatomy. These innovations quickly attracted a large influx of students. In 1538 Vesalius published *Tabulae anatomicae sex*, a set of six anatomical prints, in which he alphabetically cross-referenced the different segments of the central drawings with marginal texts. His collaborator on the drawings was the young Flemish artist Jan Stephaan van Kalkar, a brilliant draughtsman and a pupil of Titian.

In terms of the history of medicine the *Tabulae* is a transitional work: Vesalius is original in his observations, but his interpretations show him still thinking within Galenic parameters. Increasingly, though, Vesalius began to doubt the infallibility of Galen. He became convinced that in human anatomy there existed no truth other than '*the book of the human body*' itself. He became an ardent propagandist for intellectual freedom and original research in the study of anatomy. Together with Kalkar he began to plan the work that immortalised him, his encyclopaedic *De humani corporis fabrica libri septem* (Seven Books on the Structure of the Human Body). For some five years the two young men steeped themselves in Galen, relentlessly test-

Cover plate of the *Fabrica*, with Vesalius hard at work. This plate is a manifesto of Vesalius' view on anatomy and the way it should be done.

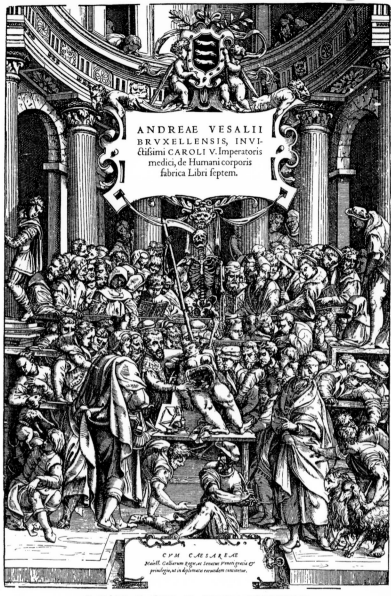

ANDREAE VESALII
BRVXELLENSIS, INVI-
étiſsimi CAROLI V. Imperatoris
medici, de Humani corporis
fabrica Libri ſeptem.

CVM CAESAREAE
Maieſt. Galliarum Regu,ac Senatus Veneti gratia &
priuilegio,ut in diplomatis eorundem continetur.

BASILEAE, PER IOANNEM OPORINVM.

ing the hallowed theories against the evidence of the dissection table. Error upon error was uncovered as the two young men examined, observed, discussed, analysed, translated into drawings, and recorded their findings. In all more than two hundred errors and inaccuracies in Galen were noted. Throughout the project Vesalius could count on the support of the Paduan authorities. Already accustomed to providing the tireless young professor from Flanders with executed criminals, they would sometimes even delay an execution until he was ready for his next subject. The *Fabrica*, meticulously printed in Basel, and with plates commissioned from the top Venetian woodcutters, appeared in 1543. This oeuvre more than any other conclusively liberated medical science, and anatomy in particular, from the shackles of thirteen centuries of Galenic compilations, exegeses, and misreadings. Vesalius's own verdict on Galen was that he had been '*fooled by his monkeys*', but he continued to hold him in honour. He reserved his contempt for Galen's misinterpreters and, above all, for his slavish followers, those intellectually constipated high academics, who '*black-garbed like crows, sit enthroned at their lecterns, arrogantly holding forth on matters they have never tested for themselves, mouthing merely what they have learnt by heart from other men's books, or have there under their noses in written form*'. Regarding the second category, which refers to the kind of anatomical lesson we see pictured by De Ketham, Vesalius adds: '*Thus everything is taught wrongly, entire days are wasted on absurd questions, and from all this confusion the observer carries away less than any butcher in his stall might teach a practitioner.*' By contrast, the cover plate of the *Fabrica* shows how it should be done: Vesalius, in person, is seen at work on an open cadaver, onlookers thronging around. For general orientation a skeleton hangs just behind the dissection table, while small animals are held in readiness for comparative examination. Max Frisch rightly called this print '*a manifesto for educational reform*'.

Kalkar's illustrations for the *Fabrica* are masterpieces of accuracy and craftsmanship. Magnificent, for example, are his 'animations', or 'musclemen': drawings in which the figure, skin peeled back to reveal the outer musculature, appears as if in motion, with every muscle shown as an independently functioning unit.

The texts, couched by Vesalius in the Latin of the finest Roman rhetorical tradition, are exemplars of Renaissance erudition. Unlike lesser writers, he never clutters up the flow of his reasoning with meaningless digressions, but when apposite will seamlessly incorporate an entertaining anecdote to illustrate a point. An example of this is his racy tale of a rapacious Spaniard who, while his whore is sunk in post-coital slumber, steals and swallows her necklace, thus proving that the duodenal valve has rather more give than Galen gave it credit for.

Predictably, the *Fabrica* was greeted by howls of protest and indignation, especially from Vesalius's one-time tutors, whose academic dignity had been insulted. One Sorbonne professor, Jacobus Sylvius, who among other things spoke of '*error-infested ordure*' from '*a presumptuous and ignorant calumniator*', went so far as to agitate for a book-burning under the slogan of '*Deliver it unto Vulcan!*' Though the tempest had little lasting effect, it was all too much for Vesalius. In 1544 he became court physician to Emperor Charles V, his dedicatee for the *Fabrica*, and quit academic life for ever.

Vesalius changed the face of medicine. In the five-year burst of blazing inspiration that generated the *Fabrica* he single-handedly inaugurated the principles of scientific medicine and paved the way for modern research methodology.

Growing pains of a new anatomy

Over the second half of the sixteenth and first half of the seventeenth centuries the terra incognita of the human body was progressively explored. In

One of Jan Stephaan van Kalkar's *tours de force* in the *Fabrica*: a so-called 'muscleman'. A number of these naturalistic yet technically precise drawings show the dissected body in different poses.

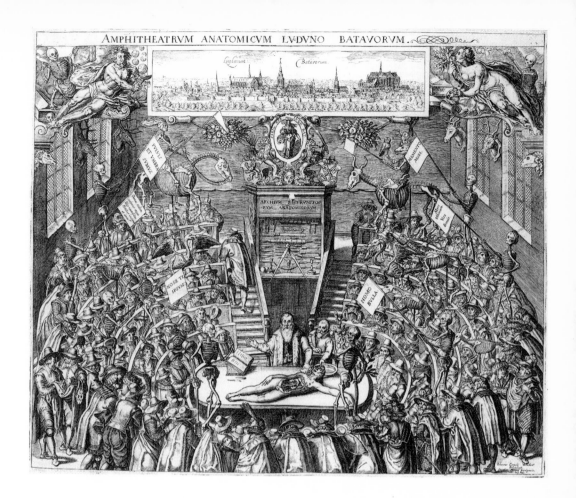

The Leiden *Theatrum
Anatomicum*, which opened
its doors in 1593, in an
1609 engraving by
Bartholomeus Dolendo,
after Jan Cornelisz.
Woudanus
(46.6 x 55.8 cm).
Rijksmuseum, Amsterdam.

the Low Countries, as elsewhere, a vernacular medical vocabulary emerged
through the increasing availability of translations from the Latin, the traditional language of learning. Within the medical profession separate surgeons' guilds were established, whose training entailed 'anatomies', or dissections of corpses, held in public and conducted by praelectors appointed
by the guild. Sessions lasted for more than a day, and always took place in
winter because corpses last longer in the cold. Though organised for educa-
tive purposes, such anatomies soon turned into spectacles of public entertainment. Such was the interest that when Leiden University opened a pur-
pose-built *Theatrum Anatomicum*, or anatomy theatre, in 1593, people were
prepared to pay for admission even when there was no dissection taking
place. A 1609 engraving of this *Theatrum* shows a circular, tiered interior.
Along the walls human and animal skeletons are displayed, holding aloft
banners emblazoned with edifying maxims, such as '*We are but dust and
shadow*' and '*Man is a bubble*', to keep the spectator in mind of the transience of this earthly life.

Although anatomy was on its way up, the way forward for teaching and
research in the subject was by no means smooth. Amsterdam acquired a
proper anatomy theatre only in 1691, while at that time dissections in Ghent
and Brussels were still taking place in the town hall, in rooms temporarily

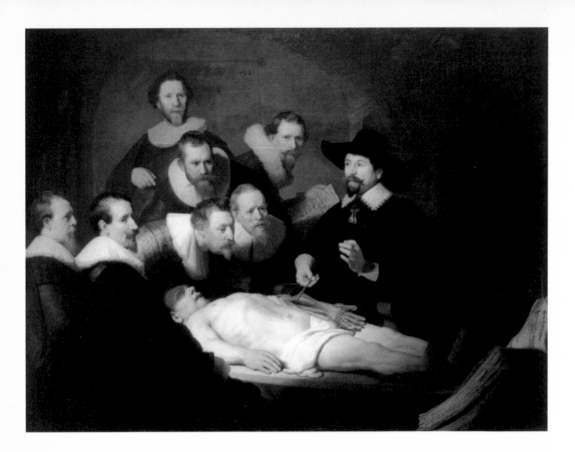

Rembrandt H. van Rijn,
*The Anatomy Lesson of
Dr Tulp*. 1632.
Canvas, 169.5 x 216.5 cm.
Mauritshuis, The Hague.

adapted for the purpose. Independent researchers could still expect to encounter active opposition. As late as c.1700 it was still possible for so eminent a scientist as Jan Palfijn to be expelled from Kortrijk on no less than two occasions for being in possession of a private collection of human bones. In 1708 he was appointed to a lectorship in anatomy and clinical medicine by the municipal authorities of Ghent. He had already carried out an unusual assignment there a few years earlier, when he had been specially engaged to dissect two '*monster children*', who were joined '*at the lower body*'. In 1718 he published his *Surgical Dissection of the Human Body* (Heelkonstige ontleeding van 's menschen lighaem) which in the course of the eighteenth century was to be translated into French, German, and Spanish, and in 1822 into Japanese as well. Profesionally Palfijn was not exclusively concerned with death; he also had a vested interest in birth, being above all known as the inventor of the obstetric forceps, although this is not entirely correct. The instrument had been developed considerably earlier in England, but was not much used until Palfijn set himself to promote it, culminating in his presentation of the '*iron hands*' to the *Académie* in Paris in 1721.

The great strides made in anatomy in the seventeenth century had surprisingly little impact on contemporary surgical practice. Together with barbers, surgeons continued to be the lowest of the low in the medical hierarchy. Guy Patin, head of the medical faculty in Paris around the middle of the seventeenth century, contemptuously dubbed them '*booted valets – a rab-*

ble of preposterous, mustachioed coxcombs brandishing razors'. It should be added, however, that not long after this the reputation of surgery sky-rocketed following the successful treatment by surgeon-barber Félix of the hitherto apparently incurable chronic anal fistula of Louis xiv.

Group portrait with corpse

During the first half of the seventeenth century, as we have seen, dissection became more or less institutionalised as the accepted medium for the teaching and study of anatomy. In this context, physicians and dissections began to feature more and more in paintings by the great and lesser masters of the Dutch School. The most famous example of the genre is Rembrandt's *The Anatomy Lesson of Dr Tulp*. When Sir Joshua Reynolds studied the painting in the Amsterdam anatomy theatre in 1781, he noted: '*The Professor Tulpius dissecting a corpse which lies on the table, by Rembrandt. To avoid making it an object disagreeable to look at, the figure is but just cut at the wrist. (...) The dead body is perfectly well drawn, (a little fore-shortened) and seems to have been just washed. Nothing can be more truly the colour of dead flesh.*'

The Rembrandt picture originally formed part of the collection of the Amsterdam guild of surgeons, which had commissioned it. The earliest work in the collection – the first of all known Dutch anatomy pictures – is *The Anatomy Lesson of Dr Sebastiaen Egbertsz* by Aert Pietersz. Looking at this piece and others like it, there can be little doubt of the intention: these were representations of the guild's collective dignity, commissioned to mark a praelectorate or to record its members for posterity. In the Pietersz anatomy picture the figure of praelector Egbertsz, scalpel in hand, stands in the midst of thirty fellow-practitioners. The ostensible focus of interest, the *subjectum anatomicum* on the dissection table, is heavily obscured: its function is essentially that of the ball in a group photograph of a football team. Indeed, the majority of pictures in the Amsterdam surgeons' collection are not anatomy pictures, but straight group portraits of the type known as 'warden portraits'. Yet another kind of painting, examples of which include Nicolaes Pickenoy's *The Anatomy Lesson of Dr Johan Fonteyn* , and Tibout Regters' *The Anatomy Lesson of Prof Petrus Camper*, makes do with a head or a skull, as tokens of the complete corpse, to signify the assembled gentlemen's occupation. In such cases we are concerned with a mixed form, a cross between the full-bodied anatomy picture and the 'warden portrait'.

Not one of these anatomies is a realistic representation of any particular dissection held on any particular occasion. For instance, the numerous spectators who habitually attended such events are nowhere in evidence. Cornelis Troost's *The Anatomy Lesson of Dr Willem Roëll* does show the praelector at work – but on the exposed knee joint of the *subjectum,* which is not in keeping with the order in which dissections had to be conducted. Correct procedure was to begin with an abdominal incision, so that the most perishable organs could be displayed first and immediately removed. The same is true of *The Anatomy Lesson of Dr Tulp*, in which we see Nicolaes Tulp clamping a nerve in the corpse's arm with the abdomen still intact. Some art historians have interpreted this as a homage to Vesalius, who in his

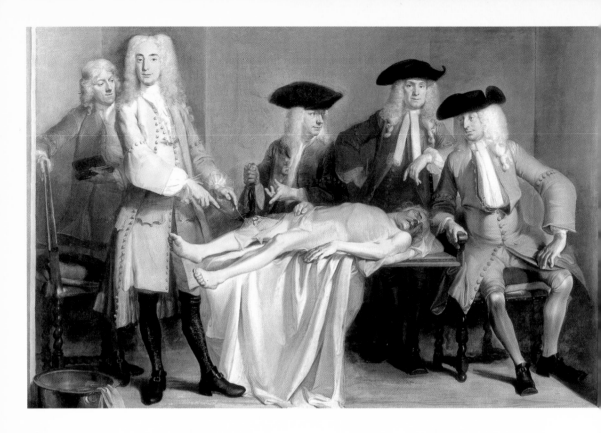

Cornelis Troost, *The Anatomy Lesson of Dr Willem Roëll*. 1728. Canvas, 195 x 306 cm. Amsterdams Historisch Museum.

well-known portrait in the *Fabrica* similarly lays bare the structure of the arm.

The one piece in which standard dissection procedure does appear to be followed is Rembrandt's other anatomy picture, *The Anatomy Lesson of Dr Jan Deijman*, which shows the *subjectum* from the front, the lower abdomen opened. Praelector Deijman is inserting his scalpel into the tough membrane encasing the brain, while a colleague holds the top of the skull in his hands. Nonetheless, here too procedure conflicts with the method advocated by Vesalius, namely that before cutting into the skull the head should first be severed from the torso. Worth noting here is that brain dissection counted as the very acme of surgical skill; only the most accomplished anatomists could hope to carry it out successfully. In light of this, it could well be that this painting was conceived as a testimony to Deijman's virtuosity in the dissection room.

The Amsterdam surgeons' collection, most of which is now in the Amsterdam Historical Museum, contains two more anatomy pictures which were probably painted to exemplify the particular abilities and specialisations of the praelector whom both portray. This was Frederick Ruysch, who enjoyed not only an international reputation as an outstandingly productive publicist, but was also a great authority on the mounting of corpses. In the latter connection, he had developed preservation techniques that allowed him to perform a number of anatomies outside the winter months. In Adriaen Backer's *The Anatomy Lesson of Dr Frederick Ruysch* the virtually unblemished, fresh-complexioned condition of the *subjectum* is presumably a testimony to Ruysch's understanding of and technique in the art of embalming. The second canvas, by Jan van Neck, which bears the same title but was painted thirteen years earlier, depicts Ruysch dissecting the corpse of a stillborn baby still clutching the umbilical cord in its tiny hand. The serene expression of the miniscule *subjectum* is strongly reminiscent of the embalmed infant heads in Ruysch's extensive private cabinet of anatomical specimens, which ranged from individual organs to complete corpses and was famed far and wide, and of which part is still in the Netherlands. Other parts of the collection went to the St Petersburg anatomy schools after their purchase by Peter the Great, the science-obsessed Russian Tsar who in his quest to modernise his country scoured Europe for new technologies and ideas.

The teeming diversity of life

Another port of call for Peter the Great in the Dutch Republic was the home of Anthonie van Leeuwenhoek, whose discovery of micro-organisms unlocked the deepest secrets of the human body, and thus inaugurated the microbiological sciences. In 1676 Van Leeuwenhoek, working with homemade microscopes which magnified objects 270 times, was the first to observe bacteria, protozoa such as amoebas (which he called 'animacules'), and many more of the most miniscule forms of life. As he recounts, he could

Rembrandt H. van Rijn, *The Anatomy Lesson of Dr Jan Deijman* (fragment). 1656. Canvas, 113 x 135 cm. Amsterdams Historisch Museum.

barely contain his wonderment on first seeing how a single morsel of food scraped from his own teeth sustained a greater diversity of tiny, writhing, miraculously beautiful creatures than there were people in the Low Countries. For this and related achievements he was elected to the Royal Society of England.

Vesalius found that the secrets of our dead bodies, as exposed by the dissection table, 'the scandal of death', were not universally welcomed. 'The scandal of life', as exposed by the microscope, received no better reception. Perhaps, with our inbuilt sense of the dignity and the importance of the human race, it will never be entirely possible to come to terms with our knowledge of the frailty of the body and its place in the teeming diversity of life.

FILIP MATTHIJS
Translated by Sonja Prescod.

Jan van Neck, *The Anatomy Lesson of Dr Frederik Ruysch.* 1683.
Canvas, 142 x 203 cm.
Amsterdams Historisch Museum.

Abortion

and the Discrepancy between Reality and the Law

Where abortion is concerned, Belgium and the Netherlands are exceptional countries: the figures there are the lowest in the world. In the United States, for example, abortion rates are almost three times higher. Yet Belgium and the Netherlands both have very liberal legislation, which is also broadly interpreted. The situation in the two countries shows that legislation has very little influence on the number of pregnancy terminations carried out. Preventing abortion would appear to be a question of efficient birth control rather than draconian laws.

In Belgium and the Netherlands abortion hardly features as a political issue, and the *status quo* is more or less generally accepted. Occasionally, Christian or extreme Conservative groups attempt to put the subject back on the political agenda, but they find little support from public opinion. Sometimes it seems as if the governments are deliberately ignoring the issue: memories of intense debates during the 1970s and 1980s are still very much alive in the minds of politicians, and they do not want abortion to become a divisive issue again. Furthermore, although the Christian Democratic parties are in opposition in both countries, there is not a single non-confessional party which will risk antagonising them by pushing the issue too emphatically to the forefront of political debate. Above all, however, it seems that the problem of the abortion issue has simply been solved, so why should politicians worry about it? Where dispute still exists on the subject, it is about more technical issues, such as the subsidising of abortion clinics.

The storm before the calm

In the past, the political debate on abortion was far from calm: from 1970 the call for liberalisation led to protracted conflicts in Belgium and the Netherlands. The legal ban on abortion met with heavy criticism, initially from the women's movement, but also from humanists and liberals. However, the Christian Democrat parties in particular, which then had much greater political influence, strongly resisted any form of liberalisation and as a result the subject was postponed indefinitely. This did not prevent the establishment of a number of unofficial, non-commercial abortion clinics, where the procedure was carried out by skilled doctors with the necessary medical care and supervision. These clinics, which often had the support of influential socialist or liberal politicians, were generally tolerated by the judiciary. Occasionally, however, there were prosecutions, and the political debate would flare up again.

In both Belgium and the Netherlands, the result of the political struggle amounted to not much more than a legalisation of current practice. Liberalisation – in the Netherlands in 1981-1984 and in Belgium in 1990 – did no more than rubber-stamp the existing situation, and had little influence on the actual number of abortions.

Adverse circumstances

Traditionally, Belgium and the Netherlands are consensus democracies, which means that the various factions of the political elite usually attempt to reach a compromise on sensitive issues. In the case of abortion too, non-confessional parties chose to take into account the sensitivities of Christian groups. Rather than introducing full liberalisation, a relatively complicated compromise was reached which met the demands of opponents as well as advocates. The Christian Democrats in particular feared the spectre of 'abortion on demand', whereby women could resort to abortion at any time for any reason. In a number of other countries, this fear led to the introduction of a 'medical grounds' rule: the legislators drew up a list of medical grounds which justified pregnancy termination, for example, pregnancy following rape, or the likelihood of congenital deformity. Experience in other countries, for example Germany, has shown that such rules are always abused. The Netherlands, Belgium and France have avoided this problem by introducing the legal fiction of an 'urgent situation': abortion is a punishable offence unless the woman finds herself in extremely adverse circumstances – a term for which there is no official legal definition. This means that the woman alone can decide whether her situation is sufficiently urgent for an abortion. In Belgium, adverse circumstances can relate to the situation within a relationship, a definite desire not to have the child, material or financial hardship, or the age of the woman in question.

By employing a term such as 'adverse circumstances', the law is indicating that abortion is not a simple everyday medical procedure, but one which should be a matter for ethical debate. The fact that there is a legal period for consideration reinforces that message. This did not, however, satisfy the Christian opponents of liberalisation. In 1990, King Baudouin of Belgium refused to sign the abortion act, and was even prepared to abdicate for several days so that the government, via a constitutional loophole, could pass the law without his signature. This royal initiative was no more than the last *incident de parcours* in the difficult realisation of a law which has since caused little social or political turmoil. One cannot escape the impression that even the Catholic Church has learned to live with liberal abortion laws. In recent years, Christian groups have taken various initiatives to provide alternative support in unwanted pregnancy, such as emphasising the possibility of adoption.

The way in which the debate on abortion has been defused in Belgium and the Netherlands is important because, in Anglo-Saxon countries in particular, the political debate on the subject is conducted in black and white terms, which by definition preclude any form of compromise. Belgian and Dutch political consensus shows that, with an ethically delicate issue such as abortion, groups with radically opposed positions can reach a workable compromise which produces a humane and fair solution. Moreover, implementing the law leads to few problems in practice because the operation has been completely lifted out of the commercial sector. In Belgium as well as the Netherlands, abortion can only be carried out in a general hospital or specialised clinic. This means that there are very few complaints about the quality of the operation or medical care.

Low abortion rates

Abortion legislation inevitably has a strong moral and symbolic dimension, and therefore seems far removed from day-to-day practice. Contrary to what the opponents of liberalisation feared, there are no indications that the number of abortions has increased significantly as a result of statutory changes in 1981-1984 (the Netherlands) and 1990 (Belgium). However, Belgium has seen a slight increase in recent years, from 10,380 in 1993 to 12,226 in 1997 (more recent official figures are not available). It is not clear whether this is a real increase, or an artificial increase resulting from a greater willingness on the part of doctors and patients to register abortions. It is clear that in the early 1990s there was still considerable reluctance to cooperate with abortion registration, given the climate of illegality in which abortions had had to be performed for many years.

Liberalisation of abortion laws did not, then, lead to an explosion in the number of terminations performed, as opponents had feared. When the figures are compared with other countries, the number of abortions in Belgium and the Netherlands is remarkably low, despite the fact that women have relatively easy access to the procedure (see Table).

Table: Abortion frequency, 1991-1996
(No. per thousand women in the 15-44 age group)

Country	1991	1992	1993	1994	1995	1996
Belgium	-	-	6.1	6.2	6.2	6.8
Netherlands	5.6	5.6	5.7	6.0	6.1	6.5
England & Wales	15.2	14.8	14.7	14.6	14.4	15.6
USA	26.3	25.9	25.4	24.1	22.9	22.9
Canada	14.7	15.1	15.3	15.5	15.5	-

Source: International Family Planning Perspectives, 1999

The low abortion frequency in the Low Countries cannot therefore be explained in terms of a lack of availability of abortion services, but has much more to do with effective contraception in all sections of the population. Access to health services in general, and to birth control in particular, is universal in Belgium and the Netherlands. And virtually everyone has access to education, too, in which relationship and sex education is fairly well incorporated. In other countries, abortion frequency is particularly high among groups subject to social exclusion. In Belgium and the Netherlands, too, the situation with regard to ethnic minority groups, where the abortion rate is high, is a worrying one. These groups have to deal not only with structural forms of disadvantage, but may also have different convictions regarding abortion. Several years ago there was a minor political row in the Netherlands when it transpired that some members of ethnic minority groups were resorting to selective abortion in favour of male children.

A further explanation for the low abortion rates in Belgium and the Netherlands lies in the success of educational campaigns. This is evident from the fact that teenage pregnancies and abortions are exceptional occurrences in both countries. In an international comparative study, the Alan Guttmacher Institute concluded that the Low Countries, together with Germany, have the lowest teenage abortion rates in the world. The number fluctuates around five per thousand women in the 15-20 age group. By comparison: in England the number is approximately four times higher, and in the USA it is as high as 32 abortions per 1,000 women in that age group. There has been some concern in recent years about a possible increase in the abortion rate in this group. The first possible cause relates to the age at which teenagers have their first sexual experiences. Both in the Netherlands and in Flanders, this age is falling. The number of 'sexually active' years for young people is therefore increasing, and is accompanied by a rise in the number of unwanted pregnancies. A further explanation could be an unintentional side-effect of AIDS prevention campaigns which emphasise the importance of using condoms. A number of healthcare specialists believe that sexually-active young people are using condoms more often and assuming that they provide effective protection against pregnancy. The message that combined use of the condom (as protection against sexually transmitted diseases) and the pill (as a contraceptive) is recommended, has not really reached young people. Figures for the coming years will show whether the increase is a significant trend, or simply an incidental fluctuation. In any case, it should be realised that the number of teenage abortions is now at an absolute minimum compared with the rest of the world. Attempts to reduce the figure even further, for example by placing more emphasis on sex education, will probably have no more than a marginal effect on teenage abortion rates. Moreover, it will be even more difficult to compare such figures in the future. Part of the current 'demand' for abortion will be absorbed by a wider distribution of the morning-after pill and the further introduction of the abortion pill RU486. The use of such pharmaceutical methods of pregnancy termination is more difficult to register precisely than the number of abortions performed in clinics. If, in the coming years, we see a fall in the number of abortions, it is more likely to reflect a switch to other methods than an actual fall in the demand for pregnancy termination.

MARC HOOGHE
Translated by Yvette Mead.

BIBLIOGRAPHY

DELMONTE, DORETTA, *Abortion Matters. 25 Years' Experience in the Netherlands*. Utrecht, 1996.
HENSHAW, STANLEY, SUSHEELA SINGH and TAYLOR HAAS, 'Recent Trends in Abortion Rates Worldwide'. In: *International Family Planning Perspectives*, 25(1), pp. 44-48, 1999.
HOOGHE, MARC, 'De liberalisering van abortus als strijdpunt in de Belgische politiek'. In: *Res Publica*, 32(4), pp. 489-509, 1990.
Jaarboek Geboortenregeling, Relaties, Sexualiteit, 1 (1985)- 15 (2000). Trefpunt CGSO, Ghent (http://www.cgso.be).
OUTSHOORN, JOYCE, *De politieke strijd rondom de abortuswetgeving in Nederland*. The Hague, 1986.

Off
with their Heads

The Death Penalty in Belgium

On 26 July 1578 three Minorites were burned at the stake in Bruges. Three more friars were whipped and exiled. They were all convicted of sodomy. This illustration was included in the late 16th-century *Descriptio et Figurae rerum Belgicae*. Stadsarchief, Bruges (Collection G. Michiels).

When France annexed the Southern Netherlands at the end of the eighteenth century, the guillotine, *the* symbol of the French Revolution, became the universal machine of death in these parts too. Under the Ancien Régime there was an abundant variety of gruesome, theatrical methods of execution: decapitation by the sword, strangling, racking, burying alive, burning at the stake, drawing and quartering, drowning, boiling and finally, the most degrading punishment, hanging on the gallows. At the height of the French Revolution feudal power symbols that were seen as cruel and unjust implements of the old jurisdiction, including instruments of torture and punishment, were publicly and ritually burnt or destroyed in several large towns in what is now Belgium.

Between the two French invasions (the first in 1792-1793, the second in 1793-1794) some of the old-style punishments were carried out, as the dreadful case of Martin Pirard in Liège illustrates. On 22 November 1793

'Old-style' execution in Flanders: in 1694 Alexander Dellguerre was convicted for a sixfold murder and executed on the Grand' Place in Brussels. These 4 prints, taken from a set of 13 by Gaspar Bouttats, show his ordeal on the wheel. Afterwards he was eviscerated and beheaded. Koninklijke Bibliotheek Albert I, Brussels.

Pieter Bruegel the Elder, *The Road to Calvary* (detail). 1564. Panel, 124 x 170 cm. Kunsthistorisches Museum, Vienna.

the man was bound to a cart and driven to the execution site whilst his executioners went to work on him with red-hot tongs. On reaching his destination he was tied to a St Andrew's cross and his limbs were broken one by one with an iron bar. His right fist was chopped off and nailed to the wheel, after which Pirard, badly battered, was himself put on display on the wheel for a couple of hours. Finally he was put out of his misery by strangling.

Equality in the face of death

The guillotine was, as its inventor Ignace-Joseph Guillotin described it in all seriousness, fast, painless and humane. This revolutionary machine combined the equality of all citizens before the law with equality in the face of death. Previously only the aristocracy had been honourably beheaded by the sword. The Counts Egmont and Hoorne, who were executed in 1568 by the Spanish Governor Alva, were amongst the 'privileged' individuals. With the guillotine the death penalty was carried out mechanically, in the same way every time. The long-drawn-out spectacles of retribution, in which the crowd was closely involved and revelled despite their horror and revulsion, were replaced by the efficient, rational, purely physical act of decapitation. The nature of the dramatic staging that was part of an execution changed. The symbolic and religious significance of public executions became blurred. But decapitation was still the culmination of a protracted ceremony which began with a procession along a prearranged route, with police escorting the condemned person(s), on foot or in a police vehicle, from the local prison to the scaffold on the market place. The public watched as the guillotine blade sliced mercilessly down. The severed head was taken from

Execution by the sword of the Counts Egmont and Hoorne on the Grand' Place in Brussels on 5 June 1568. Stichting Atlas van Stolk, Rotterdam.

the basket by the executioner and shown to the prosecutor. The eager crowds could air their various sentiments towards the condemned man verbally, ranging from compassion and disgust to indignation and hatred. It was no longer customary, either, to throw dirt, rotten eggs or stones. Nevertheless, the punishments that became fashionable with the French Revolution still contained certain highly demeaning elements, and humiliating punishments like branding and the pillory were by no means consigned to the past. The death penalty was no longer preceded by a public display, though; it had to be carried out immediately, without additional torture, in the spirit of Guillotin.

The guillotine travelled from town to town. During the night of 1-2 November 1803 it was erected on the main square in Bruges. On All Souls' Day the 23 condemned members of the infamous Baekelandt gang, 19 men and 4 women, were executed. The eager onlookers, packed together in their thousands, were 'treated to' a horrifying bloodbath. The thirty-year-old gang leader, Lodewijk Baekelandt, was one of the last to be led to the scaffold. Along with Amandus Simpelaere, Isabella van Maele and Francisca Ameye he was tried for the only murder the gang had committed. Article 13 of the French penal code required that murderers should wear a red shirt and a black cloth over their heads. As a little extra the crowd could gape at three women who were put on display for six hours, tied to posts on the scaffold. On each post you could read the woman's name, age and birthplace in large letters.

The condemned men's greatest terror was that the blade of the guillotine would not be sharp enough. Fear of that cruel death was, after all, not completely unfounded. On 29 September 1807 Michel Lancelin from Liège, who had killed his brother and his housekeeper, was uneasy about it. Exactly one hour before the execution he took his own life. In order not to disappoint the thousands of curious onlookers gathered round the scaffold and, in particular, because Lancelin came from a prominent Liègeois family, the Public Prosecutor decided to carry on with the execution and the corpse was beheaded...

Whilst 'ordinary' condemned men were usually tied to the guillotine and beheaded without much more ado, the ceremonial for patricide was particularly humiliating in the French era. The condemned person was brought to the gallows, clad in a red shirt and a black headcloth, where he or she was first put on public display whilst the charges were read out. Just before the execution the murderer's right hand was chopped off on a special chopping block, immediately followed by decapitation by guillotine. This punishment was carried out in all its gruesomeness on the Friday Market in Ghent on 25 January 1822, when 24-year-old Livinus van Butsel was executed for patricide. After Belgian independence in 1830 this ceremonial was retained in the penal code, but in practice clemency was always extended as far as chopping off the hand was concerned.

The law and reality

The Napoleonic *Code Pénal* of 1810 continued in force under Dutch rule (1815-1830), and also after the Belgian Revolution until the new Belgian penal code, which is still in use, was introduced in 1867.

Under the influence of eighteenth century ideals of humanitarian enlightenment, the abolitionist movement in Belgium found its first Belgian spokesman in Eduard Ducpétiaux. Ducpétiaux obtained his doctorate in Roman and Contemporary Law from the University of Ghent on 11 July 1827 with a thesis on capital punishment. This was a Latin translation of chapter eight of his monumental study *De la peine de mort* (On the Death

Penalty), which had been published shortly before and been well received in both the Northern and Southern provinces of the Netherlands. As irony would have it, Ducpétiaux, who played a prominent role in the Belgian Revolution, was arrested by Dutch soldiers in October 1830 for incitement to unrest and condemned to death by firing squad. But his sojourn in the damp dungeons of Antwerp citadel did not last long. The Prince of Orange intervened, and he was soon released.

After Ducpétiaux, condemned men had to rely on the Belgian King's prerogative to grant them a reprieve. Despite several legislative initiatives the stipulation that every man condemned to death should be beheaded was upheld in Belgian criminal law until 1991. Nonetheless, from a historical point of view, Belgium led the whole of Europe in renouncing the death penalty for political offences when the Penal Code was amended in 1867. The death penalty for serious crimes in criminal law (robbery with murder, patricide, matricide, poisoning and arson) has a more complicated history. From early 1834 conservative parliamentarians increased their demands for the reintroduction of the guillotine, while successive liberal Ministers of Justice had in practice suspended its use on a trial basis. However, despite the fact that crime statistics showed a drop in the number of indictable offences from 1830-1834, 9 February 1835 again saw a beheading on the main square in Kortrijk, the first since Belgian independence. On the same day, Charles de Brouckère, the future burgomaster of Brussels, for the second time presented a bill to abolish the death penalty once and for all. It was narrowly defeated. The retentionists maintained numerical superiority in the Belgian Parliament.

The abolitionists wanted to finish with the past and were critical, as they were elsewhere in Europe, of the effectiveness of the death penalty as a deterrent, as much for serious criminals as for civilisation in general. According to them, instead of instilling fear and respect for authority, the barbarism of the death penalty roused feelings of disgust and sympathy and had a pernicious effect on the spectators. The debate was influenced not only by differing views about prison sentences as a means of correction, but also by the public nature of the executions. In the mid-nineteenth century, residents of the main square in Antwerp had had more than enough of the gruesome spectacle and requested that the scaffold be erected in a less central part of the city. Initially, partly because of pressure from the shopkeepers and tradespeople, the city authorities ignored their request. A public execution on the main square brought with it an atmosphere of festivity and increased consumption in the inns and shops. During the same period there were calls in Parliament for the death penalty to be carried out within the prison walls: *'In order not to draw the people's attention to a hideous punishment that terrifies some and inures others'*. But despite criticism executions retained their public nature, even in the new Penal Code of 1867.

As far as the death penalty was concerned, the law was one thing, reality another. Of 848 death sentences passed between 1835 and 1863, 'only' 55 were actually carried out. The other condemned persons were granted a reprieve by the King and their punishment commuted to lifelong forced labour. Certain cases, where the sentence was disproportionate to the offence or where guilt was not sufficiently proved, were grist to the abolitionists' mill. Their campaign was boosted, for example, by the 'scandal of Es-

Anonymous Flemish drawing (1542), showing a condemned man on his way to the scaffold. Médiathèque municipale, Cambrai (Ms. 124, Superius, fol. 53).

canaffles' in 1844 when Fernand Duret was beheaded for his – unproven – part in the night-time arson of a rapeseed field. The case of Frans van de Weghe from Dikkele, who had killed a friend accidentally in a drunken brawl in 1846 but received no mercy, also helped. Reactions in the press to this 'judicial murder' were unusually sharp, partly because around the same time a contemporary who had poisoned his young wife in cold blood did have his sentence commuted to lifelong forced labour. However, the refusal of a plea for mercy could also be perceived as an act of justice. Count Hippolyte de Visart de Bury de Bocarmé, condemned to death in 1850 for poisoning his brother-in-law with home-made nicotine, was convinced that King Leopold I would grant him a reprieve. But the ghastly nature of the minutely planned crime and the enormous furore that the case caused at the Assizes in Hainault actually cost the aristocrat his life. His execution was presented as proof of the incorruptibility of the highest political and legal authority.

The execution of Jan Coucke and Pieter Goethals was of great symbolic value not only to the Flemish Movement, but also in the struggle against the death penalty. Coucke and Goethals, two Flemish labourers who worked in Wallonia, were convicted of robbing and murdering the widow Dubois in

Couillet and beheaded on the main square in Charleroi on 16 November 1860. Public Prosecutor de Bavay wanted to see heads roll in the case of the so-called 'Black Gang' that had been terrorising the area between the Sambre and the Meuse for some time. A few months later fourteen members of the gang were arrested and one of them, Leopold Rabet, declared that the two Flemings had been unjustly executed. Coucke en Goethals had been unable to follow the trial properly as it was carried out in French, and had most probably been wrongly convicted due to poor translation. This gave rise to heated debates in Parliament about the shortcomings of a monolingual judiciary.

Death to the death penalty

The struggle against the death penalty, however, was not only concerned with the risk of this kind of irreparable judicial error. After nine genuine members of the 'Black Gang' had been condemned to death in January 1862, Victor Hugo, amongst others, reacted with an appeal to the Belgian nation to take a stand against capital punishment in the interests of greater humanity: '*Plus d'échafaud. Mort á la mort !*' ('No more gallows. Death to the death penalty!'). Leopold I spared the lives of seven condemned men. Nevertheless, in the Hainault case Victor Hugo's plea to the people to show their magnanimity did not stop a good 20,000 people crowding into Charleroi marketplace to see the two ringleaders executed. After that, two more criminals would be put to death by a Belgian executioner. From 1863 the death penalty would, in practice, be automatically commuted to forced labour for life.

That the Belgian King exercised the '*excellent prerogative*' of the constitutional right to grant mercy does not mean that he had sovereign power over life and death. Reprieves were always proposed by the Minister of Justice and had to be countersigned by him. Without Public Prosecutor Charles de

The Brussels executioner hangs out a notice board on the Grand' Place to announce an execution. Illustration from *L'Illustration*, 23 March 1892. Koninklijke Bibliotheek Albert I, Brussels.

Oostduinkerke, 1918: Belgian volunteer Aloïs Wulput, convicted of murder, is executed by a firing squad. Stedelijke musea, Ypres.

Bavay's exceptionally strong recommendation to Minister of Justice Tesch, the King might not have refused Coucke and Goethals' petition for mercy. On the other hand, it was due more to the liberal Minister of Justice, Jules Bara, than to King Leopold II that the death penalty began to be systematically commuted to life imprisonment. Nevertheless, Leopold was very proud that he had not signed a single death warrant since the beginning of his reign. Albert I, however, was not a priori opposed to the principle of the death penalty. On 26 March 1918 a soldier who had killed a young woman in a war situation was beheaded by a French executioner in Veurne prison. The King had refused to grant a reprieve. It was the last time that a criminal offence was punished by death in Belgium. After the First World War there were about fifteen executions by firing squad for crimes against state security. The delicate issue of whether or not to carry out the death sentence arose again, in an acute form, towards the end of 1944 when collaborators were being dealt with. The war tribunals sentenced 1,202 persons to death. Of these, 242 were executed between 1944 and 1950, 106 in Flanders, 122 in Wallonia and 14 in Brussels. The summary executions were carried out by firing squad. For opponents of the death penalty this was proof that they should not accept a policy of systematic reprieves. In confused circumstances such as those after the liberation the letter of the law could indeed be used again to satisfy the collective desire for revenge.

After 1950 the Belgian Government renounced the execution of capital punishment once and for all. But, just as in the nineteenth century, a variety of bills proposing the permanent abolition of the death penalty failed to achieve a parliamentary majority. Belgium had to wait until the Government took the initiative. That happened on 25 September 1991 when Minister of Justice Melchior Wathelet introduced a bill that finally removed capital punishment from the penal code.

GITA DENECKERE
Translated by Lindsay Edwards.

'**Y**ou

must see it with your own eyes!'

The Abolition of the Death Penalty

in the Netherlands in 1870

In April 1842 a touching scene took place in front of the Kloosterkerk, a church in The Hague. The mother of a convicted murderer by the name of Van Os, who had been sentenced to death, dropped to her knees before King William I and begged him: '*Sire, Mercy! Have mercy upon my son!*'. The King stammered '*Poor mother*' and, visibly moved, helped the woman to her feet. Although he had rejected a written plea for clemency not long before, the King followed his heart. Van Os was granted a reprieve, despite the fact that he had robbed and decapitated a woman in cold blood.

But not all Queen Beatrix' ancestors were so forgiving. Between 1840 and 1870, the Kings of the House of Orange received some 400 petitions for clemency. In 75 cases, no reprieve was granted and the convicted criminals died on the scaffold. Johan Nathan, the last criminal to be hanged, had robbed and murdered his mother-in-law. He denied everything, and showed no remorse until his appeal had been rejected. '*If ever a miserable and remorseful villain has beseeched you to grant him his life in the light of the most sincere remorse for his evil deed, and insofar as that remorse has been of any weight in granting clemency*' he wrote to King William III, then it was he, Nathan, who could cherish such a '*heartfelt hope*'. The King was not in the least moved by this last-minute repentance.

'This miserable display'

Capital punishment, dropped from the civilian criminal code in 1870, is now far removed from the penal culture of the Netherlands. The subject is taboo in the higher echelons of society, and certainly among politicians (with the exception of a few small Christian parties) and lawyers. Arguments against the death penalty have been around for a long time: it does not deter potential murderers; it strikes hardest at the socially disadvantaged (as does imprisonment); it can lead to irrevocable miscarriages of justice and the death of innocent people; punishments cannot be graded (a murderer who has killed once is punished as severely as a serial killer). Finally, capital punishment conflicts with the belief in man's ability to improve himself, and therefore ultimately has an adverse effect on morality.

Pieter Bruegel the Elder,
The Triumph of Death
(detail). c. 1562.
Panel, 117 x 162 cm.
Musea del Prado, Madrid.

Such arguments were put forward as early as the eighteenth century, when executions were still carried out in a gruesome way and the rotting corpses of criminals were left to hang for weeks in gallows-fields. At that time, views on crime and punishment were still dominated by feelings of revenge and retribution. In the Netherlands after the French occupation, as in other Western countries, an instinctive revulsion against public executions began to develop and the death penalty soon became a political issue. The threatened conservative regent-aristocrats opposed its abolition, while the progressive liberal middle classes supported it. When William II was so deeply shocked by the 1848 revolution in France that he virtually handed over political power on a plate to the Dutch middle classes, matters progressed quickly. First to go, on a liberal-bourgeois initiative in 1854, were the deterrent scaffold punishments (for example, flogging and branding). More and more often, the death penalty was reduced to a prison sentence af-

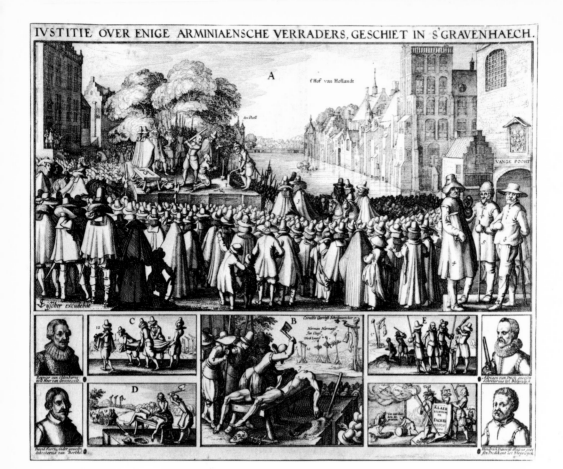

IVSTITIE OVER ENIGE ARMINIAENSCHE VERRADERS, GESCHIET IN S'GRAVENHAECH.

ter a recommendation of clemency from the King, and eventually it was abolished.

In the 1850s and 60s, people were optimistic about the level of crime; judging by newspapers, writings and debates, they felt safer than later in the century and in our own day. In the context of new political relationships, it became 'politically correct' to show disgust at public punishments, and such an attitude was equated with civilised behaviour. Conservatives in favour of capital punishment were also obliged to follow this line if they did not want to be labelled as barbarians by the liberal enlightened. Typical of the time is that eye-witnesses were often surprised at the number of women attending public executions. The tender-hearted fair sex was expected to have a greater aversion to such crude violence.

In 1859 an author in the *Weekblad van het Regt*, a weekly law journal, wrote that '*decent, peaceful citizens*' were disgusted by the death penalty, and locked themselves indoors. The '*bloody spectacle*' was, according to the journal, only witnessed by '*people of disrepute who have no decency. There is fighting, stealing and killing (on such occasions)*'. The last but one execution took place in June 1860 in Gouda, where P. Pijnacker was put to death for manslaughter and theft. The execution was a '*gruesome performance*'. It nevertheless attracted a mass of spectators, who came mainly from rural areas. According to a local newspaper, however, schoolchildren were '*kept away from this miserable display*'.

Cl.J. Visscher,
Execution of conspirators against Maurice,
The Hague, February / March 1623.
Stichting Atlas Van Stolk, Rotterdam.

The last execution to take place in Amsterdam was in 1854 when Heinrich Kemper, who had committed three murders, was hanged. The *Amsterdamsche Courant* published an extremely detailed report of the execution on its front page. The quality newspaper *Algemeen Handelsblad* heavily criticised this display of popular sensationalism in the nation's capital: '*We are too convinced of the decency of our readers to believe that they would expect from us detailed reports of the final moments, emotions, words, and last breath of a sinner such as this. Human justice has been served. The unfortunate soul now stands before the Throne of God!*'.

Between 1850 and 1860, a total of 79 death sentences were pronounced, but only 8 were carried out in public. However, opposition was so great that, in 1859, Minister of Justice Boot presented a bill proposing that executions be carried out '*at a place secluded by the walls of a gaol, or in some other way shielded from the public gaze*'. Bells were to be rung for the duration of the execution. The Minister pointed out that decent people stayed at home on such occasions, but '*people of the lower classes*' made their way *en masse* to the appointed venue well in advance. He rapidly withdrew his bill because, in the Netherlands, a secret execution was seen as an undemocratic way of 'beating up' or 'doing away with' a criminal. Secrecy would give the impression that something improper was being done. But neighbouring countries did in fact introduce secret executions (in secluded prison locations, early in the morning), and this probably explains why capital punishment was not abolished there. Capital punishment carried out in secret had become a matter of 'out of sight, out of mind'.

A scaffold sold for firewood

On 31 October 1860, Johan Nathan was put to death in Maastricht. He had the dubious honour of being the last man to die on the scaffold. After Nathan's execution, every plea for clemency was honoured without exception. Given the atmosphere which prevailed on that occasion, this is not surprising. The execution itself had the air of a forbidden act. At 9.30 in the morning, Nathan left the prison in Maastricht. Together with a minister of the church, the executioner and the executioner's helper, he walked through the deserted streets, escorted by policemen. Curtains remained closed and children were kept indoors. Even in front of the city hall, where a great scaffold had been erected, an oppressive silence descended as the procession approached. On the stroke of 10 o'clock, the executioner placed the noose around Nathan's neck and pulled the lever.

After 1860, the custom of granting a reprieve became a thorn in the side of criminal law experts, who claimed that, out of respect for the law, the death penalty should either be carried out or abolished. This was a powerful argument, but it became increasingly clear that the death penalty was abhorred primarily because executions – and especially public ones – were seen as gruesome and uncivilised. Opposition was not necessarily based on the plight of the criminal, for whom there was little sympathy. This is evident from proposals put forward at the time to make life in prison – which was already arduous – even more of an ordeal. The advocates of such arguments made it particularly difficult for themselves by pushing aside 'emo-

tional' arguments. As Minister of Justice Borret put it to the members of parliament in 1867: '*This is where reason and principles must decide, not emotion*'. But Van Deinse, an expert in criminal justice, made it clear how difficult it was to suppress emotion with 'theoretical reasoning', once one had witnessed a public execution '*with its many peculiarities and chilling spectacles*'. The Reverend Laurillard told those who were against abolishing the death penalty: '*You must see it with your very own eyes!*'.

   And so it was for many. They entered the fray with long, well-reasoned and scholarly arguments. Reading between the lines, however, it became clear to what extent their opposition to the death penalty was based on emotion, and the fact that it was regarded as uncivilised. Initiatives had also been taken outside parliament and the judiciary to abolish capital punishment. In 1863, the society promoting public welfare, the Maatschappij tot Nut van 't Algemeen, campaigned for abolition because the death penalty '*cannot be reconciled with the more proper concepts of law, morality and Christian society*'. The Zeeuws Genootschap der Wetenschappen, a society for the sciences in the province of Zeeland, and the Provinciaal Utrechtsch Genootschap van Kunsten en Wetenschappen, a society for the arts and sciences in the province of Utrecht, both petitioned the King, urging him to abolish the death penalty. The text of the petitions shows the positive way in which many well-to-do citizens viewed developments in crime and punishment. '*Other days, other ways*' announced the Utrecht society. '*Capital punishment may be considered, just as other indispensable forms of corporal punishment have been, one of the pillars of the State, one of the weapons for controlling criminals, but the evil passions and emotions of our day have been restrained, less through deterrence and violence than through the authority of reason and fair laws, and the progress of civilisation and the benevolent influence of religion.'*

Petitions and congresses followed. At the end of 1869, Minister of Justice Van Lilaar succumbed to the pressure for an abolition bill. The *Dagblad van Zuidholland en 's-Gravenhage*, a newspaper which had continued vigorously to oppose abolition, watched developments in disgust: *'Loud are the voices of those who choose to support the murderers instead of the murdered; the wolves instead of the sheep; the foxes instead of the fowl.'* Hundreds of members of Reformed churches and church committees sent letters to parliament in an attempt to halt abolition on biblical grounds. But they were fighting a lost cause. Liberal minister Van Lilaar concluded that the death penalty 'could *be dispensed with at no risk whatsoever to public order and safety, and therefore* must *be dispensed with'*. His memorandum mentions all the enlightened legal arguments of the day: the moral rehabilitation of criminals; departure from the principle of deterrence, and the argument that it is not the cruelty of a punishment which deters, but the certainty that it will follow a crime. Van Lilaar believed that as the cruelty lessened, so public order and safety improved: *'Have we in the Netherlands not de-*

Anonymous, *Execution of J.B.F. van Gogh, Amsterdam, 4 April 1778.* Stichting Atlas Van Stolk, Rotterdam.

fended flogging and branding for many years on the grounds that these bar-baric punishments would restore peace and order to our society? Have not these, too, given way under the weight of public opinion, long before the law sentenced them to death? Who would now wish for their return?'

The debates in the Second Chamber of Parliament lasted a full week. Everyone took up their positions for one last time and advocates of aboli-tion, amid all the rational arguments and statistics, pointed to the advance of civilisation, the ennoblement of feelings, the barbarity of immoral punish-ments, and the fact that an execution would *'now send tremors throughout the land'*. Those against abolition accused their opponents of *'morbid phi-lanthropy'*, and cast doubt on the statistics. They warned that chaos would ensue, and again proposed that the death penalty be carried out in secret. But abolition in law could no longer be prevented, and many Dutch had long since abolished it in their hearts. This was not only the case in civilised cir-cles, claimed Van Lilaar during the debates. He believed that it had been ex-tremely difficult to find a boatman willing to transport the scaffold from Amsterdam to Maastricht for the last execution there. Moreover, the boat-man who finally agreed to do so had demanded a fee far greater than the val-ue of his vessel.

Members of the Second Chamber abolished the death penalty on 20 May 1870 by 48 votes to 30. The First Chamber followed suit on 15 September that year, with 20 votes to 18. The Netherlands was one of the first countries in the world to take this step in penal law. The *Weekblad van het Regt* re-ported that the despised scaffold had already been *'sold for firewood'* one week previously *'for the considerable sum of forty-three guilders and sixty cents'*. The executioner and his assistant had been retained by royal decree. The *Algemeen Handelsblad* reported: *'The scaffold has now been abolished by law in the Netherlands. May it never return.'* The abolition of capital pun-ishment in the Netherlands had no measurable effect on serious crime, and to date the wish of the *Handelsblad* has been fulfilled. In neighbouring European countries, too, there was a growing aversion to the death penalty but, unlike the Netherlands, executions were carried out in private. This took the sting out of protests. Once it was no longer 'visible', capital punishment became a less central issue. This partly explains why it was not abolished in other European countries until well into the twentieth century.

Long after abolition, sensational murders, or a series of murders in rapid succession, led to campaigns for the death penalty to be restored in the Netherlands. The fact that, in 1876, the double murderer Hendrik Jut could no longer be hanged, led to the creation of a 'try-your-strength' fairground attraction which allowed visitors to strike a replica of Jut's head with a large hammer. This phenomenon even found its way into the Dutch language. The expression *'Kop van Jut'* (literally, 'Jut's head') refers to a scapegoat; someone who gets the blame for all problems. In 1880, during the discus-sions on the *Wetboek van Strafrecht* (the Dutch Penal Code), an amendment for the re-introduction of the death penalty was submitted following the murder of a 13-year-old boy. De Savornin Lohman, the anti-revolutionary and later leader of the Christian Historical Union (CHU; Christelijk-Historische Unie) put forward an emotional defence: *'The people demand – and rightly so – that justice be served, and we must support them in that, since it is through justice that a nation can be elevated.'* Other members also

Jules Malou, *The Gallows.* 1838.

spoke in this vein. The Liberal Minister of Justice Modderman responded arrogantly. He did not wish to hear exaggerated references to popular opinion, and believed that legal reform was only possible if '*thinkers and legislators have the courage to be somewhat wiser than the populace*'. The amendment was rejected by 41 votes to 21. However, this did not silence calls for the reintroduction of the death penalty, which could be heard whenever there was a particularly sensational murder or a spate of murders. But the issue never again reached the stage of a vote in Parliament.

Contemporary attitudes

In the colonies capital punishment continued to be part of the criminal law for a long time on the grounds that it was an essential tool of colonial government, given the character of the natives. In the Netherlands Indies, the Governor-General had the right to grant a reprieve, and whether the incumbent actually did so usually depended on his personal beliefs. The death penalty was not abolished there until Indonesia gained independence in 1949. It was abolished in the Netherlands Antilles in 1957. Surinam did not follow suit until it became independent in 1975, but no criminal had been put to death there since 1927.

The Second World War led to the reintroduction of capital punishment in the Netherlands. It was imposed for criminal offences committed in wartime. On the basis of the *Besluit Buitengewoon Strafrecht* (1943), an extraordinary legal decree issued by the Government-in-exile in London, 152 death sentences were pronounced under extraordinary jurisdiction (*Bijzondere Rechtspraak*) after the Liberation. Forty people were executed by firing squad. In 1981 the military penal code also scrapped the death penalty, following the inclusion in the constitution of a clause prohibiting the death penalty in all circumstances.

The percentage of the Dutch population claiming to be in favour of capital punishment is far from constant. In 1956, 36% of those asked were in favour of its reintroduction. In 1975 this rose to 47%, but fell to 31% in 1996. In a recent survey (1998) the figure was over 50%. But the figures tell us little. American police series are so popular in the Netherlands that those carrying out a survey often have to remind interviewees that there is no capital punishment in their own country. With a little extra information and discussion, opinions soon change. A recent gruesome murder, which received a great deal of publicity, could well have influenced the answers. The percentages are more an indication of the fact that people feel unsafe, and that they doubt the effectiveness of the justice system. Journalists have contributed to that feeling by portraying the Netherlands as a highly criminal society. This despite the fact that, per 100,000 inhabitants, fewer people lose their lives as a result of crime than almost anywhere else in the West.

The Dutch are not afraid to express their abhorrence of the death penalty in other countries. For many years, no criminal has been deported to a country where the death penalty might be imposed. In 1994, when the Dutchman Johannes van Damme was sentenced to death in Singapore for drug smuggling, Queen Beatrix herself appealed to President Ong Ten Cheong for a reprieve. In the media, Van Damme became a martyr. The Minister of Justice also tried to prevent the execution, but Singapore was unmoved by this Dutch pressure for civilisation and Van Damme was hanged.

HERMAN FRANKE
Translated by Yvette Mead.

A British war cemetery in Flanders. Photo by David Samyn.

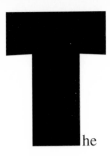

The

Decorous Dead

The Great War Revisited

'We, civilisations, we know now
that we are mortal.'
Paul Valéry, *Crisis of the Spirit (La crise de l'esprit, 1919)*

I was to start from Ypres, travel back to the beginning of the century at the end of it, drive out of town through the Menin Gate and recite Sassoon's bitter verse 'On Passing the New Menin Gate': '*Well might the Dead who struggled in the slime / Rise and deride this sepulchre of crime.*' But today the monument is reconciled with its surroundings. If things last long enough they acquire a patina which renders them abstract, untouchable. It was one of those autumn days when the quivering light hesitantly envelops everything with a warm, soft glow, not a day for commemorating eighty-year-old horrors.

I drove through the gate to the east and then turned off towards the southeast along a line that has become almost invisible. Ypres, Wijtschate, Mesen, Ploegsteert, Armentières. Provincial, language and national borders paid no attention to the line which once ran from the North Sea to the Swiss border. The rolling landscape could have been Arcadian that day, had it not been for the pig farms and golf courses. I am not sure what I marvelled at most: the resilience of this landscape that has established itself again and the talent the people who live there have for forgetting, or the magnificent and futile efforts to keep the grass cropped close in the cemeteries.

In Ploegsteert there is a monument from 1925 on the church square: a Belgian soldier, his rifle held high, summoning his mates to battle. '*To our heroes*'. The military and civilian victims of the Second World War are commemorated on the two wings built onto the monument. In the graveyard beside the church nine British soldiers lie among the messy, ostentatious graves of Belgian civilians: prominent, after all, in an impeccable lawn, behind a hedge and an unnecessary gate. '*None untimely die that die for England*' adorns one grave. A bas-relief at the town hall does Churchill too much honour: with top hat and cigar he stands at the edge of a trench peering belligerently into no man's land – as if he were, even then, the Prime Minister he was in 1940. The truth is that Churchill, who was in Ploegsteert

– five hundred metres from Hitler in Mesen, a corporal who painted the church and had a white dog, oh irony of history – wore a French steel helmet because the French were the first to start using them.

Afterwards I drove into Armentières, in France. In the marketplace a girl asked me to finance her art studies. In exchange she offered me an obscure literary magazine.

Mademoiselle from Armenteers, parley vous,
Mademoiselle from Armenteers, parley vous,
Your pommes de terre frits
They give us the squits,
Inky Dinky, parley vous.

That's what the British soldiers used to sing, when they came looking for entertainment in this town, just behind the lines. Because, make no mistake, there were British, Indian, Australian and Canadian troops here from Ypres to the Somme (excluding just the enclave of Notre Dame de Lorette and that only until 1916) defending – well, what? On 26 September 1915, 10,000 barely trained recruits walked in tidy ranks to meet the German machine guns at Loos. Later, Ludendorff was to say: '*The English soldiers fight like*

The IJzer Tower in Diksmuide. Photo by David Samyn.

Third Battle of Ypres, 1917: Australian troops on a duckboard track through Chateau Wood. This is now the site of the Bellewaerde amusement park. Imperial War Museum, London.

lions', '*True*', replied his aide-de-camp, '*but we know their leaders are donkeys*'.

So, we were in France, and the rhetoric of war hardly differed from that in Ploegsteert in Belgium. The war memorial in Armentières shows the soldiers departing and returning victorious. A woman offers a laurel to one who stands tall and proud. All the dead died for the fatherland. *Dulce et decorum est.*

'Here lie their bodies like seeds in the sand'

Which fatherland did Flemish soldiers in the Belgian army die for in the Great War? Until the First World War Flemings believed in a Flanders within Belgium. To define itself as a new country different from its French neighbour (with its secular character) the young Belgium, for the first half century at least, invoked its Flemish past, but then in French. When the Teutonic Fury rolled over Belgium in 1914, King Albert could still, without any problem, say to the army in the order of the day for 4 August 1914: '*Remember, Flemings, the Battle of the Golden Spurs and you Walloons from Liège, whose turn it is now* (i.e. against the advancing Germans), *the six hundred men of Franchimont.*' The Battle of the Golden Spurs, fought in 1302 near Kortrijk between mainly Flemish foot soldiers and French knights, has become one of the invented traditions of the Flemish movement since its literary-ideological consecration by Hendrik Conscience in his historical novel *The Lion of Flanders* (De Leeuw van Vlaanderen, 1838). But Conscience did write the book to give the Flemish a place in Belgium.

The First World War was the first and last transcendental moment in Belgian history, its finest hour. Abroad, it inspired admiration (Gallant Little Belgium) and sympathy (martyred Belgium – *la Belgique martyre*). The monarchy too, the cement of the Belgian construct, was at its strongest then: the Warrior-King stood guard over the nation. But in the trenches beside the IJzer the Flemish movement became more radical. Although Flemings provided more than 65% of the soldiers in the Belgian army their language was scorned. Flemish intellectuals, concerned at the plight of Flemish soldiers, clashed with their French-speaking superiors at the front and united in the so-called Front Movement. In occupied Belgium some Flemish nationalists (the 'activists') expected the occupiers to help them implement their political agenda. They were wrong when they thought that the Germans with their '*Flamenpolitik*' ('Flemish policy') were favourably disposed towards their struggle for emancipation.

The pro-Flemish war veterans' commemoration in Diksmuide, in West Flanders, grew into an annual pilgrimage to the (Flemish) graves beside the IJzer. Its aim was to spread the ideals of the Front Movement: 'No more war', 'Armistice' and 'Self rule'. In 1928-1929 a tower was erected in tribute. In 1946 this anti-war monument with the inscription AVV-VVK ('*Alles voor Vlaanderen - Vlaanderen voor Kristus*'; 'All for Flanders - Flanders for Christ', the Flemish Catholic student movement's motto at the end of the nineteenth century) was blown up. The culprits were never found. A verse by Cyriel Verschaeve, a priest tainted with Nazism, was daubed on the ruins: '*Here lie their bodies like seeds in the sand, / hope for the harvest, O*

Flandersland'. The new tower was dedicated in 1965 and was again inscribed with the AVV-VVK motto. Meanwhile the pilgrimage had long since grown into a major celebration of the Flemish movement and its struggle for freedom. In 1987 the tower was recognised as a 'Memorial of Flemish Emancipation' and in 1992 as a protected monument. Today the IJzer Tower is a recognised symbol of the Flemish Community, along with its flag, its shield and its anthem. A museum is currently being created in the tower, dedicated to the First World War, peace and Flemish emancipation. Perhaps that is too much for one monument. Over the years the tower and the pilgrimage have become charged with an ideological agenda. The odium of collaboration by a section of the Flemish movement during the Second World War has not been forgotten. The annual gathering at the IJzer is sometimes tarnished by the presence of extreme right-wing groups, and not only from Flanders. Besides, a large number of Flemings feel that their principal demands have been met and that they are now emancipated. Perhaps the tower should not have been rebuilt after it was blown up. The dead who were once the focus of it all have since been incorporated into another story or forgotten.

'...how bravely they died, the German soldiers'

Those who travel through Flanders and northern France looking for traces of the First World War, will come up against the absence of Germans. The signposting of German cemeteries is sparse and discreet. Tourist guides often forget them. Eighty years on '*Vae victis*' still applies: woe betide the defeated. Only in the South African National War Memorial in Derville Wood have I read in an inscription with reference to German soldiers '*how bravely they died*'. At the German cemetery in Menin, a Briton from Kent had laid a wreath with words intended to restore the balance: '*They also fought and fell*'. In Tyne Cot Cemetery in Passchendaele, the biggest British war cemetery in the world, four Germans lie buried under two tombstones near the *Blockhaus* the Canadians captured. The cemetery lies on a gently sloping hillside: you can, as it were, see the number of dead that were required to take this place. Behind the bunker, with its memorial, the geometry of the interminable rows of graves is broken. The haphazard locations of the first graves have not been changed: the dead must have been buried straight after the battle, more or less where they fell. The tombstones came later, when the cemetery was laid out in the twenties. The anomaly of this random arrangement breaks through the inexorable and comforting geometry of the cemetery and the selective outrage on which every war cemetery rests: i.e. by denying the fallen enemy.

The Germans have only cemeteries in Flanders and northern France, no proud monuments: you do not lose a war with impunity. The rhetoric of their death is in a minor key, melancholy reigns there more strongly than geometry. There are trees instead of the close-cropped grass of the British cemeteries.

In the second half of the fifties the more than one hundred German cemeteries in West Flanders were reduced to four (Vladslo, Langemark, Hooglede and Menin). The one in Menin was laid out as a collective cemetery

Käthe Kolwitz's *Mourning Parents* at Vladslo Cemetery. Photo by David Samyn.

German war cemetery, Wervicq-sud (France). Photo by David Samyn.

with remains from dozens of small cemeteries that were cleared from the area. During the reorganisation the cemeteries lost their individual crosses and acquired a more anonymous appearance. Dark stone was used instead of the blinding white English stone. The tombstones lie flat in the grass and their weather-beaten inscriptions cover groups of dead. Other building elements or ornaments are used sparsely: the grieving parents of Käthe Kollwitz in Vladslo; an octogonal building in the middle of the cemetery at Menin that looks like a Romanesque baptistery; stylised bunkers in Langemark. The reorganisation of the cemeteries has changed their design. The group, sheer numbers outweigh the individual now. Defeat has become tangible in the anonymous levelling out of the dead. The trees provide shade (which in its turn provides moss and weather-beaten inscriptions), soughing and falling leaves, that flutter down between the graves, where by 11 November they lie and decay. The Teutonic Fury fell here, a sombre German garden – a *Friedhof* – is left. Here nature is more than the backdrop it is in British cemeteries.

In Northern France the rhetoric is different again, because most of the cemeteries (there are about 200) are still there, often incorporated into the municipal burial-ground. In Pont-de-Nieppe near Armentières I saw the first German graveyard on French soil, under majestic willows surrounded by a hedge. 790 Germans lie there head to head under a black metal cross. It takes a while before you notice, amongst the black monotony, tombstones that on closer inspection prove to bear a Star of David: Jewish volunteers who died for Germany. In the light of the war that was to follow this one these isolated, and therefore all the more conspicuous, graves acquire a new significance. On the other side of the municipal cemetery, that obviously serves as a buffer, a French flag flies and French dead from the First and Second World Wars lie in two untidy rows. In contrast to the British and Germans, French soldiers could be repatriated. Right behind this a minuscule, shining British cemetery wins hands down again.

I saw the same anomaly of Jewish tombstones amongst crosses in the cemeteries at Laventie, Wervicq-sud (beautifully situated on a hill full of trees), Bousbecque and Halluin. In the latter village, close to the Belgian border, the German graveyard lay hidden away behind a hedge in the municipal cemetery. You could not reach it from the street. The records were missing from the alcove. I jumped back over the locked gate into the municipal cemetery and there lay about forty Britons under a wreath from the town council. Coincidence?

I attended the annual ceremony of remembrance in the cemetery of Langemark. In the German collective memory the name has a place similar to that of Passchendaele in the British. In 1914, some three thousand singing German students were mown down there by British machine guns. To use the memory of those inexperienced recruits, by then heroes for all time, for his war, Hitler visited the cemetery in 1940. The only sign of that on 6 November 1998 was the two motionless German soldiers solidly flanking the narrow entrance: the German helmet has hardly changed since the First World War. The speeches that day were the most pacifist and contrite I have ever heard at a memorial ceremony. Every war was labelled pointless, and the war that began in 1914 was referred to as the thirty-year war that ended only in 1945.

Cemeteries remain the purest 'sites of memory' of war, because in a war everyone loses, and the dead are absolute losers. Only they have the right to speak, and it is precisely they who remain silent. They offer no rhetoric. The organisation, the representation of the dead does that.

The Commonwealth War Graves Commission excels here in thorough organisation. Founded as long ago as 1917 – though it was called the Imperial War Graves Commission then – it chose four principles that seemed intuitively correct and were in any case convincing, which, consequently, are still respected today: every fallen soldier would be commemorated by name on a tombstone or a monument; these would be permanent; the tombstones would be uniform and no difference would be made for rank, race or religion. Relatives would have the right to add a (brief) inscription. Two monuments were permitted in the graveyards: the Cross of Sacrifice, which is a cross (the only Christian symbol) with an inverted sword on an octagonal base, and a Stone of Remembrance, a stylised altar with the quotation, taken from Ecclesiastes by Rudyard Kipling: '*Their Name Liveth for Evermore*'. All the Commonwealth countries would contribute to the costs in proportion to the number of graves.

Architects like Lutyens, Baker and Blomfield who had won their spurs planning cities like Johannesburg and New Delhi were charged with supervising the architectural design. The work was finished in the early thirties. The style was true to the refined classical style of building of the Empire at its peak.

The records of the dead, now available on the Internet, are painfully accurately kept in this fragmented garden city of the dead. John Kipling went missing at the Battle of Loos in September 1915. Despite a search by his fa-

Sir George Clausen RA,
Youth Mourning. 1916.
Canvas, 91.4 x 91.4 cm.
Imperial War Museum,
London.

ther, Rudyard Kipling, his body was never found. A few years ago research showed that Kipling lies under the tombstone of an '*Unknown British Officer*' in the St. Mary's A.D.S. Cemetery, Haisnes (Pas de Calais). They gave him a new tombstone with his name. I wondered what happened to his name on the Loos Memorial to the Missing. An enquiry to the French headquarters of the Commonwealth War Graves Commission produced, besides comprehensive information about John Kipling's dossier, the laconic sentence: '*Mr. Kipling's commemoration on the Loos Memorial has not been erased.*' Do the records yield to aesthetics then?

Why are the British cemeteries the most beautiful, in the sense of aesthetic? It has to do with the four principles mentioned above, which have led to great unity of style. However different the cemeteries may be in size, situation and respect for those buried there (the Indian Memorial to the Missing in Neuve-Chapelle has obvious oriental features), in the end they all give off the same atmosphere. It has to do with the ubiquitous white stone and green grass. War cemeteries tend towards geometry because it evens everything out and brings calm. The horror is weeded out. Tombstones refer to the dead, but you can hardly imagine human remains under the grass. The uniformity, however, never stifles the individual. Besides his official details the tombstone may also show his religious beliefs and an individual epitaph. Indeed I only saw Commonwealth mass graves in Fromelles, where some of the Australians lie in two rectangles framed by rose bushes in the grass.

But let there be no misunderstanding: for all their aesthetic consideration and serenity the British cemeteries give off the air of a political superpower that has won a war gloriously. Perhaps the British Empire has not in fact disappeared: it survives as the Commonwealth War Graves Commission. It employs an army of gardeners and handymen (more than 400 in France alone) of which I saw a regiment, dedicated and bowed, weeding in Caterpillar Cemetery by the Somme, whilst masons on scaffolding shored up the walls of the graveyard. Only in this care and determination that exacts respect because it is pointless, a useless service, does the British Empire still exist. In that sense every British cemetery is also a 'site of memory' of the British Empire. The absence of the latter is very present. All the Britons you see in all seasons wandering through Flanders and northern France from cemetery to monument are also travelling through a virtual empire.

United in diversity, the once great Empire reigns over a realm of dead. Rupert Brooke's lines '*(...) there's some corner of a foreign field / That is forever England*' has become reality.

If I had to choose just one of these impeccable British cemeteries, I would choose the unsightly, almost cosy Lone Tree Cemetery in Wijtschate. You have to open a gate and cross a meadow to find it behind a farm. There are eighty Northern Irish graves in what was once no man's land. On the other side of the road lies Lone Tree Crater where Spanbroek mill used to stand, now re-christened the Pool of Peace. It is hard to believe that this peaceful pool is the result of one of the gigantic mine explosions which heralded the third Battle of Ypres on 7 June 1917. They say the glass inkpots on Lloyd George's desk in London rattled. In Cassel General Plumer burst into tears. It was only after my visit that I could link the two sites: the eighty graves are from the same date as the explosion. Spanbroek mill exploded later than the other mines so that the Irish, who must have left their trenches too early, were most likely buried by the explosion.

Pool of Peace, Wijtschate.

'We will remember them'

In the meantime the last eyewitnesses are disappearing and the Great War will soon finally be part of great history: that which is really past, as the wars of Napoleon are past. On 11 November 1998, a few veterans wrapped up warmly, poppies in their buttonholes, sat slumped in their wheelchairs at the Menin Gate in Ypres. One of them stood to attention, straight as a die, as he recited with steady voice but wavering memory Laurence Binyon's famous lines 'For the Fallen':

They shall grow not old, as we that are left grow old.
Age shall not weary them, nor the years condemn.
At the going down of the sun and in the morning
We will remember them.

He needed a prompter to reach the end.

These centenarians were out of key under the immaculate monument. They were ... too alive, and too dead. The monument has become abstract, just like the cemeteries and memorials, and as an abstraction it is perceived aesthetically. It does not suffer them, it suffers only the chiselled names, *'these intolerably nameless names'* (Sassoon), that survive for all time like empty husks.

The forms of remembrance change. Ours is no longer that of the eyewitnesses, who have indeed grown old whilst their mates have remained eternally young. Their form of remembrance will disappear soon. Ours will remain, different, more abstract, emptier.

LUC DEVOLDERE
Translated by Lindsay Edwards.

Menin Gate, Ypres. Photo
by David Samyn.

Conrad's

Dutch Connection

Borneo has rarely proved newsworthy. Even today, Indonesia's biggest island in what was once the Dutch East Indies, is at most one among a handful of out-of-the-way tourist destinations.

A century ago, on the other hand, there was published what was to become the most widely read Eastern novel by that unique English mariner of Polish extraction 'Joseph Conrad', penname of Teodor Josef Konrad Korzeniowski (1857-1924). The novel was *Lord Jim* (1900), the tragic tale of lost honour at sea and ultimately failed redemption ashore of a young British deck-officer, exiled in the Malay Archipelago.

The area, and especially Borneo, had already been the scene of the two interconnected novels of Joseph Conrad's debut, *Almayer's Folly* (1895) and *An Outcast of the Islands* (1896). In fact, the chief locality in all three novels was a small stretch on the island's East Coast, their solitary principal characters being English, Dutch, and Asian, while their emotional climate was determined by 'ethnicity' and tragic death.

A few years later the by then internationally renowned author was to write: '*If I had not got to know Almayer pretty well, it is almost certain there would never have been a line of mine in print.*'[1]

'Almayer' has since proved to be one Charles Olmeyer, a solitary Eurasian Dutch trader whom Korzeniowski had met in 1887 when Mate of the *Vidar*, a small Arab-owned freighter flying the Dutch ensign and regularly plying between Singapore and Tandjong Redeb, a modest East-Borneo outpost at the mouth of the River Berow. 'Almayer' had been the commercial representative of the legendary Captain Tom Lingard, a maverick English sailor-adventurer known throughout the islands as the 'Rajah Laut' or King of the Sea.

Stuck in Amsterdam

Korzeniowski had obtained his berth in the *Vidar* upon being discharged from the Singapore hospital where he had convalesced after being hit by a loose spar towards the end of a Java-bound voyage in the brig *Highland*

Advertisement in *Algemeen Handelsblad*, 9 January 1887.

ISTERDAM - SAMARANG - SOERABAYA.

Het EERSTE KLASSE
snelzeilend
ENGELSCHE BARKSCHIP
Highland Forest,
Kapitein DALGARNO.
Speedige Expeditie.
itmuntende Inrichting voor Passagiers.
dres bij de Cargadoors:
HUDIG & BLOKHUIJZEN { Amsterdam, Rotterdam.
WELDRAGER, BALTUS & Co.,
Amsterdam.
MEIJER & Co., Amsterdam. (690)
toom-Snelpersdrukkerij C. A. SPIN & ZOON.

Winter Garden of Café
Krasnapolski, Amsterdam
(N. Sherry, *Conrad*, 1988,
p. 40).

Forest. He had joined her three months before in Amsterdam where she was
frozen-in opposite the Oostelijke Handelskade. With a single, '*weirdly
toothless*' old shipkeeper he had to wait there throughout February until
their cargo, likewise immobilised in '*schuyts*' up-country, could reach them
and the crew be summoned back from their unwonted leave.

To break his complete isolation, he would often go ashore and after shiv-
ering in horse-drawn tramcars alight at a sumptuous cafe in the city centre
where he would dutifully pen his umpteenth letter to the Scottish owners
who insisted on his visiting one Hudig, their Dutch charterer, in order to
press for the cargo to be shifted and 'fed up' to the ship by rail in regular
quantities.

'*Mynheer Hudig*' was '*a big swarthy Netherlander with black mous-
taches and a bold glance*'. Korzeniowski should, of course, have remon-
strated with the dusky gentleman over the inertia shown so far, but the
weather was too bitter and the office on its stately canal so warm, the coffee
and cigar so good, the fire so bright, and Hudig's sides so heartily shaking
with laughter, that his 24-year-old visitor always experienced great difficulty in making up his mind to reach for his cap.

Still, in the end the thaw did set in and in June the *Highland Forest* did
reach her Dutch-advertised destination, the port of Semarang on Java's
North coast. Only, by then, her incapacitated Number One was told by a local Doctor: '*Ach, my friend, you are young yet; it may be serious for your
whole life. You must leave your ship; you must quite silent be for three
months - quite silent.*'

Having no Dutch, he transferred to Singapore where he could indeed be
'quite silent' and, great reader that he had always been, borrow from the rich
Raffles Library all he could get hold of about that part of the world.

Fascinated by the East

The North coast of Java had not been Korzeniowski's first confrontation with the Archipelago. This had been little Muntok on Banka Island off Sumatra where, three years earlier, he had been offered unstinted hospitality by a Dutch mining-engineer after landing from one of the lifeboats of a barque that had caught fire in the Malay Straits and had to be abandoned – an experience which started a '*lifelong fascination*' for him and became the basis of his short story *Youth* (1902).

As to his life-story, Korzeniowski was born in 1857 in the Russian-occupied Ukraine to which his aristocratic, multilingual father, as an indomitable Polish patriot, had been banished with his wife and where both were to die. At 17, their French-educated and escape-obsessed son had succeeded, with the aid of a gallophile guardian-uncle, in being taken on as an apprentice-sailor at Marseilles. Then, after motley early years (which included a wild love-affair leading to gun-running for Carlists in Spain and a gambling-induced suicide attempt), he had entered the service of the British Mercantile Marine. Moving steadily on through the various stages of professional sea-

Walter Tittle, *Portrait of Joseph Conrad in 1923*. National Portrait Gallery, London.

manship, he had succeeded in obtaining his Master's Certificate in 1886, the same year as his British citizenship which had been absolutely essential in order to avoid being conscripted into the Tsar's army.

An obsessive dream

This, therefore, was how in 1887 a recovered Korzeniowski had come to find himself at Tandjong Redeb and to accept, together with his skipper, an invitation to dinner with Olmeyer, reputedly '*the only white man on the East Coast* (of Borneo)' for whom, quite incongruously, they had been asked to bring a pony – an acceptance for which he later claimed he was '*paying yet the price of my sanity*'.

In Conrad's novel the fraternity of seamen in those waters had long known about Almayer and his huge house, especially built for him on the riverbank and soon referred to with sarcastic ambiguity as the Lingard agent's '*Folly*'. With this came numerous snide digs about his forever raving of the immense treasure of gold ore that he believed Captain Lingard had discovered in the interior of the island jungle and, as his putative father-in-law, would one day share with him.

Meanwhile, the connection of the above with the confession about the link between 'Almayer' and the transmutation of Korzeniowski the seaman into Conrad the writer cannot but make one imagine that if he had really come to know the man '*pretty well*', he probably at some point must have felt: '*There, but for the Grace of God, go I*'. Why and how did the original Olmeyer make such an unforgettable impression?

The search for an answer again leads back to the Dutch. For what was emphasised in his first novel is that in his tropical solitude Almayer appeared only able to survive thanks to one obsessive dream: that of ending his life in great affluence in Amsterdam with his beautiful half-caste daughter Nina, envied and respected – and at last 'home' among his true, white compatriots!

Tandjong Redeb (N. Sherry, *Conrad*, 1988, p. 45).

Indebted to Multatuli

To Korzenioswski such a homecoming was unthinkable, with his own country ruled by a foreign power while his British naturalisation had come too late for him ever to become believably Anglo-Saxon. In fact, he was and remained a typical 'expat' – and one without a 'pat(ria)' at that.

But then, this is also what takes us to the self-exiled Dutch colonials like Olmeyer as social types from the pre-electronic age immortalised by the former Dutch East Indies government official, Eduard Douwes Dekker. Under the pseudonym of 'Multatuli', this 'long-suffering' Dutch idealist had written his passionately anti-colonialist novel *Max Havelaar or the Coffee Auctions of the Dutch Trading Company* (Max Havelaar of de Koffieveilingen der Nederlandse Handelsmaatschappij, 1860), translated in 1868 and at once bought by numerous public libraries. Actually, what may now be added to Conrad's so remarkably revealing confession about the birth of his authorship is that, if he had not come to know *Max Havelaar* pretty well, not a single chapter of his Malay novels might have been composed as it was.

Gravestone of Olmeyer's father's family vault in Surabaya (N. Sherry, *Conrad*, 1988, p. 46).

As G.J.Resink has shown in a series of highly enlightening studies[2], and R. Salverda put into the wider context of Dutch literature of the Indies[3], *Almayer's Folly* as well as *An Outcast of the Islands* and *Lord Jim* were greatly indebted to Multatuli's book. Not only is there in more ways than one a striking resemblance between the characters of the fictional Almayer and the fictional Havelaar, but compositional parallels abound as well, while there are even complete scenes in each which directly echo the Dutch plot.

One such is the dinner of the only whites at Sambir (Conrad's designation of Berow) in *Almayer's Folly*, which recalls even down to specific details the 'whites only' dinner at Lebak in *Max Havelaar*. Both are parties of four: three men and one woman, the latter being Almayer's daughter at Sambir and Assistant-Resident Havelaar's wife at Lebak (also the place of the famous 'Address to the Chiefs', whose tenor would have fitted into any of Conrad's Malaysian tales).

This brings in the similarity in writing-technique of Conrad and Multatuli which resulted from both authors' having need of a narrator (not only for plausibility's sake), viz. the ubiquitous 'Marlow' for a number of Conrad's stories and 'Shawlman' for *Max Havelaar*. As for the overall picture of the eccentric Max in Sumatra's Natal, he seems to a remarkable extent the very prefiguration of 'Tuan' Jim in the island's Patusan.

Self-exile

Needless to say, we have now come to the psychology of the Polish-English ex-sailor and the ex-Dutch East Indies civil servant. It is not only their novels' parallel starting-points, with Multatuli ostensibly owing his tale to meeting his friend-of-the-shawl in Amsterdam and Conrad owing his to meeting the man-in-pyjamas on the jetty of Tandjong Redeb. What appealed to Conrad so strongly in Multatuli was clearly the idea of a quasi-regal Western loner, dispensing justice and prosperity in an Eastern environment fast threatening to be polluted by imperialism. The good lady Tina takes her husband Max to be such a regal figure, while Almayer is described as '*liv-*

ing as a king'. And, apart from Almayer and Jim, there is Willems, the disgraced sailor from Rotterdam who as another protégé of Captain Lingard is given an – albeit shockingly ending – chance to prove himself in *An Outcast of the Islands*.

In the Archipelago more than one benign white ruler had been in evidence before *Max Havelaar*, not only 'Rajah' James Brooke of Serawak in North Borneo who was greatly admired by Korzeniowski. When regaining his strength in Singapore, he had evidently devoured A.R. Wallace's *The Malay Archipelago* (1869) and learned as much.

Crossing cultures

Of course, for Multatuli as well as for Conrad the cherishing of such idealised situations, in their positive as well as their negative effects, was an enormously potent *idée fixe*, characteristic of a particular variety of exile: i.e. the exile with roots not in one but in two cultures, national as well as racial, and therefore twice over reminiscent of Conrad's French epigraph to *Almayer's Folly*: '*Qui de nous n'a eu sa terre promise, son jour d'extase, et sa fin en exil?*'.[4]

For Korzeniowski his '*terre promise*'[7] would have been an Anglo-Polish identity as – paradoxically enough – a global seafarer; his '*jour d'extase*' the discovery of a capacity to express his feelings creatively; and his '*fin en exil*' the deeply guilt-conscious realisation that, fated to basic disloyalty through his British naturalisation, he could never return to the fatherland which his own father had given his life for and whose language he himself had 'betrayed' through his choice of English as his writing medium, his English marriage and his siring of sons ignorant of even a single word of Polish.

As shown in several autobiographical passages, Korzeniowski was not simply a political exile. He was also acutely aware that the Russian culture that dominated Poland was 'Eastern', while his 'claim to Westernism', so impressively dramatised in the opening chapter of *Under Western Eyes* (1911), dominated his every thought. In fact, seeing Poland 'colonised' by the Russians as European imperialists, this claim, when transferred to the Far East, inspired all of Conrad's feelings about 'white' colonisation in the 'coloured' tropics and the consequences of self-chosen exile.

ALMAYER'S FOLLY

A Story of an Eastern River

BY
Joseph Conrad

Qui de nous n'a eu sa terre promise, son jour d'extase et sa fin en exil—Amiel.

LONDON
T. FISHER UNWIN
PATERNOSTER SQUARE
Mdcccxcv

Title-page of *Almayer's Folly* (1895).

Colonisation

Historically, colonisation was of course the product of greed for gold resulting from the pursuit of adventure through voyages of discovery. The spice-trade, tea and coffee came next. In due course, moral justification of their forced cultivation was attempted and the 'White Man's Burden' invented while 'civilising' activities were fostered by the cynical notion that these were good for production. As a result, any exploitation of natives through economic bullying was gradually frowned upon, particularly in the Dutch East Indies after the success of *Max Havelaar*.

To Conrad this attitude became axiomatic when, after having seen the Belgian King's Congo 'Free State', the experience made him write in *Heart of Darkness* (1899): *'The conquest of the earth, which mostly means the taking it away from those who have a different complexion or slightly flatter noses than ourselves, is not a pretty thing when you look into it too much'.*[5]

It is gratifying to consider that in Conrad's self-confessed *'favourite bedside-book'* Wallace had written about *Havelaar*: *'Even if not exaggerated, the facts stated are not nearly so bad as those of oppression by free-trade indigo-planters and torturing by native tax-gatherers under British rule in India'.*[6]

He may even have felt confronted with the ghost of Multatuli when in February 1887 at Amsterdam, on the eve of weighing anchor, he would have seen the papers publish their obituaries of Douwes Dekker. Thus spiritual recognition would have actually anticipated their meeting in the Elysian Fields as so touchingly imagined in *A Personal Record* (1912).

Indeed, if there is one fact about expatriate Conrad's Dutch connection that appears to be irrefutable, it certainly is that, through his experience of the presence of self-exiled Netherlanders in the Far East, this connection was always with him and always worked creatively. For which we cannot be grateful enough – particularly in the light of his high valuation of inter-racial friendships, in the present centenary year of the story of 'Lord' Jim and the latter's sad final expiation through ethnically prompted suicide-by-proxy on his deliberate confrontation with the father of his native best friend killed by a white thug's bullet.

FRED G.H. BACHRACH

NOTES

(with thanks to Dr Jaap Harskamp of the British Library)

1. Conrad's reminiscences are mostly in *The Mirror of the Sea* (1906) and *A Personal Record* (1912).
2. See *De Gids* vol. 124 (1961) for March, pp. 178-80; August, pp. 28-35; September, pp. 107-112; October, pp. 183-86. Also *Bijdragen tot de Taal-, Land- en Volkenkunde*, vol. 115 (1959), ii, pp. 192-208, and vol. 117 (1961), ii, pp. 209-237.
3. R. Salverda, 'The Indonesian Connection. Dutch Literature in Comparative Perspective' (*The Berkeley Conference on Dutch Literature 1991*, 1993, pp. 83-109; 'Dutch and other European Literatures of the Indonesian Archipelago' (*The Literature of Colonialism*, 1996), pp. 42-62; 'Indische Letteren door een Engelse Bril' (*Extra Muros, Langs de Wegen*, 1997), pp. 120-23.
4. A.F. Amiel, *Journal Intime* under 24 April 1852 (1821-81).
5. Published in *Youth and Two Other Stories* (1902).
6. A.R. Wallace, *The Malay Archipelago*, 1869 (1962), p. 74; like Multatuli's *Max Havelaar* in English translation (1868) and Capt. E. Belcher's *Voyage of H.M.S. Samarang in the Eastern Archipelago* (1848), it is in the Raffles Library.

Brit Takes on Van Gogh

In 1 March 1997 I became Director of the Van Gogh Museum. Within weeks I could see the future of the museum clearly set out ahead of me. There was no choice. The Museum had to close. The Van Gogh Museum had enjoyed a healthy existence for some twenty-five years but for the first months and indeed, the first years after my appointment, I could boast of the somewhat dubious achievement of having brought that first phase in the Museum's history to an end by closing its doors.

Fortunately, my reasoning was sound enough. Work had just started on a major new wing to house our temporary exhibitions. This in itself would cause huge upheaval, but there was a chance also to bring forward a major renovation of the existing building so that all the construction work could be carried out in one phase. This meant closing the museum for almost a year; this massive but relatively short-lived disruption was vastly preferable to battling on in a building site for many years into the future.

The results of our labours were revealed to the public when, on 23 June 1999, the new exhibition wing and the renovated existing building were opened in the presence of Her Majesty Queen Beatrix. This was a momentous occasion for the museum and a particularly happy day for me. At last the Director who had closed the Van Gogh Museum could boast that he had reopened it in a new and revitalised form.

Every Museum Director will claim that his or her institution is unique. But to paraphrase George Orwell, some are more unique than others. From its origins as a showcase for the collections which had been cared for by the artist's family, the Van Gogh Museum has developed into one of the most popular museums in Europe. Over the years the ambitions of the museum have expanded in numerous ways: the collection has been broadened to embrace a wide range of paintings, sculptures, drawings and prints from the period c.1840-1920, offering a crucial link between the collections of our neighbours the Rijksmuseum and the Stedelijk Museum; changing exhibitions have become an essential complement to the permanent displays; new activities have been added and more stress is now laid on education and on making the collection accessible to a broad public.

A Japanese pearl

Throughout the 1980s and 1990s these ambitions placed increasing pressures on the original building designed by Gerrit Rietveld, and the need for extra space was urgent. For outsiders it is perhaps surprising that these needs were not met by Government subsidy but by an extraordinarily generous donation from the private sector. The Yasuda Fire and Marine Insurance Company Ltd provided, via The Japan Foundation, the funds that enabled the Museum to create a new building to house its programme of temporary exhibitions. Yasuda is not a household name in Europe but it is one of Japan's largest insurance companies and if the name sounds familiar it may be because that same company is the proud owner of one of the versions of Van Gogh's *Sunflowers*. This purchase back in 1987 was initiated by the then Chairman of Yasuda, Mr Yasuo Goto, whose enthusiasm for Van Gogh later prompted him to support the Museum that bears his favourite artist's name.

In Great Britain or America such corporate sponsorship of museum buildings has become relatively familiar and has largely taken the place of dwindling national or local government support. In the Netherlands such backing from the private sector (in this case 37.5 million guilders; c.$ 17.5 million / £ 11.5 million) is still a novelty. The money has provided a spectacular addition which was designed by the Japanese architect, Kisho Kurokawa.

The Van Gogh Museum before its renovation. Photo © bv 't Lanthuys / Vincent van Gogh Foundation.

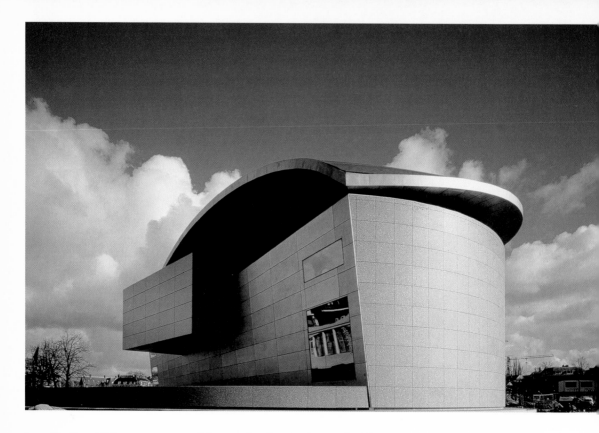

Locally, the striking space-age architecture has inspired several nicknames. For example, the shell-like exterior has been called 'the mussel'. (We prefer to think of it as an oyster; it seems more chic.) It is perhaps the interiors which are the most striking feature of the new building. The rooms are intended to be furnished in countless different ways for changing shows but the museum did not want to have neutral and character-less interiors. Kurokawa's architecture, with its fluid forms and breathtaking spaces will provide a dramatic setting for our varied programme of exhibitions.

The new wing of the Van Gogh Museum. Photo by Jannes Linders / © Van Gogh Museum, Amsterdam.

Building the new wing was a relatively straightforward affair. The renovation of the old building was, by contrast, much more complex. Whereas the funding for the new wing had been in place since 1991, the funds for the renovation (about 32 million guilders) had to be painstakingly pieced together from various sources. We raised a lot of money through our own initiatives, for example, with commercial products relating to Van Gogh, but we also had to work hard to prise funds out of government. In general, museums in the Netherlands enjoy good support through local or national funding but there is sometimes a strange reluctance to acknowledge the fact that putting money our way should be seen as a shrewd investment rather than a mere financial commitment.

The Van Gogh Museum is one of the flagships of the Dutch cultural scene and plays an important role in the gradually emerging image of Amsterdam as a cultural capital. Over the coming years millions of tourists will pass through its doors, many of them attracted to the Netherlands by the idea of visiting the world's largest collection of Van Gogh paintings and drawings.

We look with envy at the grand design and the vision that motivates major cultural projects in France, yet there are few signs that such a spirit has as yet taken hold among the practical, value-seeking Dutch authorities. It is now the turn of our neighbours, the Rijksmuseum, to undergo a major facelift for the new century. Let us hope that the relevant government bodies will grasp the nettle and find the resources to transform this national treasure into the truly great museum that it deserves to be.

Cycling to the museum

If these comments present a somewhat negative picture of museum politics in this country then I should correct this immediately. Before coming to Amsterdam I spent over a decade at the heart of the British cultural establishment as a curator at the National Gallery in London. Much of this was during the height of the so-called 'Thatcher years' when we were blessed with a Prime Minister who, whatever else her achievements may have been, will not be remembered as the darling of the arts world. In short it was a time when bewildered and beleaguered museum staff were faced with swingeing cuts accompanied by exhortations to become more efficient and more market-orientated. In the arts world we grew used to being considered at best, trivial and at worst, parasites in the eyes of politicians. I believe Margaret Thatcher came only once to the National Gallery during her long reign and she specifically asked to see the chrysanthemums by Van Gogh (no-one dared to mention that they were sunflowers).

Interior of the new wing.
Photo by Jannes Linders /
© Van Gogh Museum,
Amsterdam.

Interior of the new wing.
Photo by Jannes Linders /
© Van Gogh Museum,
Amsterdam.

It is with some relief then that one surveys a cultural world here in the
Netherlands where the arts and issues relating to culture enjoy a higher priority on the agenda of national and local politicians. I do not mind having to
compete and even battle for funds when I know that what we do is being tak-
en seriously and commands respect. If the sense of grandeur may be missing there is the advantage of a common-sense approach. For example, from
being directly run by the Department of Culture all the Dutch national museums have now been privatised and set at arm's length from Government.
This intricate process, begun in our museum in 1994, has been a success,
giving the museums more freedom to operate and develop their expertise while allowing government to concentrate on the broader picture, for-
mulating and testing the general outlines of policy. At times there is some
muscle-flexing from government as the boundaries of this still young arrangement are probed and tested but on the whole it works well and, in sharp
contrast to the British scene, one can speak of collaboration rather than competition with our funding body.

Looking back on the past three years my over-riding sentiments are warm
and positive. I have grown used to some of the paradoxes of life in the
Netherlands; the open-minded, sometimes astonishingly direct Dutch who
can also be strangely reserved and shy; the consensus culture that can be
abandoned at a stroke if circumstance so dictates. I have learned too that the

renowned tolerance here is a relative concept, more often based on practicality than on a deep-rooted belief in universal freedoms. On occasion I am nostalgic for the rougher, harsher, more brittle life of a world capital such as London but that is a nostalgia easily dispelled by a single trip on the underground to or from Heathrow airport. To complete the contrast with my former life, I can report that last year I gave Prime Minister Wim Kok and his wife a tour of our new museum. They came in their own time and without fuss on a Saturday morning simply because they were interested. They were well-informed, curious and engaging. And yes, they did come on their bicycles, attaching them to the fence outside, just like everyone else.

JOHN LEIGHTON

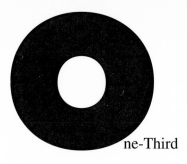

One-Third

Land and Two-Thirds Sky

As a child Holland sailed into my consciousness on the back of a disaster. I went to school in London and they scrupulously taught us London's history. I was intrigued by the three great disasters of the reign of Charles II; in 1665, the Great Plague of London, in 1666, The Great Fire of London and in 1667 the Dutch sailed up the Medway to fire cannon-shots at the Tower of London. The first two events were in the nature of Acts of God, the third was certainly an act of the Dutch. Who were these Dutch? And how come that Charles' brother was thrown out by a Dutchman? And how come we ended up having a King who spoke English badly with a Dutch accent? And who was the little man in black velvet who fatally tumbled this Dutch King onto the back of his head when his horse tripped over a molehill on Hampstead Heath?[1] This Dutch country was called both Holland and the Netherlands – to have two names was greedy – and they spoke Dutch which sounded suspiciously like Deutsch, and they had an alarming reputation for being excessively clean. And then what about double Dutch, my old Dutch, Dutch courage, Dutch trouble, Dutch caps, to go Dutch, my Dutch uncle and even Dutch Elm Disease?

Jan van Goyen, *View of Rhenen*. 1646. Canvas, 101.5 x 136 cm. Corcoran Gallery of Art, Washington, DC.

All this made for a suspicious approach to Holland. These suspicions were further assisted by my father. He was a bird-watcher in love with East Anglia, which is the closest you can get to Dutch low watery horizons without crossing the English Channel. The birds flew out to sea, eastwards from where the Dark Age invaders had come. My father dragged us, my brother and I, across those low horizons in gumboots and clutching binoculars, warning us it was even flatter and wetter in Holland.

But I am certain that the most persistent introduction to this mysterious place came later through an admiration for Dutch landscape painting. I discovered it first through English East Anglian painters like Crome and John Sell Cotman who are scarcely known outside England. I was enthusiastic for their landscapes, tried to copy them and then learnt they were copying too, copying the Dutch painters of a century before, when the strategy seemed to be to make every landscape two-thirds sky and one-third land.

I eventually came to Holland to see these two-thirds sky and one-third land paintings. I was not disappointed. Most filled the necessary criteria.

This was a land where nothing fell downhill, hill-starts in a car were unknown, and mountains were a fiction. I was seventeen and stayed in a hostel near the Railway Station in Amsterdam, sleeping in a wire-frame bed four metres from the floor. Gravity ought to have been a stranger in Holland. Yet the Dutch do not fear gravity – look at Amsterdam staircases. I saw paintings of children in the Rijksmuseum whose heads were wrapped around with bandages, a feeble protection from staircase accidents. If children did not fall downstairs, they drowned in a canal. I was intrigued by the Dutch story of a woman decapitated by the sails of a windmill. A third way to die in Holland. Gravity, drowning and windmills. The first two have given me considerable subject-matter for film-making. I await an opportunity to use the third.

Cows

Perhaps there is a fourth – bicycle-riding. I have now assiduously taken to it myself. Sitting high on a sit-up-and-beg bike along Prinsengracht, still intrigued, like so many pop-eyed tourists, about the Amsterdam bicycle cult – load it with children in front and behind, dogs in baskets, dogs dragged on

Paulus Potter, *The Bull.*
1647. Canvas,
235.5 x 339 cm.
Mauritshuis, The Hague.

leads, holding two umbrellas and a portable-phone, skipping the red traffic-lights, and singing loudly, unafraid of ridicule – no brakes and certainly no lights at night, and a most nonchalant stoicism when the damn thing is stolen yet again though you loaded it with chains and padlocks and tied it to both a tree and a lamp-post.

I enjoy the scale of the Dutch cities. Even the centre of Amsterdam is still a village, pedestrian-friendly, domestically inclined, still building good vernacular architecture in brick as it has almost continuously done since the early 1600s. And outside the cities I still enjoy those long flat horizons. I now know them better. And I have developed a particular enthusiasm for those Dutch stands and rows of trees – poplars, birches – that clump together so elegantly and stretch for metres so strictly. Planted carefully in parallel rows, their lower branches stripped away to make straight vertical trunks that play tricks on the eye as you swiftly ride past them in a car along a highway.

Being Dutch and tidy, perhaps the trees do their own de-stripping. I am now prepared to swap Dutch parkland for English parkland, it comes somewhere between the ruled edges of French Le Notre, and the accidental-on-purpose of English Capability Brown. It is friendlier, less romantically de-ranged and less aristocratically haughty. What else do I like? Picnics on the Amstel, the gaunt new armies of windmills, my walk-in-walk-out-pass to look at Frans Hals any time I wish, the new Amsterdam Museumplein that looks like the Tuileries Gardens, the confidence of tall Dutch women, the wind in Zeeland, the smell of cows when you leave Schiphol airport.

Practically the very first film I ever shot, back in the sixties, with an 8mm camera loaded with black and white film, was from a train window travelling from Rotterdam to Amsterdam at dawn, looking at cows. We have cows in England – exactly the same animals, but Holland has made a cult of the cow. It has exclusive cow-painters – Potter and Cuyp. On this train trip I was intrigued by the long black shadows of cows standing against the sun which gave them the appearance of standing on stilts. The drainage canals of a hundred small fields were set at right-angles to the train-track and catching the low winter sun, their surfaces reflected back quick, sharp, blinding reflections into the lens at regular intervals, making a mesmerising rhythmic pattern. The footage was used in a film called *Postcards from Eight Capital Cities*; one city was Amsterdam, the other Rotterdam. The film is now lost. My films were first shown to an international audience in Rotterdam, where I subsequently made a movie about Vermeer set in Rotterdam Zoo which curiously possessed a rarity – a Dutch mountain – some thirty metres high, the home for goats and monkeys. And I now live in Amsterdam. In a house close to the Rijksmuseum. I can see its south tower when I paint in the attic and I know there are four Vermeers under that roof, and a considerable number of those one-third land and two-third-sky paintings, and also quite a few painted cows.

Casual and confident

The enthusiasm for Dutch painting remains. How could they produce so many, and not just in the Golden Age – Rembrandt, Vermeer, van Gogh and Mondrian? The Van Gogh Museum is close. And so is the Stedelijk. Way back in 1963, way before Rudi Fuchs, I accidentally listened there for the first time to the music of Stockhausen, and saw paintings by his companion, Mary Baumeister. I tried to paint like her for several years. And he was my introduction to modern music. I later traded Stockhausen for Cage and Baumeister for RB Kitaj, but the train of influences in and via Holland is strong and they continue. I am now a collaborator at the Amsterdam Muziek Theater with the music of Louis Andriessen, and I was given licence, not at the Amsterdam Stedelijk, but at the Rotterdam Boymans van Beuningen, to make a first curatorial exhibition – it was called *The Physical Self* and we displayed human nudes in glass-cases to demonstrate where painters from Memling to De Kooning had taken their inspiration. I doubt if you would be allowed to do such a thing anywhere else. I have since tried to exhibit a dead swan in the Louvre and a live pig in the Vienna Hofburg Palace but met with rejection on both counts. A live human nude was not even to be dreamt of.

This freedom, this nonchalance, this toleration and these opportunities are often praised as being very Dutch characteristics. The necessity to trade, the smallness of the country and the impossibility of hiding in it, have no doubt contributed to these characteristics. The need to get along with foreigners has generally made the Dutch tolerant and more open, and curiously more honest – sometimes brutally honest. Holland is an old democracy – everyone can be part of a decision-making process, and curiously success is not

feted. Stick your head above the parapet and, watch out, you might get it lopped off. This attitude is strangely present in a Dutch aptitude to invent and instigate, but not to follow through. There is a reluctance to self-promote, which makes the embarrassment of riches an endearing characteristic, but also a fearful one, because it implies so much confidence. Self-promotion, the Dutch seem to be saying, is a characteristic of the unconfident. Which might be why the Dutch in their relaxed way are probably the best Europeans – they have been Europeans for so long. It is of course to do with trade and communications. The English are also supposed to be a trading nation. But one of the differences between Dutch and English attitudes which is touching – and I sympathise – is that although both nations were curious to travel the world, the English always regarded themselves as superior to their trading partners, yet they were not always so happy to return home – look at America, Australia, India – whereas the Dutch, though they had colonies, always came back. They knew home was best – to sit in their own convivial company comfortably – you can see it in Dutch seventeenth-century painting as you can see it now in cafés, restaurants, Amsterdam parks, domestic togetherness, families, and a liking for the very word that the English feel uncomfortable about – coziness. The Dutch kiss is threefold. The English find this excessive. I like it.

1. 'The little man in black velvet' being the mole who built the molehill that caused William III's horse to stumble and throw him, with fatal results. Political correctness not having been invented yet, supporters of the exiled Stuarts gleefully devised a new and now famous toast 'To the little gentleman in black velvet'.

2. The libretto of *Writing to Vermeer* was written by Peter Greenaway and Louis Andriessen put it to music. The director was Saskia Bodeke. The opera opened in Amsterdam in December 1999.

Rags and flags

It is said that Dutch William who became the English King William III – Sweet William to the Protestants, Stinking Billie to the Catholics – didn't want to leave his children in England far from home, so he didn't have any. We have an English nursery rhyme for him. '*Hark hark the dogs do bark, the beggars are coming to town, some in rags and some in flags and one in a silver gown.*' The beggars were the Dutch sea-beggars, the flags were orange, and the one in the silver gown was William. We have learnt many of our four-letter swear-words from Dutch sailors, orange flags still haunt Anglo-Irish politics, and with William, modern Protestant Britain really begins. The little man in black velvet on Hampstead Heath could not halt the changing times.

In an opera at the Amsterdam Muziek Theater[2], there was a modest attempt to return some of these Dutch enthusiasms back to the Dutch. The very title was an homage – *Writing to Vermeer* –, and on stage there were tall and confident Dutch women, a cow, bridges, excessive cleanliness, a certain amount of coziness and much – very much – water.

PETER GREENAWAY

**F**ascinated

by the House

The Paintings of Hans Broek

There are many examples in art history of how a painter's work can be influenced by travel or a long stay in another country. I would just like to draw attention to the hundreds who left northern Europe and crossed the Alps to see the works of their great predecessors and to experience the clarity of the light, as in Venice. Generally, the real work did not begin until their return, when sketches were turned into paintings.

Ever since then, travel or some time spent abroad has been if not a prerequisite for full artistic development, then an essential element in many an oeuvre, with effects lasting over years. Examples include Paul Klee and August Macke and their journey to Tunisia, which in both cases crucially affected their work.

The determining factor in the work of the Dutch painter Hans Broek (1965-) was a journey he made in 1993-1994. At that time his girlfriend was living in Los Angeles and a visit to her provided an opportunity to explore the surrounding region. He was captivated and amazed by the unique beauty of the landscape and the light, and by the colours, especially those of the desert and – by his own account – the purple and brown mountains.

What struck him most of all was the Californian light. It gives everything in the landscape contours that stand out sharply against the morning, midday or evening sky. Every moment of the day shows this almost tangible presence of light; it offers an unreal and magnificent spectrum of colours which are not hidden from view by majestic passing clouds, as in the more atmospheric Low Countries by the sea. These are colours of a magical splendour, of stunning beauty, but sometimes also slightly fake, as in a kitsch technicolour film. Perhaps this is why on occasion they seem to contain a certain menace and to evoke an indefinable foreboding.

Broek was quite familiar with the qualities of the Californian landscape – not from personal observation but, like most of us, from films and television. Moreover, this recognition at one remove, this sense of déjà vu on seeing the landscapes on the West Coast, arises in part from the information presented to contemporary artists through exhibitions and catalogues. The American urban landscape was not completely unknown, of course; art, too, has contributed to our knowledge of it.

Hans Broek, *Untitled*. 1996
(no. 1).
Canvas, 170 X 170 cm.
Private collection (Photo by
Thys Quispel / courtesy De
Pont Stichting, Tilburg).

Broek has of course seen David Hockney's Hollywood paintings, the swimming pools in which the water makes fanciful scrawls with white movements on the blue tiles. And whether in Rotterdam, at the Museum Boymans-van Beuningen, or in Los Angeles, at the Museum of Contemporary Art, Broek will have seen work by the American painter and printmaker Edward Ruscha, perhaps a painting like the one showing three dark houses of the same shape, a shadow made concrete, seen in a monochrome, pitch-black perspective. In this information age no one, not even Broek, can paint without being influenced. By Ruscha, and Hockney, and the Canadian Alex Colville. And perhaps René Magritte as well. His *Empire of Lights* (1954), with the house half hidden behind a tree in the light of a streetlamp, is virtually unavoidable for anyone who paints houses. Which is what Broek does.

The house is the theme he returns to most often. And then the differences from the other artists mentioned are immediately apparent. Broek does not grant us a glimpse of the interior, as Colville and Hockney do; we are shut out. There is no suggestion of a story, as there is with Magritte's solitary streetlamp, and there is no question with Broek of the kind of perspective in which Ruscha places his houses and sailing boats. However broad the view of the landscape, everything, each house, each building, is seen frontally, reduced to its essence: a white block with a few lines (for the storeys) and some squares (for the windows). This reduction goes so far that it sometimes seems as if the painting does not depict bungalows or flats, but that instead

grid paintings (by Agnes Martin) or drawings (by Jan Schoonhoven) have been scattered over the landscape, in a small format admittedly, but nonetheless...

Hans Broek, *Untitled*. 1996 (no. 6).
Canvas, 148 x 148 cm.
Private Collection, Poppel (Photo by Thys Quispel / courtesy De Pont Stichting, Tilburg).

No trace of man

Thus Broek is not concerned with the landscape, or perhaps only in part. What matters to him above all is the painting, the artefact of paint and canvas with its own laws and traditions. Nonetheless, in the conversation I had with him, Broek said the image was more important to him than the painting. He makes that secondary to the subject, whereas the viewer is deeply impressed – well at least I am – by how Broek makes the observed reality secondary to his painted interpretation of it. I particularly admire the way in which Broek turns reality into art and how he does this by painterly means.

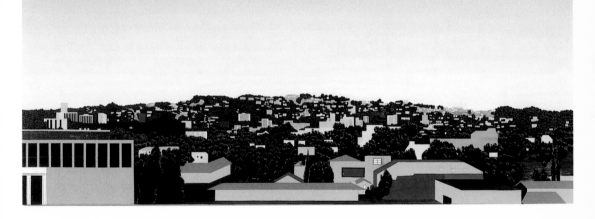

Hans Broek, *Untitled*. 1996
(no. 2).
Canvas, 148 x 300 cm.
Collection KNP, The Hague
(Photo by Thys Quispel).

Hans Broek, *Untitled*. 1996.
Canvas, 120 x 300 cm.

I admire the contrasts which Broek constantly creates in his work: contrasts between light and dark, nature and culture, colour and the absence of colour, space and enclosure. And I admire the reduction of reality to an austere and tightly controlled composition, which is generally based on the picture plane being divided in two by the horizon or an incline.

An excellent example, bringing together almost everything that is typical of a Broek painting, is the untitled work of 1996, no. 6. It is a square canvas (148 x 148 cm) showing a bungalow on a slope with a dense covering of bushes. The house, not quite a square, is not in the centre of the painting; this prevents the composition from becoming too static. A similar effect is achieved by a line – a terrace, a balcony? – which protrudes from the dark block into the light space.

The dividing line, from top left to bottom right, between sky and slope works as a diagonal in a composition that is as a result suddenly very geometrical, though achieved with figurative means. The contrasts are striking:

between the smoothly painted, almost luminous sky and the dark bushes, whose outlines are marked by a pattern of white, shining dots, and between the severe lines of the house, a dark block with two light grids (the windows), and the irregular vegetation. Mondrian versus the seventeenth-century landscape painter Hercules Seghers.

No trace of people. In none of Broek's paintings or drawings is man physically present. He is seen only through what he has left behind in the landscape and nature. Perhaps man is found only indoors; he may be in the interiors which we are not shown. Broek appears to be fascinated by houses alone. Whether it is a dark, rather mysterious-looking gardener's cottage in Wassenaar or near Arnhem or a shoe-box of a bungalow among eucalyptus trees makes no difference. After all, their common characteristic is that they are closed spaces in which anything can take place and anything can be hidden. Looked at in this light, Broek's paintings have certain cinematic qualities, not only because of the sometimes very broad, panoramic format but also because of an element of suspense underlying his arrangements of reality. They are sets waiting to be acted on and brought to life with drama. The colours of the sky, glowing mysteriously, add to this effect.

Unreal silence

Only occasionally does the viewer get some idea of what is going on, as in *Pursuit and Possession*, painted after an etching by the Japanese artist Hokusai. What we see is a long, low, dark bungalow – yet again with grids for windows – surrounded by high snowdrifts. The house is on fire; at least that is what is suggested by the highly stylised flames emerging from an opening in the roof and the ominous orange glow behind the windows. There is no sign of the occupants. Everything takes place in an unreal silence.

The same is true of the large panoramas of the desert or the urban landscape. Paintings do not generally speak – though some of them do! – but Broek's are unusually quiet, even when they depict part of the busy metropolis of Los Angeles. No noise, nothing of the permanent hum of traffic, just the silence of the landscape arranged by the painter. He even manages to surround a car, one of those big American models, with silence - and mystery. It is very close to being the kind of abstract painting in whites and greys of which Robert Ryman would have been proud.

There remains the question whether the Broek of the paintings is the same as the Broek of the drawings. Judging by the subject-matter, he is, with at most a slight preference in the drawings for another typically Broek theme – densely growing, broccoli-like bushes. In the drawings he seems to be primarily concerned with texture. The drawing *Thousand Oaks* shows the rhythmic orderliness of trees planted by man. But superimposed on that is a second layer, shading with short diagonals, a pure use of graphic means. Broek does this again in the more freely designed *Case Study* in which the clouds with green shading are surrounded by a slightly undulating, blue outline which turns the bushes into islands, as it were, an archipelago of bushes.

Both drawings and paintings show very clearly the extent to which the desert around Los Angeles and the buildings in it have influenced Hans Broek's work. With the possible exception of Flevoland, in the crowded Netherlands he would certainly never have found that kind of space or the light arching over it.

CEES VAN DER GEER
Translated by John Rudge.

Hans Broek, *Glendale*.
1995. Crayon on paper. De
Pont Stichting, Tilburg.

Rhapsody of facades

The Zurenborg District in Antwerp

Right at the end of the nineteenth century, as a result of a strong economic revival, Antwerp acquired a new district: Zurenborg. Its name refers to low-lying '*zure*' (acidic) pastures squeezed between the suburbs of Berchem and Borgerhout and bisected by a brick railway-viaduct. This new development was in part made possible by the proximity of rail links to Brussels and the Netherlands, and by the advent of trams and local trains. On the northern side, near Borgerhout, streets of rather modest houses were constructed for deserving workers and the lower middle class. The liberal Antwerp city council named the streets after the signs of the zodiac, possibly in the hope of bringing the people closer to the ideals of the Enlightenment. But to the south of the railway, raised high above ground level on its viaduct, arose an extremely curious group of residences, which the developer of the district described as villas, in the most diverse Revival styles. The main thorough-fare of this elite neighbourhood was named after the two prominent families who had invested in Zurenborg, Cogels and Osy.

Rampant eclecticism

The Cogels-Osy neighbourhood was in the main the work of one man, Louis Luyckx. This 'town planner', working under instruction but also rather self-willed, loyally served the financial interests of his employers. He gave the architects he commissioned free rein when it came to their fantasies for the facades, but at the same time he maintained firm control as regards the general concept laid down for the construction of the district. The decoration of the facades, and not least the diversity of styles, were meant to provide an abundance of nostalgic elegance. It was precisely by means of its striking facades that this area of urban villas, standing neatly in rows with their small front gardens, was intended to impress the citizens of Antwerp and at the same time evoke the grandeur of God's creation. The district's rampant eclecticism, which was deliberately not allowed to become a strongly architectural Art Nouveau masterpiece, is explained by the militant Catholic inspiration of the project developer and his rich directors. The progressive architects of the day lived and worked in Brussels, and were inspired by masonic and social-liberal ideals. At the request of Zurenborg's conservative 'town planner', the Antwerp architects in the main looked back towards the past glories of Antwerp and Europe.

Ostensibly, the unabashed eclecticism of the Cogels-Osy neighbourhood also seems to be a logical consequence of Antwerp's chaotic expansion in the second half of the nineteenth century. But the tight control exercised by the developer gives the neighbourhood, even today, the paradoxical and deceptive unity that is so appealing. The names given to the streets also contribute to this apparent coherence. The clash of arms is to be heard in the streets named after Kruger, Pretoria and Transvaal, referring to the then highly topical Boer War. The streets named after General Capiaumont, General Van Merlen and Waterloo remind us of the most famous battle ever fought on Brabant soil. The range of Revival styles in the facades provides visitor and resident with a summary of the entire history of Western civilisation. Here one finds medieval Flanders cheek-by-jowl with French Renaissance, but one also comes upon Greek antiquity, Venetian *palazzi* and contemporary Jugendstil. In almost every case these involve straight copying of architectural elements – never of real insights into the use of

Impression of Pretoriastraat and Cogels-Osylei seen from the railway near the Eastern Station.

The Battle of Waterloo,
a wide residence with
a gateway door in a very
heterogeneous Art Nouveau
style (F. Smet-Verhas,
1905, Waterloostraat 11).

space or innovations such as one finds in Victor Horta.

The weird coherence of the Cogels-Osy area is a consequence of its unsubtle references to the cosmos. The decorations and inscriptions on the facades leave no room for doubt: they seek to point the passer-by in the direction of such philosophical profundities as the passage of time and the movement of the heavenly bodies. The various times of day, the seasons, the classical pantheon, the Christian world (with particular emphasis on the Carolingian Renaissance) and even the various stages and protagonists in the struggle for national freedom: nothing was too great or too small for the 'town planner' and his associates.

It was preferred practice for the architects to work on groups of houses. This led to the identifiable accents that are distinguishable in this strange cohesive whole: traditionalist facades by Ernest Dieltiens and Frans van Dijk, neoclassicist pseudo-palaces by Ernest Stordiau and the Cols and Defever team, facades dripping with nostalgia by J. Bilmeyer and J. Van Riel, and fortunately also elements of the contemporary Art Nouveau style in the work of F. Smet-Verhas, Jules Hofman and J. De Weerdt.

A miraculous house on its way to the stars

The Art Nouveau creations of Joseph Bascourt in particular deserve more than a modest mention in the history of Belgian architecture. Whereas most of his colleagues religiously followed the lead of the Brussels masters, fashions and successes, Bascourt found a tone of his own, mostly oriental in style, which gradually became clearer in spite of the somewhat confusing diversity of his designs. This tone became apparent in the twenty or so Art Nouveau houses he built between 1898 and 1908, most of them in Zurenborg.

Bascourt made his debut in the Cogels-Osy neighbourhood with a crazy castle-like facade behind which stand three separate homes called *In de Sterre, de Sonne* and *de Mane*. In his monograph on Bascourt (Archives d'Architecture Moderne, Brussels, 1993), the architectural critic Francis Strauven calls this staggering work *'the absolute pinnacle of neo-Flemish Renaissance'*. In terms of harmony, however, Bascourt reached the peak of his inventiveness in *The Four Seasons*. These are four almost identical cor-

A neoclassicist pseudo-palace, clearly inspired by Chambord Castle on the Loire (E. Dieltiens, 1899, Cogels-Osylei 39-41-43).

ner houses at the cross-roads of Generaal Van Merlenstraat and Water-loostraat, a few dozen metres from the small roundabout in the Cogels-Osylei. All the elements, as simple as they are appropriate, contribute to the natural and shining unity of this group of houses: the crenellated garden walls, the conspicuously narrow and restrained vertical windows, the white glazed-brick sections of the facades, with several brightly coloured bands lower down at eye-level, the Spanish-looking bay windows that converse with each other across the street, the enchanting mosaics of the four emblems, each with a festoon bearing the name of the house: *Spring, Summer, Autumn, Winter,* and the varied colours of the paintwork on the doors and windows.

The Morning Star glitters like an architectural gem in the otherwise excessive Cogels-Osylei. This modest little facade seems slightly oppressed by the violence erupting in those to the left and right of it, which reaches paroxysmal proportions in Frans van Dijk's *Scaldis* group – the Antwerp version of Venice's *palazzi*. In the midst of this eclectic jumble, Bascourt's little masterpiece shines in spite of its simplicity, as insistent as the planet Venus in the sky before sunrise. This house was built a year later than the monumental *Scaldis* and its simple forms are seamlessly linked to the *Lotus* and *Papyrus* double house that Bascourt built in Transvaalstraat in 1901. In each case there is a small, flat, restrained facade into which the door and windows of the ground floor and first floor are cut. In *The Morning Star* the

An ode to the Carolingian-Romanesque art of building: Detached group of four residences, brought together behind a single symmetrical facade (J. Bilmeyer and J. van Riel, 1897, Cogels-Osylei 12-10-8-6).

striking double window on the first floor cuts the facade open precisely in the middle; this doubling gives it the harmonious calm which is totally lacking in the built environment of Cogels-Osylei. The pointed outlines of the decoration on the small basket arches pull the simple architectural composition upwards so that the facade seems to taper – as if this miraculous house might at any moment set off to take its place as a luminous heavenly body in the firmament.

Winter, one component of the *Four Seasons* housing group (J Bascourt, 1899, Generaal Van Merlenstraat 29).

A miniature city of illusion

The Cogels-Osy neighbourhood has never been the object of unanimous appreciation. The splendour of its facades struck many people as typical Antwerp ostentation. It was also quickly understood that the motive driving the 'town planner' was by no means purely aesthetic or ideological in nature. For the investors and their developer it all hinged on money. These fine-looking houses were to be let as soon as possible, and at substantial

The Morning Star,
a residence in Art Nouveau
style (J. Bascourt, 1904,
Cogels-Osylei 55).

rents. Preferably to well-off foreigners who settled temporarily in Antwerp with their family and staff, often with an eye to their business in or involving the port. It was only after 1914 that increasing numbers of residents were able to buy their houses.

In the thirties the area faded as a curiosity and in the sixties it resurfaced as a problem. At that time most of the houses were occupied by their ageing owners. They hoped for a spectacular rise in the value of the land, since it was intended that nearby Berchem station would entirely take over the international function of Antwerp Central. Once again, the railway appeared to be playing a crucial part in the life of the district. Plans soon appeared for the demolition and redevelopment of the Cogels-Osy area, this time with luxury flats and comfortable hotels. It was precisely at that moment that architects, critics, writers and artists stood up for the preservation of the district. They did not want a repetition of the world-wide disgrace that Belgium had faced after the demolition of Victor Horta's Volkshuis in Brussels.

The struggle between the old people with their avaricious dreams and the young ones fighting for preservation was not settled until 1984. For the first

Contemporary design in Zurenborg. Part of this house is inspired by the *Mercurius* villa, which occupied this site before its demolition in 1933 (Chr. Conix, 1991, Cogels-Osylei 29a).

time in Belgian history an entire urban district was classified as 'a land-scape', and several notable buildings within this 'urban landscape' listed as monuments.

The new residents of the rescued Cogels-Osy neighbourhood were of course of a different social class to the well-off lower middle class that had so forcefully resisted the area's preservation. After 1968 some original, vaguely creative and bizarre characters settled in the neighbourhood, as well as journalists, philosophers, musicians, writers, designers, artists and architects.

Architects! But had they in fact played the leading part in creating the district? With the Cogels-Osylei as the central axis of the smarter part, Zurenborg is the product of a strange *Kunstwollen*. This resplendent but somewhat dream-like part of the city owes its unmistakable character to the supervision of a 'town planner' with a capitalist mandate. The eclectic outburst that took place round 1900 resulted in a rhapsody of facades, but by no means in a transformation of living spaces. These were still bound in the strait-jacket of the typically Belgian expanded and deepened pipe-drawer: three or four rooms behind each other alongside a passage. That is where the real unity of the district lies, in the predictable middle-class domestic culture. By contrast, the coherence mentioned above is based on imagination. Because in spite of the coherence that was *wished for*, what today's visitor *actually* sees is fragmentation. Each house, even each group of houses, is '*chilled to the heart by silence*' (after the well-known poem by Maurice Gilliams, the great Antwerp poet of decline).

It is not so much that the typical Cogels-Osy house protects the intimacy of the citizen, because every decent residence does that. It is much more that every facade evokes a dream of unity and harmony in time and space, while tight cohesion is precisely what is utterly lacking in this relatively small area. The Cogels-Osy district preserves an illusion. And yet its chaos of styles and paranoid madness are fascinating, since both are typical of the Antwerper who obstinately disregards his decline into provincialism and continues to cherish his mythical past.

A century ago the district already had a restorative function. At that time too it was a miniature city of illusion, megalomanic in its littleness, and a permanent showcase for itself and its visitors.

FRANS BOENDERS
Translated by Gregory Ball.

All photos taken from:
Hans Roels and Serge Vermeir, *Belle époque: Zurenborg, Antwerp*. Antwerp: Pandora, 1996.

hate messages'

The Work of Willem Elsschot

For me, literary history is littered with 'might have beens'. Last year, amid the centenary commemoration of Guido Gezelle, I found myself fantasising about what might have happened if Gezelle, on one of his stints as a supply priest in England, had chanced upon work by his contemporary, fellow-Catholic priest and nature poet Gerard Manley Hopkins circulating *samizdat*-style before its eventual posthumous publication in 1918, nineteen years after both their deaths.

In the case of Willem Elsschot (the pseudonym of Alfons de Ridder, 1882-1960) two more or less wild surmises preoccupy me. First, what if Elsschot had met his fellow-townsman, the modernist poet and Flemish activist Paul van Ostaijen, who died in 1928? Would the mutual incomprehension of the dedicated avant-garde artist and the part-time writer have prevented any real communication, or would creative sparks have flown? We shall never know, but if any playwrights read this, it could make a wonderful piece of theatre.

More substantial evidence justifies a second question: what might have happened to Elsschot's international career and reputation abroad, had a number of initiatives to publish English translations of his work during his lifetime borne fruit?

In the correspondence of the Dutch writer Edgar du Perron – incidentally, a link between Elsschot and Van Ostaijen – we find a mention of an English friend of Du Perron's, Anthony Gishford, living in The Hague and so taken with the novella *Cheese* (Kaas,1933) (a '*small masterpiece*') that he has translated it into English. Gishford, however, is inhibited from pursuing the project further because '*the very concept of Dutch or Flemish literature is non-sensical to English publishers*'.[1] Nevertheless, an enthusiastic notice subsequently appeared anonymously in *The Times Literary Supplement* of 26 April 1934 and may have been written by Gishford.[2] The tone and rarity of such a paean justify quotation in full:

As a tragi-comedy this unpretentious story, told against a lightly sketched background of Flemish middle-class life, is extraordinarily moving. In a prefatory essay Elsschot reveals himself as the possessor of a highly de-

veloped artistic consciousness, and his book is a striking affirmation of that quality.

Laarmans, a middle-aged shipping clerk who embarks on an untimely adventure in cheese salesmanship, is not, by the grace of his creator, the grotesque figure that from description he must appear, but an average type who at a rather late age makes the elementary mistake of trying to realise his life in terms of romance. Introduced more or less fortuitously into a milieu that is just beyond the range of his experience: associating once a week with men who talk about shares which he does not possess, families with whom he is not acquainted, restaurants at which he cannot afford to eat, he snatches at the first opportunity that seems to offer him a chance of moral and material equality with them. The former is quickly achieved. No sooner has he saddled himself with twenty tons of cheese to sell on commission than they welcome him as a 'big wholesale dealer in foodstuffs' and are lavish in their praise of the specimen of his products he has brought for them to taste. But their orders do not help very much towards the disposal of the twenty tons. Nor does an order from the father of one of his children's schoolfellows. Nor do his own eventually desperate attempts to peddle it from shop to shop in a suitcase. Up to this point he has been spared an impact with reality, but the daydream rapidly becomes a nightmare, from which he is finally delivered only by a supreme act of cowardice and defeat that cuts the knot and serves to restore him to the security of the shipping firm and his former unambitious domesticity.

Sadly, though perhaps unsurprisingly, the notice remained without resonance in the UK publishing world, and no trace remains of Gishford's labours.

Gishford's translation was not the only one: the Archive and Museum of Flemish Culture in Antwerp holds the typescript of an undated version by A.J. van Riemsdijk,[3] while I am aware of a further translation by an Englishman long resident in Belgium, Vernon Pearce.[4]

In the 1950s we find the translator Hans Koningsberger negotiating unsuccessful with Scribner's Sons in New York for the publication of a translation of the novella *Soft Soap* (Lijmen, 1923) and its sequel *The Leg* (Het been, 1938).[5] The two works finally appeared in 1965, together with Elsschot's last story, *The Will-o'-the-Wisp* (*Het dwaallicht*, 1947) in a translation by Alex Brotherton in the scholarly, prestigious, but commercially unsuccessful hardback series *Bibliotheca Neerlandica*.[6] Who knows what impact a well-marketed translation of one or more of Elsschot's tales might have had in interwar and post-war Britain and America?

The editors of Elsschot's collected correspondence, published in 1993, suggest that his literary career was thwarted twice over by the two world wars in which his country was embroiled,[7] but whether a more peaceful environment and a warmer critical reception for the early work would have turned Elsschot into a prolific or full-time writer, remains yet another 'might have been'.

Rather than continue what may appear a somewhat plaintive account of unrecognised genius, I shall give newcomers to Elsschot's work without a knowledge of Dutch a brief factual and critical framework. The best and

The Elsschot family at Wenduine, 1922. Collection Ida de Ridder.

most eloquent plea for wider international recognition is the work itself.

An early painting of the author shows a gaunt, intense, moustachioed face beneath a broad-brimmed hat, and evokes the pen-portrait of Elsschot's *alter ego*, Frans Laarmans, as a young literary enthusiast and nationalist tearaway, remembered by the anonymous narrator at the beginning of *Soft Soap*:

I'd known him as a shabbily-dressed idealist with long hair that made his collar greasy and a big pipe with a bowl shaped like a death's head, and a heavy walking stick that he waved menacingly whenever he'd drunk too

much or marched in a demonstration. No one else could shout Flemish bat-
tle-cries as loudly as he used to, and he had been arrested twice, to my
knowledge, for crimes that he hadn't committed, simply because he looked
such a dangerous character.[8]

However, the tearaway was destined for a life in business, and specifically
advertising, with literature as a sporadic, secondary activity. Not, though,
a marginal one: his modest output of eleven novellas and a volume of poetry is an impressive monument to economy and trenchancy of style, a language without regional or descriptive embellishment, as well as scathing wit
and irony overlaying a deeper charge of emotion.

After some early derivative verse, later largely disowned, Elsschot's literary career falls into two main periods: from 1910 to 1923 and from 1933
to 1947. After graduating from business college he worked first in Paris
(a period he was to draw on in *Villa des Roses*, 1913) and later in Rotterdam,
where, encouraged by a Dutch colleague, he wrote the first of the poems later collected as *Verses from the Past* (Verzen van Vroeger, 1937). Among the
poems is the bleak 'Marriage' ('Het huwelijk'), aptly described by the
Dutch writer S. Vestdijk as '*a novel in miniature*':

Perceiving how the creeping mists of age
had left the sparkle in his wife's eyes quenched,
her cheeks all worn, her forehead deeply trenched,
he turned away and fumed in helpless rage.

Furiously tugging at his beard he'd swear,
survey her, with no passion left to feel,
see sin once splendid turn to an ordeal,
while she gazed up like some poor dying mare.

She would not die; though like a fiend from hell
he sucked her marrowbones, they'd still not crack.
Afraid to whine, beseech or answer back,
she shook with fear, yet stayed alive and well.

He thought: I'll kill her, set the house ablaze.
I'll wash the mildew off my stiffening frame,
escape through water and through cleansing flame,
and find new love, new pastures I can graze.

He didn't kill, as giving dreams their head
raises both practical and legal snags,
and, puzzlingly, one's spirit always flags
in the evenings when it's time for bed.

His children grew, as year on year passed by,
and saw how the man that they called their sire
was sitting still and tight-lipped by the fire
with godforsaken grimness in his eye.[9]

Willem Elsschot (1882-1960). Photo by Paul van den Abeele.

It is hard to look at later portraits and group photographs without hearing the chilling echo of that poem.

The last sentence of *Villa des Roses*, where the chambermaid Louise, having been seduced and abandoned by the philandering commercial traveller Grünwald, returns to her one-horse village in the provinces, evokes the desolation unforgettably, with the utmost economy: '*It was her village sure enough.*'

The disposal of Louise's aborted foetus over a fence had earlier been commented on in equally terse terms: '*It was a simple funeral.*'

The book was well enough received to encourage Elsschot to continue writing. *A Disappointment* (Een ontgoocheling, 1921), set in his native Antwerp, describes a doting father's disillusion with his hopeless son, while *Salvation* (De verlossing, 1921) is his only treatment of one of the major themes in Flemish fiction: the power of the Church in rural Flanders. *Soft Soap* (1923) introduces the recurring figures of Laarmans and the larger-than-life, Svengali-like business guru Boorman, who re-invents Laarmans as his personal assistant under the name 'Texeira de Mattos' and grooms him as his successor in the dubious profession of '*salesman in printed paper*' selling formulaic advertising copy to small businesses. The climax of the story is the foisting of thousands of copies of the *World Review* on a small lift-making firm. Truth was in fact stranger than fiction, since in real life De Ridder and his partner pulled off a similar coup with their *Revue Continentale Illustrée,* except that the target was a convent![10]

Lack of critical response led to a hiatus of almost ten years in Elsschot's literary production. In 1933, encouraged by the editors of the new Belgo-Dutch magazine *Forum,* which advocated the primacy of content over formal conceit in literature, Elsschot produced first *Cheese,* written in a matter of weeks, and a sequel to *Soft Soap.* His principal supporters in *Forum* were Jan Greshoff and Menno ter Braak. The latter particularly had a formidably intellectual view of literature and culture, and Elsschot, who declared '*I hate messages*', felt unable to deliver the '*profundity and philosophy*' that Ter Braak seemed to expect. Ter Braak, undeterred, persisted in seeing Elsschot as '*a writer who represents an idea, without having ideas himself*'. It is touching to find the quintessential non-intellectual asking Greshoff about this Freud who is mentioned so frequently in the pages of *Forum.* Anecdotes abound about his sparse library and his need to refer to his children for copies of his works.

The next two books, *Cheep* (Tsjip, 1934) and its sequel *The Lion Tamer* (De leeuwentemmer, 1940), which chronicle the writer's daughter's marriage to and subsequent divorce from a Pole and his relationship with his grandson, the 'Tsjip' of the title, are both his most directly autobiographical and his most optimistic works. In *Pension* (Pensioen, 1937) and *The Tanker* (Het tankschip, 1942) Elsschot returns to the murky world of business.

The last major work, *Will-o'-the-Wisp* (1947), is the first-person account of Frans Laarmans' abortive nocturnal sexual and religious quest through the Antwerp docks in the company of three Afghan seamen for a whore tellingly named Maria van Dam. Though tempted to continue, Laarmans, like his earlier incarnation in *Cheese,* abandons the search and returns to the bosom of his family, since, as Elsschot had written long before, '*giving dreams their head raises both practical and legal snags*'.

In the Low Countries a measure of recognition came belatedly to Elsschot with the publication of his *Collected Works* in 1957, and a series of readings – he was often overcome with emotion when reading aloud – and since his death in 1960 he has become an undisputed modern classic.

More recently my own translation of Elsschot's prose debut, *Villa des Roses,* a lugubrious yet hilarious tale set in the seedy Paris boarding house of the title, appeared in the prestigious Penguin Twentieth-Century Classic series in 1992. Sadly the book received virtually no publicity or reviews. The following blurb in the publisher's list seems to have been written entirely without reference to the book itself: '*A Dutch diary of a nobody, displaying the foibles of the European lower bourgeoisie at a high point in their fortunes.*'[11]

In 1997, still convinced that there was a potential English readership for Elsschot, I completed a translation of *Cheese* (of which an extract follows after this essay) – after all, besides the obvious French and German versions, the book had by now appeared in Italian, Serbo-Croat, Indonesian and other languages. I entered into negotiations with an American publisher about a paperback edition, which it is hoped will appear in the near future.[12] The climate may now be more favourable, because of the two recent film adaptations, *Lijmen / Het been* with a screenplay by Fernand Auwera and *Kaas,* directed by Orlow Seunke. If the 'tie-in' potential is realised, the necessary synergy may be generated, and the appeal of this neglected Flemish master to English-speaking audiences at the start of a new century can be put to a proper test. Elsschot's international breakthrough is perhaps still to come.

PAUL VINCENT

NOTES

1. E. du Perron, *Brieven,* R. Spoor & L. Uding (eds.), 9 vols, Amsterdam, 1977-90, I, 508.
2. Page 303. (TLS, 26 April 1934)
3. Archief en Museum voor het Vlaamse Cultuurleven, catalogue no. 52.900.
4. Personal communication from the translator, 26 January, 1998.
5. Willem Elsschot, *Brieven,* V. van de Reijt & L. Paris (eds.), Amsterdam, 1993, pp. 890, 892-893, 923-926, 932.
6. Willem Elsschot, *Three Novels*, Leiden / London / New York, 1965.
7. Elsschot, *Brieven,* pp. 7-8.
8. *Soft Soap,* pp. 9-10.
9. Transl. P. Vincent, *De Tweede Ronde* (Autumn 1982), supplement.
10. See M. Somer, *Willem Elsschot en het Wereldtijdschrift*, Antwerp, 1983.
11. Twentieth-Century Classics, Catalogue 1992-93.
12. Green Integer Press, Los Angeles.

PUBLISHED TRANSLATIONS

Will-o'-the-Wisp (fragment) (Tr. A. Brotherton). In: *Delta* 4 / 2 (Summer 1961), pp. 67-99.
Three Novels: Soft Soap / The Leg / Will-'o-the-Wisp (Tr. A. Brotherton). Leiden / London / New York: Sijthoff / Heinemann / London House & Maxwell, 1965.
Four Poems ('At a Child's Deathbed', 'One of the Poor', 'Marriage', 'The Hunchback Speaks', Tr. P. Vincent). In: *De Tweede Ronde* (Autumn 1982), supplement.
Drie gedichten / Three Poems (Tr. by W. Woods, P.J. Large and B. Bird). In: *Dutch Crossing* 18 (December 1982), pp. 4-9.
Vier gedichten / Four Poems (Tr. by P.Vincent and P.J. Large). In: *Dutch Crossing* 19 (April 1983), pp. 50-58.
Brief aan Walter / Letter to Walter (Tr. by D. Cartwright *et al.*). In: *Dutch Crossing* 37 (December 1989), pp. 109-19.
Villa des Roses (Tr. with an introduction and notes by P. Vincent). Harmondsworth: Penguin Books, 1992.

SECONDARY LITERATURE IN ENGLISH

MEIJER, R.P., *Literature of the Low Countries* (2nd rev. ed.). Cheltenham, 1978, pp. 333, 334-336, 337, 338.
SEYMOUR-SMITH, M., *Guide to Modern World Literature* (2nd ed.). London, 1976, p. 394.
THORLBY, A.K. (ed.), *Penguin Companion to Literature,* 4 vols. Harmondsworth, 1969, II, p. 251.

Two Extracts from *Cheese*
by Willem Elsschot

Introduction

'Style is the man,' said Buffon. It's hard to imagine a more succinct and accurate way of putting it. This slogan, though, standing there like a model waiting to be immortalised by a sculptor, is not much good to a person of sensibility. But is it possible to give any notion in words of what style is?

The tragic is born of a maximum of stylistic tension. Everything about the human condition itself is tragic. Think of Job's words: 'There the wicked cease from troubling, and there the weary be at rest', and at your feet you see a mass of writhing, copulating, eating, praying humanity, with a rubbish tip next door for those whose last convulsions are over.

Style is closely allied to music, which developed from the human voice, a vehicle of rejoicing and lamentation before words on paper were thought of. Tragedy is also a matter of intensity, of tempo and harmony, of rests, an alternation of exultation and slow passages and gong strokes, of simplicity and sincerity and sardonic grimaces.

Picture a sea and above it the sky. At first the blue sky is a gigantic canopy of uninterrupted splendour. Anyone taking a blue sky as their starting-point must be capable of making the sky bluer than any sky has ever been in reality. The spectator must be immediately struck by the strange blue of the firmament, without being told that 'that sky is very, *very* blue'. After all, he has a soul to tell him that, style being comprehensible only to those with souls.

The sky must remain blue and pristine till the blue has fully permeated his soul. But not for *too* long, or else he'll think, 'So, the sky's blue, that's all there is to it, I've got the message.' And he'll turn his back on you and become absorbed in reflections which are on his personal level. And once he's escaped your clutches you won't get him back to where he's supposed to be watching or empathising, or at least not with another blue sky. The more intense the blue the better, since then it will fill him all the sooner. And if you begin with a black sky, then the black must immediately run all over his skin.

Once the blue splendour has lasted long enough, a first little cloud appears to remind him that he is not standing there to gaze at that blue sky for the rest of his days. And gradually the blue disintegrates into a chaos of lowering clouds.

A gong stroke heralds the first cloud and each new stroke a procession of grotesque new shapes.

The first gong stroke plays a crucial role, like the first birth in a family. The others are born in exactly the same way, but one gets used to everything, even to birth, and the element of surprise gradually diminishes.

That first gong stroke must come when everything is pure and blue, all love and happiness, when the last thing that anyone expects is a gong stroke. It should warn, unsettle, but not alarm. Something like the monastic 'Brother, you too must die' on a summer's afternoon. It must be oh so soft. The man must wonder what it was. If it was rejoicing then it was a funny way of going about it. After that first stroke, he must start distrusting the blue sky, like someone who suddenly tastes something odd in their food or sees something moving in the peaceful grass when there isn't a breath of wind. He must wonder if he has heard something suspicious and if that isn't perhaps a cloud there in the distance. It is best if a little later he comes to the conclusion that it wasn't a gong stroke, but that one of those rejoicing got a frog in their throat. That can only be achieved if the first stroke is soft and is not sustained for too long.

You are sitting alone at night reading in a deserted house. And you suddenly imagine you may have heard something. No, the silence persists and your heart resumes its listless rhythm.

If that first gong stroke is too loud, then nothing else that follows will have any impact. He'll think, 'Oh, so that's the point of it? Right then.' And he will at once block up his ears. Or he'll pit his willpower against the fairground din you are kicking up and keep his eyes wide open, knowing that soon he won't hear a thing. Because constant noise is the same as absolute silence. And the man who suddenly makes all those gong strokes himself seems like a man possessed.

After that strange blue sky has continued for a little longer, there follows a second stroke.

Next, this man of yours sees a cloud and thinks, 'So, I was right. It wasn't rejoicing.' And so as to be sure, because that blue is still on his mind, he searches his memory of what has happened for the first gong stroke. If he tries hard enough he will find it and think, 'You see, it didn't escape my attention.' However, he is still not sure if that first stroke was deliberate, it was so faint and so unexpected.

The man in his deserted house gets up and listens. And that's when they start closing in. Gradually, in an accelerating tempo, the blue is overwhelmed and massive banks of cloud pile up. The gong strokes fall thick and fast and your man can already foresee the strokes still to come. He wants to take charge himself, because he thinks he is in control and doesn't realise he is being controlled. And just when he says, 'Now comes the stroke that will bring the tower crashing down, that's what I want', the gong falls silent and a patch of blue becomes visible.

He thinks, 'Well, it's better than I thought. It could have been worse. I could have brought the whole lot tumbling down, and that would have been the end of it.' He doesn't know that the stroke couldn't come now, because the blue has been forgotten, because the impression of the blue has been erased from his soul. And that stroke by itself is not the point, the point is the blue *and* the stroke, the blue when the stroke is expected and the stroke when one is starting to absorb the blue again.

The man in the empty house sits down again.

And when the spectator has seen the blue for the tenth time, each time more briefly, and thinks, 'Yes, now I've got it, the secret is the constant alternation of blue and masses of clouds,' *that's* when the stroke comes. It judders right through his body and speckles his skin. The man in the silent house tries to get up, but can't. He is not afraid, but paralysed by the majesty of that single gong stroke. He thinks, 'You won't catch me out like that again.', and gets ready to face the next stroke, like at the circus where one always expects more pistol shots after the first one has been fired.

He's wrong, that was *the* stroke.

If you want to end with a blue sky there may be a few more strokes, but they are just a last echo, a mopping-up operation, a bird's final flutter. But if you yourself have had enough of that blue sky, then that's that, Amen and good night.

He goes on sitting there when there's nothing left, no gong strokes and no masses of cloud. Not even a blue sky.

He closes your book and leaves, forgetting his hat. On the way he stops and mutters, 'That was quite a story.' He turns back one last time, and then continues on his way in a dream and disappears over the horizon. His soul has been touched by tragic tension.

In nature tragedy resides in the things that actually happen. In art it is more a matter of style than of what happens. A herring can be depicted tragically, even though there is nothing intrinsically tragic about such a creature. On the other hand it is not sufficient to say, 'My poor father is dead' to achieve a tragic effect.

In music the abstract nature of tragedy is seen even more clearly. The tragic quality of Schubert's *Erlkönig* is not heightened by Goethe's words, even though a child is strangled in it. On the contrary, all that strangling distracts one from the tragic rhythm.

The same applies to literature, although there one has no scales to use but must make do with woefully inadequate words. And since the fact is that every word evokes an image, the sequence of words creates a framework which can be coated with style. One cannot paint without a surface. But the framework itself is incidental, as the greatest stylistic tension can be achieved with the most insignificant of events. The whole of Rodin is just as much present in one of those hands as in the whole group of Burghers of Calais, and the miracle is that he was able to sustain it for seven burghers. It's just as well there weren't seventy of them. It follows that the same standard framework may be clothed so completely differently by different temperaments that no one would suspect that there was the same framework underlying such totally different products. The main thing is that one is given something to work with on which one can let loose one's stylistic urge in a satisfying way. That is why one should give schoolboys a free choice of essay subjects and not force those fifty-seven unfortunates, all so different, to describe Spring or Mother's Funeral on the same afternoon. And if one of them were to send his teacher a letter explaining why he could not be bothered to write an essay on any subject at all, then that letter should count as his essay.

The effect one is seeking to achieve must accord with one's frame of mind. Someone in a genuinely happy mood should not try to evoke a tragic impression, or false notes will be struck that spoil the effect of the whole. Unless the cheerfulness is used as a foil for serious tension. But in that case there should be something odd about the cheerfulness, like the blue of that sky. Right from the opening (for a book is a song) one must keep the final chord in mind, and something of it should be interwoven through the whole story like a leitmotif through a symphony. The reader should gradually be seized by a feeling of uneasiness, making him turn up his collar and think of his umbrella while the sun is still out in all its glory.

Those who do not lose sight of the end will automatically avoid all verbosity because they will constantly be asking themselves if each of their details actually contributes to their aim. And they will soon discover that every page, every sentence, every word, every full stop, every comma either brings the object nearer or delays it. Because there is no such thing as neutrality in art. What is not necessary should be excluded and where one character will do a crowd of them is superfluous.

In art there are no prizes for trying. Don't try to swear if you are not angry, or cry if your soul is dry, or rejoice if you aren't full of joy. One may try to bake a loaf, but one does not try to create. If there is a genuine pregnancy, birth will follow automatically, in its own good time.

III

That Mr Van Schoonbeke comes from an old and wealthy family. He's a bachelor and lives alone in a big house in one of our nicest streets.

He's got bags of money and all of his friends have money too. They're mostly judges, lawyers, businessmen or ex-businessmen. Every member of the group has at least one car, except for Mr Van Schoonbeke, my brother and myself. But Mr Van Schoonbeke *could* afford a car if he wanted, and no one knows that better than his friends. Which is why they find it strange and sometimes say 'that blessed Albert'.

With my brother and myself it was a different matter.

As a doctor he has no valid excuse for not having a car, all the more so as he cycles, thus making clear that he could use one. But for us barbarians a doctor is sacred, on a par with priests. So that by virtue of his being a doctor my brother is more or less presentable, even without a car. For in the circles he moves in Mr Schoonbeke really has no business cultivating friends without money or titles.

When they come in and catch him with a stranger, he introduces the newcomer in such a way that they all think at least a hundred percent more of the man than he's really worth. He calls a head of department a manager and introduces a colonel in civvies as a general.

But I was a difficult case.

You know I'm a clerk with the General Marine and Shipbuilding Company, so that he had nothing to latch on to. There's nothing sacred about a clerk. He's naked in the world.

He thought for a couple of seconds, no longer, and then introduced me as 'Mr Laarmans from the shipbuilding yards'.

He considers the English name of our company too long to remember and also too precise. For he knows that there's not a single large firm in the whole town, but one of his friends knows someone on the board who could have told him at once of my social insignificance. He would never have dreamt of saying 'clerk', as that would have been my death knell. And for the rest I had to get by as best I could. He had given me that coat of chain mail, but he could do no more.

'So you're an engineer,' asked a man with gold teeth sitting next to me.

'An inspector,' said my friend Van Schoonbeke, knowing that being an engineer involves a particular university, a degree and far too much technical knowledge for it not to cause me problems in my first conversation.

I laughed, to make them think that there was a big secret about it which might be revealed when the moment was ripe.

They sneaked a glance at my suit, which was thankfully almost new and could pass muster, even though it wasn't particularly well cut, and proceeded to ignore me.

They first talked about Italy, where I've never been, and I travelled with them through the whole land of Goethe's Mignon: Venice, Milan, Florence, Rome, Naples, Vesuvius and Pompeii. I've read about it, but Italy remains just a dot on the map to me, so that I kept silent. Nothing was said about the artistic treasures, but Italian women were marvellous and passionate.

When they had had enough of that, they discussed the difficult situation of landlords. A lot of houses were standing empty and they all maintained that their tenants paid irregularly. I wanted to protest, not on behalf of my tenants, as I haven't got any, but because I myself have always paid on time up to now, but by that time they had already got onto their cars: four and six cylinders, garage charges, petrol and oil, things that I of course know nothing about.

Next a survey was given of what had happened in the past week in those families worth mentioning.

'The Gevers boy got married to Legrelle's daughter,' said one.

It isn't mentioned as a news item, because everyone already knows apart from me, but rather as an item on the agenda on which a vote was necessary. They either approve or disapprove, depending on whether or not both parties are bringing equal fortunes to the match.

They're all of the same opinion, so no time is wasted on discussion. Each of them expresses only collective thinking.

'So Delafaille has resigned as chairman of the Chamber of Commerce.'

I've never heard of the man, but they not only know he exists and has resigned, but usually also know the real reason behind it: official odium because of bankruptcy, some secret illness or other, a scandal involving his wife or daughter, or simply because he was fed up with the job.

That 'radio news bulletin' takes up the greater part of the evening and is the most uncomfortable time for me, as I have to limit myself to nodding, laughing or raising my eyebrows.

Yes, I'm in a constant panic and sweating more than when mother died. You now know how I suffered then, but at least that was over in one night, while at Van Schoonbeke's it starts all over again every week, and the sweat I've already shed isn't subtracted from what still lies in store for me.

As they have nothing to do with me outside my friend's place they can't remember my name and at the beginning gave me all kinds of names which only vaguely resembled my real one. And since I couldn't keep correcting them, by repeatedly saying 'sorry, it's Laarmans', they finally started first looking at my friend Van Schoonbeke and saying to him, in my presence 'your friend maintains that the Liberals...' And only then would they look in my direction. That makes the use of my name unnecessary. And at the same time 'your friend' carries the meaning that Van Schoonbeke is starting to have fine friends.

In fact they prefer me to say nothing at all, because whenever I say anything it means a whole palaver for one of them. Out of politeness to the host one of them is obliged to give me a sketch of the birth, childhood, studies, marriage and career of some local celebrity or other, whose funeral was all they wanted to discuss that evening.

I can't stand restaurants either.

'Last week I had snipe with my wife in the 'Trois Perdrix' in Dijon.'

Why he should say that his wife was there too, I have no idea.

'So, a dirty weekend with your lawful wedded wife, lad,' says someone else.

And then they start mentioning restaurants, competing with each other, not only in Belgium but far and wide in foreign parts too.

The first time, when I wasn't yet so shy, I felt it my duty to mention one too, in Dunkirk. A school friend had told me years ago that he had once dined there on his honeymoon. And I had remembered the name because it was named after a famous pirate.

I kept my restaurant at the ready and waited for an appropriate moment.

But this time they were talking about Saulieu, Dijon, Grenoble, Digne, Grasse and were obviously on their way to Nice and Monte Carlo, so that I could scarcely mention Dunkirk. It would have been like suddenly bringing up Tilburg while the restaurants on the Riviera were being summed up.

'Believe it or not, but last week in Rouen, at the 'Vieille Horloge', I had a selection of hors d'oeuvres, lobster, half a chicken with truffles, cheese and dessert,
all for thirty francs,' said someone suddenly.

'The lobster wasn't tinned Japanese crab by any chance, old man, was it?'
someone asked.

'And the truffles minced prostate?'

Rouen isn't that far from Dunkirk and it was a perfect chance that I couldn't let
pass. So I took advantage of the next silence and suddenly said 'The 'Jean-Bart'
in Dunkirk is excellent too.'

Even though I'd geared myself up for it, I was alarmed by the sound of my own
voice.

I lowered my eyes and waited for the reaction.

Fortunately I hadn't claimed that I'd eaten there myself in the last few weeks,
because someone immediately said that the Jean-Bart had been closed for about
three years and is now a cinema.

Yes, the more I say the more clearly they can see that not only do I not have a
car, but that I never will have one. So silence is the best policy, since they're beginning to keep an eye on me and must be wondering how Schoonbeke came to
be offering me his hospitality. If it were not for my brother, who occasionally gets
patients through Van Schoonbeke, I'd have sent the whole lot of them packing
long ago.

Week by week it became clearer to me that my friend has a troublesome protégé in me and that it couldn't go one like this, when suddenly last Wednesday
he asked me if I was at all interested in becoming Belgian representative for a big
Dutch firm. They were very enterprising people, for whom he had just won a big
court case. I could get the agency right away. It would enough for him to put in
a word, and he was very happy to do so. No money was needed.

'Think about it,' he advised me. 'There's a lot of money to be made and you're
the right man.'

That was a bit presumptuous of him, because I don't think anyone should think
I'm the right man before I think so myself. But still it was nice of him to give me
the chance with no strings attached of shedding my simple clerk's togs with the
General Marine and Shipbuilding Company and becoming a businessman
overnight. His friends would be bound to drop fifty percent of their haughtiness.
Just because they had a penny or two!

So I asked him what kind of business his Dutch friends were in.

'Cheese,' said my friend. 'And there's always a market for that, since people
have to eat.'

From *Cheese* (Kaas, 1933. Em. Querido's Uitgeverij, Amsterdam)

Translated by Paul Vincent (Translation © Paul Vincent).

Jewellery

in the Low Countries

Jewellery – a vehicle for vanity and social display or a minor cultural phenomenon? The first view of jewellery is generally accompanied by a certain arrogance; a few platitudes about human, preferably female weaknesses, and jewellery is quickly dismissed as a topic worthy of serious consideration. This view is reinforced by the fact that jewellery has long since lost its immediate usefulness as a means of holding clothing in place; with the advent of the button, the shoelace, the zip and Velcro jewellery has become virtually superfluous as a practical item. A jewel today serves only to decorate.

The other view, of jewellery as a contemporary cultural phenomenon, is supported by a small group of believers such as the designers of modern jewellery themselves, gallery-owners, a handful of museum curators and three handfuls of collectors who meet each other at every jewellery event and, adorned with a few good pieces, profess their devotion.

In reality, the two approaches are not mutually exclusive. On the contrary: few topics are as interesting as human weaknesses and the human need to regard one's own appearance as a vehicle for personal expression.

Precisely because jewellery has lost its practical function over time, it has become an important carrier of meaning. Designers now undertake academic training in order to realise their own ideas about jewellery and the bedecking of modern man or woman in their own particular idiom. The nice thing about jewellery, however – in contrast to the visual arts, for example – is that it really only comes to life when it is worn. The messages contained in an item of jewellery can vary with the context imparted to it by the wearer, his or her personality and the way in which the jewel is worn. The old adage 'the viewer completes the work of art' is particularly true of modern jewellery.

Elegance or democracy

Flanders and the Netherlands may in principle share the same language, but this does not extend to their attitudes to the artistic display of vanity and social success. People in the South (Flanders or, more generally, Belgium) at-

Truike Verdegaal, Jewel
made from Old Jewellery.
Elect 1. 1992.
Gold / Silver / Gems,
L = 21 cm. Photo by
Gerhard Jaeger / courtesy
of Galerie Louise Smit,
Amsterdam.

tach value to external appearance and a certain degree of frivolity in clothing and accessories – as is quite apparent from the wide range of attractive
fashion items available there. In the last 10 or 15 years cities such as Antwerp have developed into avant-garde fashion centres.

In the years following the Second World War contemporary jewellery,
particularly expensive jewellery, held its own in Belgium, drawn on by developments in fashion. It was acceptable to spend money on one's appearance, including on jewellery and other accessories. The right to make and
wear jewellery was uncontested. This probably explains why in Belgium
modern jewellery has never been seen as something particularly special.

In the Netherlands, developments in the jewellery business have been
subject to much more pressure. A long struggle has been fought to have jewellery accepted as a serious art form. As long ago as the sixteenth and seventeenth centuries, under the Republic of the Netherlands, there was resistance to the bodily display of prosperity. It was a moral question, which
turned out to have a major influence on Dutch society and its culture. In the
rich North, prosperity was mainly kept indoors and spent on the home and
its contents. This explains why Dutch jewellery has always set itself apart
from jewellery from other countries by a certain contrariness. In the twentieth century in particular, *gravitas* has been more valued in the Netherlands
than a desire for beauty and accentuating the wearer's physical characteristics. This emphasis on *gravitas* is another legacy from the time of the
Republic, and fits in with the long and inalienable tradition of freedom of
expression still to be felt in the far-reaching individual liberties which Dutch
society maintains and defends.

Throughout the twentieth century the most interesting Dutch jewellery designers have sought to put their mark on their time, always in conflict with the fact that adornments of any kind, and jewels in particular, in some way or another represent a financial value. This conflict has been expressed among other things in a preference for inexpensive materials. This trend reached its culmination in the late sixties and seventies: factory-made pieces of aluminium and stainless steel, all kinds of plastic, rubber, old tin cans, scouring sponges, garden hose, bottle tops and chewing gum packaging were used as material for jewellery. The Netherlands became *the* country where jewellery was subjected to the democratic ideas of the time. With a resistance to status and authority which was as youthful as it was vehement, Dutch jewellery came to symbolise optimism, irony and personal fascinations.

These democratic views meant that modern jewellery had to be accessible to every Dutch person, to wear as they chose. Price must no longer be a barrier. The ideal solution would be for these new jewels to be mass-produced. This view also had to do with the ideas of functionality prevailing at that time. The shape of the jewellery had to flow naturally from the material and its working and had to fit the body. Fasteners had to be an integral part of the design. Although the price of this type of jewellery was not high at the time, the combination of cultural interest and social confidence needed to wear stove pipe and shower hose as a necklace or bracelet was rare indeed.

Looking back, these views of functionality and the scope of modern jewellery were very oppressive and narrow. But the conviction with which they were propagated was powerful enough. The offensive fought by the avant-garde designers, with Emmy van Leersum, Gijs Bakker, Françoise van den Bosch, Onno Boekhoudt and Marion Herbst as the first generation of innovators, led to an international appreciation of the work of Dutch jewellery designers. In the eighties and nineties the work of Dutch designers was represented at all major international jewellery exhibitions.

In the same way as the Dutch now look with some envy at the position of Flemish fashion designers, so the Flemish looked enviously at the position which Dutch jewellery designers have acquired for themselves in the past thirty years.

Attitudes

The exhibition *Attitudes*, which began in Antwerp in 1985 and toured through Germany, the Netherlands and Great Britain, makes a good starting point for looking at developments in modern jewellery in the Low Countries. This exhibition and its accompanying catalogue was a Flemish initiative, intended to provide an international platform for Belgian jewellery, something which was sorely needed at the time. It brought together work by representative jewellery designers from Belgium, Germany, Britain and the Netherlands. The title of the exhibition is very telling: in the mid-1980s designers of contemporary jewellery were characterised by the attitudes adopted and expressed through their work.

In the accompanying text, the Fleming Johan Valcke wrote that the zenith

Siegfried de Buck, Ring from *'Spina'* Series. 1999. Gold. Photo by Michèle Francken / courtesy of Galerie Siegfried de Buck, Ghent.

of jewellery design in Belgium in the first decades after 1945 lay with a number of plastic artists. Starting from their own personal design ideas, they sketched or modelled designs which were then made up by professional jewellery-makers at home and abroad. They were miniature sculptures, usually cast in gold. Valcke is fairly derogatory about the 1970s, referring to *'tasteless abominations dripping with gold and stuffed full of diamante or natural pearls'*. He contrasted them with *'the occasional very well thought-out jewel'*. At this moment, as a Dutch writer on and collector of jewellery, I am really very curious about those *'abominations'*, because 30 years of cerebral jewellery design, constantly rejecting the history and traditions of the discipline and the status of expensive jewellery, has become rather too much of a good thing.

In 1985 the work of the Belgian participants in *Attitudes*, namely Hendrik Bijl, Pia Clauwaert, Siegfried de Buck, Anita Evenepoel, Pascaline Goossens, Jean Lemmens, Linda Liket and Daniel Weinberger, was well able to hold its own in this international context. The work of Anita Evenepoel formed – and still forms – a bridge between the worlds of fashion and jewellery. Siegfried de Buck and Jean Lemmens are pioneering Belgian jewellery designers who have each undergone their own development, with De Buck remaining faithful to precious metal and Lemmens moving into lacquerwork. Pia Clauwaert's powerful work has made her an important figure for a younger generation of Belgian jewellery designers.

The Dutch contribution to *Attitudes*, assembled and described by the gallery-owner and jewellery designer Paul Derrez, began with a more self-

assured claim. After introducing the five Dutch participants, Onno Boekhoudt, Marion Herbst, Birgit Laken, Annelies Planteijdt and LAM de Wolf, he stated: *'It is no coincidence that this work has great intensity and quality. In the last 20 years experimental jewellery has undergone continuous development in the Netherlands. The radical break with tradition which was given form after 1965 in the jewellery of Emmy van Leersum and Gijs Bakker in particular, set something in motion which has now achieved its own identity as a fully developed discipline.'*

The choice of these five participants was a careful one. Both Onno Boekhoudt and Marion Herbst belonged to the first generation of innovators in their field. They were co-founders of the BOE group, the 'Federation of Rebellious Precious Metal Workers', which in 1974 opened the eyes of colleagues and the public to the diversity of visual qualities which can be incorporated in a piece of jewellery. In their work they followed movements in the visual arts, such as geometric abstraction and kinetic art. They sought to achieve a logical form in their jewellery, adding an unusual effect by some unexpected twist. Marion Herbst's work had become very playful and colourful by the late seventies and early eighties, while Onno Boekhoudt concentrated more on making sculptural objects than on jewels in the eighties. Despite this, he was represented at *Attitudes* by fine rings and bracelets.

The large, wearable textile objects by LAM de Wolf made a big impression. They were in the exhibition to represent a group of designers, trained in textiles, whose colourful work added lustre to Dutch jewellery design in the early eighties. These textile jewels did not look expensive, and were not

Onno Boekhoudt, Ring. 1999. Silver / Brass (cast & mounted). The figure is worn in the palm of the hand. Photo courtesy of Onno Boekhoudt.

meant to; they had a formal, decorative quality, they broadened the scope of jewellery and were eagerly used as high points in many jewellery exhibitions of the time. British jewellery artists at the exhibition, such as Caroline Broadhead and Julia Manheim, also worked with textile and paper. The German participants mainly used metals, including a great deal of precious metal.

The return of gold

Whilst this exhibition was on tour, another small revolution occurred in the world of Dutch avant-garde jewellery. Partly influenced by the work of German and Italian colleagues, precious metal slowly but surely made its way back into the work of Dutch jewellery designers. Robert Smit led the way as early as 1985, quickly followed by Annelies Planteijdt, Philip Sajet, Willem Honing and then by a new generation of Dutch jewellery designers. Working with precious stones remained problematic in the Netherlands, however, with a few exceptions such as Gijs Bakker, Hans Appenzeller and Philip Sajet. The consequence of this second revolution was that Dutch jewellery, whilst retaining some of its traditions, became ever richer in appearance. The harnessing of high-calibre training to a contemporary spirit of individualism resulted in the eighties and nineties in ever more personal statements in the profession.

Since the late eighties Dutch jewellery design has been enriched by the

Iris Eichenberg, Brooch.
Organic material.
Photo by Ron Zijlstra /
courtesy of Galerie Louise
Smit, Amsterdam.

emergence of first-class designers such as Rian de Jong, Nel Linssen, Peggy Bannenberg, Petra Hartman, Lucy Sarneel, Francesca di Ciaula, Ted Noten, Dinie Besems, Jacomijn van der Donk, Truike Verdegaal, Danielle Koninkx, Peter Hoogeboom, Iris Eichenberg, Felieke van der Leest, Katja Prins and Evert Nijland. And this while many of the first generation of innovators such as Bakker, Boekhoudt and Smit are still fully active.

Subjects which have featured in Dutch avant-garde jewellery design in the last ten years have included homosexuality and male-female patterns. Jewellery has been used to refer to the functioning of the body, with external embellishments referring to internal processes. Just as in the visual arts, domesticity and even simpering sentimentality were embraced, for example in happily conjoined hearts, pigs and frogs' legs. Some jewels incorporated small ceramic bowls, which have a domestic look. Photographs encased in laminated plastic were used to refer to the world of the media and advertising. And the history of jewellery design became an accepted starting point once again, provided it was accompanied by a certain irony. A new, personal form was given to old and sometimes broken jewels which still had sentimental value. With a delight in doing 'something daring', designers experimented with traditional objects such as strings of pearls, charm bracelets, coral necklaces and cameos. Even the Kosovo crisis has been addressed in contemporary Dutch jewellery.

Alongside all this 'meaningful' jewellery, the Netherlands, just like other countries, was still making beautiful jewels in which the main concern was with formal qualities such as material, colour, form and treatment of the surface.

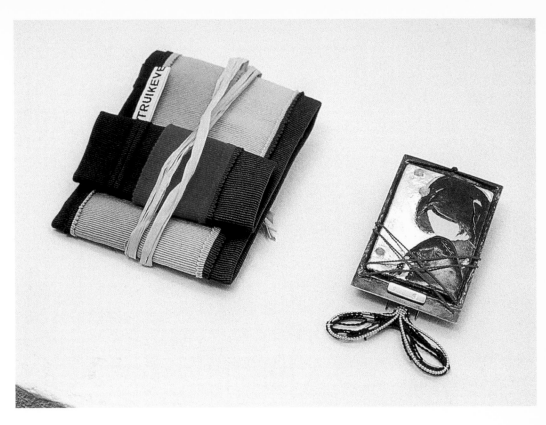

Truike Verdegaal,
'Sagiurusume'. Brooch and
wrapping from *Japan* collection. 1999.
Photo by Eddo Hartmann /
courtesy of Galerie Louise
Smit, Amsterdam.

Petra Hartman, brooch from
Kosovo Jewellery. 1999.
Photo courtesy of Petra
Hartman.

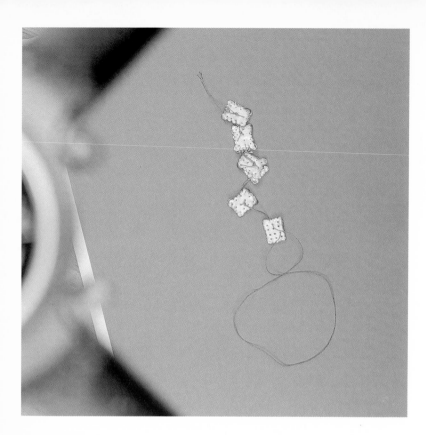

Hilde de Decker, Cookie
Necklace. 1996 / 1997.
Silver / Cord.
Photo courtesy of Galerie
Marzee, Nijmegen.

At the end of the twentieth century, the revolution in Dutch jewellery design can be regarded as a success in terms of the gains which have been made and the great wealth and diversity of approaches which now exist side by side. In the Netherlands, modern jewellery has indeed become a minor cultural phenomenon. Museums of modern art follow developments and purchase striking pieces. Jewellery designers can obtain subsidies from cultural funds. Instrumental in these developments were the jewellery galleries, a specialised field within the gallery sector which manifested itself in the Netherlands in parallel with developments in avant-garde jewellery design.

Equally, of course, the revolution can be described as a failure if the original ideas of the first generation of innovators are taken as a criterion. The production and distribution of mass-produced jewels is just as problematic now as it was thirty years ago. Modern jewellery has become quite as elitist as the expensive jewels of the past. Today's top pieces can actually fetch higher prices than the jewels made from precious metal against which the modern designers had so rebelled. With the return of gold and such traditional classics as the pearl necklace, the snake – a favourite motif in jewellery! – has bitten its own tail.

Interaction and cross-fertilisation

Together, all these results provide the perfect basis for a better relationship between Flemish and Dutch jewellery designers. Since the *Attitudes* exhibi-

David Huycke, Brooch. 1997. Silver / Black pearl, Ø 3.5 cm. Photo courtesy of Galerie Marzee, Nijmegen.

tion and other events, young Belgian jewellery designers have begun a catching-up exercise. The Belgian home of modern jewellery is now in Flanders, where Antwerp and Ghent offer trend-setting training courses, museums and galleries. Interesting designers include Hilde de Decker, who produces ironic work with themes such as female vices and virtues; David Huycke, a genuine goldsmith, makes splendid, formal jewels in precious metal; the work of Anne Zellien is refined and Els Ongenae works with organic forms. The work of Sophie Lachaert, Annemie de Corte, Hilde van Belleghem, Hilde van der Heyden, Patrick Marchal and Marguerite Servais also deserves mention. And under the name Wouters and Hendrix two Belgian designers have succeeded in building up a successful brand of fashion jewellery, which is mass-produced and sold primarily through fashion outlets.

Apart from the developments in the jewellery industry, since the late sixties the Netherlands has become generally more fashion-conscious. Dutch colleges offer high-quality training in fashion, with graduates often finding employment outside their own country, whilst a few Dutch fashion brands have also come to the fore. The success of Belgian fashion designers has turned out to be a major stimulus. A similar process is now occurring with avant-garde jewellery; the Dutch success is proving infectious in Flanders.

These days, Flemish and Dutch jewellery designers are collaborating on an increasing number of projects, workshops and exhibitions. This fits in with the general trend. Jewellery may be a small discipline, but this is precisely what makes it a highly international one. Contemporary jewellery has

Felieke van der Leest,
'Little Roses' Charm
Bracelet.
Photo by the artist / courtesy of Galerie Louise Smit,
Amsterdam.

become a vehicle for cultural interaction. Designers from Australia, Japan, the United States, Canada, Norway, Finland, Spain, Portugal and, of course, the Netherlands and Belgium soon learn about each others' latest collections via their own networks. Sometimes they clearly react to each others' work.

Despite their different backgrounds, however, this is a time of many parallels between the work of Dutch and Flemish designers. And if one is looking for differences, one might observe that the work of Flemish jewellery designers is somewhat more refined and elegant than the 'up-front' work of their Dutch counterparts. And that makes for a proper balance, in modern jewellery as in other things, between these two who share a common language: enough correspondences for the two sides to understand each other, enough differences for them to observe each other with curiosity.

MARJAN UNGER
Translated by Julian Ross.

BIBLIOGRAPHY

DERREZ, P., J. VALCKE *et al.*, *Attitudes* (exhibition catalogue). Antwerp, 1985.

DORMER, P. and R. TURNER, *The New Jewellery; Trends +Traditions*. London, 1985 (revised edition 1994).

MARTENS, H., L. DEN BESTEN and M. MOKVELD, 'Jewellery'. In: *Holland in Vorm*. The Hague, 1987; pp. 195-212.

UNGER, M., *News from the Netherlands* (exhibition catalogue). Lisbon, 1990.

'Bravely

enjoying life in the face of death'

Gerrit Kouwenaar, Poet

When he was seventeen Gerrit Kouwenaar (1923-) decided to leave school in order to become a poet. And he succeeded in realising his ambition most convincingly: beyond doubt he has developed into one the greatest Dutch poets of the second half of this century, not only because of the many excellent poems he has written, but also because he has proved to be one of the most influential forces on later developments in the poetic landscape of the Netherlands.

A very curious aspect of his literary career, however, is that it took him nearly as many years again to discover his unmistakable poetic self. Of course he wrote a great number of poems in the meantime, showing evident traces of surrealism and expressionism; he played a noticeable part in the international CoBrA-movement of painters and poets during the late forties, he was one of the politically engaged young writers who started a noisy revolution in Dutch poetry during the early fifties, but it was not until he was thirty-five that he published his first incontestibly authentic book of verse: *using words* (het gebruik van woorden, 1958). After so many years he had at last discovered that it was not in the spontaneous expression of subconscious motives, nor in exuberance, that his talents and character lay. On the contrary. The essence of his new-found attitude towards his art was restraint, precision, soberness, avoidance of anecdotal elements. A poem had to be a well-considered construction of complex word-buildings, the poet's task was to control the language and at the same time to respect its structure and its components. In short: Kouwenaar had developed into a poet in the symbolist tradition, in the vein of such writers as Wallace Stevens, who gave him his shock of recognition, and Paul Valéry.

'One could not smash a window with a poem'

Lacking any faith in superhuman powers and hating abstractions, he tried to find his way in the unremitting poetic exploration of the inscrutable *conditio humana*: '*I am not a scholar, not a counsellor / I can't explain to you the impossibilities of earth and air / I make them*', he wrote. This is to say that he was very much aware of the fact that there is no solution to the riddles of life: '*I have failed to get my mind round human existence; I accept it.*' And what he tries to do in his poetry is to make its readers suddenly and deeply aware of his and their position: '*To shock people by their own reality.*' A striking example is: '*One protects oneself by flesh against nothing.*' That is to say: flesh does not amount to much as a protection against attacks from outside or from within, man is extremely vulnerable, but at the same time the flesh is all he has to protect him against that which lies in wait for him: annihilation.

Now the central problem for the poet Kouwenaar is that this effect must be produced by means of '*deceitful and ambiguous language*'. At best '*poetry is something that stands its ground on the verge of losing*' he once said, '*but in spite of that one must try again and again*'. So he feels his efforts forever frustrated by the limitations of his means of expression. '*What I am trying to do in my poems is to make things tangible.*' And of course this is impossible: words are but words, not objects you can hold in your hands: '*One could not smash a window with a poem*'.

I have built a whole world
with nothing and I suffer
not poverty

This is what writing poetry amounts to for our poet – he succeeds in building a complete, a perfect world in his verse: in this way it is a triumph, a *creatio ex nihilo*, but frustration is built in because words are not and cannot be concrete objects, they are just sounds or a series of black spots on paper, and so the poet suffers. But at the same time writing a well-made poem does give a measure of satisfaction, and so he suffers not poverty. In thirteen words Kouwenaar has turned a number of somersaults, and in a way all of his pronouncements are legitimate and meaningful. It is no wonder that a man who has the nerve to see his power and his limitations in this way, often resorts to paradox and irony.

What a poet tries to do in his verse, is '*to grasp something out of time and to give it some kind of immortality*', and of course this too is impossible. '*Once contaminated with words / the landscape will not exist any longer.*' This is one of the reasons why Kouwenaar is fascinated by photographs: each of them a fixation of one infinitesimal moment of the past. Part of his *a hundred poems* (100 gedichten, 1969) is called 'today, a photograph album' ('heden, een fotoalbum'). It is a series of autobiographically inspired poems, making clear that one's 'now' is not a single moment in the course of time, but in fact an accumulation of past experiences. The most fascinating example of photograph-inspired verse however, is a group of poems called 'le poète y. sur son lit de mort', based on a picture of the Russian poet Esenin (1895-1925; the French call him Yesénin, hence the 'y.' in the title) on his deathbed after committing suicide. In these four poems Kouwenaar has managed to evoke an extremely complex combination of experiences and insights into life and death, transience and eternity, and into the power and the impotence of poetry, flawlessly and succinctly.

'One still has to count one's summers'

Gerrit Kouwenaar (1923-).
Photo by David Samyn.

Many poets tend to become repetitive once they have discovered their individual way of writing, particularly so when they grow older. Kouwenaar, however, has succeeded in continually renewing his style, in varying his approach and his means of expression, while remaining immediately recognisable in the twelve collections of verse he has published over the forty years since *using words* appeared. At first he concentrated almost exclusively on the nature and limitations of poetry, but then he realised: *'If I go on in this way I shall ultimately finish off on a blank page.'* Therefore he decided *'to draw more reality into the poems'*. And so he wrote *the voice on the third floor* (de stem op de 3e etage, 1960), starting:

The city: this peaceful soldiers' camp
in which in the early frost-morning
streetcars chirp
like the whetting of swords

And once again he makes clear that he has renounced every trace of idealism: *'I don't believe in mankind / being good // I believe in man the way he murders and doesn't murder'*. *'I must live with death / with all those fellow-beings head-over-heels / in this stinging focus of time'*.

In his next book, *without names* (zonder namen, 1962), Kouwenaar's (self-)irony plays an important part, his language becomes even more concentrated, and paradoxical statements abound, especially in a group of poems 'gone / disappeared' ('weg / verdwenen') about the demolition of a once-famous theatre, which he conjures up in his verse: absence made concrete one might say. Several poems in *a hundred poems* are written in a lighter key and the book contains the autobiograpical section already referred to. A process of increasing self-relativation and of growing ever more conscious of his own transience is an important theme in two new collections bearing the paradoxical titles of *dates / scenery* (data / decors, 1971) and *landscapes and other events* (landschappen en andere gebeurtenissen, 1974). It is in these collections that an important change in the designation of the lyrical subject takes place: instead of *'ik'* ('I') Kouwenaar now uses *'men'* ('one'), an indication that he is not dealing with private experiences and sensations, but that the reader himself is involved as well; it has become a shibboleth in his later work. Growing older, he clearly needs fewer words to express his experiences: his poems become shorter, even more highly concentrated and restrained, without loss of intensity and vitality. Of course by now Kouwenaar is compelled to face the oncoming end: *'One sees / the end of the garden'*, *'future has been degraded to short sight'* and *'what one clearly sees is framed in black'*. But in spite of that he does not lose his taste for life:

One still has to count one's summers, pass
one's sentence, one still has to snow one's winter

one still has to get the shopping done before
darkness asks the way, black candles for the cellar

'*Bravely enjoying life in the face of death*', the poet Herman de Coninck called it. The loss of friends and relatives has inspired a number of poems in which Kouwenaar openly admits his sadness but at the same time reminds himself and his readers of the love and friendship shared, without ever falling into sentimentality.

In short, Gerrit Kouwenaar is an ever-fascinating poet, a man who has had the courage to face the full extent of life's complexities with impressive honesty.

A.L. SÖTEMANN

Five Poems
by Gerrit Kouwenaar

farewell

Something falters, one has smoked too much, flees
coughing to the orchard, autumn breathes

narrowly, silent as a bed this is, it's silent
a mouth, only the snails on dead wood move

sitting on a stone one would like to stay here
for hours or centuries, living off a brimful

beaker left behind when for a moment summer flesh and spirit
in a near-mute three-voiced choir remortalised themselves –

From *a smell of burnt feathers* (een geur van verbrande veren, 1991)

afscheid

Er hapert iets, men heeft te veel gerookt, vlucht
kuchend in de boomgaard, najaar ademt

ternauwernood, stil als een bed is dit, het zwijgt
een mond, alleen de slakken op dood hout bewegen

men zou hier willen blijven zitten op een steen
uren- of eeuwenlang, terend op een boordevol

achtergebleven beker toen zomer vlees en geest
zich in een hees driestemmig koor even onteeuwigden –

a smell of burnt feathers

One comes home, it's march, one opens up
the wintered house, absence and want
have knotted webs, consumed scavengers, driven
the owl through the chimney to death

the floor full of helpless down, the books
shit chalk-white, the glasses in smithers
on the eternal bed a neat carcass
with huge wings

what did one do to-day?
picked up branches, bewailed the withering
elderberry, fuelled a fire with trash –

From *a smell of burnt feathers* (een geur van verbrande veren, 1991)

the last days of summer

Slower the wasps, scarcer the gadflies
greenflies greyer, angels none, nothing
that heavens here, all burns lower

these are the last days, one writes
the last halt of summer, the last
flames of the year, of the years

what was keeps being there barely
and what one clearly sees is framed in black

one must sign off here, imply
the garden in the garden, spare the open book
the ending, one must withhold oneself

keep secret how language comes caving in at the lips
how the ground swamps the poem, no mouth
shall speak what winters here –

From *a smell of burnt feathers* (een geur van verbrande veren, 1991)

---

een geur van verbrande veren

Men komt thuis, het is maart, men ontsluit
het verwinterde huis, afzijn gebrek
hebben webben gestrikt, mee-eters verteerd, de uil
door de schoorsteen de dood in gedreven

de vloer vol hulpeloos dons, de boeken kalk
wit bescheten, de glazen aan gruizels
op het eeuwige bed een proper karkas
met machtige vleugels

wat heeft men gedaan vandaag?
takken geraapt, de kwijnende vlier beklaagd
vuur gestookt van afval –

de laatste dagen van de zomer

Trager de wespen, schaarser de dazen
groenvliegen grijzer, engelen gene, niets
dat hier hemelt, alles brandt lager

dit zijn de laatste dagen, men schrijft
de laatste stilstand van de zomer, de laatste
vlammen van het jaar, van de jaren

wat er geweest is is er steeds nog even
en wat men helder ziet heeft zwarte randen

men moet zich hier uitschrijven, de tuin
in de tuin insluiten, het geopende boek
het einde besparen, men moet zich verzwijgen

verzwijg hoe de taal langs de lippen invalt
hoe de grond het gedicht overstelpt, geen mond
zal spreken wat hier overwintert –

a winter evening

Sat a long time looking at the gangrenous trunk
of the old elder burning down

beyond words this slow self-absorbing leave
this natural birth of cinders

and not to be grasped how meanwhile next to time
in a neighbouring snowed-under now
the dormouse awoke and the radio
was singing the song of the glittering chalice

and how, later, the white room was blacker and later
than ever and the luminous watch
held its breath, listening for
the immortal ticking of the woodworm –

From time is open (de tijd staat open, 1996)

een winteravond

Lang zitten kijken hoe de verkankerde stam
van de oude vlier verbrandde

niet na te vertellen dit trage eenzelvige afscheid
deze vanzelfsprekende geboorte van as

en niet te rijmen hoe onderwijl naast de tijd
in een belendend dichtgesneeuwd heden
de zevenslaper ontwaakte en de radio
het lied zong van de fonkelende beker

en hoe later de witte kamer zwarter en later
dan ooit was en het lichtgevend horloge
zijn adem inhield, luisterend naar
de onsterfelijke klok van de houtworm –

winter stands still

Write winter stands still, read a day without death
spell the snow like a child, melt time
like a clock mirroring itself in ice

it's ice-cold today, so translate what one writes
into a clock that won't run, into flesh
that's there like snow in the sun

and write how her body was there and bent over
supple in flesh and looked back
straight in the eye of to-day, and read what this says

the sun on the snow, the child in the sled
the track snowed under, illegible death –

From a glass to break (een glas om te breken, 1998)

de winter staat stil

Schrijf de winter staat stil, lees een dag zonder dood
spel de sneeuw als een kind, smelt de tijd
als een klok die zich spiegelt in ijs

het is ijskoud vandaag, dus vertaal wat men schrijft
in een klok die niet loopt, in het vlees
dat bestaat als sneeuw voor de zon

en schrijf hoe haar lichaam bestond en zich boog
gelenigd in vlees en keek achterom
in het oog van vandaag, en lees wat hier staat

de zon op de sneeuw, het kind in de slee
het dichtgewaaid spoor, de onleesbare dood –

All poems translated by Lloyd Haft.

E

verywhere

a Tourist

Wim Delvoye's Lively 'Almost-Art'

Wim Delvoye, *Cement Truck*. 1990-1999. Carved teak wood, 325 x 670 x 225 cm. Photo courtesy of the artist.

At the last Venice Biennale Wim Delvoye (1965-) exhibited a full-size cement-truck sculpted in teak. A decorative, sculptural statement from which one could conclude not only that contemporary art can be beautiful, but also, and most significantly, that mobility is the most important condition for the mingling of ideas and that this cultural mix is the potential wealth of our future society.

The truck was made by the best woodcarvers in Indonesia. It kept twenty craftsmen from three villages busy for eleven months. Decorative wood-carving is a local tradition that was introduced by the Dutch in the seven-

teenth century. They did not carve in the Dutch style, however, but in Flemish Baroque, because at the time there was a more lucrative market for this. Instead of exotic motifs, Wim Delvoye found elements he was familiar with from the choir stalls, pulpits and confessionals of his youth. Nowadays these woodcarvers are best-known for their clever copies of European antiques.

In a historical context, this sculpture, whose most striking features are its monumentality and its startling 'surrealist' mutations, raises critical questions regarding such social phenomena as colonisation and tradition, distribution and speculation, the retention of cultural identity and the chances of economic survival.

And so multiculturalism and artistic crossover also form the background to Wim Delvoye's art. His cement mixer is an obvious symbol of the ease with which the global and the local are blended together in today's society. Delvoye has an ironic name for this cultural phenomenon: 'glocal'.

In order to give contemporary shape to his artistic view of society he has translated the concept of the ready-made, now almost a hundred years old, into terms of labour. His most important tools are the telephone and the Yellow Pages.

Almost-art

Wim Delvoye's work is based on the simple principle of duality, whereby an image is confronted with the identity of its material support. This leads to new objects and new images, each evoking a whole series of associations and creating links between craft practices, popular traditions, historical references, artistic interpretations, economic consequences and social relations. They somehow still refer back to an earlier life, but on Delvoye's operating table the encounter between an umbrella and a sewing machine assumes a new significance.

The ambiguous nature of his objects reflects the ambivalence of today's culture, which is in search of a new harmony between the reality of the moment and the romantic glorification of the past.

The tension in Delvoye's work is brought about by this confrontation between an object and an image which ostensibly have nothing to do with each other. For example, he paints expressionist scenes on classical tapestries, Delft motifs on gas cylinders and circular saws, and heraldic arms on shovels and ironing boards. In the same way he replaces the net in a handball goal with stained glass showing religious and popular scenes (*St Stephen*, 1990; *Panem et Circenses*, 1989), hacks little notes into majestic rock faces and tattoos pigs with women's hearts and Harley Davidson motifs.

Unjustly, Delvoye's work is always associated with kitsch. But kitsch is characterised by a loss of meaning, whereas Delvoye's work incessantly generates new meanings. Nor is the way the objects are embellished or enhanced purely decorative, since the nature of the object is radically altered.

The simple, direct visual language of his art appeals primarily to a broad public, while its references to art history and clever inversions, double meanings and visual word games also make it attractive to the knowledgeable art-lover.

Wim Delvoye, *Shovel.*
1989. Enamel print on shovel, H c.150 cm. Photo courtesy of the artist.

This makes Wim Delvoye both a Flemish primitive and a conceptual artist, a craftsman and a *provocateur*, a popular painter and a philosopher of art, a provincial and a citizen of the world.

On the one hand Delvoye's art of camouflage and disguise is a lively reflection on our ethnic, social and cultural identity. On the other, his work is evidence of a cautious search for the artist's role and the meaning of art in a postmodern society. Flung back and forth between his Flemish roots and the global village, he tries to unite the two worlds.

His work displays tremendous powers of imagination that systematically renew themselves. It is characterised by great diversity, in terms of both the materials used and the genres into which he ventures: he steps lightly from painting to sculpture, from woodcarving to ceramics; he works in stained glass, porcelain, tattoos and, most recently, in film and video too.

Delvoye throws himself into a different world every year. From the stained-glass workers and the ceramists via the tattooists and the pig-fatteners to film production and the music industry. Yet he remains everywhere

Wim Delvoye, *Eddy & Marcel*. Installation view at Frac des Pays de la Loire, Nantes, 1999. Live tattooed pigs, born 1998 (Eddy) and 1997 (Marcel), dimensions: growing. Photo courtesy of the artist.

Wim Delvoye, *Paper Aeroplanes*. 1998. Video still. Photo courtesy of the artist.

a tourist. By exploring the outskirts of art he tries to shift his own boundaries. This is why he uses the phrase 'almost-art' to describe his work, an activity intended to make life more exciting than art itself. And the greatest compliment he can be given for this is 'street credibility'.

Apart from the formal aspects of his work, he naturally also deals with subjects common in contemporary art: the relationship between form and content, the figure and its background, sign and signification, words and images, the problem of style, the role of ornament, the questioning of artistic categories, subverting the hierarchy of high and low, initiating discussion on the consensus, the present meaning of the avant-garde, the value of cultural individuality, strategy and speculation, taste and fetishism, heritage and tradition.

But the importance of his work also lies in the precision with which he has charted the range of images now available not only to artists but to anyone, and in the fact that he has recorded the way they are handled (consciously or unconsciously) at the end of the twentieth century.

The social relevance of teenage spots

Delvoye has recently been concentrating on film and video. The media he uses are never entirely innocent. They are always used for their intrinsic qualities, which are critically analysed, though never without the necessary humour. There is no limit to the possibilities engendered by the perversity of the moving image. In his films and videos he simultaneously exploits and denounces both the authority of what is shown and its impact on society, as well as the moral and aesthetic problems thrown up by its ideological manipulation.

Paper Aeroplanes (1998) shows a fictional politician, barely visible over a mass of microphones. He is making a speech in a huge hall to an audience of confirmed supporters. The video emphasises the form: the magnificent setting, the immense crowd of people, the unceasing applause, the speaker's rhetorical gestures and the intonation of his voice. This could not be in greater contrast to the content, which is a poetic plea for making paper aeroplanes, a practical explanation and a eulogy on the relaxing nature of this childlike occupation: '*Paper aeroplanes are a source of immense pleasure*'.

In terms of form, he pulls out all the propaganda and indoctrination stops. In a short period such topics as politics and the media, narcissism and power, and art and propaganda are appositely touched upon. The caricatural cliché is easily recognisable and at times disquieting, since form and content are subtly blended together. This work demonstrates that all aesthetic and social conventions are reversible and that the significance all too often derives from the decoration and not the essence. As always in Delvoye's work, *Paper Aeroplanes* can also be interpreted as a metaphor for art and the artist. The same media laws of seduction and the powers of persuasion apply here too.

Sybille is an ode to youth. In shades of pastel-pink and with Bilitis-like background music, we see slow-motion movements we cannot immediately identify. As is usually the case in Delvoye's work, here too our perception is manipulated by the images. After some time there is a shift from sensuality to aggression, from eroticism to pornography; how squeezing teenage spots changes into a highly emotional experience.

Like the two versions of *Sybille*, *Angel* was also shot on 16 mm film. It consists of a close-up of a young woman with angel's hair being pawed for several minutes by various male hands. While the image itself is shock-

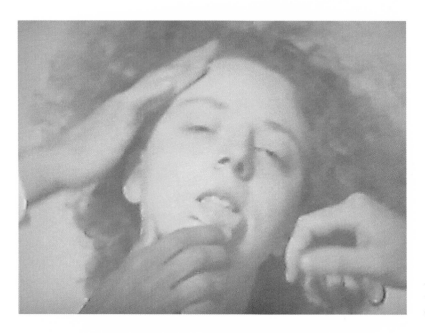

Wim Delvoye, *Angel*. 1999. Video still. Photo courtesy of the artist.

Wim Delvoye, *Love Letter* (*'Mohammed'*)(detail). 1998. 36 panels (80 x 40 cm each), cibachrome. Photo courtesy of the artist.

ing, the accompanying soundtrack of laughter makes it even more distressing.

There is here an obvious criticism of what we see on television every day, but in an artistic context the images form a commentary on the social relevance of art and the boundaries of morality as accepted in art and society. The artist is outside the law. Art is the last refuge where ideas do not have to be politically correct. But its 'icon' is pawed and violated by one and all.

Multicultural potato peel

A good example of the social relevance of Wim Delvoye's work is a fairly recent clash he had with the political world. Having been requested to design a work of art for the assembly chamber of the Flemish Community Commission in the Brussels parliament building, he came up with thirty-six identical panels bearing photographs of potato peel arranged in elegant curls.

On closer inspection these abstract arabesques form Arabic letters and this calligraphic text turned out to be a love letter from a certain Mohammed to Caroline. The triviality of everyday reality was suddenly transformed into a display of idealised love. When the politicians involved became aware of this fact, the work was promptly rejected. But as long as some politicians think that they have to impose limitations on multicultural expressions of art and love, artists like Wim Delvoye have a bright future and a long life ahead of them.

LIEVEN VAN DEN ABEELE
Translated by Gregory Ball.

Poetry

in Print

Hendrik N. Werkman, Master Printer

Hendrik N. Werkman,
*'De Ploeg in Pictura'
Poster.* 1925.
Hand-press, 92.5 x 41 cm.
Groninger Museum.

If he hadn't hit upon the idea of using his printing tools in a radically new way, it's almost certain that Hendrik Nicolaas Werkman (1882-1945) would never have carved himself such a unique place for himself in Dutch art history. He may have been known in the annals of the Groningen art association De Ploeg (The Crew) as a painter of some distinction, but today he is remembered as a master printer who managed to fashion an entirely unique world with his experiments in type.

He produced his printed works from 1923 until his death in 1945. Working with the letters in his typecase, inking rollers and stencils, he made countless illustrations and compositions, all of them infused with a wondrous beauty.

Werkman the Crew man

Werkman started his art career rather late in life. In the milieu in which he grew up, a life as an artist was not regarded as a possible livelihood. At first he earned his living as a journalist, and from that background he moved on to the world of printing, where he succeeded in building up a thriving business.

When he was thirty-five, Werkman made his first hesitant attempts at painting during his free time, and two years later he was accepted as an active member of De Ploeg. This association was founded in the city of Groningen in 1918, and its primary goal was to increase the opportunities for artists to exhibit their work. De Ploeg became the stronghold of modern, expressionist tendencies in the northern part of the Netherlands.

Werkman became a prominent Ploeg member, a 'Crew man', partly because he was extremely active and undertook all the printing for the group. As a painter he was far from the most conspicuous member. He set his subjects in compositions consisting of large surfaces worked in a limited number of often subdued tones.

In 1921 Ploeg member Jan Wiegers returned from Davos where he had become acquainted with the work of Ernst Ludwig Kirchner, and Werkman,

Hendrik N. Werkman,
Churchgoers in the Snow.
1919-1920.
Canvas, 50 x 60 cm.
Groninger Museum.

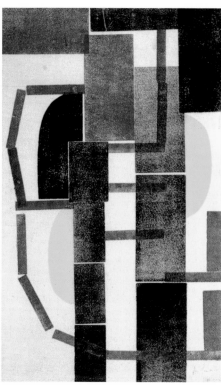

Hendrik N. Werkman, *View
of a Town in the Snow*.
1922.
Canvas, 70.5 x 48.5 cm.
Groninger Museum.

like so many other Ploeg painters, fell under the expressionist's spell. He too began painting in bright colours, and he also adapted the techniques Kirchner had developed for painting large, evenly covered surfaces. Kirchner diluted oil paint with petrol, which quickly soaks into the absorbent layer beneath, creating a matt surface. He also mixed diluted oil paint with beeswax, a mixture that spreads easily and dries quickly.

Werkman employed this technique for the first time in the painting *Sunflowers with Painting*, dated 1921. Besides that of Kirchner, this work also betrays influences of Vincent van Gogh and Edvard Munch in its choice of theme and its elongated, lively brush strokes.

Typeface and inking rollers

His first printed work dates from 1923, when Werkman was going through a serious crisis. He had become entangled in financial problems, forcing him to dismiss almost all his employees and to relocate the large, thriving printing business to a single floor of a warehouse.

Seen in retrospect, this period was an extremely fortunate one for the development of Werkman's artistry. He began to experiment with materials in his typecase and discovered the expressive possibilities inherent in the letters and inking rollers. He started using letters as pure forms and even inked the other sides of the type, printing with a hand-press. What emerged were compositions constructed entirely of rectangular forms in a wide range of colours and tones. An example is *Composition*, dated 1924. This printed work consists of elongated rectangular shapes in black and red, combined with narrower and shorter rectangles and black line segments. The work is filled with staples and twists, thickly printed areas and very transparent surfaces.

Later, writing about this period in a letter to his friend August Henkels, Werkman commented: '*But like a wet poodle I shook off everything that was in the way, and for a while I was almost completely alone. To tell the truth, I sometimes didn't even understand myself. But there was one thing I never forgot: everything you don't lose is profit.*'

The *painter* Hendrik Nicolaas Werkman experimented with the expressionist styles that had by then pervaded all of the northern Netherlands. But the *printer* Hendrik Nicolaas Werkman was his own man. Since he had mastered the art of printing down to the minutest detail, he enjoyed an unparalleled knowledge of the expressive possibilities inherent in the materials, which gave him enormous freedom.

The technical limitations he confronted as a painter were no longer a hindrance to him. The materials in the typecase held possibilities that forced him in a new direction, with his compositions now determined by the rectangular shapes of the letters. He no longer looked for inspiration in expressionistic styles but in the abstract geometric language of constructivism. He also found himself somewhat outside the artistic currents that had become so interesting to members of De Ploeg. His little publication entitled *The Next Call*, which Werkman printed in a limited edition and distributed among friends and kindred spirits, was hardly taken seriously within his old circle.

In *The Next Call*, Werkman printed his compositions alongside accompanying text. The compositions often formed the basis of the larger coloured works he executed later. With their transparency, bright colours and frequently tumbling shapes, these works possess a casual quality, as if they had emerged entirely on their own. But in fact quite the opposite was the case. First the most important coloured surfaces were applied. Werkman was able to create endless nuances by printing either heavily or very lightly, by inking the blocks with a thick or a thin layer, or by making an initial printing with the block first before printing on the original. After this he started in on the detail, and even then he used every means at his disposal in order to achieve just the right colour, tone and transparency. Frequently a single print would make fifty passes under the hand press. And this is where Werkman's mastery became apparent. Despite the enormous amount of labour that went into his work, each one was clear, light and sensitive.

Undogmatically abstract

Although Werkman received only very limited support within De Ploeg, he was increasingly appreciated in international avant-garde circles. He exchanged *The Next Call* with journals such as *Merz* and *Zenith* and occasionally had contact with champions of abstract geometric art such as Michel Seuphor of the magazine *Het Overzicht* and later *Les Documents de l'Esprit Nouveau*. Even so, Werkman felt isolated. In 1943 he wrote to August Henkels: '*In one of my airings in "The Next Call" I once wrote, "einen wirklichen Freund habe ich nie besessen" (I have never had a real friend). I regret that this is the bitter truth in my case, which I nevertheless was able to write at the time without any hesitation.*'

Nor did Werkman throw himself heart and soul into the avant-garde world. Often it was Seuphor who re-established contact with the Groningen artist and drew him in. This timidity may have had to do with the fact that Werkman was never a convinced abstract geometric artist. The typesetting material seemed to elicit abstract work almost automatically, but unlike so many other international avant-garde artists he was not preoccupied with questions about how to separate himself from his work. Frequently even images from Werkman's daily life, such as the roof with its chimneys that he viewed from his window, resulted in a composition. '*I alternate between abstract and non-abstract, first without any particular subject, then with a subject taken from nature. The technique lends itself most particularly to abstraction, and that's the way I like to work, because the results can often be pure expressions. Yet it's surprisingly difficult to find just the right abstract form for what you want to say or communicate.*'

During the thirties Werkman discovered the stencil, infinitely increasing the possibilities for his printed work. He made abstract lyrical compositions with an endless variety of forms, but he also produced figurative works. For example, between 1935 and 1937 there appeared the 'South Sea Islands' series in which Werkman depicted an earthly paradise. During that period he and a group of others had plans to follow in the footsteps of Gauguin and go to live in Tahiti.

The most narrative of his works are the prints he produced for *Hasidic*

Hendrik N. Werkman, *The Next Call 6*.
October-November 1924.
Hand-press, 27.2 x 21.5 cm / 44.5 x 50 cm (leaflet).
Groninger Museum.

Hendrik N. Werkman,
*Ballad for an Imprisoned
Poet.* October 1943 (30).
Stencil, 32 x 24.5 cm.
Groninger Museum.

Legends. During the first years of the war, Werkman made two series of ten prints in an edition of twenty for the underground printer known as De Blauwe Schuit (The Blue Barge). This business had been set up in reaction to the anti-Jewish regulations issued by the Nazi occupier in 1940. August Henkels, one of its founders, had Werkman read Martin Buber's *The Legend of Baal Shem*, which describes the stories and deeds of Baal Shem Tov, a simple man from Poland who managed to provide the Jewish community there with faith and trust in difficult times and was the father of Hasidism. Werkman was touched by the stories and designed illustrations to accompany them. They form a moving account of episodes from the life of Baal Shem, but they are also magnificent prints quite apart from the story.

This underground work was to have fatal consequences. Werkman was arrested for producing illegal printed material and shot by the Germans on 10 April 1945.

SASKIA BAK
Translated by Nancy Forest-Flier.

Anne

Frank's Literary Connections

In the award-winning 1959 film *The Diary of Anne Frank*, we see a mercurial Anne on the first day of her arrival in the secret annexe finally wind down with a book. She reads the last sentence out loud and we recognise *A Tale of Two Cities*, Charles Dickens' historical novel set in eighteenth-century French revolutionary times. In the film the camera zooms in on the title page in Dutch, translated as *Verhaal van twee steden*. There is something wrong with this picture, because it is highly unlikely that the real Anne Frank ever read this book. First of all, she had just started to learn English, and this would have been too difficult for her. Secondly, the Dutch translations published up to 1942 were entitled *In Londen en Parijs,* and thirdly, it is unlikely that she was reading this, because this kind of book did not fit in with the other books she was interested in at the time. The book is not mentioned in her diary. The screenwriters, Frances Goodrich and her husband Albert Hackett, who also wrote the theatre version, must have come up with the idea from the diary itself, in which Anne mentions four times that her father is reading his Dickens. Once he even entertained the entire annexe company with readings from *The Pickwick Papers*. One can argue that choosing *A Tale of Two Cities* was very appropriate for dramatic effect and added thoughts of revolutionary violence to the certain ominous suspense so apparent in other small details in the film. However, it is probably not historically accurate.

What were the books that Anne Frank was interested in, and was allowed to read? Let us go back to 12 June 1942. On the second floor of a townhouse on Merwedeplein 37 in Amsterdam, a young Jewish girl celebrates her thirteenth birthday. She has been living in Amsterdam since 1934, following the persecution of Jews in Germany, where she was born in Frankfurt. Her father, the son of a banking family, starts a business selling pectin for making jams and jellies and spices for meat processing. Together with her sister Margot she goes to the Montessori elementary school. After the German invasion of the Netherlands, May 1940, they attend the Jewish Lyceum, a high school. After Margot receives a summons to report for transport on 8 July 1942 the entire family goes into hiding, together with the Van Pels family. They are joined later by dentist Frits Pfeffer. Anne Frank starts keeping a diary two days after her birthday. She knew she was getting a diary, because she had already bought it together with her father in Blankevoort's book-shop. I will come back to the diary itself, but for now I would like to draw your attention to her other presents on that birthday. I quote: '*From Daddy and Mama I got a blue blouse, a game, a bottle of grape juice, which to my mind tastes like wine, a puzzle, a jar of cold cream, 2.50 guilders and a gift certificate for two books. I got another book as well, "Camera Obscura" (but Margot already has it, so I exchanged mine for something else)... They (her schoolfriends) gave me a beautiful book, "Dutch Sagas and Legends", but they gave me Volume II by mistake, so I exchanged two other books for Volume I. Aunt Helene brought me a puzzle, Aunt Stephanie a darling brooch and Aunt Leny a terrific book: "Daisy's Mountain Trip". I had my birthday party on Sunday afternoon. The Rin Tin Tin movie was a big hit with my classmates. I got two brooches, a bookmark and two books.*'

As one can see, books were an important part of her cultural baggage and an obvious treasure and pleasure to get as presents. Of course one should re-alise that there was no TV and that books were cherished, partly because they were expensive in the pre-softback era. Dutch books still are. After the German decrees against the Jews, which forbade them to go to the theatre, the cinema, to own a telephone, to travel by tram, to have visitors or keep the windows open after 8 p.m. and other horrid absurdities, the Jews had limited entertainment. In the hiding place even listening to the radio was very much restricted to the hours when the personnel downstairs had left. Therefore, books and reading must have been greatly appreciated. On 11 Ju-ly 1943 we read in the diary: '*Miep (one of the main helpers, Miep Gies) brings us 5 library books every Saturday. We always long for Saturdays when our books come, just like little children receiving a present. Ordinary people simply don't know what books mean to us shut up here. Reading, learning and the radio are our only amusements.*'

What were they reading? Anne gives us the answer herself when she made a list of the members and their interests: '*Mr Van Daan: detective sto-ries, love stories; Mrs van Daan: biographical novels and occasionally oth-er kinds of novels; Mr Frank: is learning English (Dickens), never reads novels, but likes serious, rather dry descriptions of people and places; Mrs Frank: reads everything except detective stories; Mr Dussel: reads every-thing, goes along with the opinion of the majority; Peter van Daan: seldom reads, sometimes geography; Margot Frank: reads everything, preferably on religion and medicine; Anne Frank: likes to read biographies, dull or ex-citing, and history books (sometimes novels and light reading).*' She men-tions also that among her courses are art history, mythology, Bible history and Dutch literature.

This entry of 16 May 1944 gives a general idea of Anne's broad interests and it indicates that she prefers informative biographies and history books. This is a marked change from her earlier entries, full of novels and ro-mances. Then again, the last year of her diary sees much less mentioning of books in general, in favour of romanticising about her relationship with Peter, life in general and matters of survival.

Anne's first diary, which she received on her thir-teenth birthday, 12 June 1942. Photo © AFF/AFS, Amsterdam, The Netherlands.

Anne Frank in the first class at the Jewish Secondary School, 1941.
Photo © AFF/AFS, Amsterdam, The Netherlands.

'I'm allowed to read more grown-up books lately'

When we try to get a picture of the books she was reading, we come across a few obstacles. First of all, the diary does not cover the entire hiding period. Secondly, she doesn't always give full titles and authors' names, nor is it always clear that she has indeed read them. She writes on 29 October 1942: '*Daddy has brought the plays of Goethe and Schiller from the big bookcase. He is going to read to me every evening. We've started with Don Carlos.*' Does it follow that Anne Frank read Goethe? This was stated once in the *New York Times*, in the review of the Oscar-winning Anne Frank documentary. I think it is a silly attempt to make a young genius out of a regular teenager, who doesn't need this.

On other occasions Otto Frank wanted her to read German classics like Koerner and Hebbel, projecting his own education onto his daughters. It doesn't mean that she obliged and at the tender age of 13 was reading beyond normal teenage interests. She did like Theodor Koerner, however, now regarded as a mediocre playwright from the early nineteenth century, more famous for his war-songs. '*Now I can buy "Myths of Greece and Rome"* - great!' she writes also about her birthday presents on 14 June 1942. Did she buy this? Probably. Was it a strange choice? It might sound very learned in 2000, but it is not really, for someone who goes to a school called a Lyceum, where the literature of the Greeks and Romans is being taught, in Greek and Latin, although not in her first year. It is even likely that the book was on the list of recommended school books. Still, she had a mind of her own and certainly liked to enjoy and explore her interests to the full as she writes, months later, on 27 March 1943: '*I'm mad on Mythology and especially the Gods of Greece and Rome. They think here that it is just a passing craze, they've never heard of an adolescent kid of my age being interested in*

Mythology. Well, then I shall be the first!' She calls this one of her time-killing subjects, and indeed what better topic than myths and legends, where anything is possible and fantasy knows no bounds.

I mentioned *Camera Obscura* (1839), one of her birthday presents together with the diary. This Dutch novel by Nicholaas Beets is often regarded as the Dutch equivalent of Dickens' *Pickwick Papers*. However, Anne only mentions the title and nothing about the content. The same goes for other works like *Dutch Tales and Legends, Daisy's Mountain Trip*, a book called *Good Morning Milkman* and *Lydia's Problems*. In 1944 we read about her interest in biographies of Liszt, Galileo, and Emperor Charles v, but also on a different topic: Margot's book *Palestine at the Crossroads*. On 12 June 1944, for her birthday, which would be her 15th and last one, she marvels at the 5-volume *History of Art* by Springer.

We don't really get to hear what Anne thought of these books, or who suggested these titles. However, we have some information about other books and I quote from her diary for 3 October 1942 : *'I have such a lovely book, it's called "Eva's Childhood". The Eva in it thought that children grew on trees like apples, and that the stork plucked them off the tree when they were ripe and brought them to the mothers. But her girlfriend's cat had kittens and they came out of the cat, so she thought cats laid eggs and hatched them like chickens, and the mothers who wanted a child also went upstairs a few days before their time to lay an egg and brood on it. After the babies arrived, the mothers were pretty weak from all that squatting. At some point, Eva wanted a baby too. She took a wool scarf and spread it, and then she squatted down and began to push. She clucked as she waited, but no egg came out. Finally, after she'd been sitting for a long time, something did come, but it was a sausage instead of an egg. Eva was embarrassed. The maid thought she was sick. Funny, isn't it?'*

The novel she is referring to was written by Dutch author Nico van Suchtelen and describes the development of a young girl, born out of wedlock to a frail woman who dies when Eva is a baby. Her grandfather, a kind old notary, brings her up, together with a friendly maid. We see her go to school, become a lovely but outspoken, honest, inquisitive, naughty teenager with a positive outlook on life. The author, who died in 1948, was a humanistic writer with an interest in the philosophy of Erasmus, Spinoza and Freud. He was part of a Thoreau and Tolstoy type of communal living in the early decades of the century and as a religious humanist had strong pacifist ideas. In the book one of Eva's friends, whom she loves dearly, becomes a conscientious objector and ends up in prison at the end of the novel. The story ends when the grandfather dies and Eva, who has just finished high school, decides to learn typing and shorthand to get a job. She goes to live with her uncle Herbert, who has returned from Australia after having stolen and squandered her inheritance, but is accepted back in forgiving grace.

Although the novel and its author have now largely been forgotten, he was well known at the time, and Anne Frank had definitely taken to the book and certain topics in it. She writes on October 29, 1942: *'I'm allowed to read more grown-up books lately. I'm now reading "Eva's Childhood" by Nico van Suchtelen. I can't see much difference between this and the schoolgirl love stories. It is true there are bits about women selling themselves to unknown men in back streets. They ask a packet of money for it. I'd die of shame if anything like that happened to me.*' Anne must have identified very strongly with the ever curious Eva, who tries to understand what goes on in these so-called 'houses of pleasure' as she ponders: '*So they had fun these women. Perhaps they danced with the men that came. And of course they would sing, and they would make them drunk... But then? They were paid... some of them became filthy rich. Not here of course but in Paris and Vienna and the like. They were paid for their love, they sold their bodies, as they say. How was that possible? How could love become something ugly? It was incomprehensible. But surely there was no love between these women and their visitors? How could there be one man, who wanted to buy a woman's dedication, and how could there be found one woman who sold herself?*'

Other important female questions occupy Anne's thoughts as she writes in the same entry about this book: '*It also says that Eva has a monthly period. Oh, I'm so longing to have it too; then at least I'd be grown up.*' In the book, Eva thinks about her mother and what it would be like to be one herself. This is the passage that Anne refers to: '*Strange, that she had to think of that now, after the doctor had told her, the great, miraculous, that she now...a woman...imagine: she was...a woman, that she could now be a mother. She had known before that the time would come one day...(her girlfiend) Jet's had already started half a year ago and she thought it was quite normal (doodgewoon), only annoying..But now it was her turn, it seemed so strange- important, so....responsible, so... official. You could only think of it a little bashful, half-fearful, and yet it was wonderful.*' When Anne refers to this regarding herself she uses the phrase '*it seems so important*' which sounds literally taken from the novel. A later note of 22 January 1944 says '*Today I couldn't write a thing like that anymore*'.

Anne is obviously interested in other facts of life, as we read: '*I have learned something new again: "brothel" and "cocotte", I have got a separate little book for them but it's kept with the letters, otherwise nothing special.*' Unfortunately, this separate little book was lost.

One should realise that Anne's quotes do not represent the entire novel and one might wonder whether an impressionable 13-year-old should read such books. It was certainly the case until the sixties that in Dutch libraries most books were classified according to a system of cataloguing numbers, indicating the targeted reading public. Of course access was a matter of parental discretion, also in Anne Frank's case, as she writes on 17 March 1944: '*every book I read must be inspected. I must admit that they are not at all strict, and I'm allowed to read nearly everything.*' As other instances show, Otto Frank was a fairly open-minded person. There was discussion in the annexe about other books; the Van Pels' commented more than once on the too liberal education of the Frank children.

This doesn't mean that Anne Frank read only risqué books. Far from it. Her favourites when they first went into hiding in the Autumn of 1942 (21 September) were a series of books by Cissy van Marxveldt, a pseudonym for Sietske Beek-de Haan, with titles relating to the main character Joop ter Heul. Anne read the five books in a week and one of them four times. Joop or Josephine ter Heul is one of three children of succesful businessman Ter Heul. His wife, Joop's mother, seems mainly worried about the right etiquette, the latest fashion and her daughters' marital candidates. We follow Joop, mainly through a diary and letters to a friend, from her childhood, especially her early teens, to adolescence, marriage at 19 to a bank manager, and motherhood.

Especially in the novel called *Joop ter Heul's High School Times* (De H.B.S.tijd van Joop ter Heul) we see parallels with the young vivacious Anne Frank, who like her novel's hero founds a club of girlfriends to share secrets and go out together. In Anne Frank's case it was called Little Bear minus Two (De Kleine Beer min twee), with referral to the heavenly body; as Anne explains: '*because we thought the Little Bear had 5 stars, but we were wrong there, because it has seven stars, just like the Big Bear; minus 2 therefore means that Sanne is the Leader and Jacque is the secretary, and that we (Ilse Hanneli and I) are left to make up the club. It's a ping-pong club.*' They play table-tennis in the Wagner family's dining room and go to the ice cream parlour to cool off afterwards. If we go by the examples of her novels, they also have evenings together spent gossiping about boys and teachers, eating sweets and planning parties.

The similarities abound when reading Anne Frank's early diary. She had not yet decided on Kitty as her soulmate, but wrote to several people named Connie, Pop / Emmy, Marjan, Pien, Lou, identical names to those in the Joop ter Heul books. In fact, until 21 September 1942 it seems that Anne doesn't get a grip on her diary. She has not decided on a form yet, just personal notes or a 'letter' to a friend, imaginary or not. Until she writes on that same day: '*I haven't written anything for ages, but no doubt I'll make up for it*', and continues: '*I really feel like corresponding with some one, and I'll do that in future with my diary. I'll write in future in letter form, which is in fact the same*' and '*I have some time left tonight dearest Emmy, and so I shall drop you a few lines, this afternoon I wrote a fairly sheepish letter to Yettje, but I had hardly sat down for a minute when I had to peel potatoes for "her ladyship my mama" she says it in such commanding tones, and if I don't hop to it she shouts "loos". That is German but I don't know exactly how you spell it. Just as in "Joop ter Heul". Incidentally, have you read Joop ter Heul?*' Joop ter Heul uses English phrases from her sister to show off, sometimes German, and occasionally doesn't know how to spell them. It's amusing to realise that she asks in a letter to Emmy, one of the characters in a novel, whether she had read the novel. One letter is addressed to the whole club in general and she has a few lines for each member, singling out one person who in the Van Marxveldt novel was called Kitty Franken. '*Dear Kitty, Yesterday I wrote to Emmy and Yettje, but I prefer writing to you, you know that don't you and I hope the feeling is mutual.*' Why she chose Kitty is not quite clear. The character in the novels comes across as sympathetic, lively and naughty like Joop, great company, but she doesn't stick out as special, doesn't finish high school, marries a stockbroker and is not one of the main characters. Perhaps her last name 'Franken' inspired her choice. Perhaps the name Kitty comes from a real life friend called Kitty. The fact is that the letters to Kitty become more frequent, and on 13 November 1942 she addresses the last one to Yettje. In the revised version it is Kitty all along from 20 June 1942 when she writes the well-known lines: '*In order to enhance in my mind's eye the picture of the friend for whom I have waited so long I don't want to set down a series of bald facts in a diary like most people do, but I want this diary, itself to be my friend, and I shall call my friend Kitty.*'

Anne Frank was enamoured of the Van Marxveldt books, as she states on 3 October: '*As a matter of fact Cissy van Marxveld is first class. I shall definitely let my children read her.*' The comparisons with the books are striking: the diary form, the direct referrals, the letters to the girls, the club, the reports about classroom and school activities. A French pop quiz and especially Anne's constant talking in class and the composition she had to write about 'a chatterbox' for punishment, could have been lifted out of a Joop ter Heul book.

These books have lost much of their charm nowadays, and no teenager reads these stereotypical novels anymore, in which fathers are grumpy old darlings, mothers followers of fashion or marriage counsellors for their daughters, the maid-servant is either old and kind, or young and absent-minded, the sister older and silly, and the brother understanding. Emotions in these books are never very passionate, most important issues are school matters, like being promoted to the next grade. In 12th grade, several girls fall in love with young intellectuals, students with promising careers. Joop in the books is a lively, intelligent, bubbly girl, what Americans would call 'a swell bobbysoxer'. She sometimes feels stifled by her family and conventional sister, likes to go against the grain, i.e. when expressing an interest in theatre, and lets her impulses steer her in unforeseen directions. One might think of nineteenth-century examples like Alcott's *Little Women* or Austen's *Pride and Prejudice,* but these Dutch works never reach that level. Nevertheless, these books give an interesting insight into the stereotypical view of a certain type of woman in the twenties in the Netherlands. Anne must have identified with this carefree upper-middle-class existence, and when we take this into account her diary gains this extra dimension.

'Advanced' themes

A far more interesting book that must have widened her horizons, was called *The Rebels* (De opstandigen), and Anne is quite informative about this one. On closer examination, however, one cannot maintain that Anne gives an accurate rendition of the whole novel, nor that she has quite understood the basic theme: women's emancipation and struggle (or rebellion, hence the 'rebels' of the title) to find a place and life of their own, as portrayed in the history of three generations of one family. In half a page she sums up nicely all the names of the protagonists and their children. The reason is simple: this was given at the end of the book, where some 40 characters are put in their family tree. The novel has some nice aspects, which have escaped Anne's inexperienced eye. I spoke earlier of Nicolaas Beets' *Camera Obscura* as the work that Anne was going to read, and the first part of this work is written in a similar vein. One interesting detail is the appearance of Beets in the flesh, fulminating in a lecture against suffragettes. This was based on a true story, and among his reasoning was the bad example set by women in America, who sit in their clubs, with crossed legs, smoking cigars.

It may be surprising that Anne is actually not more outspoken about one of the main protagonists in the novel, the woman who leaves her dictatorial uncle's house to become a governess abroad. She returns after 30 years as a writer, a profession that was not 'done' for a woman in 1870. Anne's summary leaves most of the second part of the book out, and gives no indication about the third part, mainly a view of contemporary life in the twenties. The author to my mind doesn't seem to grasp it all either and gets a little tedious, with a midlife-crisis modern man who falls in love with a 20-year-old and his midlife crisis wife, member of parliament, who acts out her hot flushes.

There is also a Kitty in this book, an 18-year-old with a gorgeous body, who wants to go to Berlin to join a dancing troupe and express herself like Isadora Duncan, the famous dancer. I don't think that Anne was inspired, and although she was very interested in film stars, she doesn't indicate any sympathy for this person. I suspect that it was mainly the first part that really interested her, for reasons of readability, or historical interest. Two years later, she had developed stronger ideas about the treatment of women in society when she writes: *'I merely condemn all the men, and the whole system, that refuse ever to acknowledge what an important, arduous, and in the long run beautiful part, women play in society.'* (15 June 1944)

The author of the book *The Rebels*, Jo van Ammers-Küller, who died in 1966, had a few other best-sellers in the twenties, with for that time 'advanced' themes. It was risqué even to mention matters like 'divorce' or an 'affair', let alone illegitimate children. Many educators, librarians and parents made sure that only adults would be able to read this.

A bitter personal detail must be mentioned about the Dutch author Jo van Ammers-Küller. Several of her books were translated into German at the time, and, perhaps carried away by success, she became a staunch Nazi sympathiser. She was forbidden to publish for several years after the war. It is one of those ironic twists of history to realise that Anne was reading her books, while the author was collaborating with her tormentors.

In their second year in hiding, on several occasions she makes informative inventories of things like daily routines, or people's reading habits. She writes on Thursday April 6, 1944: *'Dear Kitty, you asked me what my hobbies and interests were, so I want to reply, but I warn you that there are heaps of them, so don't get a shock!*

First of all: writing, but that can hardly be reckoned as a hobby.

No. 2 is family trees. I have been searching for family trees of the French, German, Spanish, English, Austrian, Russian, Norwegian and Dutch royal families in all the newspapers, books and pamphlets I can find. I have made great progress with a lot of them, as, for a long time already, I've been taking down notes from all the biographies and history books that I read; I even copy out many passages of history.

My third hobby then is history, for which Daddy has already bought me a lot of books. I can hardly wait for the day that I shall be able to comb through the books in the public library.

No. 4 is Greek & Roman Mythology. I have various books about this too. I can rattle off the 9 muses or the 7 loves of Zeus. I have the wives of Hercules etc. etc. at my fingertips.

Other hobbies are film stars, and family photos. Mad on books and reading. Have a great liking for history of art, poets and painters. I may go in for musicians later on. I have a great loathing for Algebra, Geometry and figures. I enjoy all the other school subjects, but history above all!'

The wall of Anne's room with photos and film star collection.
Photo © AFF/AFS, Amsterdam, The Netherlands.

'Anyone who doesn't write doesn't know how wonderful it is'

While the helpers Miep and Mr Kleiman brought books[5] from the library, Mr Kugler brought Anne the magazine *Cinema and Theatre*. She had a collection of postcards and film stars: in the Anne Frank House one can still find the pictures of Deanne Durbin, Ginger Rogers, German film star Heinz Ruhmann and Dutch actress Lilly Bouwmeester pinned to the wall. In a charming short story entitled *'Dreams of Movie Stardom'*, she addresses the question put to her by Mrs Van Pels: *'Why she doesn't want to become a movie star'*. She tells the story of her fictitious correspondence with a film star called Priscilla Lane and subsequent travel to Hollywood to meet her. She is well received and has a wonderful time. A photo session is arranged and Anne gets a modelling job. But *'I had to stand, sit, and smile continuously; walk up and down, change clothes again, look pretty, and put on fresh make up. At night I was so exhausted that I had to drag myself to bed. On the third day it hurt me to smile.'* She finds out that this life is hard work and the story ends: *'As for dreams of movie stardom, I was cured. I had had a close look at the way celebrities live.'*

Her story is one of the more than 40 short stories, observations and unfinished fragments that Anne Frank wrote besides her diary. We know when she started: on August 7, 1943 she writes: *'An interruption in my sketches of life in the "Secret Annexe". A few weeks ago I started to write a story, something that was completely made up and that gave me such pleasure that my pen-children are now piling up.'* She called the story *Kaatje*. It was written when she was observing a little girl through the window of the secret annexe, playing in the garden. It is a two-page fantasy about the girl, who Anne describes as being one of seven. She has lost her father, has a kitten, and she is a nice and sometimes naughty girl. Kaatje can't wait to grow up so she can earn money in the factory for her mother. She wants to get married but have only two children. '*Kaatje go to bed says mother, you have been daydreaming again*'. Thus ends the story.

Anne Frank is very clear about her ambitions as a writer (11 May 1944) : '*Now, about something else: you've known for a long time that my greatest wish is to become a journalist someday and later on a famous writer.*' Interestingly enough, she had already written on 3 April: '*I must work, so as not to be a fool, to get on to become a journalist, because that's what I want! I know that I can write, a couple of my stories are good, my descriptions of the "Secret Annexe" are humorous, there's a lot in my diary that speaks, but – whether I have real talent remains to be seen. Eva's dream is my best fairy tale, and the queer thing about it is that I don't know where it comes from. Quite a lot of "Cady's Life" is good too, but, on the whole, it's nothing! I am the best and sharpest critic of my own work, I know myself what is and what is not well written. Anyone who doesn't write doesn't know how wonderful it is....*'

It's a hypothetical question whether Anne Frank would have been a good writer. Take her story called *Fear,* in which fire and bombs go off like a cheap B-movie, the main person is constantly running away, but also tries to keep her parents to finally find peace in nature, on a meadow. Compare this example of bad creative fiction writing to a realistic albeit cynical entry in the diary of 2 June 1944: '*I have a brand new prescription against gunfire: during particularly loud bangs hasten to the nearest wooden stairs, run up and down a few times and make sure that you fall gently downstairs at least once. What with the scratches and the noise of running and falling, you are too busy to listen to the gunfire let alone worry about it. The writer of these lines has certainly used this ideal recipe with success!*' A much better description of the fear and panic of people who had no hiding place within their hiding place!

One of the most interesting parts of her diary from a literary point of view is her growing into a writer, her shifting interests from teenybopper into a more serious thinking woman, her growing in spurts, her doubts, self-criticism etc. In the early days, she was a little schoolgirl, reading Joop ter Heul, but at the abrupt end we already see an interesting style unfolding, to be brutally cut off. And she loved writing, as shown on April 5, 1944: '*I can shake off everything if I write; my sorrows disappear, my courage is reborn. But, and that is the great question, will I ever be able to write anything great, will I ever become a journalist or a writer? I hope so, oh, I hope so very much, for I can recapture everything when I write, my thoughts, my ideals, my fantasies. I haven't done anything more to "Cady's Life" for ages; in my mind I know exactly how to go on, but somehow it doesn't flow from my pen. Perhaps I shall never finish it, it may land up in the wastepaper basket, or the fire...that's a horrible idea, but then I think to myself, "At the age of fourteen and with so little experience, how can you write about philosophy?" So I go on with fresh courage; I think I shall succeed, because I want to write!*'

She certainly got carried away about her writing when she said: '*I want to send in to "The Prince" (a popular magazine) to see if they will take one of my fairy tales, under a pseudonym, of course, but because all my fairy tales so far have been too long, I don't think I have much of a chance.*' (April 20,

1944). More realistically: '*I want to try and finish the story of Ellen, the fairy. I can give it to Daddy for fun on his birthday, together with all author's rights.*' (6 May 1944) These last words were more prophetic than she ever wished, considering the rights of the last definitive edition.

Shirley Temple in wartime?

The Dutch are a reading people. Unlike the Americans, they have less capacity for adoration, hollywoodising or sensationalism. Anne Frank's *Tales from the Secret Annex*, a number of short stories, are examples of not very great literature, and she was never regarded as a great Dutch author by the official literary canon. Anne Frank's diary does not deal with themes and motifs like guilt about collaboration, or at being a bystander, love in wartime, death, coincidence, or choices with a lifelong impact etc. Also, her diary was a work in progress. Still, events and thoughts reappear. Opinions about education and recurring guilt feelings are combined with a great sense of honesty, especially towards herself. She is also a careful chronicler or journalist of daily events. Besides these, she is full of desire for a true friend, and although she starts with a paper friend, she wants a real one, which leads to a love in which she only half-heartedly believed herself. Amazing is her enormous sense of discipline and her work ethic. She studies mercilessly, French irregular verbs, translations from Dutch into English etc. Here is an entry from April 27, 1944: '*At the moment I'm reading The Emperor Charles V, written by a professor at Goettingen university; he worked at the book for forty years. I read fifty pages in 5 days; it's impossible to do more. The book has 598 pages so now you can work out how long it will take me – and there is a second volume to follow. But very interesting.*' All this in addition to her stories and her diary. Isn't she every teacher's dream student?

This doesn't mean that we should simplify Anne Frank to that famous last line of the play and film: '*in spite of everything I still believe that people are really good at heart.*' In fact, it is not the last line in the Diary at all, but the entry of July 15, 1944, which continues: '*I simply can't build up my hopes on a foundation consisting of confusion, misery, and death, I see the world gradually being turned into a wilderness, I hear the ever approaching thunder, which will destroy us too, I can feel the suffering of millions.*' But it is easy to take these lines too out of context, because the entry finishes : '*and yet, if I look up into the heavens, I think that it will all come right, that this cruelty too will end, and that peace and tranquillity will return again. In the meantime, I must uphold my ideals, for perhaps the time will come when I shall be able to carry them out!*'

However, let's not be afraid of a less hopeful, a less saintly image, and take a slightly more critical view when painting Anne Frank's historical portrait. Anne Frank, bubbly and sweet as she might have been, also had her limits and shortcomings. Her age and immaturity prevented her sometimes from seeing different points of view in her mother or dentist Dussel, made her write romance-style stories better forgotten, and although she shows remarkable growth over a short period of time, she was not a completely rounded person yet. She should also be seen in the larger perspective of a persecuted Jewish family in the Netherlands and not simply as a cute Shirley Temple in wartime.[6]

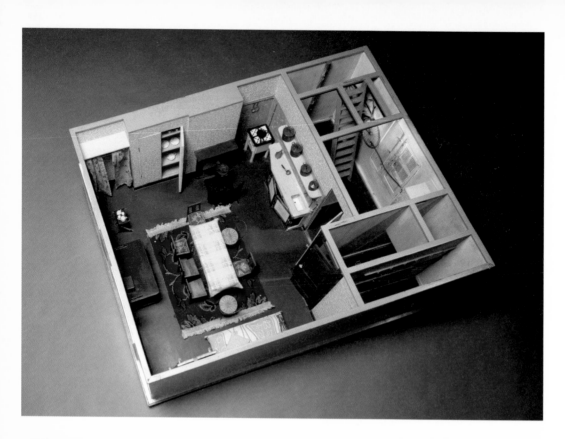

Would she have written the famous lines: '*In spite of everything etc*' knowing that she still had 7 months of excruciating pain, torture and humiliation to go through? We don't know, but we can inform ourselves about those last months. Here is a quote from an eye witness: '*The Frank girls were so emaciated. They looked terrible. They had little squabbles, caused by their illness, because it was clear they had typhus. ...They had those hollowed-out faces, skin over bone...You could really see both of them dying, as well as others. But what was so sad, of course, was that these children were still so young. I always found it so horrible that as children they had never really lived.*' This quote comes from Rachel van Amerongen in the documentary *The Last Seven Months of Anne Frank* by Willy Lindwer. It is perhaps a sign of the times that the catalogue in which this video was offered for sale has the warning: '*contains delicate matter*'. Do we have to guard ourselves from shock when the rosy picture of Anne Frank threatens to be destroyed, when real facts from real life take over? Will we have an anti-cruelty chip built into our TV's to guard us from '*delicate matters*'? I like to think that Anne Frank herself would have been much more open and forward. She deserves more than a rosy picture. On May 26, 1944 she writes in unusual desperation, with compassion for her helpers and only a glimmer of hope: '*Again and again I ask myself, would it not have been better for us all if we had not gone into hiding, and if we were dead now and not going through all this misery, especially as we shouldn't be running our protectors into danger any more. But we all recoil from these thoughts too, for we still love life; we haven't yet forgotten the voice of nature, we still hope, hope about everything. I hope something will happen soon now, shooting if need be- nothing can crush us more than this restlessness. Let the end come, even if it is hard; then at least we shall know whether we are finally going to win through or go under.*' This was a few months before she wrote: '*I trust to luck, but should I be saved, and spared from destruction, then it would be terrible if my diaries and my tales were lost.*'

Little did she know that her luck would soon run out, and that the consolation prize for us would only be her diaries and tales, which were not lost. But what a prize!

TON J. BROOS

Two models made in 1961 to Otto Frank's instructions to give visitors an idea of how the annexe looked when it was a hiding place. Photo © AFF/AFS, Amsterdam, The Netherlands.

BIBLIOGRAPHY

AMMERS-KÜLLER, J. VAN, *De opstandigen, een familieroman in drie boeken.* Amsterdam, 1925; translated as: *The Rebel Generation*, New York (1925).
BARNOUW, DAVID (ed.), *The Diary of Anne Frank: the Critical Edition.* New York, 1989.
FRANK, ANNE, *Tales from the Secret Annex.* New York, 1983.
MARXVELDT, CISSY VAN, *De H.B.S.tijd van Joop ter Heul.* Amersfoort, 1930 (9th edition, many other editions).
SUCHTELEN, NICO VAN, *Eva's jeugd.* Amsterdam, 1923 (Anne might have used: Amsterdam, Wereldbibliotheek,1942, the 15th edition).

The

Containment of Chaos

The Work of Gerard Reve

A dalliance with the English language nearly caused the Dutchman Gerard Reve to become an English writer. In 1951 the Dutch government awarded him a travel grant to write his novella *Melancholy* (Melancholia), but when the Minister for Culture got wind of the fact that the book contained a masturbation scene the grant was instantly withdrawn. The indignant writer boldly decided that henceforth he would write only in English, to which end he settled in London and set about mastering his new language. In 1956 Reve published *The Acrobat and Other Stories*, but the difficulties of writing in English proved too much for him and a few years later he went back to his mother tongue. His efforts to learn English, however, were not in vain, for his mastery of the language enabled him to produce excellent translations into Dutch of a number of plays, including *The Caretaker* by Harold Pinter and *Who's Afraid of Virginia Woolf?* by Edward Albee.

Reve is a controversial writer whose literary career has been filled with such upsets as the above-mentioned incident. Born Gerard Kornelis van het Reve (the shortened form of his name dates from 1973) in Amsterdam on 14 December 1923, he grew up in a Communist family. His brother, Karel, became a professor of Slavic languages and one of the Netherlands' best post-war essayists. As an adult Gerard would develop into a fierce opponent of the ideology his parents had pinned their hopes on.

His first novel, *The Evenings* (De avonden), published in 1947, provoked a storm of criticism. Some critics reacted positively and others were dismissive, but none was indifferent. The novel describes in ten chapters, corresponding to the last ten days of the year 1946, the attempts made by Frits van Egters, a young man in his early twenties, to get a grip on his life, which he perceives as nothing but a fragmentary collection of meaningless moments. Despite his good intentions ('*Let us make sure our time is well spent*'), he does not succeed in spending his time – and especially his evenings – in a satisfactory way. He's bored, and irritated with his parents, with whom he lives. Frits carries on listless conversations with his friends, and their small talk is interspersed with horror stories and cynical jokes: '*Elephantiasis, that's a good one, you can sit on your own balls as though they were a* pouf.'

The spiritual vacuum to which *The Evenings* testifies was attributed by a number of critics to the enemy occupation of the Netherlands which had ended only a short time before. Reve's novel was said to interpret the mentality of post-war youth, formed during a period when traditional moral principles were being trampled upon. The writer himself was bewildered by all the commotion caused by his first-born and made the following matter-of-fact comment: '*I wrote "The Evenings" because I was convinced I had to write it: that seems to me a good enough reason. I hoped that ten of my friends would accept a free copy, and that twenty people would buy the book out of pity and ten others by mistake. Things turned out differently. It's not my fault it caused such an uproar.*'

The novella *Werther Nieland*, published in 1949, was largely ignored by the critics. It is the story of a younger version of Frits van Egters, who – if such a thing is possible – is even more unable to face up to an incomprehensible and therefore terrifying reality. Despite the scant attention originally paid to the book, it is now regarded as a high point in Reve's oeuvre, also by the author himself.

Letter from Edinburgh

The 1950s were a rather unproductive period for Reve, in which he had very little to show for his efforts. This is evidenced not only by his adventure with the English language, but also by his attempts to make a name for himself as a playwright. The production of his tragedy – *Commissioner Fennedy* (Commissaris Fennedy), written in 1962 – was a complete fiasco.

In the meantime Reve was searching for a form other than the traditional story, the constraints of which he had come to perceive as a straitjacket. The form he was seeking was found by accident, when, as editor of *Tirade*, lack of copy compelled him to contribute a 'travel letter' describing a writers' conference he had attended in Edinburgh. This 'Letter from Edinburgh' was well received, and was followed by other letters, which became more and more personal. In 1963 Reve compiled a selection of them in *En Route for the End* (Op weg naar het einde), which was followed three years later by *Nearer to Thee* (Nader tot U), the latter also containing a section of poems. These books sold by the tens of thousands, and the author fanned the flames of his success by making conspicuous appearances in the media, testifying to his reputation as a master of the provocative and humorous statement.

In *En Route for the End* and *Nearer to Thee* Reve replaced conventional narrative with a looser, epistolary form, in which recollections, outpourings and reflections effortlessly settle into place. Stylistically, too, Reve was able to move about more freely. Whereas the first work is characterised by syntactical soberness and frugality in his use of words, in the 'travel letters' Reve made use of long sentences – often interrupted by parenthetical expressions and exclamations – as well as a frequent change of register. A special effect was achieved through the use of language inspired by the Bible. For example, the famous pronouncement by Paul the Apostle, '*And now abideth faith, hope, charity, these three; but the greatest of these is charity*' (*I Corinthians* 13:13) was profanely varied by Reve to read, '*Sex, Drink, and Death, these three, but the greatest of these is Death.*'

Despite these differences, there is a great deal of thematic continuity in his early work up to and including the 1960s. Such themes as writing, religion and homosexual love are developed to the full. Frits van Egters in *The Evenings* can be viewed as a prospective writer. Admittedly, he doesn't put pen to paper, but he forces himself to observe keenly and to express his observations clearly. It is a way of getting a grip on a world that appears to him to be meaningless and absurd. The same cathartic function is fulfilled by writing, which is now being practised in earnest by the author who is the main character of the collections of letters.

'Revism'

Religion plays a comparable role in Reve's work. In *Becoming a Writer* (Zelf schrijver worden, 1986) – four treatises that in no way offer the instruction manual promised by the title, but contain instead Reve's poetics – he calls art and religion *'twin sisters'* with the task of *'interpreting reality'*. At the end of *The Evenings* the protagonist turns to God in a heart-rending monologue, in which he sums up his parents' exasperating idiosyncrasies, nonetheless begging God to have mercy on them. God has seen everything, just like the budding writer Frits van Egters. The same interpretive function is given to religion in the travel letters.

When Reve's characters turn to God, they do so in a tone suggesting equality between God and man. In the letters in particular, God appears as a figure with human traits. Just as man needs God, so God cannot do without man. The poem 'Epilogue' from *Nearer to Thee* ends with the lines, *'But sometimes, when I think that You do truly live, / I think that You are Love, and lonely, / and that, in selfsame desperation, You seek me / as I seek You.'*

Despite the frankness found in *The Evenings*, the near absence of sexuality is striking, as contemporary critics also pointed out. There are only a few passages from which one may gather that the protagonist's feelings of lust are closely connected with torture or at least fantasies thereof. A story dating from Reve's English period but published only in 1968, *A Prison Song in Prose*, displays a similar connection, this theme finally unfolding completely in the prose written by Reve in the 1960s. Sexual love is directed at members of the same sex and is strongly aroused by pictures of torture, usually not of the lover, but of boys offered to him as a sacrifice. Satisfying one's own desires is subordinated to the pleasure of the beloved. Uninhibited by modesty, the writer has labelled this seemingly religious constellation 'Revism'.

The interweaving of the various themes, already visible in the writings discussed so far, is nowhere so apparent as in a passage from the 'Letter from the house called The Grass', which supplements this article. Here the main character thinks about the book he himself is going to write, which will be the deliverance of man and nature. Literature serves to realise a religious goal: salvation. In accordance with Christian messianism, God returns to earth. On this day of the parousia, the glorious Advent at the end of time, God assumes the shape of a *'one-year-old, mouse-grey donkey'*, who submits a full three times to the sexual advances of the protagonist, the love of God thus receiving sexual confirmation.

Reve himself is very attached to this passage, but representatives of the Dutch Reformed Church objected to the representation of God as a donkey (in the author's opinion, *'the dearest, most innocent creature I can think of'*), who, to make matters worse, has sexual relations with a person. In 1966 Reve found himself faced with a charge of blasphemy in a court case that became known as the 'donkey trial'. The writer defended himself in a brilliant address to the court, in which he showed as little respect for the bench as his characters did for the Supreme Being. He expounded his image of an immanent God, based on the quintessential identity of God and man: *'God has just as much need of our love and comfort as we do of His, and is just as dependent on our saving Him as we are on His saving us.'* He contrasted this picture with the God of his opponents, *'a wrathful, unfathomable petty tyrant, but one who cannot possibly be duped...'*. The author, who converted to Catholicism that same year, was acquitted.

His conversion, which meant supporting a conservative institution, did not make Reve popular among the progressive intelligentsia in the Netherlands. His political views became more conservative. He supported the United States intervention in Vietnam and was also able to discern the positive side of South African apartheid policies.

Reve could count on more sympathy, though, when defending the rights of homosexuals to their own sexual proclivities. He openly declared his homosexuality and was for a short time the editor of *Dialoog, tijdschrift voor homofilie en maatschappij* (Dialogue, a Magazine for Homosexuality and Society), thereby making his own contribution to the emancipation of homosexuals.

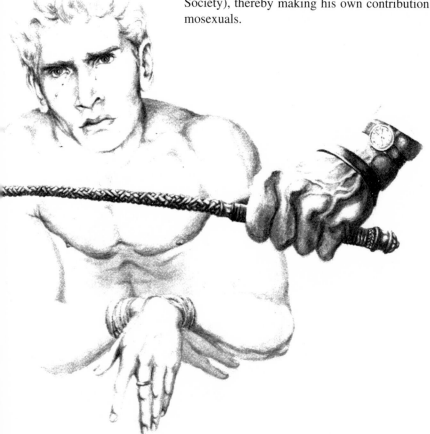

Illustration from *A Prison Song in Prose* (1968).

Gerard Reve cheers the Pope in Brussels on 4 June 1995. Photo by Klaas Koppe.

My Mother, the Church

The travel letters written in the 1960s were not the end of the line in Reve's development. Although his work has since been characterised by a loose structure, the actual letter form disappeared into the background and the story came into its own again. Reve demonstrated a predilection for the frame narrative, which guaranteed him optimum freedom of movement. His return to the story was compensated for by the publication of a long series of authentic letters, such as *Letters to Wimie 1959-1963* (Brieven aan Wimie 1959-1963, 1980), *Letters to Skilled Workers* (Brieven aan geschoolde arbeiders, 1985) and *Letters to my Personal Physician 1963-1980* (Brieven aan mijn lijfarts 1963-1980, 1991).

This development may create the impression of a neat division into fiction and non-fiction, but nothing could be further from the truth. Reve is an elusive author, who takes pleasure in causing confusion, as emerged from the biography he invented for himself in the late 1960s. This hoax maintained that he was descended from Baltic-Russian parents, and – destined for a career in the military – served as an officer in the Indies, or present-day Indonesia. His career was supposedly cut short when he entered into an illicit relationship with a Javan prince. This so-called biography has nothing whatsoever to do with the facts of Reve's life.

Reve became increasingly aware both of his subject matter and of his stylistic capabilities. The dark side of this realisation caused him in a number of works, such as *The Silent Friend* (De stille vriend, 1984), to cling unabashedly to his old routine. A new dimension was added to his work, however: starting in the mid-1970s, Reve produced a number of writings providing explication of his subject matter. The essence and technique of the arts, and literature in particular, was treated in the above-mentioned book *Becoming a Writer*. His religious development is the subject of *Mother and Son* (Moeder en zoon, 1980). The title already reveals that Mary, introduced as a traditional mother figure, has by now supplanted God in Reve's religious universe. At the same time the title suggests that a craving for religious security may be traced back to one's relationship with one's parents: '*If I dared to be very honest, then one thing was extremely clear: I was searching for my mother, whom I had lost for good, and a Church now presented itself to me which called itself our mother and which, moreover – not* de jure *according to the statutes but* de facto *according to the house rules – was run by a Mother.*'

Literature as exorcism

In *Old and Lonely* (Oud en eenzaam, 1978) the first-person narrator declares his particular sexual inclinations, in which lust and cruelty are inextricably linked, from the vantage point of what he calls '*Communistic pornography*': the detailed description of the torture inflicted on youthful Communists by capitalist bullies during training sessions. (An early example of this is to be found in 'The Foreign Boy' in *The Acrobat and Other Stories*.) The narrator of *Old and Lonely* expresses it as follows: '*Communistic pornography instilled in me a preoccupation with cruelty, which pushed all other feelings and thoughts into the background. In my imagination, sadistic scenes of dungeons and interrogations would henceforth accompany every feeling of sexual lust, and only by summoning up these scenes or permitting them to appear could my desires be satisfied.*'

Despite this tendency to offer rational explanations, Reve's view of the world remains essentially irrational. In *Becoming a Writer* he expounds the notion that the part of writing which he finds most important – the Conception ('*the light in which the writer sees the world and existence*') – does not bear close scrutiny. Another example of the limited role that reason plays in Reve's thinking is the fact, revealed in *Mother and Son,* that his decision to become a member of the Catholic church was an impulsive one, taken as an expression of gratitude for being reunited with a lover.

The Revian hero is invariably confronted with a reality whose incomprehensibility harbours all manner of danger. In order to exorcise this reality and the fears it inspires, Reve seeks refuge in literature, which fulfils the same function as religion. Whether this involves seeking careful formulations, as Frits van Egters trains himself to do in *The Evenings*, or indulging in compulsive narration, such as the first-person narrator in *The Book of Violet and Death* (Het boek van violet en dood, 1996), the stakes are always what Reve himself regards as the essence of all art: '*overcoming and containing chaos*'.

G.F.H. RAAT
Translated by Diane L. Webb.

The Acrobat and Other Stories. Amsterdam / London, 1956 (Original in English).

'A Circus in Miniature' (Tr. James S Holmes and Hans van Marle). In: *Delta*, VII, 1964, 2, pp. 52-63.

'The Decline and Fall of the Boslowits Family' (Tr. James S Holmes and Hans van Marle). In: *Modern Stories from Holland and Flanders* (ed. Egbert Krispyn). New York, 1973, pp. 126-154.

'Gerard Reve: an English Sampler' (Tr. Paul Vincent). In: *Dutch Crossing*, 12, December 1980, pp. 55-57.

Parents Worry (Tr. Richard Huijing). London, 1990.

'Werther Nieland' (Tr. Richard Huijing). In: *The Dedalus Book of Dutch Fantasy* (ed. Richard Huijing). Sawtry (Cambs.), 1993.

Four Extracts

by Gerard Reve

'Almighty and everlasting God,' he said softly, 'cast your eyes upon my parents. See them in their hour of need. Do not avert your gaze.' 'Listen,' he said, 'my father is as deaf as a post. He hears so little it's not worth mentioning. Fire a cannon next to his ear as a joke and he'll ask if the doorbell is ringing. He slurps when he drinks. He uses his dessert spoon for the sugar. He eats meat with his fingers. He farts when it's not called for. He has pieces of food stuck in his dentures. He never knows where to insert the coin. When he peels an egg, he never knows what to do with the shell. He asks in English if there's any news. He mixes all his food up on his plate. Almighty God, to whom all things are known, I know these transgressions have not gone unseen.'

He was passed by six girls with their arms slung around each other, alternately racing forward and then checking their pace. 'He makes a mess knocking the ashes out of his pipe,' he whispered, when they were past him. 'He loses stamps. Not on purpose, but he loses them all the same. You can't find them any more, that's the point. He wipes his fingers on his clothes. He turns off the radio. If I strike a G with the fork, he thinks I'm crazy. And he pokes around in the serving plates. That's uncleanly. And often he doesn't wear a tie. But great is his goodness.' He stopped and stared out across the water. 'Look at my mother,' he said softly. 'She says I should be sociable and go on living at home. She tells me to wear my white sleeveless pullover. She makes apple fritters with the wrong kind of apple. I'll tell you about it sometime when I have the chance. She makes lots of smoke when she lights the stove. And she let the attic keys burn up. Almighty and everlasting God, she thought she was buying wine, but it was fruit juice. Dear soul. Blackcurrant-apple. She moves her head back and forth when she reads. She's my mother. See her infinite goodness.' He wiped a tear from the corner of his right eye with his sleeve and walked on.

'A thousand years are nothing in Thy sight,' he continued. 'Behold the days of my parents. Old age is approaching, they are racked with disease, there is no hope. Death is near, and a gaping grave. Not a grave, actually, because they're going to be put in an urn: we make a weekly payment on it.' He shook his head.

'Look at them,' he whispered. 'There is no hope for them. They live in loneliness. Wherever they reach out all is emptiness. Their bodies are deteriorating. He still has hair on his head, a whole head of hair. No, he's not bald. But that will come too.'

From *The Evenings* (De avonden. Amsterdam: Van Oorschot, 1967[15], pp.194-195). *Translated by Diane L. Webb.*

My interest in death and undertaking was acquired at a very early age. Long before I reached adulthood I founded the *Club of Tombs*, whose purpose was to provide a decent burial for dead birds and other small animals. The graves were earthen pyramids or conical elevations designed to have passageways and an air shaft. They've all disappeared because everything was dug up, and houses were built everywhere that are now ready to be demolished. Everything gets knocked down sooner or later.

My early youth has not yet been the subject of sufficient study. I myself have no recollection of the first five years of my life. From my sixth year I have vague memories of a corridor, a view of a playground, and from the balconies a view of a row of houses in which people lived who didn't exist, because the walls were made of yellow bricks. And that's all. Décor, therefore, but without actors or sounds. Did anything terrible happen during those first five years? It wouldn't surprise me if it had, but I don't remember anything: it defies historical observation. All in all I've had a strange life, when I think about it. Not special, but unusual, that's probably the right word. Something providential seems to inform that life, not anything that guides or advises me, but a providence that always ensures that I escape, without knowing what I'm escaping from. These acts of providence have not made my life any happier, though perhaps they've given it direction. Nevertheless, we are faced with a mystery: we look in the mirror of a dark reason, and I think it has to be like that.

From *The Book of Violet and Death* (Het boek van violet en dood. Amsterdam / Antwerpen, Van Oorschot, 1996, pp. 71-72) *Translated by Diane L. Webb.*

Turning back at the intersection in front of W.'s cafe, I actually took the way home. Drank too much again, God, God damn. 'I'll kick the habit, I have to, I swear I will. As it was in the beginning, is now, and ever shall be, I'm going to stop drinking, I swear it in the sight of God. But I don't know when exactly.'

I had to fight – with God and people I would struggle, and I would overcome, this I now saw. No, oh no, never would I give up the hope of writing what had to be written but which no one had ever put into words before: the book, once again, that would make all other books unnecessary; the book, which, when finished, no other writer would have to worry about writing ever again, for all of humankind, yes, even the whole of nature, still fettered by hate and fear, would be redeemed. Then the children of man would see a sunrise such as was never seen before, and music would sound, sighing as though from a distance, which I had never heard yet nonetheless recognised. And God Himself would come to me in the shape of a one-year-old, mouse-grey donkey and stand in front of the door and ring the bell and say, 'Gerard, that book of yours – did you know that parts of it made me cry?'

'My Lord and my God! I will praise Thy name for ever and ever. I love you so very much,' I would try to say, but halfway through I would burst into tears, and start to kiss Him and pull him inside, and after a lot of grabbing and clutching on the way up the stairs to the bedroom, I would take Him, protractedly, three times in a row in his Secret Opening, and afterwards give him a complimentary copy, not cloth-bound, but hard cover – none of that petty stinginess – with the dedication: *For the Everlasting. Without words.*

From *Nearer to Thee* (Nader tot U. Utrecht / Antwerpen: Van Oorschot, 1990[20], pp. 117-118)
Translated by Diane L. Webb.

'So you're the new member,' Larry said. 'What's your name?'

'Yes, I'm the new member,' Darger answered. 'I'm Willem's brother.'

'So you're a brother of Willem,' Larry said, putting his hand on Darger's shoulder. 'Is that so? Well, I don't have to tell you much about the struggle we're waging. Because Willem knows everything a boy of his age should know about it, and I'm sure he's told you a lot about it.'

'Yes, yes,' Darger answered. He would have liked to take a few steps backward, but he was already standing against the wall.

'So I suppose you know what they do to comrades of ours in other countries,' Larry said. His shirt was open at the top, and some hairs on his chest stuck out.

'I. Yes, yes,' Darger said hastily.

Larry put his tongue between his lips and closed his left eye.

'For instance, did you know that they beat them with iron rods?' he asked. 'So that they die with the blows, and that their backbones are broken? You know that, do you?'

'Yes, yes,' Darger said quickly. Larry's hand was still on his shoulder.

'But we'll make them pay for it,' Larry went on. 'Don't you think we'll avenge our martyrs? We will, and we'll do a lot worse than they did, believe that.'

From *The Acrobat and other Stories*. Amsterdam / London, 1956, pp. 123-124.
Written by the author in English.

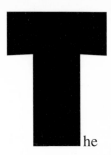

The

Quest for Sparkling Light

Emile Claus in a European Perspective

The Flemish painter Emile Claus (1849-1924) already had a productive career behind him when he espoused Impressionism in 1889. He had graduated from the Academy of Fine Arts in Antwerp in 1874 and for 15 years participated in the cultural life of that city, which was invariably classified as a bastion of arch-conservatism by modernist circles in Brussels. However, he enjoyed success from the very start, as evidenced by his painting *Two Punished Friends*, which found its way into the highly diverse collection of King Leopold II as early as 1876. Like many of his contemporaries he was interested in orientalism and in late 1878 and early 1879 he travelled to North Africa and Spain, though this had little effect on his work. In fact until 1882 he confined himself to unadventurous romantic and realistic genre scenes, and made his name primarily as a portraitist.

Emile Claus, *Riches and Poverty*. 1880. Canvas, 110 x 165 cm. Private collection. Photo by Hugo Maertens.

Emile Claus, *The Picnic*. c. 1887. Canvas, 129 x 198 cm. Royal Collection, Brussels. Photo by Hugo Maertens.

But nature was to assume an increasingly important role in his work. In 1882 he rented a dilapidated country house on the banks of the River Leie in Astene in East Flanders. The wide landscapes surrounding Villa Zonneschijn were to beguile him from that moment on. In the meantime, he became acquainted with the rising tide of Naturalism at the Paris Salons in the eighties, and the confrontation with artists such as Jules Bastien-Lepage (1848-1884) also led him down this path. *The Picnic*, also in King Leopold II's collection, displays to the full Claus' alliance with the naturalist movement. Man and nature come together in an informal scene, a monumental composition in which rural figures appear in bright light, true to life and with a gentle critical undertone of social criticism.

The call of light

Enthralled by the French Impressionists' controversial exhibitions and their participation in the salons of *Les XX* in Brussels, he rented a studio in Paris in the winters of 1889 to 1892. But Claus by no means developed into a thoroughbred Impressionist. Or as the prominent Parisian critic (and Claus' friend) Gabriel Mourey summarised it in *The Studio* in August 1899: '*He is an Impressionist to this extent – that he possesses the gift of feeling with the utmost keenness the true meaning of Nature in all her manifestations; while he is bound by no rule, subject to no formula, in his endeavour to interpret that meaning on his canvas. But, unlike most Impressionists, he has the rare capacity to know how to choose his impressions, to test them to the uttermost, and never to rest until he has translated them to his full satisfaction, disdaining the haphazard attempts which are sufficient for the majority of modern landscapists.'*

The appreciative support Claus received from progressive art critics was in sharp contrast, however, to the lukewarm reaction of the Belgian public. As late as 1890 and 1891 many collectors still had reservations about Impressionism. In this period Claus' work drew a positive response from collectors in Paris and also in Britain. One such was John Maddocks from Bradford, who knew Claus' work from the Paris salons. Although his main interest was in the naturalism of such painters as George Clausen and Léon Lhermitte, he also owned early impressionist paintings by Claus. The artist himself actually mentions this in a letter to an English friend: '*Mr Maddocks has always strongly encouraged me, and had the courage to buy my work at a time when everybody in Belgium found me by far too audacious, because, as you may know, the leaders, the standard-bearers as it were, of the young Belgian school of painting are not at all in sympathy with the beautiful art of Monet and his school.*' The friend in question, Wynford Dewhurst, included the letter in a much-talked-about book, *Impressionist Painting. Its Genesis and Development*, published in London by George Newnes in 1904. In this book Dewhurst, a critic on *The Studio* and himself a painter, made a significant contribution to the theory that French Impressionism originated in part from the early nineteenth-century achievements of John Constable and William Turner, referring to Claude Monet and Camille Pissarro's stay in London in 1870 and 1871. In support of this thesis the author quoted Claus' account of his time in London: '*I have all too quickly glanced at the Turners and Constables of London, nevertheless it was a revelation to me, and those great artists Monet, Sisley and Pissarro continue simply what that giant Turner discovered.*' However, Dewhurst was also greatly impressed by the work of Claus himself: the first pages of chapter 10, '*La peinture claire*', are devoted entirely to Claus and backed up by seven plates.

Emile Claus, c.1895.

Emile Claus, *Impression at Night*. Drawing on paper, 12 x 16 cm. Private collection. Photo by Hugo Maertens.

Emile Claus, *Villa Zonneschijn*. 1899. Canvas, 80,5 x 116,5 cm. Musée d'Orsay, Paris. Photo Réunion des Musées Nationaux – Jean Schormans, Paris.

According to Dewhurst, public access to Maddocks' collection and its inclusion of paintings by Claus were '*a revelation to those artists who found themselves in Bradford at that period. Unknown and a stranger, Claus received in spirit silent congratulations for his splendid achievement, which aroused in several breasts a keen feeling of emulation*'. That Emile Claus also had a soft spot for this British author is clearly apparent from his dedication of *La ferme 'en souvenir au peintre Wynford Dewhurst'* in October 1904.

The trendsetting periodical *The Studio* also kept a close eye on Claus' development from his beginnings in 1893. This meant that the English public was familiar with his striking entries for avant-garde exhibitions in Europe and the United States. In fact Claus was also invited to exhibit in Britain, by the Pastel Society and The International Society of Sculptors, Painters and Gravers in London, among others. *The Studio* saw him as more than just a dot on the artistic map of Europe. As a consequence of the Paris *Exposition Universelle* of 1900, where Claus snapped up the gold medal, Gabriel Mourey covered the Belgian section in the November issue of *The Studio*. Only two Belgian artists stood out with distinction in the face of international competition, and they were Albert Baertsoen and Claus. But Mourey was charmed primarily by the monumental *Passage des vaches*, which has still lost none of its seductive powers in its present home at the Royal Museums of Fine Arts in Brussels: '*It is a large canvas of extraordinary luminosity, intensely powerful, and admirably rich in colour. I do not think any open-air picture of equal importance has yet been produced.*' In this work Claus attained a literally dazzling mastery of the pictorial depiction of the country life surrounding him. '*It is wonderful to observe the play of light* on the sparkling waters, the contrasts between the patches of sunshine piercing through the trees, and the clear shady places around; to note the difference in the colouring of the superb animals, ... the exactitude of their movements and their various expressions, if one may say so'. The Studio included a plate of *Passage des vaches* to back up the writer's superlatives. Mourey had in fact already written extensive articles on the two artists: on Claus in August 1899 and on Baertsoen the previous September. The Belgian correspondents Fernand Khnopff (in Brussels) and Pol de Mont (1857-1931) repeatedly brought Claus' work to the attention of their English readers.

Exile in London

On the outbreak of the First World War Claus fled to Britain, where he stayed until 1919. After a short time in Rhubina in Wales his artistic activity only really reached full flow when he rented a studio in Norfolk Street in London. He replaced his cheerful pre-war luminism with a colour harmony of subdued, soft half-tints. The subject was no longer dominant: the constantly changing panoramic view over the Thames and Victoria Embankment, under clouds, sun, mist or rain, time and again provided marvellous ephemeral river views that came close to the true spirit of Impressionism. This mettlesome sixty-year-old rarely appeared in London society, but took part all the more in the round of exhibitions. He was a notable guest in group exhibitions at the Goupil Gallery, The Royal Academy, The Grosvenor Galleries, the Grafton Galleries and the Dowdeswell Galle-

Emile Claus, *Passage des vaches*. 1899. Canvas, 67 x 100 cm. Private collection. Photo by Hugo Maertens.

ries, but his high point came in May and June 1917 when the Goupil Gallery mounted a one-man show of his work.

The latter days of a luminist

Claus was active as a painter until his death in 1924. In its August issue of that year *The Studio* published a commemorative article about him. *'The death of Emile Claus, the great Belgian artist, is another cruel loss for the country,'* wrote Paul Lambotte, who as director of the government's Fine Arts Department was later to exclude Claus' work from retrospectives abroad! Nevertheless, Claus' work was highly successful in exhibitions at home and abroad during his lifetime, at the Belgian and Paris salons to start with, but equally in dozens of exhibitions in Germany, Great Britain, Italy, the Netherlands and the United States. But the lack of appreciation for his work after 1924 had its roots in Belgium, and was due to the overpowering rise of Flemish Expressionism and to a lesser extent abstract art, as well as the first shoots of the successful Belgian Surrealist school. James Ensor was the only artist to be absorbed by avant-garde circles; such artists as Claus, Léon Frédéric, Fernand Khnopff and Theo van Rysselberghe, who had given Belgian art just as much of a guiding impulse in the early 1890s, were doomed to utter contempt. But nowadays we can give Claus his full due.

JOHAN DE SMET
Translated by Gregory Ball.

Emile Claus, *Sunset (London).* 1918. Canvas, 59 x 49,5 cm. Private collection. Photo by Hugo Maertens.

From

Belgian Unity to Flemish-Walloon Duality

The Story of Socialism in Belgium

The grim working conditions of Belgian miners, as depicted in *Descent into the Abyss*, an engraving in *La Cigale* (Brussels, 1868). Collection IEV, Brussels.

Social issues thrust their way onto the political scene in Belgium in 1885 with the formation of the Belgian Workers' Party (*Belgische Werklieden-partij*, BWP), in 1945 renamed the Belgian Socialist Party (*Belgische Socialistische Partij*, BSP). The BWP had developed regionally out of the founding in 1877 of a Flemish Socialist Workers' Party and a Brabant Socialist Party. The main driving forces were urban craftsmen's associations. Although a number of Walloon groups joined it in 1885, in the industrial areas of Wallonia the BWP's influence remained practically non-existent. This changed after a wave of revolutionary strikes in the Walloon industrial heartland which had to be put down by the army. The leaders of the BWP, as shocked as anyone, responded by linking socio-economic concerns still more closely to their main political campaign for one man, one vote. This, they thought, would lead to a socialist majority in Parliament and thence to government intervention in social matters. The political weapons deployed were large-scale peaceful demonstrations and general strikes. Having now gained the support of the Walloon industrial proletariat, the BWP developed into a national workers' movement. From now on, within the nineteenth-century nation state, it had sufficient extra-parliamentary disruptive capability to exert constant pressure on the national ruling elite. At the same time the BWP became the first mass party with a centralised structure: as political organisation, as trade union organisation and as health insurance provider. But it still relied on the organic local growth and development of a network of local organisations which enclosed members in their own socialist world in the face of the 'hostile bourgeois state'.

Concerned at the BWP's capacity to cause trouble and fearing a social revolution, the political elite soon recognised the party as a power player, initially within its own sphere of interest. There then followed a stop-go process of social and political integration of the BWP into the bourgeois parliamentary system. Political integration was achieved in 1893 with the abolition of the qualified franchise based on taxation and the introduction of universal multiple voting, followed in 1918 by universal single suffrage. Social integration came about gradually through fundamental concessions on social issues, recognition of trade unions by the state and employers and

the emergence in the 'golden sixties' of the national consultative economy, development of a national social security system and the welfare state. What emerged was a mixed economy with social checks and balances, a compromise which left the economic foundations of the bourgeois state in place. In the course of this process the socialist party evolved into a fully-fledged partner in government. While in the inter-war years its presence in the unavoidable coalitions was only grudgingly tolerated, all this changed after the Second World War. The BSP, its programme and its leaders alike, had become part of the national ruling elite. Working its way into areas of government power, it helped to infiltrate the state by means of political appointments and patronage. But despite all this, in 1978 the BSP ceased to exist as a unitary party. It split into two independent parties: the Walloon *Parti Socialiste* (PS) and the Flemish *Socialistische Partij* (SP).

The *via dolorosa* of Belgian factory workers in the nineteenth century in A. Bentos' *The Clock Strikes 5...Half Asleep They Make their Way to the Factory.* Collection ABVV, Ghent.

Two processes of modernisation

The emergence of socialism was bound up with the process of industrialisation in the nineteenth century and the presence, or absence, of a concentrated industrial proletariat. Events took very different courses in Wallonia and in Flanders. In contrast to Wallonia's 'golden age' (the coal-mining areas and industries of Hainault and Liège, the two largest of the four Walloon provinces), in 1850 the economy of 'poor Flanders' still depended predominantly on agriculture and cottage industry, with a few exceptions such as the textile mills of Ghent and the Antwerp docks (the birthplace of Flemish socialism). An underdeveloped region which, among other things, served as a labour pool for the industries of Wallonia. Not until towards the end of the nineteenth century would Flanders begin to develop the momentum to catch up economically, starting with small and medium-sized enterprises (and resulting, even today, in a different economic fabric). It also led to a difference in the parties' relative power in the two regions. This became apparent when universal single suffrage was introduced in 1919: in Wallonia the socialist party won 51% of the vote, while in Flanders the Catholic party had 47.7% (the socialists 25.58%). A different dominance, then, which was to endure *mutatis mutandis* until the 1965 elections; and even today these two parties are still the largest in their respective regions. Nationally, however, partly as a result of demographic developments, the socialist majority in Wallonia was negated by the even larger Catholic majority in Flanders. The socialist strategy, of gaining a majority in the Belgian national parliament through universal single suffrage, consequently became dependent on the industrial development of Flanders, which was expected to produce the same results as in Wallonia. But historical circumstances had changed. By now Christian Democracy had emerged and was able to accommodate social and occupational shifts within the Catholic pillar; alongside the Boerenbond (the farmers' union) there was now also a Christian workers' movement.

The second modernising process in the nineteenth century was the creation of nation states, in our case the emergence of the Belgian state following the 1830 revolution. French became the standard language, the high-status language. The result was a francophone monopoly of all senior posts in government, the judiciary and education. An artificial situation, since in Flanders the overwhelming majority of the population spoke only Dutch and they were the demographic majority in Belgium. Walloon socialism was to

Banner of the Ghent Bond Moyson health insurance organisation. In Ghent nineteen such organisations merged into one federation and joined the BWP in 1889. Collection AMSAB, Ghent.

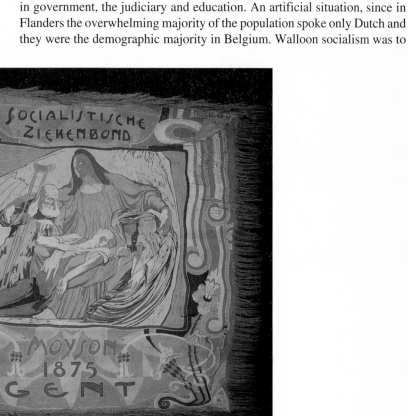

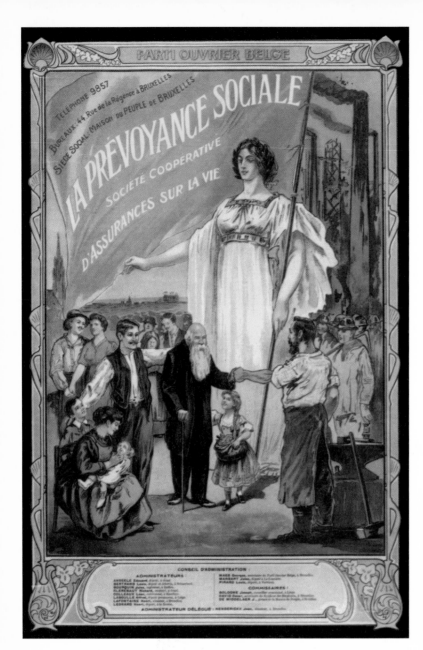

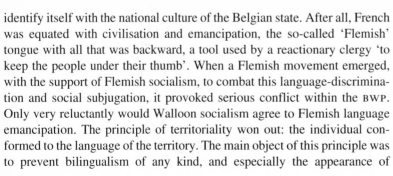

identify itself with the national culture of the Belgian state. After all, French was equated with civilisation and emancipation, the so-called 'Flemish' tongue with all that was backward, a tool used by a reactionary clergy 'to keep the people under their thumb'. When a Flemish movement emerged, with the support of Flemish socialism, to combat this language-discrimination and social subjugation, it provoked serious conflict within the BWP. Only very reluctantly would Walloon socialism agree to Flemish language emancipation. The principle of territoriality won out: the individual conformed to the language of the territory. The main object of this principle was to prevent bilingualism of any kind, and especially the appearance of

Flemish minorities with language rights in Wallonia. This option resulted in the development of a language-frontier dividing Flanders and Wallonia.

Walloon discontent and Flemish socialism

A 1952 BSP poster, calling on people to join the party. Collection AMSAB, Ghent.

Walloon socialism's dissatisfaction with the unitary structure first manifested itself in 1912, when following defeat at the polls (especially in Flanders) Jules Destrée threatened administrative partition. Three significant frustrations came to the surface: universal multiple franchise robbed the socialists of what was rightfully theirs, in socio-economic terms there was a sense of being ignored by the Flemish-Catholic government, and in cultural terms the rise of Dutch as a rival official language meant the loss of power and jobs. The Walloon socialists began to take over the leadership of the Walloon movement. After the First World War the 'one man, one vote' system was very rapidly implemented. It made the socialist party roughly as strong as the Catholic, peaking in 1925 when it won 40% of the national vote. More than ever, a national majority strategy seemed a realistic proposition. Belief in this and participation in coalition governments pushed the federal idea into the background; it even gave way to a unitary Belgian nationalism, which manifested itself strongly after World War I. This was curbed, though, by the establishment's negative attitude to socialist participation in government and the party's electoral decline.

After the Second World War the idea of federalisation gained new impetus. Wallonia's demographic position as a political minority, which was becoming more and more apparent, gained a new economic dimension with the decline of its heavy industry, starting with the closure of the coal mines. There was also the political fact that the BSP, despite being the majority par-

During the great 1960 - 1961 strike serious riots broke out in the centre of Liège on 6 January 1961. At the end of the day there were over eighty people injured, of whom two died.

ty in Wallonia (46.8%), was again in opposition in the national Parliament. This led to the great strike in the winter of 1960 / 1961, known as 'the strike of the century'. The strike's main base was in Wallonia, where it was led by the populist leader André Renard. Again the army had to be called in. In its declining phase the strike took a federalist turn, assuming the character of a revolt by left-wing Wallonia against central government in Brussels ('*l'Etat Belgo-flamande*') which was seen as financially, economically and politically responsible for Wallonia's decline. The region was now convinced that anti-capitalist structural reforms could only be achieved through federalism. Which meant that it no longer believed in a socialist majority strategy at a national, Belgian, level. The strike failed; but it had profound political consequences. For the next decade governments were based on a Flemish Christian Democrat-Walloon Socialist axis: a formula which, because Belgian unity was so important to the monarchy, was from now on also the king's preference. But the foundations had been laid for further polarisation of the communities. As the economic balance shifted from Wallonia to Flanders, now entering its golden age, Walloon socialists worked strenuously for economic powers to be transferred to the Walloon region, but financed from the centre. Such a regional power-base would enable them, as the strongest party, also to influence Belgian decision-making.

Flemish socialism found itself in a difficult position. It had opposed federalism to avoid becoming a minority in an autonomous 'Catholic' Flanders. Arguing for some kind of cultural autonomy, between the wars the socialists continued to work with the Flemish Movement. Internally, there was growing discontent in the party over the language situation. The break with the Flemish Movement came after the Second World War. With a few exceptions the generation then emerging, who remained in place into the seventies, tended to stay aloof from the Flemish demands to avoid fuelling Walloon federalism. They tried to justify their stance by pointing to the many Flemish Nationalists who had collaborated during the German occupation. However, this approach failed to take account of the way in which Flanders' industrial development was heightening language sensitivity among ever larger groups on the Flemish side.

The split in the socialist party and the process of federalisation

As the relationship between the communities came to dominate the agenda more and more, and people began to tinker at remodelling the unitary state, a clash became inevitable. The first conflict occurred in the BSP's Brussels federation. When during the 1968 parliamentary elections Dutch-speaking candidates were relegated to unelectable positions so that the socialists could better compete with an extreme francophone party (the FDF), the result was political discord and the splitting of the Brussels federation. This heralded the split in the party itself, again after a period in opposition from 1974 to 1977. During the subsequent inter-community negotiations a new generation of Flemish socialists, led by co-chairman Karel Van Miert, began to take a more specifically Flemish stance and wanted to develop more confederal party structures, while also seeking a more modern social

democracy; and in 1978 the Walloon chairman André Cools severed the party's unitary connection. The BSP's defensive strategy, which in practice restricted both its wings, had proved untenable. Meanwhile, the party had lost ground; from its highest post-war electoral result, 37.3% in 1954, it had dropped to 25.4% in 1978: from 28.7% to 21.4% in Flanders, from 48.2% to 36.7% in Wallonia, from 45.1% to 16.2% in Brussels.

The constitutional reforms of 1988 and 1993, building on the foundations laid in 1970 and 1980, have transformed Belgium from a unitary to a federal state. What now exists is a party confederalism, with each party having electoral responsibility only in its own part of the country. In Wallonia, helped by the resurgence of Walloon nationalism, the PS succeeded in retaining a very strong position and so exerting an influence at the national level. De-industrialisation continued, leading to high unemployment (twice as high as in Flanders). At first this could be blamed on asset-stripping by finance capitalists. Now, a couple of decades on, questions are being asked about the PS's political responsibility regarding the restructuring programme and the use made of hundreds of billions of francs. Had it not, from an out-dated vision of state intervention, sought first and foremost to safeguard its power-structure and patronage? It is striking that within the PS too the regionalists gained the upper hand: those who wish to expand Wallonia into a Walloon nation by transferring cultural authority from the French Community in Belgium (Wallonia and francophone Brussels) to Wallonia. This would round out the political and socio-economic project by creating a greater sense of cultural solidarity. It would stimulate the Walloon sense of identity, thus helping achieve the transition to the post-industrial age. Meanwhile, a francophone-Walloon alliance appeals to Belgian solidarity to safeguard the considerable financial transfers from Flanders.

The process of modernisation brought profound changes to Flanders. By the mid-sixties it had become the strongest region economically, enjoying exceptional prosperity. At the same time the decline of the Christian Democrats, whose vote fell by more than half, meant that the Flemish socialists no longer faced the spectre of becoming a minority group in a state dominated by the CVP (*Christelijke Volkspartij* ; Christian People's Party). The SP followed its own line, among other things in Foreign Affairs, Defence and the former colony of Zaire (now again the Congo). It cooperated in developing the Flemish Parliament. It is divided, however, on the further federal development of the state. One group, like the majority in the Flemish parliament, wants to shift the institutional centre of gravity further towards the member states, though it would retain structural and financial solidarity with Wallonia. Its aim is efficient government: each region, having its own perspective, would be better able to deal with its own problems in a context of economic globalisation. A neo-Belgian group prefers the status quo, including maximum possible funding from federal government. In this the group is closer to the PS and the position of the trade unions and health insurance providers. Faced with the considerable political fragmentation in Flanders, the success of the Greens and its own political decline, in 1996 the SP attempted to launch a radical-democratic plan which was to lay the groundwork for a broad progressive regrouping; so far this has met with little success.

Indeed, the whole socialist movement is showing signs of crisis. A child

A 1978 PS campaign poster: '*Building the future of Wallonia with the socialists*'. Collection IEV, Brussels.

Karel van Miert as SP chairman in 1984. Van Miert later served as a EU commissioner.

of the industrial age, in the sixties its ideological dogmatism and pillarised networks meant that it was not attuned to the new movements in society: the emancipation of women, youth protest and the environmental movement. Thanks to the welfare state which the socialists had fought for, the sense of collective oppression has greatly diminished; a sizeable proportion of the great-grandchildren of the nineteenth-century workers now belong to the 'new middle class'. This individualistic new generation rejects authoritarian, paternalistic organisations and traditional establishment values. Political depillarisation is proceeding at a faster pace. Moreover, with the switch to a post-industrial society the industrial base is shrinking and the social model based on it has to be modified accordingly. Finally, the liberalisation of the market meant that state monopolies lost their meaning. In Belgium, meanwhile, the Agusta-Dassault scandal (backhanders to the socialist parties in connection with arms purchases) and the dioxin crisis in the pig, cattle and poultry sectors (while the socialist parties participated in government) also exacted their toll in the elections of June 1999. The SP fell to a historical low of 15% in Flanders, barely managing fourth place. It had lost much of its traditional support to the far right, while the better-educated voted for the Greens. In Wallonia the PS also dropped to below 30% and its lead as the largest party was greatly reduced. Whether the two Social Democratic parties will continue to exert an influence consequently depends very largely on how far they can modernise themselves.

Blair's 'Third Way'? Yes, but...

This is the same challenge as is faced by all Europe's Social Democratic parties as they seek to adapt to globalisation and the communications revolution, with the aim of creating a new European social and economic model focused on employment and a modern welfare state. In electoral terms, this means they must break through to the centre groups. There is also a growing consensus regarding the scheme for an 'active welfare state'. True, this project is not free of ideological confusion. On the one hand, its rhetoric is modified to fit each country's realities. On the other, it is still largely a matter of pragmatic-dynamic planning aimed at producing practical policies in which many parties can recognise themselves.

This is why after the latest elections in Belgium Tony Blair's ideas on the 'third way' and the 'active welfare state' helped bridge the ideological gulf between liberals and socialists. In July 1999, for the first time since 1954-1958, a liberal-socialist government came into being, a 'purple coalition' after the Dutch model, albeit with Green Party participation. Along with a number of convergences and introducing the concept of the 'active welfare state', the present SP minister Frank Vandenbroucke also saw some weaknesses in the construction of Blair's 'third way'. Social investment (education, training) as a means of reintegrating semi- and unskilled workers, in particular, into the labour market must not be seen as replacing social expenditure (benefits) but as supplementing it. Additionally, a macro-economic policy is necessary, as a response to the europeanisation of European economies. This presupposes a European economic authority as a reference-point for the Central Bank and, among other things, fiscal coordination, supplemented by forms of organised social consultation between employers and employees at a European level.

A further difference from the British situation is that the SP has already been in government for over a decade and has been involved in crisis management. Self-examination led the party to conclude that it had confined itself too much to defending social gains, had thereby acquired a conservative image and no longer seemed to have a critical offensive theory of change. This has meant renewed talk of the importance of internal and external communication strategies (the 'spin doctors'), of reaching new target groups and the concept of the active welfare state. The government must ensure a rising level of employment by eliminating from the social system mechanisms which discourage working (the so-called 'unemployment traps') and by providing stimuli (reduced labour costs, work experience) to steer the unskilled, in particular, into the working community. Central to this are equal opportunity and social justice, with regard for self-respect and well-being. This is tied up with a socialism of values, of rights and duties (Blair again), an ethic of citizenship and personal responsibility which applies also to the rich. This topic, so it is said, like the problems of crime and public safety, can no longer be left to the right-wing parties.

However, according to Karel Van Miert, ex-chairman of the SP and former EU commissioner, the debate on the Third Way obscures the deeper issue of whether, with the huge increase in company size, the evolutionary trend is still towards a free market economy. Above all, is there not a need, he asks, for a 'Competition Authority' to ensure that the market-economy game is played according to the rules, and to provide a framework for this.

HARRY VAN VELTHOVEN
Translated by Tanis Guest.

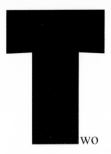

Two

Tales of a City

Ghent, Tale No. 1: A Mind of its Own

Emperor Charles v was born in Ghent on 24 February 1500. 500 years later the people of this Flemish city wish to commemorate this event, though they have no desire to celebrate it. Their memories of this Emperor are predominantly unpleasant ones. He occupied the city when in 1539 Ghent refused to continue paying the high taxes imposed by the ruler in order to finance his campaigns. He abolished the traditional mid-Lent procession and the centuries-old privileges of the crafts guilds. He decided to execute the chief insurgents, obliged the prominent citizens to come with bare feet to beg forgiveness, and had fifty of the most vociferous protesters parade in their undershirts, with a hangman's rope round their necks. This was his way of making it clear to them that they had deserved to be sent to the gallows (later on the people of Ghent adopted the honorary title of 'noose-wearers', in commemoration of this). In addition, he removed all political autonomy from Ghent and had the abbey of St Bavo turned into a fortress. Finally, it was during his rule that the bloody persecution of the Protestants was instigated. Historians take a somewhat kinder view of the Emperor's actions; but they cannot alter the fact that the people of Ghent would rather use Emperor Charles' Year to treat themselves to a festive end to the millennium, and at the same time give more publicity to the attractions of their city.

The annual procession of 'noose-wearers' leaving the Castle of the Counts in Ghent. The procession recalls Charles' punishments of the rebellious city in 1540, when its officials were forced to appear before the Emperor bare-footed, in their undershirts and with nooses around their necks.

From worsted to cotton

In the late Middle Ages Ghent, which grew up at the confluence of the Scheldt and its tributary the Leie, was one of the most important cities in Western Europe. Its inhabitants numbered 65,000. That was only slightly fewer than Paris, and far more than London. Its prosperity rested on three pillars.

In the first place Ghent had developed into an important centre for the production of high quality worsted. The wool came from England. Specifically in order to safeguard the supply of this raw material, in 1340 the city's leader, Jacob Van Artevelde, concluded a treaty with the King of England against the latter's enemy in France. On the Friday Market in Ghent

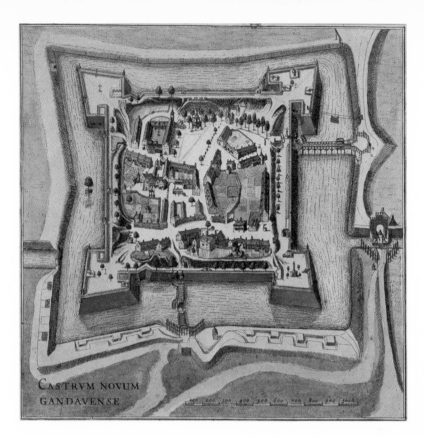

Coloured engraving after Sanderus' drawing of the Spaniards Castle, which Charles v had built on the site of the abbey of St Bavo. Stadsarchief, Ghent (Atlas Goetghebuer).

Miniature showing an armed scuffle on the Friday Market. In the 14th century it was not unusual to settle social conflicts and private grudges in a violent manner. Wells-next-the-Sea, Norfolk, Ms. 695F.

homage was even paid to Edward III as . . . King of France. When in the second half of the nineteenth century the young state of Belgium went looking for historical heroes, Artevelde was one of their romantic discoveries. That is how Ghent got the title of 'Artevelde City'.

Furthermore, in the Middle Ages the skippers of Ghent held the monopoly on the Scheldt and the Leie, which meant they controlled shipping in the entire county of Flanders. Finally, the people of Ghent had introduced the grain staple. This meant that every ship carrying grain that passed through Ghent must deposit part of its cargo there. By this means they ensured that the city was never without the necessary quantity of grain to feed its abundant population.

From the sixteenth century onwards things did not go so well for Ghent, as the three pillars of its prosperity came increasingly under attack. However, from 1750 on the city experienced an economic resurgence, and in the course of the nineteenth century Ghent developed into the most important centre of industrial growth in Flanders. On account of the dominance of the textile industry, concentrating on the processing of cotton and flax, people even referred to it as the Manchester of the Continent. Industrial expansion took over the last remaining building land within the sixteenth-century city walls. The gardens of existing properties were frequently commandeered to build the necessary housing for workers. Expansion outside the city walls was difficult, because the city council imposed taxes at the city gates on the import and export of goods.

When in 1860 the Belgian government did away with all municipal tariff barriers, a process of suburbanisation was begun which is still continuing to this day. The medieval harbour in the heart of the city was reduced to a harbour for inland shipping. An industrial harbour was developed to the north of the city, round the end of the canal that connects Ghent to the Scheldt in Terneuzen. Moreover the industrialists preferred the sites to the north of the city, because they needed the harbour for the import and export of their products. New workers' areas rose up among their factories, always with a minimum of public services and poor quality housing. This expansion rolled further out towards the boroughs to the east and south-east of the city.

The first train in Ghent in 1837. A railway station was erected on this site in 1850, but was demolished in the 1930s to make room for Zuid Park. Stadsarchief, Ghent (Atlas Goetghebuer).

House of the 'Tied Skippers' on Korenlei (1740).

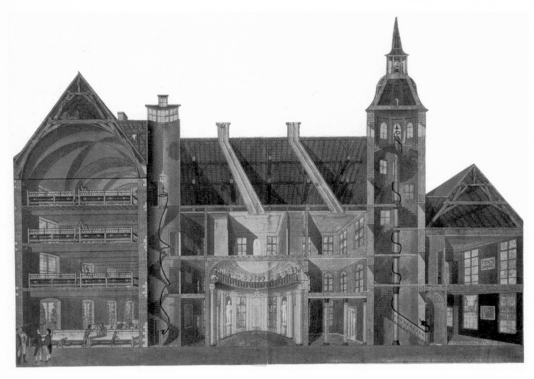

In these proletarian areas a strong socialist movement developed under the leadership of the charismatic tribune of the people, Edward Anseele, better known as '*Vader Anseele*' ('Father Anseele'). He was particularly concerned with the expansion of the cooperative movement, which was active not only in the distribution sector but also in the production sector, under the name of '*Moeder Vooruit*' ('Mother Forwards').

In the south of the city military defence works initially hindered expansion. The citadel, built after the battle of Waterloo, did not disappear until the end of the last century. The city council allocated the land to a park surrounded by middle-class streets. After the First World War the city expanded further to the south, with housing for those in higher income brackets. One of these areas is still called the Miljoenenkwartier (Millionaires' District). Eventually the villa builders got hold of the picturesque village of Sint-Martens-Latem (also: Laethem-Saint Martin), where up to that time the Flemish Expressionists (the Laethem School) had sought and found inspiration in the rural peace of the Leie landscape and its inhabitants. This north-south polarisation within the city of Ghent still exists today; in a lower-class district such as Voormuide the average income is three times lower than in a more chic area in Sint-Denijs-Westrem.

Inexorable exodus

The expansion beyond the city walls lessened the pressure on space in the centre. Thus the medieval patterns were preserved for the most part. The only completely new district to be built by the city government was around 1885 in the area between the station (demolished in the 1930s and now King Albert's or Zuid Park) and the cathedral of St Bavo – a new district with handsome middle-class houses and wide streets. After the Second World

Lieven Bauwens' cotton spinning mill in Ghent, 1808.

Cité ouvrière (working-class neighbourhood) at Blandijnberg, 1929. AMSAB, Ghent.

War the city centre lost its appeal as a residential area. The new generation dreamed of comfortable houses with gardens and garages. Such a thing was not to be found in old Ghent. An inexorable exodus from the city began. Crumbling buildings, often nonetheless of historical value, had to make way for architecturally worthless blocks of flats. These provided a solution only for older inhabitants and thus contributed to the ageing of the population. In past decades the population has declined every year by at least a further 1,000 inhabitants. Ghent now has 225,000 citizens, and so remains the third largest city in Belgium, after Brussels and Antwerp. The elderly outnumber the young by 15%.

The high figures for exodus and ageing are kept down by the immigrants (mainly of Turkish origin) who have come to live in the inner city with their relatively large families. Officially Ghent has 8% of people of other nationalities and that is decidedly less than Brussels and Antwerp. The true number of people of other ethnic origin is higher, because in recent years a great many people of other nationalities, and their children, have taken Belgian nationality.

In spite of the declining population the city centre has had to deal with increasing traffic problems. These inhabitants who had moved to the green outskirts continued to come back to take their children to school, to go to work or for shopping. The medieval streets were definitely not suitable for the influx of the Automobile, and even the wider streets of the last century were soon to appear too small. The construction of a motorway entry and exit in the heart of the city merely exacerbated the problems.

From the end of the 1970s a new wind began to blow through the city hall. There came an end to the laissez-faire politics of town planning. In the first place more attention was paid to heritage buildings. Various restoration works were started, which took care of clearing up a few dilapidated patches in the city's fabric. In the case of large buildings, such as the city hall or the church of St Nicholas, it is naturally a matter of long-term work, the 'final touch' of which we shall only be able to admire in the course of the twenty-first century. In addition the city authorities produced action-plans, aimed at bringing new life into a couple of neglected medieval neighbourhoods. In the Patershol, a district in the shadow of the Gravensteen, once a castle of the Counts of Flanders, the good intentions still failed to prevent the renovated streets from being taken over by restaurants. The restoration of the residential function was more successful in the Prinsenhof, the district around the Burgundian court where Emperor Charles was born. The little houses of the St Elizabeth beguinage seemed suddenly very much in demand.

From the beginning of the nineties the municipality's main concern has been with the densely populated district of the 'nineteenth-century girdle' round the old centre. This is home to many people on limited incomes, socially deprived people, and above all immigrants. In these districts you find an accumulation of social problems: few public amenities and a lot of unhealthy housing, a low level of education and a high level of unemployment, tensions between the indigenous and non-indigenous life-styles. Both the municipality and the social housing associations are investing millions in order to put up new houses and improve existing properties. Schools are being given extra staff. Community centres are appearing, with community workers who are trying to encourage cohesion among the inhabitants and some input from them. With generous government subsidies, social workers are setting up programmes to encourage the integration of immigrants, albeit with respect for their own culture. Other initiatives offer opportunities for retraining and reabsorption into the normal labour market. The results are clearly to be seen. The problem districts look totally different from how they were ten years ago. Many of the immigrants, particularly those of the younger generation, speak better Dutch than their native-speaker neighbours, who know only the Ghent dialect. The ambitious ones are pushing through to university and higher education, so that gradually there are lawyers and doctors of other ethnic origin obtaining their degrees. The number of non-indigenous tradespeople is growing, and they are also getting a lot of regular indigenous customers, on account of their low prices.

However, the great efforts the authorities are making to improve the quality of life in the nineteenth-century girdle are grist to the mill of the Vlaams Blok, a right-wing nationalistic party which, under the slogan of 'Our own people first', challenges the fact that they are spending so much money on immigrants and doing far less for the 'ordinary' people of Ghent, and persistently fights against evolution towards a multicultural society. In the local elections of October 1994, the party won 13% of the votes. In the parliamentary elections of June 1999 its score increased to 20%. The traditional political parties await the result of the October 2000 local elections with great trepidation, all the more because the massive influx of refugees from Eastern Europe has already led to a rekindling of the delicate debate on hospitality and security.

The Rozier buildings of the
Faculty of Sciences of
Ghent university, c.1900.

Restricting car traffic in the inner city is an equally sensitive issue. A first
attempt to contain the flow of traffic by only allowing vehicles to drive
through the centre in one-way loops fell to the black flags of the protesting
traders. Thereupon the municipality decided first to build a series of car-
parks. Only when these were ready did they dare to introduce a traffic plan
which would drastically curtail traffic in the centre. At the same time various measures were taken to stimulate cycle traffic. The Mayor, aldermen
and senior city officials are regularly to be seen on their bicycles. Now one
needs a special permit to drive a car into the city centre. Other drivers are directed to a small ring-road, along which are a number of multi-storey car
parks. Electronic signs at the roadside indicate the number of vacant spaces
in these parks.

At work

The economy of Ghent is in a fairly healthy state. Employment is increasing, mainly in the service sector. Here the proportion is slowly approaching
70%, while employment in industry has fallen to 30%. The 'white collars'
have superseded the 'blue collars'. Unemployment is slightly over 10%.
This figure is comparable to Antwerp, but better than Brussels and the large
cities of Wallonia. However, it is disturbing that half of these are long-term
unemployed. Equally disconcerting is the fact that there is more than 20 percent unemployment among people of other nationalities and young people.
These are mainly people with a low level of education.

A truck on Graslei in the
late 1970s. The lettering
says: 'Ghent flowers
throughout Europe'. The
high-quality floriculture of
the Ghent area still enjoys
international fame.
Photo by Paul van den
Abeele.

That is surprising when one considers that education is the largest employer in the service sector. Ghent is a veritable city of Academe. The university boasts more than 20,000 students, with a further 25,000 in the poly-
technics. Because the principal campuses are situated within the town, these
students give Ghent a youthful appearance, both during the day and in the
evenings. The presence of the university, with its internationally famous de-
partments of biotechnology, led to the establishment of businesses that try
to valorise the results of research. Plant Genetic Systems and Innogenetics

have already become firms of world renown. To the south of the city people even want to expand an entire industry park into a *Biotech Valley*.

In 1983 Ghent hosted Flanders' first Technology Fair. Flanders Technology International was launched as a forum for advanced technology talent in Flanders and a place where scientists and businessmen could meet. Public interest was so great that the initiative subsequently evolved into an exhibition designed to present science and technology to a wider audience. Since interest in the Fair has declined over the last few years, in 2002 there will be an exhibition which under the title *Flanders Valley 2002* will provide an overview of innovative research in Flanders' Technology Valleys.

To provide a fitting home for Flanders Technology International a new exhibition complex was built on the site of a disused airfield; as well as all manner of exhibitions this also regularly resounds to pop concerts. In the Spring of 2000 the halls of Flanders Expo housed the 32nd Floralies, a vast exhibition held every five years to draw international attention to the high-quality floriculture of the Ghent area (especially its azaleas and begonias).

In addition to an extensive network of banks, insurance companies and firms offering services to business, Ghent is well provided with medical and social services, chief among them the University Hospital. Because Ghent is also the capital of the province of East Flanders, public services are also very well developed. Despite considerable competition from shops outside the city, which are easy to reach by car and have generous parking, the centre remains an attractive place for shopping for the entire region. On a Saturday in Veldstraat, the main shopping street, you can hardly move for the crowds.

Industrial activity continues to be important. After the textile industry had almost disappeared from the Artevelde City following the Second World War, because it could no longer compete with low-wage countries, the extension of Ghent's harbour was mainly responsible for the creation of new employment in the industrial sector. Ghent is connected to the sea via Terneuzen, and from 1968 has been accessible to ships of up to 60-70,000 tons. 24 million tons of goods annually are imported into, or exported from, Ghent in ocean-going vessels. In recent years there has been an attempt to diversify, in order to reduce dependence on the variable fortunes in certain sectors. A handful of major companies are located in the canal zone. Sidmar manufactures steel plate, which is used mainly in the car industry. Volvo assembles both cars and lorries. Honda has moved its distribution centre for Western Europe to Ghent. The right bank of the canal zone has ready access to the E17 and E40 motorways which intersect in Ghent.

Alive – and kicking

Tourism has developed into a flourishing sector. Although the city can pride itself on the *Adoration of the Lamb*, the world-renowned triptych by the Van Eyck brothers, and the splendid view from St Michael's bridge is mentioned as a must in every tourist guide, for years Ghent was merely a stop-off for tourists on the way from Antwerp (or Brussels) to Bruges. That has changed in recent years, partly thanks to the building of new hotels. Even the city hall is flanked by representatives of two international hotel chains.

Ghent probably derives much of its charisma from its abundance of cultural activities, on account of which the city even dares to call itself the cultural capital of Flanders. For years it has played a leading role in the Festival of Flanders, inaugurated by the Ghent professor, Jan Briers, which every autumn brings to Flanders an impressive list of famous orchestras and soloists. Ghent also provides the location for the International Film Festival, which the Ghent film enthusiast, Jacques Dubrulle, succeeded in developing into an event of international acclaim.

Ghent has a variety of museums, small and large. The SMAK, alias the Stedelijk Museum voor Actuele Kunst (Municipal Museum of Current Art), under the direction of the flamboyant personality of Jan Hoet, is undoubtedly the one which has attracted most attention in recent years, but the more classical Museum of Fine Arts, or the Museum for Industrial Archaeology and Textiles both have fine collections.

There are also ten or so smaller halls to be found in Ghent where people regularly bring traditional productions and also try out newer forms of stage art. The Flanders Opera plays in a restored heritage building dating from the middle of the previous century. One of the most active organisations is the Vooruit Art Centre, housed in the imposing Feestpaleis (Festival Palace) built by the Ghent socialists just before the First World War.

The annual Ghent Festivals have been loudly acclaimed in Belgium and in the Netherlands. These are ten-day summer festivals with street theatre, public concerts, theatre productions, exhibitions and markets, at which the hotel and catering industry sees to it that visitors do not die of thirst or starvation.

In a word, Ghent is alive and kicking. Charles V could be proud of the city of his birth. But the reverse cannot be said. At the beginning of the Emperor Charles Year a memorial plaque was unveiled at the Donkere Poort (Dark Gate) in the Prinsenhof, his birthplace; it bears the names of 56 citizens of Ghent who, having been accused of Protestantism, lost their lives under his rule. The contrary-minded citizens responsible have ordered the names methodically: beheaded, burned, buried alive...

The Castle of the Counts in Ghent.

DANIËL VANACKER
Translated by Sheila M. Dale.

http://www.gent.be

wo

Tales of a City

Ghent, Tale No. 2: Clouds – Home

I cannot write about my own city; it is little more than *clouds – home*. Yet from the window where I write I see it lying like a faded postcard, but life-sized, so that the postcard becomes the world: the stubby tower of St Michael's, that never acquired its spire because the fifteenth-century parishes, in endless competition with each other, ran out of funds; the battlements of the eleventh-century fortress, the Castle of the Counts, behind the uniformly grey roofs of a renovated former monastery; at hardly any distance the steep roof of a 1607 chapel and, when I reach the highest point of the house, behind the chapel appear the three high towers that are said to be so distinctive that they are praised in American tourist brochures as a '*medieval Manhattan*' – so all one sees is history, the flags of Ghent, Flanders and Belgium meaningless at half-mast on a rainy day above the castle, in all weathers, against the clouds, against home.

Bart Verschaffel wrote an essay on this city that I found superb, in which he

The Castle of the Counts, c.1860: note the factory chimney inside the at that time not yet renovated fortress. MIAT, Ghent.

puts the impossibility of characterising Ghent into an historical perspective, even in actual spatial terms. He says it is a city that has not grown out of a fullness, a being too full, but out of an empty space – originally this was probably the space where the Rivers Scheldt and Leie merged, and centuries later the over-spacious area within the new city walls. With the keen eyes of someone who is not at home here, but has just come to astonish himself and to take note of things, Verschaffel points out to what extent this city is built out of empty spaces, that its cohesion is in fact no more than a clinging together, an *Aufeinanderfolge* that allows no centralisation, and from which the average Ghent inhabitant seems to have learned his indifferent tolerance.

In the same way as Belgium produces inhabitants who see things in relative terms and only half identify with their state, Ghent has produced citizens who see things even more relatively (of course I don't mean this is a fundamentalist quality, but an acquired habit, a cultural sphere, an attitude that has arisen from living together in a particular place).

Ghent Gothic 'reserve'. Photo by Paul van den Abeele.

Ghent has always been a bilingual city, because its upper classes spoke French and Ghent dialect. Later, from about 1930, the dialect was replaced among these upper-class citizens by 'proper Flemish', which they were shocked to find was still incomprehensible to the Dutch; later still, in the sixties, this gave way to 'ABN' (*'Algemeen Beschaafd Nederlands'*; 'civilised Dutch'), which because of the horribly grating and gurgling accent the average Ghent speaker gave to the Dutch language, and to their great horror, was still called a dialect by their northern cousins. To this very day the youngsters at Ghent's secondary schools are proud of their absolutely unbearable gibberish, a mixture of 'suburban Flemish' and Ghent dialect – fashionable, deliberately finicky mannerisms and pep talk, the pleasure of using which increases in proportion to the irritation it causes. For this reason Ghent people to some extent always remain naturalists of the old school: their *'vree wijs'* ('really cool') dialect is their certificate of rebelliousness, their signal to the world that they will still not let themselves be subdued – formerly this may have been an heroic attitude, but now it is only the un-

Ghent author Raymond de Kremer, who wrote in French as 'Jean Ray' and in Dutch as 'John Flanders'. This is the cover of the 1970 Dutch translation by Hubert Lampo of his French-language novel *Malpertuis* (1943).

mistakable mark of provincialism, the passionate hobby of people who, at the end of the century, feel that boundaries everywhere are fading and fear that the differences that gave them their identity will rapidly disappear.

Ghent people have a predilection for secrecy, in sharp contrast to the first impression they give of big-talking cordiality. Ghent author Jean Ray, who wrote in French and whose *Œuvres complètes* were published in Paris in the sixties, wrote a novel entitled *Malpertuis* which became well-known internationally, in which the dying, haunting remnants of the Greek gods terrorise and torment the occupiers of a typically sombre mansion such as can still be found in Ghent. A house like this, with dark nooks and crannies, with secrets that appear only very gradually from behind the peeling plaster, seems the perfect biotope for citizens who have learnt to combine sociability and secrecy. But of course it is also recognisably the setting for the symbolist epoch. It is perhaps no coincidence that it was precisely then that the city enjoyed a literary heyday.

It may well be that the penchant for reserve is more logical in a city whose identity developed in the gothic age than in one that grew up during the Baroque. Antwerp's extroversion is reflected in its baroque heritage, its facades and broad, straight avenues. Ghent's reserve is equally reflected in the labyrinthine street pattern and the close, intimate atmosphere of the old neighbourhoods that were built in the fifteenth and sixteenth centuries. It is clear to anyone standing in St Bavo's Cathedral what Baroque was later able to do with the spirit of a gothic city: the old, stylish and restrained Flemish Gothic was in later centuries submerged under masses of exuberant marble, which was intended to demonstrate the emancipation and assertiveness of the citizens at the dawn of the modern age. Squashed between historical reserve and emancipatory boastfulness lies an area that's hard to define, which combines provincialism with a certain worldly disdain for the outside world.

    'Ghent has had a rough time under every form of dominion: kings and emperors, Catholicism, Belgianism and capitalism. But its rebellious response may have more to do with a distrustful, stubborn resistance to everything open and foreign than with pride and the urge for freedom.' – Bart Verschaffel.

One of the bromides regarding Ghent is that it is located not only literally but also figuratively between Bruges and Antwerp: a gothic city with the occasional minor historical modification by the Baroque. However, it does not have a town plan that has torn open its streets, and in the historical centre nothing has been widened, there are no major nineteenth-century building projects to be seen such as those by Hausmann in Paris and Emperor Franz Josef in Vienna, nor has any self-confident main street been built as in Antwerp: just this continuing withdrawn life within a chaotic, historically evolved logic-free street pattern, the bane of the car-driving tourist and only questionably offering protection to the inhabitants, now the cars are gradually beginning to give up roaring through the narrowest streets as if they were driving along a boulevard in a metropolis. The medieval organisation of the space is exposed for all to see. Now, all at once, tourism presents them as a fetish: the splendid sixteenth and seventeenth-century buildings, the

'Au quai du grand Marais', a part of Ghent which has disappeared.

Children playing on Vlaamse Kaai. Between 1894 and 1902 the architect J.G. Semey built a number of picturesque houses along this quay. Each house was dedicated to a Flemish artist. Most of these houses were demolished to build a ring-road. Stedelijke Commissie voor Monumenten en Stadsgezichten, Ghent.

few eighteenth-century mansions that are still intact, the spacious nineteenth-century buildings, deceptively discreet from the outside, but also those typical alleys of the textile-working proletariat that have survived the building acts, the unsightly squares in the bend of a connecting street. Now it has been completely restored, the gothic seclusion of the narrow streets in the late-medieval Patershol has been actively stripped of any historical individuality by its staging of itself as an historical setting, by the smell of roasting that rises from the ludicrous accumulation of restaurants and bistros, frantically raking in whatever can be extracted from the casual passing tourist, as if this were a remote spot where one had to hoard things for the winter. In this neighbourhood, where the alternative generation is starting to become financially secure, the only exoticism is by now probably to be found among the better-integrated immigrants. Unlike other cities, the immigrant population has not ended up in a ghetto, but has to a certain extent integrated itself into small-scale retailing, carpet sales, catering and small, self-supporting building firms. This is probably the only way to stand up to the still menacing power of such extremist groups as the Grey Wolves. Immigrants often have an identifiable place there, most of them speak decent suburban Flemish and make jokes about the somewhat uncomfortable native Belgian who comes into their shop for the first time.

In a Moroccan greengrocer's I saw a Ghent woman scold her two-year-old child and give it a good smack. The Moroccan saleswoman, a self-confident woman wearing elegant North-African clothes and a *chador*, stepped in and in perfectly articulated Flemish said that *'you won't achieve much like that, a little diplomacy works better'*. She smiled broadly and affably at the astounded working-class woman who could only speak the coarse dialect, not 'proper Flemish' like the self-assured Moroccan woman. On another occasion, in a Tunisian butcher's, I heard an old middle-class Ghent woman complaining, in French, that the butcher's assistant had addressed her in Dutch. *'C'est encore plus bizarre ça, il parle flamand!'* she exclaimed indignantly. When I responded to her in French that the boy was simply well integrated and was speaking the national language, and that it was called Dutch and not Flemish, I got a good pasting myself: *'Vous êtes quand-même tous des gens fanatiques vous.'* The Tunisian butcher winked at me and laughed. But I don't know whether the man realised that the two people standing in front of him were both born and bred in Ghent, though one of them thought she did not belong to the same culture as the other.

The few broad avenues built on the outskirts in the nineteenth century were swallowed up by the ring-road in the brusque functionalism of the sixties. The handsome *'burgershuizen'* (middle-class houses) – which in Ghent are different from *'herenhuizen'* (mansions), being one category smaller, but also fitted with marble chimneypieces and fine wooden floors – have for a generation languished, abandoned and decaying, as a result of the devastating hold the car has on the city. The lofty rows of trees in front of the

The Coupure at the start of the 19th century. As well as an important economic artery, the Coupure was also a popular scenic promenade for the people of Ghent. Stadsarchief, Ghent (Atlas Goethgebuer).

shipowners' houses on the Vlaamse Kaai or the picturesque calm of the then Heirnislaan with its double line of trees have been absorbed into a sort of motorway in the city. All the greenery has gone and the asphalt has been spread as wide as possible – in many places it is now again being made as narrow as possible. For decades architectural objects devoid of context stood with dirty windows and dark soot-encrusted facades. Over recent decades these buildings have in fact been saved by the fact that Ghent is also a university city – of the numerous provincial graduates who stay on in the city when their studies are complete, many have chosen the cheap housing offered by these half-decayed buildings. Now this generation has become affluent, it is repairing the houses on the Coupure canal, which was dug in Napoleon's day, on the big avenues near the municipal park, around the station and in the quiet backstreets, and is fitting them out in accordance with the grammar of its own desires: walls with a southern tinge, simple Italian furniture, polished floorboards and renovated plasterwork. The enterprising alternative and fashionable lifestyle is the only one that has found a feasible answer to nineteenth-century life in these oversized rooms, the light on the courtyards and the echo in the coach-house behind a facade one has walked past without a thought. These big houses had their hardest time in the decades after the Second World War, when there was insufficient capital to maintain them and the functionalism of the sixties disapprovingly passed this sort of architecture by. It was not only Eastern Europe that mistreated its heritage in the sixties as a result of the dogmas of functionalism. In this way part of the urban memory of the middle-class Ghent mentality is even now unexpectedly restored by a contemporary *lifestyle* citizen. Habitation with a sense of history, habitation by '*leaving everything its value*', as Heidegger said, is of course also the indication that a certain world has disappeared.

The penchant for what is characteristic, the modesty of the big hidden houses behind inconspicuous facades, the workshops of the freemasons' lodges and temples that are impossible for the layman to find, the sometimes shocking emptiness of the churches and squares when there are no tourists to give the city any appearance of importance, the way the almost stagnant water slices through the city – all this is sometimes reminiscent of Bruges on a winter's day, but a single event is sufficient to rouse Ghent a little from its provincial lethargy and make it seem like a great city for a while.

This unstable self-image fuels the nervousness of local politics, since every event, however local or trivial, may suddenly go off at a tangent and assume an importance that transcends local politics. The vision, the courage or the critical mind needed to resolve this are usually lacking. The critical minds of provincial cities prefer to become absorbed in their own cleverness rather than in coherent views. It is for this reason that Ghent has often behaved wantonly towards its historical infrastructure, and its urbanisation has been characterised most of all by a highly *à la carte* approach. Politicians who have grasped that the listing of step gables signifies tourist profit are not necessarily therefore convinced that industrial buildings from the thirties deserve preservation too, that open spaces of historical significance do not necessarily have to be filled up, that demographic networks are subtler than the plans of municipal architects, that the constantly grumbling, immorally egocentric retail trade should not hijack debates on urbanisation;

The shopping centre at the Zuid, known to the people of Ghent as the 'Ceauçescu Palace'. The statue of socialist leader 'Father Anseele' shows the way. Dienst Toerisme, Ghent.

that buildings that now appear worthless may in twenty years' time be of great sociological value, and that in ten years neighbourhoods given up by the politicians are able, of themselves, to develop a new demographic fabric which no one could have predicted. It is a fact that the combination of provincialist urbanisation and the self-esteem of a half-large old city of culture almost always leads to the wrong compromises which please nobody. The umpteenth lamentable example of this was the plan drawn up by a totally uncultured architect to squeeze the valuable old fish market behind a gigantic, already outdated, postmodern display case blazing with artificial light. Fortunately such plans are increasingly thwarted by the actions of inhabitants who still retain some degree of historical awareness.

The urban planners sitting at their drawing boards with their jobs for life do not usually have a clue about the subtle demographic shifts in the urban fabric, they receive these signals too late and immediately convert them into functionalist terms, whereby meaning and 'magic' disappear as soon as they have the idea of 'organising' them into something. Officials who try to get a grasp of urban planning are like children catching butterflies: they are usually left with nothing but a paltry smear of colour on their fingers. Where the attempt *is* made to develop an overall outlook, the projects degenerate into misplaced delusions of grandeur, such as the shopping centre at the Zuid, which the people have rechristened 'the Ceauçescu palace'. No one wanted this building except the developers and the politicians.

At the same time it has to be said that Ghent is the first city in the country to see the rejection of a large-scale project for an underground car park in the historic centre, in a popular referendum exacted by massive petitions. Nor was that achieved, as the press suggested, by a hard core of ecology and left-wing groups. On that day I saw them walking to the polling stations in their best clothes: the elderly, headstrong people of Ghent, who, with heads held high, came to register their vote and declared to anyone prepared to listen that '*them in the town hall shouldn't think they can wreck our town*'. No, they said, and 'no' it was: the required number of votes were cast and the city council had to put its ambitious plan, for which planning permission had already been granted, back in the drawer.

Ghent's former covered cattle market, known to the people under its older name of Beestenmarkt (Animal Market), was a gem of a particular sort of architecture, whose importance was not understood. The complex, once abandoned by the livestock trade, could have been developed as a sort of small Covent Garden, which the surrounding neighbourhoods could have made into a superb meeting place in an organically evolved environment. It was mercilessly demolished and replaced by blocks of housing of a shocking lack of imagination, right next to the roaring traffic of the ring-road. There is not the slightest indication that any reflection on the quality of life or the urban fabric played any part at all in this plan, which has largely robbed a neighbourhood of its centre of gravity and meaning. Where there was once a place that is branded deep into my memory, with its ominous smell of blood and the unforgettable eyes of the waiting cattle next to the red-smeared posts under the successive low roofs, and also with its whole entourage of workers' cafés and lively activity round the sheds, the umpteenth no man's land has now appeared, a contemporary built wasteland concerning which later generations will shake their heads in outrage, just as we do now regarding so many blunders committed in the sixties, that last tasteless repetition of the totalitarian Bauhaus dream. Here too the void behind the housing blocks is conspicuously devoid of meaning, creating a feeling of desolation, a lack of direction, as if one wanted to create a space for a sort of being one did not oneself understand. Being aware of a city means not just protecting the picturesque centre, but also understanding what an intricate urban fabric has, or had, developed on the outskirts too. This has nothing to do with nostalgia – on the contrary, it is part of an efficient civic policy of enabling people to feel at home in centres that have grown through the course of history – that particular nowhere where we feel we are somewhere.

In the meantime the nonconformist element of the younger population has been moving to other parts of the outskirts, the outport with its docks, buildings still empty, big old houses and cheap lofts. There too, in ten years time, the urban planners will undoubtedly pick up on a few of the ideas that the common sense of the residents themselves is already putting into practice in all their simplicity, but without money or the politics of the fine facade.

It is also there, in the enchantment of the emptiness and desolation on a Sunday afternoon, that I sometimes seem to detect the remnant of a smell, a fleeting wisp or flash from the corner of my eye that reminds me of a distant past. Not that this has a value in itself, but it is something that can give value to the smallest of things, a value that had been forgotten.

Now, have I actually said anything about this city? I get the distinct feeling I have said nothing at all, done no more than capture something fleeting. I must have felt very much at home.

STEFAN HERTMANS
Translated by Gregory Ball.

NOTE

The original full version of this essay was published in *Cities. Stories on the Road* (Steden. Verhalen onderweg, Amsterdam / Leuven: Meulenhoff / Kritak, 1998).

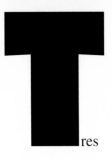res

Fratres Belgae

Brothers, Poets and Civil Servants in the Sixteenth Century

This article is based on an extensive study of the works and lives of Janus Secundus (1511-1536), Adrianus Marius (1509-1568) and Nicolaus Grudius (1504-1470), three brothers who became famous as the '*triga*' , the 'team of three' poet-brothers.[1] For once, I have decided not to stress the fact that one of them, Janus Secundus, ranks among the foremost poets of the world.

Rather, I shall address the position of the three brothers in the bureaucracy and court system of the Burgundian Netherlands, on the occasion of the five-hundredth anniversary of the birth of Charles V, and I have selected for translation the end of the elegy that Secundus wrote at his father's death. It has been my good fortune that Peter Brodie has been willing to translate this fragment into heroic verse.

The generation born during the first decade of the sixteenth century no longer had to fight for humanism. The brothers were able to study in Leuven at the Collegium Trilingue, set up in 1518 in the spirit of Erasmus, where the three sacred languages, Hebrew, Greek, and Latin, were taught according to modern philological principles.[2]

They wrote their poems in Latin and also wrote each other letters almost daily in that language. At home they spoke Dutch and as attorneys and magistrates they could write Dutch and French, but Latin was the only language in which they were able to write down intimate or poetic nuances. Even at the beginning of the next century humanists still felt that poetry in Dutch was unartistic.[3] Secundus is the only famous Dutch poet, because he wrote in Latin. He became famous because of his *Basia*, his 'kisses', but he was also one of the first medallists in the Low Countries.

Humanists may be recognised by the fact that they want to go back to the sources which, in their eyes, became sullied during the Middle Ages. Thus, back to the Bible and the Church Fathers and away from the barbaric Latin of scholastic theologians; back to the *Corpus Juris* and away from the authority of commentators in barbaric Latin; and back to the exemplary poetry of the classic Roman poets.

Linguistically informed research on the sources of Christianity boiled down to the question: Is this the true text, is this the true interpretation, and is this really true? Erasmus too occupied himself with critical editions of the

New Testament and the Church Fathers. All too often the answer, as far as the Vulgate and the Roman Catholic tradition were concerned, had unfortunate consequences for the tradition of the Church. And what in earlier times might have remained restricted to an argument among monks and complaints about corruption now became everybody's business, due to the spread of paper manufacturing and the invention of printing. The result was that heresy could no longer be contained. The critical point was the iconoclasm of 1566. Philip II sent the 'Iron Duke' Alva to the Netherlands with wide-ranging powers. The atmosphere had already turned bitter, certainly after the abdication of Charles V in 1555 when Philip came into power.

The reign of the Archduchess Margaret of Austria, who was the regent of the Netherlands from 1507 until her death, was in retrospect seen as an ideal era. Music, tapestry and the fine arts thrived in line with the Italian Renaissance; the language at her Court in Mechelen was French, her court poet was a Savoyard rhetorician; there were many Dutch-language rhetoricians' associations, and the highest court of justice, the Grand Council, was of course humanistic, as was the Collegium Trilingue in nearby Leuven.

Janus Secundus was born in The Hague, lived in Mechelen, and died at not quite twenty-five years old near Doornik, on a visit to his employer, the Bishop of Utrecht. So, he lived in the yet undivided Netherlands. In those days you were not travelling from one country to another when you went from The Hague to Mechelen.

First, I shall discuss his fame, then his life in connection with his two brothers Grudius and Marius, likewise poets, along with that of their wise older brother Everaart (1497-1561).

At the end of my essay, I shall record a conflict between bureaucracy and court; a conflict that was Grudius' downfall. I am able to do so thanks to some highly personal letters. They seem never to have been intended for publication; they are so disadvantageous to Secundus' and Grudius' ambitions.

I will conclude with the Revolt, insofar as it occurred *libertatis ergo* (*'haec libertatis ergo'* became the motto of the University of Leiden), 'for the freedom' of the old system of government – to which the family was attached, and which was abolished by Alva in 1567. In this liberal vision the Revolt was not caused by religious strife: *religionis ergo*.

The fame of Janus Secundus

Secundus was revered by one of the founders of Leiden University, the hero of the siege, Janus Dousa, who himself had wanted to become another Secundus by writing *Basia*. Dousa cultivated this poetic passion when he was studying in Paris. The French Pleiad poets honoured Janus Secundus by imitating him, alone of the poets north of the Alps. A Janus Secundus conference was held in 1998 in Paris, in which many *seizièmistes*, or sixteenth century scholars, participated. Among the Dutch philologists Harm Jan van Dam presented a paper on Latin Poetry in the Netherlands during the sixteenth century, in which he emphasised the veneration for Secundus in the north as well as the south, but particularly in Leiden.[4] It is very important for the history of Dutch culture that at the foundation of this university, the founders on the rebel side wanted to link themselves to Secundus *and*

Erasmus (they died in the same year, 1536, for its founders only forty years ago). Poetry overcomes religious antitheses. In 1561 the Dutchman Cripius published an edition of Secundus' *Opera* in Paris; a second edition, after the 1541 edition published by Secundus' brother Marius. During the Revolt Cripius chose the Catholic side, and became chancellor of Spanish Guelders. By contrast, one of Everaart's sons, and thus a nephew of Secundus, Aarnout, chose the side of William of Orange even though he remained a Catholic. He continued the family tradition and became the first president of the new Grand Council in The Hague. This Aarnout took along the poetical archives of Marius and Grudius that he had inherited from his father. And so it was that the poems by the two other brothers were published in Leiden.[5] The brothers lived to be old, and practised genres other than love poetry. Secundus was planning to do this as well, but he died too soon. Only his juvenile poetry is left us, including the erotic poems that made him so famous.

How are we supposed to imagine the fame of a love poet in Calvinistic Holland? But Latin love poetry did become a Dutch speciality, along with classical philology. The Calvinist Daniël Heinsius, one of those child prodigies who adorned the University of Leiden at the end of the sixteenth century, and who became a professor of Greek as well as poetry at a very young age, made his poetic debut writing erotic poems. Many philologists followed his lead and it was only around 1800 that complaints were rising that the Dutch were neglecting poetry in the vernacular.

Medal by Janus Secundus, May 1533, with the portrait of Frans van Craneveld, a Christian humanist, as tolerant as his friends Erasmus, Vives and Thomas More.
Stone matrix, 4.9 cm.
Koninklijk Penningkabinet, Leiden.

Loyal to Emperor and King

The brothers' father, Nicolaas Everaarts (1462-1532) was born in Walcheren as a sea-captain's son. He made a career in law. In 1505 he became a councillor at the Mechelen Grand Council, the highest Court of Appeal of the Netherlands, in 1510 president of the Court of Holland in The Hague, and in 1528 president of the Grand Council in Mechelen. He built up a reputation as a great and irreproachable lawyer and governor. His sons followed in his footsteps. Everaart and Marius were equally irreproachable magistrates; but Grudius and Secundus were not. They couldn't stand the fact that with all their erudition, with their great poetic talent, they had to live like poor courtiers.

Let me briefly pursue the careers of four brothers (from a total of eighteen children). In 1523 Everaart became a lawyer at the Court of Holland presided over by his father, and in 1526 he became a councillor at the Court of Friesland. In 1533 he became a councillor at the Grand Council of Mechelen. He returned to the Friesian Court as president, and in 1549 he became president of the Grand Council of Mechelen, as his father had been a quarter of a century earlier.

In 1534 Marius became a lawyer to the Grand Council of Mechelen, in 1540 councillor at the Court of Utrecht, a year later councillor at the High Court, in 1546 chancellor of Gelderland.

In 1526, Grudius became a lawyer to the Court of Holland, in 1532 Secretary under Nicolas de Granvelle, who was in charge of Netherlands affairs. He travelled to Spain with the Court and after his return in 1538 he became Secretary of State and Secretary of the Privy Council. In 1540 he became the Registrar of the Order of the Golden Fleece and Receiver of Subsidies of the province of Brabant. However, he handed over not one cent and was arrested in 1554. He had invested the collected tax money in a failed project to reclaim land from the Zijpe in the North of Holland. He died in 1570 in Venice, destitute and on the run.

Secundus was also trained as a lawyer. He followed Grudius to Spain from where the brothers were sure to return loaded with gold. After a year he got a job as secretary to the Spanish Archbishop Tavera and hoped for a clerical career; he wanted to become the priest and provost of Haarlem! However, he contracted malaria in this to him barren, hot, impoverished, and uncultured country, returned home ill and died of anaemia, the consequence of malaria.

From this brief summary it appears that these middle-class young men (the family was ennobled in 1535) pursued judicial and administrative careers, in the jumble of provincial governments, including the Court of Holland (legislation and administration of the law were not separate), the Subsidies of Brabant, and central Councils, and the summit of such a bureaucratic career, the Grand Council, the highest court of appeal in the country. These civil servants, trained in Roman and ecclesiastical Law before which all are equal, were supposed to serve as a counterweight to the privileges of nobility, clergy, and cities, and so were part of the road to centralism.

Taxes were called 'Beden', 'Quêtes', literally 'Entreaties': the sovereign had to ask for them. And because wars kept getting costlier, the central administration was getting into ever deeper financial trouble, and national bankruptcy threatened more than once.

The watchword 'Haec Libertatis Ergo' means that the Revolt was a protest against the centralism that Alva ultimately wanted to push, including central taxation. And indeed, the Republic of the Seven Provinces later persisted with the old system, as faulty as it was, with their Provincial States, their States General, and their Council of State; and the Dutch are still accustomed to discussing everything along the 'polder model'. In this way the Dutch, unlike the Spanish, escaped absolutism. The Nicolaï family remained loyal to the Emperor and also to King Philip. Grudius bore the title of councillor of Charles v, and Philip kept him on in that capacity, even after his arrest. The family remained loyal to the system. However, Marius ended his career in the Council of Troubles that Alva had instituted, to repress the opposition.

Times had changed halfway through the century, although even in 1567, one year after the iconoclasm, an Italian, Guicciardini, described the Netherlands as an idyllic nation, a 'vera e felice repubblica' ('a true and prosperous republic'), because he encountered everywhere the same 'cività e politia' ('civil and political culture').[6]

Bureaucracy and the Court

Lawyers are bureaucrats and bureaucrats are, in principle, incorruptible. Over and against this stands the royal court, which to us, in principle, is corrupt. The former statement sounds idealistic and the latter cynical; but they are tautologies: the rule of law, as opposed to favours. The Sovereign is the source of all law and therefore stands above it. He dispenses favours and mercy, or the contrary, at his will. A courtier is grateful for the charity the sovereign has been pleased to offer; or else he dreads his capricious wrath.

Medal by Janus Secundus, 1531, with the portrait of Emperor Charles V. Bronze, 4.6 cm. Koninklijke Bibliotheek Albert I, Brussels.

Medal by Janus Secundus, 1530, with the portrait of Nicolas van Busleyden at the age of 24. Disc of boxwood, 6.9 cm. Koninklijke Bibliotheek Albert I, Brussels.

Although of course father Everaarts was appointed President of the Grand Council on his merits, Secundus yet calls his appointment 'a gift' from the Emperor in his poem on his father's death.

Secundus exhibits his courtier mentality in his letters to his brother Everaart when he has his eye on privileges in the form of clerical sinecures. When Secundus has finally been appointed secretary to Archbishop Tavera of Spain, he writes to Everaart on 31 May 1534:

I am going to have a brilliant career and if I behave myself, which I certainly plan to do, I will presently be counted among the foremost of his court. I can imagine all manner of things, whatever you want, due to the friendliness, the culture, the power of my Lord. Besides stipends, favours, and exceptional honours which are not to be slighted, is a hardly indubitable expectation of the most generous privileges for me. For, because he is Cardinal, all the dignities of the church and the privileges that become vacant all through the year wait for his and only his decision, to such an extent that each week he can help one of his people to a handsome amount of loot.

Grudius with his office of Receiver of Subsidies in Brabant ended up entangled in the bureaucracy. As a bureaucrat, he was now under the control of the Auditor's Office (this, too, is an institution we are still familiar with today). However, after his arrest, aside from his legal defence, he also kept appealing to his role as one of King Philip's councillors and to the orders of his lord, which he could not have refused.

It is even the case that after his first arrest Grudius was released by order of the King. When Philip left the country in 1559, Grudius had to flee; his possessions were sold on the street. The States of the province of Brabant still had a claim on him for two hundred thousand guilders, hundreds of millions in today's terms.

I have selected the conclusion of Secundus' elegy on the death of his father in the verse translation by Peter Brodie. I include it in order to show another side of the young poet (he was then twenty-one) than the one of the very well-known *Basia*. He was capable of more, and was planning an epic on the Emperor's victorious expedition to Tunis. He would, had he persevered in his clerical aspirations, certainly have set himself to writing religious poetry, as Grudius did at the end of his life.

Secundus has summoned his father's ghost from Elysium, or paradise, in order to give his political testament to his son. Father Everaarts is introduced as the man who was to make an end to the exploitation of the nobility and the general lawlessness in Holland by introducing Law, which applies equally to all.

Secundus has his father' s speech end in praise of his incorruptibility. He added later (as appears from his manuscript) an encouragement to consider that as his first and foremost legacy. However, at precisely this juncture an inappropriate yearning to become rich had come to possess him; and a bit later Grudius was exposed as a swindler.

Janus Secundus, Fun. 1, lines 145-218
(Englished by Peter Brodie)

My son, sweet comfort of my latest years
(Who, late my care, yet still my care appears –
If blessed Shades can care for mortal things),
What is it that such lamentation brings?
'Tis not my death that should these tears evoke,
But theirs, whom Death has finished at a stroke.
How long the threads that timely Clotho spun
For nascent me – and now my life is done!
(That life whose years unblemished I have passed,
Whose scant remains the dark earth hides at last.)
The rest of me is bound by no small tomb,
But part to airy seats, its regal womb,
Has sped; and part aloft the future sings
On snowy Reputation's plaudent wings.
As life is glossed by toil elaborate,
So virtue glistens, exercised by fate.
For when (and these endeavours I confess,
That thus your wounds may trouble you the less),
My primy youth's achievements set aside,
I took my place of Senatorial pride

One of eight watercolours, copies of oilpaintings made by Gillis Smeyers of Mechelen for the Vestry of the High Court. A summary of the long legend: The subject is derived from the history of the *Troubles of the Low Countries* (Troubles des Pays Bas) by Joachim Hopperus, counsellor in the Great Court. The painter made a great effort to work from authentic portraits. On the occasion of his departure to Spain in 1559 Philip II told the Council among other things that he had appointed Margaret, duchess of Parma, as regent and had charged her with the upkeep and execution of the proclamations of his father in order to maintain the true religion, and to exterminate heresy....

On the representation: The Counsellors sit along the wall, a bit like ancient Roman senators. Above them are the portraits of Emperor Charles V and King Philip II. The King stands on a platform holding a speech. To the left two guards; one of them looks at us and must be the painter himself. Behind him stand: the Duke of Alva, Cardinal Perrenot de Granvelle, the Count of Horne and Viglius, a high ranking friend of the three brothers, assisted by two pages. Before the platform sits a watchdog.

Everaart, the President, is the first in a long line of magistrates (7); the fourth is Van Craneveld (10). Everaart shows that he follows every point of the King's speech with great attention, others make clear that they find what the king says evident, and that they will keep everything in their hearts. The two registrars prove that the speech is based on documents, while a dog keeps an eye on the ordinance books. To the far right two secretaries. Photo courtesy of Stadsarchief, Mechelen.

(The gift of our unvanquished Emperor,
Under whose laws the Belgic towns of yore
And potent peoples bore Submission's yoke,
To worship Justice, Fairness to invoke),
Despatched was I to rule Batavians –
Their savage cities and unbridled clans –
Who, then by bonds of Justice scarce restrained,
The fairest fields with bloody slaughter stained,
Embracing evil in contempt of law,
Mingling uncivil wounds in civil war.
What ills, what disarray did I not sense,
While I the crimes of haughty malcontents
Strove to confound, then finally to free
Innocent beings from rapacity.
With the just gods' and a just Emp'ror's aid,
Their onrush I so resolutely stayed,
By fraud and threat and wicked sword beset,
That I with Justice's brave standards met
Th'opposed host, whose enmity's surcease,
By statute sanctified, engendered peace.
Full eighteen times had Phoebus' cart gone round
Neptune's salt wash and Tellus' orbed ground –
Rare were the remnants of so great an ill –
Since I began to check Batavia's will,
When I was honoured with a task supreme,
To supervise our Senate's mighty scheme
For storied Mechlin, where rich Delus swings
Its saffron tide in swift meanderings,
And temples of the gods the heavens touch,
And chieftains' palaces uprise as much,
And walls ne'er trampled by the hostile throng.
To peoples glad I gave, with lordship strong,
A gentle jurisdiction – this you find,
My son – e'er prompted by an honest mind.
No love, nor hate, nor favour did impress,
Nor fear: money, of things the tyranness,
Oft saw her gift disdained with lofty look,
And from my threshold back her step she took,
Amazed; her mischief now in vain, she wept
That I my own integrity had kept.
So I, to my lord no advisor mute,
The fairest judge to loose a tangled suit,
Amassed no heap of malesuasive pelf;
Amassed instead what's precious in itself,
Which I bequeath – no age may dim its fame:
A stainless reputation and a name.
Let my parts prosper you, and happy live;
Enjoy what time the laws of nature give.
You, too, in time, shall grace the dusty tomb;
Your name, a single ray amid the gloom,

Shall shine in vain, and all our bones shall be
Mindlessly trampled by posterity.
Meanwhile my image shall live on in yours
(A visor of a visor) – who ignores
My prophecies? Whomever would it please
To have my precepts scattered to the breeze?
But if you, too, shall meet a slender fate,
Your labours lauded at a lowly rate,
Be not ashamed, my son, to emulate
A father; let not grasping greed for great
Riches entice you step by step to go
The divers paths of life you do not know;
If to be like your father it should gall
In this one thing – be not alike at all.

J.P. GUÉPIN
Translated by Wanda Boeke.

NOTES

1. *De Drie Dichtende Broers*, Groningen, STYX 2000. The Latin texts are on the Internet: http://www.let.leidenuniv.nl/dutch/Latijn/Drie Broers.html. I thank my good friend Hugo de Schepper for his careful reading of the manuscript.

2. The *Collegium* was financed by Jeroen van Busleyden. Secundus made a medallion of one of his sons.

3. The great philologist and poet, D. Heinsius (1580-1655), gave a speech in 1603 entitled *De Poetis et Eorum Interpretatoribus* on the occasion of his appointment at the age of twenty-three as professor extraordinary of poetry. He starts out by expressing the hope that there are few people among his audience who hate poetry, and even fewer people who throw themselves at the task overly hastily and without erudition. This was directed at the rhetorical poets in Dutch.

4. H.J. van Dam, 'Jean Second et la poésie neolatine du 16e siècle aux Pays Bas'. In: *Cahiers de l'Humanisme*, 2000, in which the other contributions to the conference have also been published.

5. By B. Vulcanius, Professor of Greek, who added one poem by Secundus to the collected poems by Grudius and Marius in order to give the book the title of *Poemata et Effigies Trium Fratrum Belgarum...* (Leiden, 1612). This edition is rare, but most of the poems written by the two brothers were included in an anthology edited by Ranutius Gherus (Janus Gruterus), *Delitiae Poetarum Belgicorum*, in 5 vols. (Frankfurt am Main, 1614), which enjoyed wide distribution. The first publication of poems by Janus Secundus, *Opera* (Utrecht, 1541), is reprinted by B. de Graaf (Nieuwkoop, 1969).

6. L. Guicciardini, *La Descrittione di tutti i Paesi Bassi*, first edition 1567. In later editions comments have been added about the '*incivilissime guerre civile*' ('barbaric civil war') and the '*pestifere hersie*' ('pestiferous heresies') or the '*si perverse imprese*' ('perverse enterprises') of William of Orange. Grudius and his friends were friends of Guicciardini's.

G rown

Up but not Full-Grown

Children's Theatre in the Low Countries

Huis aan de Amstel /
Maccus / Combattimento
Consort, poster of the semi-
opera *King Arthur* for the
1999 Holland Festival.
The painting is by Marlene
Dumas.

The 1999 Holland Festival, probably the most prestigious performing arts event in the Low Countries, opened with Henry Purcell's semi-opera *King Arthur*, coproduced by the Combattimento Consort of Amsterdam and the theatre companies Huis aan de Amstel (Amsterdam) and Maccus (Delft). This sort of combination of theatre and opera is not in itself unique or even exceptional. However, what does make it exceptional – and even unique – in this case is that it involved two *children's* theatre companies.

One can hardly imagine better proof of the current regard for children's theatre in the Netherlands and Flanders than the privilege of this opening performance. The artistic management designed a comprehensive programme book to accompany the performance, as well as an informative CD-ROM and a Website full of playful surprises. In addition to this there were also opera workshops, including one for parents and children. So the education of the young audience, with a target group of eight years and up, was not neglected.

From education to experience

After a new generation of young dramatists had started to see children as a legitimate audience in the sixties and seventies, there was a gradual shift in children's theatre during the eighties: from theatre focusing mainly on social and political education towards theatre in which experience and fantasy prevailed. In the mid-eighties this led to the eventual disappearance of all educational ideals: theatre had become primarily an aim in itself, and no longer a means of communicating a message or imparting a particular view of life. The leading performances of the last decade include those by Teneeter (Nijmegen) and Artemis ('s-Hertogenbosch). Their performances very obviously appeal to the child's own experiences. A good example of this is Teneeter's play *Princess Iphigenia* (Ifigeneia Koningskind), in which Euripides' well-known tragedy is seen through the eyes of the young Iphigenia, which means that the young audience is witness to the real drama in Aulis: the inner conflict of a girl about to be sacrificed to please the gods.

In Artemis' *Tell, Medea, Do Tell* (Vertel, Medea, vertel), the point of view is similarly shifted from Medea, the murderess, to the victims, her two young sons. They plague their mother from the Underworld with troublesome questions about the reasons for her gruesome crime.

Both these plays were adapted by Pauline Mol, who has also become highly renowned for her theatre work abroad, mainly in Germany. For example, in 1999 the Hans Otto Theatre in Potsdam included her *Sometimes I Get Lost in a Dragon* (Soms verdwaal ik in een draak) in its repertoire, a fascinating play based on four famous fairytales by the Brothers Grimm. Here too the focus is on experience: the children overcome their fear, symbolised by an evil dragon, through the power of their imagination. In their own imagination the young audience share the experience of the threatened children and the happy ending has more or less the same effect as a classic catharsis.

Dynamic handling of the imagination, now the trade mark of children's theatre in both the Netherlands and Flanders, radiates to all performing arts disciplines. One example is the Flemish dancer Pascale Platel, who worked for years in adult theatre before being invited by BRONKS (Brussels) to do a solo play for children of eight and older. As she herself has said, in this play, *The King of Paprika-Flavoured Crisps* (De Koning van de Paprikachips), Platel discovered the form for which she had been searching for years: a form based mainly on direct involvement, both with the action and with the audience, and with constant interaction between reality and imagination.

Various repertoires

It is not only Teneeter and Artemis who have recently shown that the classical repertoire can be made perfectly accessible to a young audience. Other companies have also been able to make superb performances out of major dramatic works. Of Shakespeare alone there has been an impressive number of recent adaptations. In 1991 Ignace Cornelissen, the artistic head of Het Gevolg from Turnhout, adapted and directed *A Winter's Tale*. A year later his company won the Hans Snoek Prize, the most important children's theatre award in the Netherlands and Flanders, for an adaptation of *Henry V*. For this play Cornelissen chose a conspicuously light, playful tone, in which a language of images replaced that of words, but in such a way that the essence of Shakespeare's play was retained, even for the very youngest spectators.

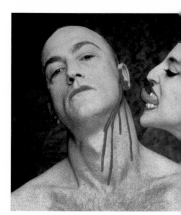

A year later, the MUZtheater (Zaandam) failed to achieve the same standard with their *Othello*, partly because the director, Allan Zipson, more or less smoothed the story out into a contemporary soap opera and dared not rely sufficiently on the powers of imagination of the teenagers of fourteen and over for whom the play was intended. However, with the thriller-style play *A Macbeth* (Een Macbeth), the same director and company did succeed in capturing the hearts of youngsters (and adults), due primarily to the surprising part played by the witches.

In 1997, at the Growing up in Public theatre collective in Utrecht, the director Jeroen Kriek unashamedly mutilated *Hamlet*, making of it a perfor-

mance bent on creating effects, but which was nevertheless emotional, and was performed both for and by young people. In autumn 1999, Xynix (Amsterdam), an opera company for children, produced an adaptation of *The Taming of the Shrew* entitled *Bitch* (Kreng): in this libretto the old noble Baptista has become a lady singing teacher, and Katherina's suitor Petruchio becomes a well-known tenor who comes to ask her for singing lessons. During the same period BRONKS brought out an unusual *Romeo and Julian* (Romeo en Julien), for an audience of sixteen and older. In this adaptation of Shakespeare's tragedy of love, which uses a lot of contemporary music, the female element is completely absent, and this one-sided view focuses on the gang of youths associated with the young Romeo.

The children's theatre companies naturally produce their own plays too, and sometimes they draw on existing prose writings: stories, novellas, and novels. For example, in 1999 Theatergroep Maccus (Delft) created the play *Otherland* (Anderland), for all ages from six up: this was a stage adaptation of a novella by the Dutch children's writer Paul Biegel, who in his turn was inspired by the well-known Brendan legend. Also in 1999, the Ibycus company from Antwerp won the Hans Snoek Prize for *De Tolbrug*, a dramatisation of the children's novel *The Toll Bridge* by Aidan Chambers, in which the author himself was closely involved.

Material for a play may of course also emerge from improvisation in rehearsals. Amongst the various examples in this field we must certainly mention Victoria (Ghent), a company whose purpose is as a production company for young dramatists making their debut, providing them with an outlet for their ideas. The 1996 production *Little Bernadette* (Bernadetje), the second part of a trilogy by the writer and director Arne Sierens and the choreographer Alain Platel, is undoubtedly one of the most striking plays for young people (and everyone else) in recent years. In this piece, which could be described equally well as a play, a dance performance or a circus act, the director, choreographer and actors concentrate the energy generated during improvisation into a sensational theatre experience. This production, in which the pilgrimage-centre of Lourdes is transformed into a fairground attraction with dodgems, was also extremely well received on its extensive international tour.

At the end of 1999, also with Victoria, another Sierens / Platel collaboration again combined various theatrical disciplines in *All Injuns* (Allemaal Indiaan). This highly acclaimed production, in a collage-like form, gives the spectator a glimpse into a realistically-portrayed deprived neighbourhood. The production won a place in the 2000 Holland Festival.

Between toddler and young adult

Victoria was established in 1992 on the foundations of the children's theatre company Oud Huis Stekelbees, which in its day performed mainly for very young children and was also particularly active in primary schools. Soon after taking the helm at Oud Huis Stekelbees, its new artistic director Dirk Pauwels decided to change course and produce works *for* and, more especially, *with* adolescents and young adults – an audience which had for a long time been neglected by the theatre.

With the newly-named Victoria, Pauwels set a course that was widely imitated, even in the Netherlands. Several years ago, a number of adult theatre companies there finally started to take older children seriously as a theatre audience. This recognition was undoubtedly prompted in part by the disturbing statistics on the ageing of the Dutch theatre-going public: investing in young people meant investing in one's own future.

At the same time the companies at last became aware of the government's strong desire to promote young people's participation in cultural activities by, among other things, a radical review of the final years of secondary education.

Toneelgroep Amsterdam alertly latched onto what was going on and made several productions using non-professional actors from fifteen to twenty years old, for an audience of about the same age. January 1999, for instance, saw the opening of *Bad Angel (Sonnet 144)*, a very loose adaptation of Shakespeare's *Love's Labour Lost*. At the same time, in a sort of parallel production, the company's entire actors' corps performed the musical stage-carnival *Dark Lady*, based on several of the Bard's sonnets. In early 2000, the company repeated this 'double hit' of young people's and adults' productions side by side, in two pieces based on the life and work of Bertolt Brecht.

In 1999 the Onafhankelijk Toneel (Rotterdam) created a memorable play for youngsters of twelve years and older, called *Tingeling*, having previously produced a theatre / dance performance with ten actors aged between fifteen and twenty and a so-called 'family show' based on a children's book by the German writer William Steig (*Abel's Island*). In this play the use of a television screen allows the spectator to look, in the most literal sense, into the mind of the remarkable Mr Tingeling, a character comparable with Jacques Tati's Monsieur Hulot. The things going on his mind are acted out elsewhere on stage in a maze of mini-sets and filmed live using a video camera. Seldom is such a pressing appeal made to the young audience's associative powers and seldom is fantasy made into such a concrete subject in the performance itself as in this production.

Back to involvement

Tingeling is a good example of a play which is pure entertainment, without educational pretensions. Nonetheless, even here the Onafhankelijk Toneel tried to meet the wish of the educational world that plays should be usable for educational ends. Secondary school pupils were, for example, able to take a workshop on the creation of the 'toy sets' and if so desired build this sort of scene themselves.

The relationship with schools is naturally much more intense in the children's theatre companies. Both in the Netherlands and in Flanders, roughly half of all performances by subsidised companies are for schools. This may be in the company's own theatre, a theatre elsewhere or in the schools themselves. In this respect there is very great diversity. One company may perform as often as possible in the 'open' circuit of theatres, while another will put on the majority of its performances in schools. Theatergroep Wederzijds from Amsterdam, for instance, even performs almost exclusively in schools,

Onafhankelijk Toneel, *Tingeling*. Photo by Maarten Laupman.

and sometimes in other locations such as centres for asylum-seekers.

In 1990 Wederzijds won the Hans Snoek Prize for its play *Hitler's Childhood* (De jeugd van Hitler), with which they showed they did not intend to avoid important politically and ethically charged subjects. This was followed three years later by *Mirad, a Boy from Bosnia* (Mirad, een jongen uit Bosnië), a gripping play in which, with limited theatrical resources but no less effectively for that, the company sketched the fortunes of Mirad the refugee. This play, which has been translated into many languages and performed with great success outside the Netherlands, questioned the attitudes (political and otherwise) of the young audience, in the same way as *Rupa Lucian, Child from Rumania* (Rupa Lucian, kind van Roemenië), another, in some ways comparable, play by the company was to do in 1999.

Wederzijds is one of the few companies in the Netherlands and Flanders to show that even in our day and age enthralling, penetrating theatre for children and young people can be made on the basis of the ideals of the politically instructional theatre of the seventies. It is not the educational element that is missing from children's theatre – in a certain sense it has always been there – rather, slowly but surely, the pursuit of a certain commitment, a political and social awareness among the young theatre-going public. It is striking enough that in the jury reports for the many prizes Wederzijds have received in the nineties, it is repeatedly the company's social commitment that is praised.

Limits to growth

At the present time, a substantial part of the organisation of children's theatre in Flanders rests with three major children's arts centres. There is BRONKS in Brussels and then Villanella in Antwerp and Speeltheater / Kopergietery in Ghent. In Antwerp, HetPaleis, a continuation of the Royal Children's Theatre under a new name, occupies a somewhat aberrant position, in terms of both organisation and ideas. The artistic management's aspiration is mainly to create plays for six to twelve-year-olds, whereas the arts centres, and now a growing number of companies, intend to work primarily for teenagers and young adults.

Dirk Pauwels, the artistic head of Victoria, has already been mentioned as someone who has turned his back on theatre for the youngest audiences. He did so because of an inner resistance against both the lethargy of colleagues in other youth theatres and against Flemish culture policy. According to him this policy keeps youth theatre in an artificial isolation and prevents it from achieving actual emancipation. In 1997 Ignace Cornelissen also took his company, Het Gevolg, down the road of adult theatre. And he too criticises the limitations within which youth theatre has to work. The necessity (financial and otherwise) of close contact with education and schoolchildren is only one example of this.

As far as the Netherlands is concerned, in the report entitled *Children's Theatre in the Future* (Het jeugdtheater van de toekomst, 1999), the thirteen fully subsidised children's theatre companies complain of the exploitation of staff and the financial and organisational obstructions that frustrate their desire to take up new challenges. In parallel with this it seems, paradoxically enough, that it is precisely the recognition of youngsters as an 'adult audience' that hinders the continued development of youth theatre. On the *Moose* Website, a 'virtual theatre magazine' set up several years ago by five young theatre academics in Amsterdam, the large-scale *King Arthur* project was described as *'the play that marked the end of the heyday of youth theatre in the Netherlands'*. Of course, a rather provocatively formulated statement like this does not say it all, but it does say something. After all, *King Arthur* does indeed show to what extent the establishment has now embraced youth theatre and how much of the inspiration of the companies' early years, and of the pure, genuine wish to create interesting and exciting things for children, has been lost as a result.

It seems the time has come for renewed reflection, which will only lead to a successful outcome when everyone joins forces, all the arts centres and companies, both Flemish and Dutch, subsidised and unsubsidised. One initiative that makes one hopeful is the Tweetakt Festival, a full-scale arts event for children and young people. This festival first made its appearance in 's-Hertogenbosch in 1983 under the title Kunst Jr. Festival, a meeting place for play-makers and organisers, on the initiative of De Bundeling, the Dutch children's theatre organisation set up in 1981. From 1999 the festival is to be held alternately in Antwerp and 's-Hertogenbosch, and this has given new force to the existing cooperation between Dutch and Flemish children's theatres. The organisers expect an intensive exchange of ideas about art and art education for children and teenagers and mutual improvement in methods of production and attracting audiences.

In the Low Countries, both north and south, children's theatre has achieved an artistic standard regarded with envy by the rest of Europe. There is no lack of achievements on which to build, nor of ideals to pursue. Opening up the magic of theatre to children and teenagers, enabling the continued growth of children's theatre: this is a challenge for every play-maker in Flanders and the Netherlands who attaches importance to passing on a valuable cultural possession to a new generation.

JOS NIJHOF
Translated by Gregory Ball.

FURTHER INFORMATION

Flemish Theatre Institute
Sainctelettesquare 19 / 1210 Brussels / Belgium
tel. +32 2 201 09 06 / fax +32 2 203 02 05 / e-mail: info@vti.be

Dutch Theatre Institute
Herengracht 168 / 1016 BP Amsterdam / The Netherlands
tel. +31 20 551 33 00 / fax +31 20 551 33 03 / e-mail: info@tin.nl

These organisations jointly publish the bilingual magazine *Carnet* (English / French).

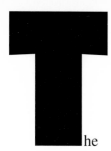

The

ther Languages of the Netherlands

Pieter Bruegel the Elder, *The Tower of Babel* (detail). 1563. Panel, 114 x 155 cm. Kunsthistorisches Museum, Vienna.

Today, multilingualism is a fact of life in all the world's large metropolitan conurbations. Globalisation, trade, migration, tourism, war and refugee crises have all contributed to the increased mobility of products and people – and of the languages and cultures they bring with them. In New York we find sizeable communities of immigrants who speak Spanish, Italian, German, Hebrew, Yiddish, Chinese, Vietnamese and other Asian languages. In Jakarta there are speakers of many of the 300 different languages to be found in the Indonesian archipelago. In Moscow one may encounter speakers from the 176 recognised linguistic minorities within the former Soviet Empire. And in London today some 300 different languages are spoken, and 25% of its schoolchildren speak a language other than English at home.

Multilingualism is also a key characteristic of the history, culture and society of Europe, with about a hundred languages in active use today. The European Union (EU) is operating on the principle of Unity in Diversity, and in 2001 the European Year of Languages will celebrate the great linguistic diversity of the continent. The EU has adopted the 11 languages of its member states as its official languages, and uses two of these – English and French – as daily working languages. A further 40 to 45 languages – ranging from Basque in Spain and the Celtic languages in Brittany, Wales, Ireland and Scotland to Ladino in Italy, Macedonian in Greece, and Sami (Lapp) in North Scandinavia – are covered by the Charter for Regional or Minority Languages (1998) of the Council of Europe. And, of course, there are the many languages of recent immigrant communities from outside the European Union, such as Turkish, Arabic and Chinese.

In the Netherlands today we find a similar situation, especially in the urban areas. Over the past 25 years there has been a rapid rise in immigration, and the presence of speakers of perhaps a hundred different languages is now an everyday reality. With a strong and open economy and society, the Netherlands attracts people from all over the world: not only nurses from Surinam and South Africa, call centre operators from France, football players from Africa and Latin America, and IT specialists from Britain and the USA, but also teachers from Austria, Turkish businessmen, Columbian street

musicians and Kosovan refugees. In this new Babylon one can watch cable TV in the major European languages and buy newspapers in a variety of foreign languages ranging from Arabic to Swahili. All this makes for interesting patterns of multilingualism, bringing Dutch into contact with an ever widening range of other languages.

Below, I will first of all discuss the present situation of the various categories of languages and speakers we can distinguish. Secondly, I will consider what kind of language policy the Netherlands will need in order to meet the challenges and opportunities of multilingualism.

The Dutch language

Dutch is the national language of the people of the Netherlands, and also one of the official languages of neighbouring Belgium and of the European Union. With a total of some 21 million speakers in the Netherlands and Flanders, Dutch ranks between number 35 and 40 in the linguistic top hundred of the world.

Dutch has a well-developed standard and is widely used as the common language in society and education, in politics and government, the courts, the churches, the media and publishing. The Dutch and the Flemish are actively working together to develop and promote their language, and have established a strong resource structure via the Dutch Language Union (Nederlandse Taalunie), which is responsible for the spelling, grammar, dictionaries and terminology of the language. The association Our Language (Onze Taal) offers an active and popular Language Advisory Service, and there is an ongoing, lively public debate concerning the recent rise of so-called 'Polder-Dutch' and other informal varieties of the language.

The Dutch constitution does not stipulate that Dutch is the official language. But the Netherlands has long operated a single language policy as the key to building up the Dutch Kingdom as a centralised nation state. Education is normally in Dutch, and throughout the nineteenth and well into the twentieth century, this policy was aimed at unidirectional assimilation of speakers of Frisian, Yiddish and the many different dialects of Dutch. More recently, the 300,000 Dutch colonials repatriated from Indonesia in the 1950s and the Mediterranean migrant workers ('gastarbeiders') of the 1960s faced strong assimilationist pressures to adopt standard Dutch as the common language.

Given the large numbers of Dutch speakers, the elaborate support structure that is available, and the great weight of the state behind it, the Amsterdam sociologist De Swaan predicts that the language will certainly survive. Leading linguists expect Dutch to thrive and develop in the coming century, amalgamating and incorporating influences from other languages, in particular from English. Needless to say, this will only happen if the Dutch continue to invest in the maintenance, promotion and development of their own language.

Indigenous regional or minority languages

Apart from Dutch, the Netherlands today recognises five other languages – Frisian, Low Saxon, Limburgs, Yiddish and Romany – as indigenous regional or minority languages under the European Charter mentioned above, which the Netherlands, unlike its neighbour Belgium, has ratified. The recognition of Low Saxon (*Nedersaksisch*) in the eastern provinces and of Limburgs in the southeast was mostly symbolic: no resources have been allocated for their introduction in education or the media. As a symbol of regional pride, though, these two languages reflect the growing tendency of rural areas to identify themselves as different from the more dominant urban west of the country. Already, the province of Zeeland is clamouring for the recognition of its dialect as another indigenous regional language.

Amongst these five, Frisian ('*Frysk*'), the nearest relative to English on the continent, holds a special position. As an official language in its home province of *Fryslân*, it is the common language of some 400,000 native speakers who produce a lively output of literature, theatre and films in Frisian. It is supported by an inventive language policy with good academic input, a clear presence on the world wide web, and a resource structure fostering the teaching and study of both language and culture. From the 1950s onwards, the Frisian language has gone through a process of increasing recognition, culminating in the Administrative Agreement of 1989 that defines the joint responsibility for Frisian of both the Dutch national government and the Frisian provincial administration. The Agreement was renewed in 2000 to take into account the many obligations stipulated in the European Charter.

The official status of Frisian provides considerable support. But it is a matter of what a former Dutch prime minister called the 'narrow margins', which are defined by the Dutch national government, in particular in education. Thus, for example, in secondary schools Frisian is only available as a subject like other foreign languages, and not as a daily contact language. Higher education as a path to economic success is available only in Dutch, and not in the rural areas where Frisian is spoken. Dutch continues to carry a higher prestige, and without Dutch one does not have good career prospects in the Netherlands. As a consequence, there is a significant brain drain away from *Fryslân*. The pattern traditionally has been for Frisians to migrate, often to Amsterdam, where they have gone over to Dutch, while sometimes retaining Frisian for use at home, with their family and friends and when they visit relatives back home in *Fryslân*. The Director of the European Central Bank, the Frisian Wim Duisenberg, is a good example.

Due to the various pressures that Dutch society brings to bear on Frisian, the future of this language gives some cause for concern. The fact is – and in this respect, as the *Euromosaic* survey of 1996 has shown, Frisian is typical of all the other linguistic minorities in Europe – there are no monolingual speakers of Frisian any more. However, with its large number of native speakers, Frisian is still well above the critical threshold for linguistic survival.

European languages

Over the past 20 years, and especially after the abolition of the internal European borders in 1992 (Schengen Treaty), there has been a strong influx of fellow citizens of the European Union (EU). No overall figures are available, but the category of 'Other non-Dutch people' in the Netherlands numbered a total of 1.6 million people in 1997. This includes 143,000 immigrants from Southern Europe, with sizeable communities of Spanish (30,000), Portuguese (15,000), Italians (33,000) and Greeks (10,000) living in the Netherlands today.

There are no separate figures for European citizens from Great Britain, Germany, France or Scandinavia, nor for people from the European Economic Region. But clearly there are large numbers of English-speaking immigrants in the Netherlands today: chippies from Ireland, English nurses, museum directors and translators, American and British consultants working in the media and advertising, trade, transport and information technology, in the financial sector and in Dutch multinationals such as Unilever, Shell and Philips. As a result, in Amsterdam today speakers of English constitute the largest foreign community.

Many of these English-speaking migrants come to the Netherlands for economic and personal reasons. Neither the Europeans nor the Americans are obliged to take courses in Dutch, because – unlike the ethnic minorities discussed below – the new 1998 law on integration does not apply to them. Many of them therefore do not learn Dutch, and this strong English presence adds considerably to the pressures that English, as the language of globalisation, is already exerting on Dutch. Many Dutch multinational companies operate in English in any case, and want the EU to follow suit as soon as possible. In 1985, the Dutch made English a compulsory subject for all children from the last two years of primary school, and so one can predict that in thirty years time there will be no monolingual speakers of Dutch left. The Nijmegen linguist De Bot even envisages a scenario of a gradual, sector-by-sector transition of the country from Dutch into English, beginning in the economy, in science and (information) technology, the universities and academic publishing, then in entertainment and the media, and finally also in education, the law, politics, public life, and society in general.

The languages of the ethnic minorities

In addition to European migrants, the Netherlands also attracts large numbers of immigrants from outside the European Union. The total number of the so-called ethnic minorities was at least 1.4 million people in 1997. A first subcategory, that of ex-colonial subjects, consists of some 287,000 people from Surinam, another 95,000 from the Netherlands Antilles and Aruba, an estimated 40,000 Moluccans, and some 10,000 Javanese. They often know Dutch and for that reason achieve better results in the Dutch education system than other newcomers, such as the economic immigrants and, more recently, the refugees and asylum seekers. The largest minorities here are the Turks (280,000), the Moroccans (233,000), the Chinese (90,000) and people from the former Yugoslavia (60,000). In addition, there are many small minorities from all over the world, from Eritrea, Kurdistan, Sri Lanka, Thailand and Vietnam, to Cape Verde and Brazil.

The key plank of the government's minorities policy is the new law on integration ('*Inburgering*') of 1998, which makes it obligatory for all newcomers who are not citizens of the European Union, the European Economic Region and the United States to take courses in Dutch, and to learn the customs, conventions and values of Dutch culture, in preparation for their integration into Dutch society. Given the numbers mentioned above, it is clear that the implementation of this *Inburgering*-programme will require a massive, long term investment in the teaching of Dutch as a second language. There is an urgent need to improve the quality of these courses, and also their accessibility within the existing education system and via local libraries, social clubs, the mass media and the internet.

There is every reason to do this, because the integration of immigrant minorities into Dutch society is becoming a matter of very serious concern. Speaking Dutch, achieving good results in the Dutch education system, and doing well in employment – these are the three key features that set the native Dutch apart from many immigrants in the ethnic minorities. This in turn brings the threat of a downward spiral for newcomers, of low proficiency in Dutch, followed by low educational achievement – often in poor, segregated schools – and low success in employment, leading to the formation of a new proletariat, a badly educated, hardly integrated, non-Dutch-speaking underclass, faced with exploitation and exclusion, and the risk of a life in crime.

On the positive side we note that, increasingly, the new minorities are organising themselves into a wide range of cultural, religious and political organisations, often with interesting European and global connections; and that all the larger Dutch political parties now have members from the minorities in the national parliament. The multicultural economy of today is generating jobs for the enterprising new Dutch who can speak other languages: in translation, language teaching, travel agencies, journalism (newspapers in Arabic, Kurmanji, and Hindi) and in the media, such as the new Turkish-Dutch Radio and TV, and Migrant Television Amsterdam. Many immigrants are making a valuable contribution to Dutch culture, producing world music, adding spice to the Dutch diet, and enriching the Dutch calendar with ethnic holidays. Meanwhile, immigrant writers such as Moses Isegawa, Abdelkader Benali, Kader Abdollah and Hafid Bouazza are adding a whole new dimension of linguistic creativity and creolisation to contemporary Dutch literature.

The Netherlands as a multilingual society

The Netherlands today, especially in the urban areas, is a multilingual society, with Dutch as its common language, English as the dominant outside influence, and a wide range of indigenous and immigrant minority languages. Many speakers of minority languages, especially the smaller ones, will make the transition to Dutch for social and economic reasons; others, for personal, social and cultural reasons, may not do so. Individual newcomers may achieve varying degrees of proficiency in Dutch, but in general Dutch

will become the common language for contact and communication between people of very different background and origin.

In the process we can expect an enormous increase in bilingualism, which will expose the Dutch language to many different linguistic influences. In Amsterdam today, more than 60% of school pupils are of non-Dutch speaking background, and schools where some 80 different home languages are spoken are not exceptional. The result will be a *koinè* Dutch with all kinds of new accents and idioms, new meanings and expressions, as we already see in the rise of new varieties such as *Smurf speak*, *Nethermix* and *Netherenglish*.

Processes of linguistic contact and interaction such as these – with complex patterns of mixing, switching and rivalries between languages, between the extremes of Dutch purism on the one hand and unfettered creolisation on the other – are likely to continue for the foreseeable future, since the influx of immigrants of every kind is projected to continue apace. By 2015 the ethnic minorities will reach 2.4 million, the other (European) migrants perhaps 2 million. Such numbers dwarf anything the Dutch have dealt with in the past. It is high time, therefore, to wake up to the fact that the Netherlands today is an immigration country, and so, just like Australia, will need to develop a well-considered language policy.

Dutch for all ?

Dutch will continue to dominate in the Netherlands, as the common language of the people, the media, politics, trade and commerce, education, sports and literature. From here it is only a small step to argue – as many Dutch people do – that there should be just one single official language for the public domain, since this will create equal conditions for everyone. This view goes well with the egalitarian character of Dutch society and with its long tradition of assimilation of newcomers. It also addresses a crucial practical point, viz. that without Dutch one faces great difficulties of integration and participation in Dutch society. And in effect, the new *Inburgering*-law of 1998 has already made Dutch the obligatory common language for a wide range of newcomers.

But the *Inburgering*-law, important as it is, can only be the first step towards a fully-fledged language policy. A single language policy may have been sufficient in the monolingual Dutch nation state of the past, but it will not do as an answer to the complex issues involved in contemporary multilingualism in an increasingly multicultural society. There is a host of questions concerning the other languages of the Netherlands that this policy does not address. For example, if Dutch is obligatory for the ethnic minorities because Dutch society needs a common language, then why don't we extend this requirement also to the sizeable numbers of European newcomers, and in particular the English speakers? Should we continue to exempt our fellow Europeans from any obligation to learn Dutch – remembering that in the near future Hungary, Bulgaria and Turkey may become full members of the European Union? If so, how much scope should there be for teaching in mother tongues other than Dutch? And what about the Frisians?

If there is anything these questions make clear, it is that there is no one single linguistic remedy that will suit all situations. What is needed here is a differential language policy that works, and that can produce a fair balance between the various linguistic needs and rights involved. This should be developed, naturally, in the wider context of a European language policy framework.

Promoting customer-friendly multilingualism

In the meantime, we would do well to accept that multilingualism is a living reality in the Netherlands today, and to realise that people who do not speak each others' languages, especially when their behaviour, customs, traditions and taboos are quite different from what the Dutch may be used to, will sooner or later have problems in communicating. Schools, hospitals, museums, the police, the courts, the social services are all increasingly aware that language and communication are crucial to the success of their operations. So, taking a practical approach, we should develop what Nelde has called '*customer-friendly multilingualism*'.

Already one can observe interesting developments here. In Amsterdam-Bijlmer, efforts are made to recruit labourers in their own language, using Papiamento, English and the languages of Ghana. In Utrecht, police officers take lessons in Arabic in order to be able to communicate with the local community in the multicultural suburb of Lombok. Dutch TV offers news bulletins for the deaf in Dutch Sign Language. The Dutch government uses Frisian in its Culture Plan, and is making an increasing amount of information on e.g. education, the social services and taxes available in Moroccan Arabic, Turkish, Chinese and other languages.

Initiatives such as these contribute to better contact. And we may well ask what other steps can be taken to facilitate communication. A basic first requirement here is to establish a database of the other languages of the Netherlands, of existing linguistic / communicative needs and available resources. Such central statistics are simply not available at the moment.

For the longer term, the Netherlands will need large numbers of well-trained linguists who can facilitate communication between speakers of different languages. To help people and organisations when they get stuck in insurmountable linguistic problems, there should be an essential provision such as the *Language Line* of Great Britain, a telephone service that connects them to speakers of the other languages involved. Beyond this, linguists will have to be trained who can audit and assess the growing linguistic needs of individuals, communities and organisations. There is work here for interpreters and translators, and for language managers who can match the various linguistic needs with available resources. The linguistic skills of bilingual people should be rewarded, and models of best practice for running the increasingly multilingual populations of schools, jails and hospitals need to be developed and disseminated. And, building on its longstanding tradition of effective foreign language teaching, the Netherlands will need to produce the language teachers, translators and technologies that can bridge existing communication gaps and turn them into productive opportunities – especially now, when the non-English use of the Internet is expected to quadruple over the next few years.

What is needed is a commitment to invest in high quality language training, education and resources, and to develop a fair and effective approach to the problems as well as the opportunities presented by the growing multilingualism in contemporary Dutch society.

REINIER SALVERDA

BIBLIOGRAPHY

BAKER, C. and S. PRYS JONES (eds.), *Encyclopaedia of Bilingualism and Bilingual Education.* Clevedon, 1998.

BAKER, PH. and J. EVERSLEY (eds.), *Multilingual Capital. The Languages of London's Schoolchildren and their Relevance to Economic, Social and Educational Policies.* London, 2000.

BOT, C.L.J. DE, *Waarom deze rede niet in het Engels is.* Inaugural lecture, Catholic University Nijmegen, 1994.

BROEDER, P. and G. EXTRA, *Language, Ethnicity & Education.* Clevedon, 1999.

CRYSTAL, D., *English as a Global Language.* Cambridge, 1997.

DORREN, G., *Nieuwe tongen. De talen van migranten in Nederland en Vlaanderen.* The Hague / Antwerp / Utrecht, 1999.

EXTRA, G. and T. VALLEN, 'Migration and multilingualism in Western Europe. A case study on the Netherlands'. In: Grabe, W.(ed.), *Multilingualism and Multilingual Communities,* 1997 (=American Review of Applied Linguistics, 1997).

NELDE, P., M. STRUBEL and G. WILLIAMS (eds), *Euromosaic. The production and reproduction of the minority language groups in the European Union.* Luxembourg, 1996.

SALVERDA, R. (1998), 'Frisian'. In: Price, G. (ed.). *Encyclopedia of the Languages of Europe.* Oxford, 1998; pp. 177-184.

SMEETS, H.M.A.G., E.P. MARTENS and J. VEENMAN (eds.), *Jaarboek Minderheden 1999.* Houten / Tiegem / Lelystad, 1999.

SMEETS, R., 'Talen en taalpolitiek in de Europese Unie'. In: Sijs, N. van der (ed), *Taaltrots. Purisme in een veertigtal talen.* Amsterdam / Antwerp, 1999; pp. 381-416.

SWAAN, A. DE, 'The Evolving European Language System: A Theory of Communication Potential and Language Competition'. In: *International Political Science Review* 14 (1993), no. 3, pp. 241-255.

WEBSITES

European Bureau for Lesser Used Languages - http://www.eblul.org
Euromosaic - http://www.uoc.es/euromosaic
Forum Instituut voor Multiculturele Ontwikkeling - http://www.forum.imo.nl
Fryske Akademy - http://www.fa.knaw.nl
Meertens-instituut - http://www.meertens.knaw.nl
Onze Taal: http://www.onzetaal.com
Polder Dutch - http://www.hum.uva.nl/poldernederlands
SIL Ethnologue Database - http://www.sil.org/ethnologue
Nederlandse Taalunie - http://www.taalunie.nl
Tolkencentrum - http://www.tolkencentrum-non.nl
Voor Allochtonen Door Allochtonen - http://www.vada.nl

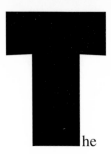he

Scattered 'I'

The Ambivalent Work of Paul de Wispelaere

The work of the Flemish writer, essayist and critic Paul de Wispelaere (1928-) is highly characteristic of the development of literature and literary criticism in Dutch during the second half of the twentieth century.

When he came on the scene in the mid-sixties, De Wispelaere was much impressed by both the French *nouveau roman* and the *nouvelle critique* which at that time was coming to the fore in the Paris-based group Tel Quel. Like the representatives of this *nouvelle critique* who were developing a European variant of the American New Criticism, De Wispelaere opted for a formal structuralist approach to literature. For him, literature was and still is primarily a question of form and language. But unlike the New Critics, whose main emphasis in their 'close reading' was on the study of poetic language and the 'unity' of the closed, complete literary work, De Wispelaere showed a great affinity with the ideologically charged criticism, or *critique d'interprétation,* which engages the entire personality of the critic. This he found in the multi-faceted example of Roland Barthes. Like Barthes who in *S / Z* (1970) and *The Pleasure of the Text* (1973) proposed a way of reading that recognises the pluralism of a literary text, De Wispelaere also resisted looking for and finding *the* meaning of a text: he prefers openness and mutability, incompleteness and elusiveness.

De Wispelaere's cultivation of ambivalence and contradiction is apparent not only in his analysis of literary texts, but also in his own creative work. Ambivalence can be seen as the key to his oeuvre: according to him uncertainty, doubt, is the great theme '*that gnaws at the heart of modern literature*'. In this respect he is a typical postmodern author of the late twentieth century whose themes are the fundamental unknowability of the world and the problematic relationship between language, literary work and reality.

Between garden and world

De Wispelaere's interest in 'modern' forms (which from the 1980s onwards have been known as 'postmodern') was already evident from his editorship, from 1956 to 1962, of the Antwerp avant-garde magazine *De Tafelronde,* and afterwards of *Komma* (1965-1969), a magazine in which, paradoxically, the preference for formal analysis went hand-in-hand with an explicit appreciation of the egodocument and diary.

From the start, self-reflection has been central to De Wispelaere's creative prose, as in the essay 'The problematic "I"' ('Het problematische ik' in the collection entitled *With a critical eye* (Met kritisch oog, 1967)) in which the critic describes the fragmentation of the 'I' in modern literature in the work of authors such as Amiel, Proust, Valéry, Gide, Benn, Pirandello and Sartre, using the myth of Narcissus. In the early creative works – the novella *Scherzando ma non troppo* (1959) and the novels *Becoming an Island* (Een eiland worden, 1963) and *My Living Shadow* (Mijn levende schaduw, 1965) – the main preoccupation was the elusive intertwining of living and writing. The main character of *My Living Shadow* attempts through writing to '*excavate causes and connections from the past in the search for a pattern in which everything happened as it had to happen*'. Writing is, and will remain, a form of living, of vital reflection: it is a unique exploration of consciousness which strives constantly to achieve the fullness of authentic existence and which is also constantly trying out new, modern forms. Eventually this quest resulted in a unique form of autobiographical prose in which various genres – storytelling, criticism and essay – flow harmoniously into one another and in which the search for authenticity of the scattered 'I' forms the thematic core.

This mixed form was first realised in *Paul contra Paul* (Paul-tegenpaul, 1970) which, as the title already indicates, has a basic structure that is fundamentally dualistic. In this diary of a writer, it is the duality of the writer's personality which has become the central theme. His '*ambivalent knowing*' also returns in subsequent purely creative work, for example in the well-known triptych *Between Garden and World* (Tussen tuin en wereld, 1979), *My House is Nowhere* (Mijn huis is nergens meer, 1982) and *Letters from Nowhere Houses* (Brieven uit nergenshuizen, 1986), in which the writer's 'in-between position' is established using a number of typical romantic motifs. The need to come to terms with a world which forces itself aggressively upon the writer is set against to the need expressed in earlier work to fold in on oneself, to isolate oneself or '*become an island*'. And modern society now stands opposed to the earlier narcissism as a focus of problems. From this point on, De Wispelaere explores the opposition between on the one hand a pure, paradisiacal existence (expressed through the image of the garden), where there is room for unfettered erotic experience with the adored young woman, and on the other hand the vulgar, uncultured, corrupt society which is destroying nature, or the natural, and silence with its technological inventions.

The alphabet tastes of ash

The masterly *The Charred Alphabet. Diary 1990-1991* (Het verkoolde alfabet. Dagboek 1990-1991,1992) is one of the high points of De Wispelaere's work. It has the previously tested amalgam of critical-contemplative and storytelling elements, mixed with shreds of memories and autobiographical reflections. The diary in the strict sense of the word, the observation of what takes place in the writer's surroundings and in his life, occupies a relatively small space in *The Charred Alphabet*. Direct perception in which, as ever with De Wispelaere, nature plays an important part, is linked by means of associations to remembered images from the near and distant past, but is also determined by numerous reading experiences, by critical consideration of the work of both others and himself. But the unfolding egodocument is still a means of preserving the integrity of the past, a form of 'literary archeology'. The aim of the diary is '...*to restore fragments of the disappearing world*'. So the use of fragments which is part and parcel of the diary form is not a handicap, but contributes to the achievement of his aim. For the incompleteness of the fragment, or '*the brief glint of shards*', indicates a higher unity, or expresses a desire for synthesis: '*From the fracturing and impermanence which give rise to them* (the fragments) *and which are their natural seedbed, they express through their very form-energy a desire for permanence and unity.*'

There is another respect in which fragmentary writing that expresses a desire for unity is a dual act: for the act of writing, as Gustave Flaubert had noted before, produces an image of writing itself. Writing is dual, *ambivalent* work: it is a means of creating distance, of looking back at oneself, in retrospect. This ambivalence is present formally in *The Charred Alphabet* in the doubling of 'I' with 'he': '*I focus on* him *as he stares listlessly through the skylight of his study*'. All the themes, motifs and characters from De Wispelaere's earlier work are present in this diary: the women who have played a role in his life and who he has presented as characters in earlier novels; the many travel recollections connected with these figures and which are evoked through looking at photographs or repeating the journey. And the fascination with literature remains undiminished, the preferences well known: Rilke and Leiris, Flaubert, Brodsky, Frisch and the Flemish novelist Louis Paul Boon, about whom De Wispelaere has produced pioneering critical studies, alongside newer, more recently discovered writers. And there are the emotional outbursts protesting against the destruction of nature by the tasteless, vulgar, noisy activities of humans and their machines, set in counterpoint to the lyrical images of events in nature and the animal kingdom which are reproduced in their rich sensuous diversity. And here too, finally, are the familiar outbursts against stupid, hypocritical politicians, against the absurdity of some scientific experiments, and against the degradation of language through levelling-down in the mass media. This is where the book's title comes from: '*actually there are fewer and fewer words which you can savour, the alphabet is charred and tastes of ash*'. The title also refers to a motto borrowed from Octavio Paz in which by means of '*flaming resurrections / from the charred alphabet*' a paradisiacal, prelapsarian world is evoked which is still free from an awareness of time, of time passing and thus also from decline and mortality.

The book itself contains the suggestion that through language, through writing, a world can be called into being in which a regained unity is conceivable, in which a conciliatory synthesis of contradictions accepted as complementary is a possibility. In this sense, *The Charred Alphabet* can be called the diary of acceptance, of ultimate peace: a high point in the oeuvre of Paul de Wispelaere and in the genre of romanticised autobiography.

ANNE MARIE MUSSCHOOT
Translated by Jane Fenoulhet.

October

Starting a book is a terrible thing.
Is there something I can do? Ilse has asked again, with insistent concern. Through what she cannot do for me, I escape her or become alienated from her. It's of no use that I smile reassuringly at her. Are you coming for a swim in a minute? she goes on to ask, then at least you'll be doing something healthy. No, I don't feel like doing anything, and definitely not something healthy. And what are you doing? She is halfway through *Boquitas pintadas* by Manuel Puig: 'a wonderful book'.

Duplication: I focus on him as he stares listlessly through the skylight of his study. He is past sixty, greying at the temples, balding at the crown. He is small but solidly built, with the first signs of fleshiness. In his youth he did a lot of gymnastics, cycling, football and boxing. Those distant days, which are still right there in his brain cells and his bones, but which for her belong in a history book. When all things are considered, he, through his parents, has one foot in the nineteenth century, while her future lies in the twenty-first. That's more than a century difference. He reels at the thought. The conversation that has just taken place is still murmuring in his ears. From where he is standing, behind glass, he looks down into the garden and orchard which he laid out nearly twenty years ago and which seem to have grown without him. Through a pane of glass: increasingly he has the impression that this is the way he looks at life, his own too. The trees, still in leaf, are wrapped in cotton-wool layers of mist. All the wonderful books in existence have been wrested from a paralysing unwillingness, that is why at this moment he never wants to see one again.
Rilke, in a letter from 1907: 'For weeks, apart from two short interruptions, I have not spoken a word; at last my loneliness is complete and I feel enclosed in my work like the stone in a fruit.' This haunts his mind. He thinks: if only I had reached that point.

The garden, drizzled with autumn colour, is starting to sink into itself again. The lawn feasts on rotting cooking pears, apples, rose-hips, berries and leaves. It sucks the lost summer days into the swampy ground. That seed must die before it can germinate is a poet's cliché but nevertheless a certainty to which I cling.

An exercise. Look at the hand lying on the oak top of my work table. The hand is stuck to my arm, or my arm is stuck to my hand. I (someone minus the hand) am stuck with the whole thing. Every year the number of age spots has increased, there is more of a greenish tinge to the swollen veins. The skin is a maze of fine lines. If only it were someone else's hand. But I need it to write.

Exciting news today from the genetics front. French researchers report in the journal *Science* on a successful experiment to transplant brain tissue from quails into chickens. Twenty of the chickens lived for over two weeks and could walk and peck as normal. But five did not make typical clucking noises, they cheeped like young quails. At last science has produced the quailchicken that the world had been waiting for. Oh why didn't they transplant tissue from a peacock into my brain stem? Then today I would be sitting on the roof-ridge, paradise blue, writing merry stories.

It is evening. We are sitting under the lamp which illuminates our figures and movements. Only our faces and hands are exposed, and so that is what we look at. Between my thumb and curved index finger I crack walnuts for her. Sometimes they are too hard and then I don't succeed. You have strong, soft, dear hands, she says. Not true, I say, but I am glad that she speaks her own truth. Of course, it is the truth of love, but all other truth is unbearable.

Writing a diary is itself a way of living, the diary writer lives in the light of his diary and with his eyes fixed on his diary, the content of the diary consists of the writing of it. As the caterpillar is already the butterfly, lived reality is already diary-literature. There is a risk that an apparently spontaneous gesture is already looking for the words in which it will soon appear on paper. Every kiss can be a Judas kiss. When I opened the bedroom window this morning, a flock of startled starlings flew with a great commotion straight into these lines of my diary. The diary creates the events of the day (of the year, of the remembered life).

'While working you must forget everything and it should be as though you are writing for yourself or for the person you love most on earth' (Paustovsky). That person is you: do not forget.

This afternoon, gathering walnuts, another wicker basket full, I suddenly became aware that I was planting my feet further apart than I used to when I bent forward. I quickly straightened up – a twinge in my lower back – as though I'd been caught doing something I shouldn't, and scanned the side of the house to see if Ilse was standing behind one of the windows. No, she hadn't seen. Surely she would not have wanted to see anything other than me, sprightly and lithe, gathering nuts for her? What hasn't been seen doesn't count. It can be suppressed and forgotten.

A little later, while I'm reading in the newspaper with a shock that Moravia has died at eighty-two, struck down by a brain haemorrhage while his Spanish wife – his third, half a century younger than him – was in Morocco, I hear a sharp tap on the window and just glimpse of something falling past. Wrenching open the front door, I am a split second faster than the ginger tom Peanut and grab the tiny colourful bird lying on the path against the wall. Peanut looks at me indignantly. Back in the sitting room, I see that it is a little goldcrest, pretty rare in these parts. He isn't limp, just stunned. I put him in an empty flower pot on the window sill. After half an hour I hear rustling and see that he is on his little feet again. Not long after, he flies up and flaps against the window. I take hold of him again and put him outside in one of the spherical clipped hawthorns at the edge of the lawn. At the end of the afternoon I see Peanut coming across the lawn with a little bird in his mouth. Swiftly I pull the door open again and see him putting the goldcrest down on exactly the same spot where I had picked it up.

Everything in the garden is growing, flowering and ripening, and you hear none of it. The big, important things come about in silence in the way the text is surrounded by white. The sun shines noiselessly. And the rain? The rain makes the kind of sound that is the obverse of silence: its temporary interruption and the expectation of its return. Writing makes no noise either.

Silence makes the slightest sounds audible. Something like the rustling of sunshine in the leaves. When the beloved speaks, silence is the echo of one word and the intimation of the next. Sometimes, at moments of intensified living, silence and sound lose their deep connection, they are torn apart and collide. That's how it was, in my memory, when G. had an orgasm: the taut silence out of which her body suddenly cried out and into which, dying away, it subsided again. Ilse's words of love are completely different: in her mouth, panting, the silence swells warm and damp without ever being broken.

These still, sunny October days are the most beautiful of the year. They have something of a subdued final festival about them. They pass like a yellow-spoked wheel turning very slowly. They are meant for stories about the summer which has gone. When a gentle wind ruffles the grass, the leaves under the walnut tree tremble like the wings of fallen birds. There are still some shrub roses out, but they are already tinged with death. The hollyhocks, yellow, white and red, have retreated to the tops of their stems. They can go no further.

From *The Charred Alphabet. Diary 1990-1991* (Het verkoolde alfabet. Dagboek 1990-1991. Amsterdam: De Arbeiderspers, 1992, pp. 9-13).
Translated by Jane Fenoulhet.

Paul de Wispelaere (1928-).
Photo by David Samyn.

'The

Orpheus of Amsterdam'

The Life and Work of Jan Pieterszoon Sweelinck

Let Sweelinck's image attract your eyes,
The ears he charmed, while still alive:
And know that, though he lived and died in Amsterdam,
It was from Deventer this great bard came.

This verse by the seventeenth-century poet Jacobus Revius refers to the one major event in the life of Jan Pieterszoon Sweelinck (1562-1621) that is not associated with the city of Amsterdam, namely his birth in Deventer. In his day this internationally famed composer, organist, expert in organ building and teacher was rightly praised as the '*Orpheus of Amsterdam*', the city where he lived from his boyhood and where he played the organ in the Oude Kerk from around 1577 until his death. Jan actually succeeded his father in that position and his son Dirck Janszoon in turn inherited it from him, so that this important musical post was held by three generations of Sweelincks, over a period of almost a century (1564-1652).

Jan Pieterszoon, who later added his mother's surname to this patronymic, can be seen as the last great representative of two centuries of European dominance by what is known as 'Netherlandish polyphony'. His contribution to both instrumental and vocal music was outstanding, particularly if we consider that his predecessors and contemporaries concentrated mainly on the religious and secular repertoire for the human voice. Thanks to the flourishing music printing industry, his vocal works enjoyed a wide circulation. His keyboard music, though, survived only in manuscript, showing that this repertoire was still overshadowed by vocal music. However, thanks to Sweelinck's fame as a teacher at home and abroad and, of course, to the exceptional quality of his work, instrumental music in general gradually grew in importance; it was the beginning of a triumphant progress that was to continue into the seventeenth century.

Sweelinck is a typical exponent of the Dutch municipal musical culture within the religious context of the Reformation. Whilst in other regions such as the Catholic Southern Netherlands the practice of music was 'directed' mainly by the Court and the Church, in the Calvinist North it was the municipal magistrates, the burgomasters and the municipal 'parliament' (the so-called 'vroedschap' or 'city fathers') who were responsible for artistic and cultural life. So as an organist at the Oude Kerk, Sweelinck was also a civil servant employed by the city's Calvinist administration. We can judge what this meant from his duties; these consisted not so much in enriching the liturgical services with organ music – as was the case in the Catholic south – but in giving a kind of public concert twice a day. Since the Calvinists had largely banished music from their services, the church building became a concert hall. This was the background against which most of Sweelinck's keyboard works originated. They were often performed not only on the organ, but also on the harpsichord, an extremely popular household instrument at the time. Indeed, the living room was a lively centre for part-song: family members and friends would gather round the table, especially after the midday meal, to perform religious motets or psalms, secular French chansons and Italian madrigals. So Sweelinck's contribution to vocal music concentrates on these genres, which also found a ready market in the flourishing 'collegia musica', or 'musical guilds', organisations of (highly skilled) amateurs who met every week to make music under the direction of a professional musician.

Sweelinck's work illustrates extremely well the diversity of musical life at the beginning of the Golden Age. Despite the blossoming of the arts at the end of the sixteenth century and in the early decades of the seventeenth and the presence of many extremely good musicians, Sweelinck's productivity, versatility and the superior quality of his oeuvre make him unique in the Netherlands.

Music for man
He made his mark in the field of the polyphonic French chanson, which reached a last peak of brilliance in the second half of the sixteenth century, thanks, among others, to Orlandus Lassus. In 1594, the year of Lassus' death, in Antwerp Pierre Phalèse published a collection of chansons for five voices entitled *Chansons ... de M. Iean Svvelingh organiste, et Cornille Verdonq nouvellement composées ...,* consisting of eighteen works by Sweelinck and four by his contemporary Cornelius Verdonck, then a singer with Philip II's celebrated 'capilla flamenca' in Madrid, who later lived and worked in Antwerp. Sweelinck proved right from the outset that he was a composer who had fully mastered current compositional techniques and at the same time followed the latest stylistic developments within the genre. On the one hand, he demonstrated his command – taken almost for granted in a composer from the Low Countries – of imitative counterpoint, in which all parts are equally involved in the presentation of the musical material. At the same time, his chansons betray the then ubiquitous influence of the Italian madrigal, in which particular attention was paid to the expressive rendition of the text. Yet Sweelinck's approach to the text remained fairly reserved. For example, he attempted none of the chromatic experiments that were coming into vogue at the time. Nor, in his own madrigals, did he succumb to the exuberant 'irregularities' preferred by some Italians, and in particular by the Neapolitan Carlo Gesualdo and to some extent also the young Claudio Monteverdi. This somewhat conservative, though certainly not inferior, approach is characteristic of the madrigal in the Netherlands in gen-

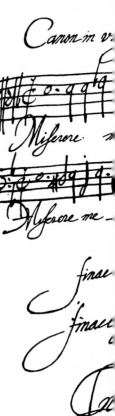

eral. Knowing the rather old-fashioned tastes of his public, in his numerous, highly-popular Antwerp publications Pierre Phalèse concentrated on more traditional madrigal compositions, such as the early works of Luca Marenzio. It is abundantly clear from his *Rimes françoises et italiennes* for two and three voices, published by the Leiden branch of the Antwerp firm Plantin in 1612, that Sweelinck was familiar with Phalèse's publications. A few of the madrigals are adaptations of existing compositions by, for instance, Marenzio and Andrea Gabrieli. These arrangements for just two or three voices were very popular in amateur circles. Sweelinck probably drew inspiration from the work of the polyphonist Jean de Castro from the Southern Netherlands, the top 'specialist' in, mainly, three-part arrangements of chansons and madrigals. Phalèse published numerous collections by him from 1569 onwards and they remained in great demand until well into the seventeenth century.

Engraved portrait of Jan Pieterszoon Sweelinck, made by J. in 1624, three years after the composer's death.

A canon by Sweelinck (autograph).

Music for God

In his religious music Sweelinck concentrated on two target groups: the members of the Dutch Reformed Church with his polyphonic settings of the French Geneva Psalter (four books of *Pseaumes de David*, published in Amsterdam and Haarlem between 1604 and 1621), and the still numerous Catholics in the North with his Latin motets, published in the Catholic stronghold of Antwerp (*Cantiones Sacrae*, 1619). Though Sweelinck converted to the new doctrine once the Calvinists assumed power in 1578 (he may have had no choice in the matter), he was not unsympathetic to his former Catholic faith. In fact, a relative religious tolerance prevailed and we know that Sweelinck's circle of friends did not include religious fanatics.

Sweelinck's Geneva psalms, in which he set Clement Marot's and Theodore de Bèze's translations to music based on the original monophonic melodies by Louis Bourgeois, form the absolute culmination of a development that had begun in the 1540s. Possibly he chose the French translations rather than the Dutch, which were also available, because the French repertoire was widely known in the Netherlands (especially the polyphonic adaptations by Claude Goudimel, one of the victims of the infamous St Bartholomew's Day Massacre, and Claude Lejeune), and also because the Dutch translations were poetically very weak. In the Latin motets of 1619, his '*opus ultimum*' (the final part of his French psalms appeared posthumously), Sweelinck showed in particular that 'classical' polyphony, based on imitative counterpoint and madrigalian expression, had lost none of its power, despite the growing European success of the 'modern' Italian style, the so-called '*accompanied monody*' in which a single voice, with instrumental accompaniment, carries the musical structure. However, these innovations only penetrated the Netherlands very slowly. The *Pathodia sacra et profana*, by the polymath Constantijn Huygens, published in Paris in 1647, is a good example of this Italian influence.

Pioneering in Perfection

Sweelinck's madrigals, of course, showed a marked Italian influence; but so also did his instrumental music, especially in the fantasias and the toccatas.

The fantasias, including the brilliantly conceived *Fantasia chromatica*, usually elaborate on a single theme which is ingeniously surrounded by ever-changing contrapuntal motifs and is itself manipulated using *augmentatio* and *diminutio*, increasing or diminishing the note values, techniques which Sweelinck employed with great skill to build a climax. The toccatas are extensive improvisations in which virtuoso ostentation alternates with more contrapuntal passages, which betray the Dutch heritage. The works of the Venetian San Marco organists, such as Andrea Gabrieli and Claudio Merulo, may have been his models, but the influence of the English virginalists is also very apparent. With virtuoso keyboard composers like John Bull, William Byrd and Peter Philips, English keyboard music flourished as never before around the turn of the century. Sweelinck was a personal friend of Bull and Philips, whose Catholic convictions had forced them to flee to the Southern Netherlands. In 1593 Philips travelled to Amsterdam '*only to sie and heare an excellent man of his faculties*', undoubtedly a reference to Sweelinck. The English influence is particularly noticeable in his variations on secular songs (*Est-ce Mars, Ick voer al over Rhijn, Mein junges Leben hat ein End*', etc.).

But it was especially with his variations on chorales and Gregorian chant (*Ich ruf zu dir Herr Jesu Christ, Ons is gheboren een kindekijn, Da pacem Domine*, etc.) that Sweelinck made history. His chorale adaptations began a tradition which spread to Northern and Central Germany, in particular, and eventually culminated in Johann Sebastian Bach's unsurpassed contribution to the chorale repertoire for organ. Sweelinck's name is in fact very much associated with his fame as a teacher: German organists in particular came to study under him. The most important of these were Samuel Scheidt and Johann Scheidemann, both masters of the chorale variation; they were taken as models by Dietrich Buxtehude and Johann Pachelbel, the very two composers who paved the way for Bach. Hence the inestimable historical importance of Sweelinck's instrumental work. He may not have been a true innovator, certainly not in vocal music. But he perfected a number of genres, and in instrumental music in particular he laid the groundwork for the lasting success of keyboard music in the baroque. His oeuvre does not overwhelm with spectacular dramatic effects, but, like seventeenth-century Dutch art in general, it excels because of '*a loving cultivation of detail, picturesque representation and mathematically contrived balance*', as the Sweelinck authority Frits Noske aptly expressed it. Consequently, – and I quote the last line of Noske's very worthwhile monograph on the composer – '*his genius does not reveal itself spontaneously; it is disclosed only by dint of insight and knowledge*'. The year 2000, when the 250th anniversary of Johann Sebastian Bach's death is being widely commemorated, would seem an appropriate time to re-evaluate one of the pioneers who prepared the way for Bach's monumental art; not only because of Sweelinck's historical importance, but equally because of the undeniable merit of his music.

IGNACE BOSSUYT
Translated by Alison Mouthaan-Gwillim.

FURTHER READING

Edition of Sweelinck's *Opera omnia*. Amsterdam, 1957 - .
Noske, Frits, *Sweelinck (Oxford Studies of Composers*, 22). Oxford, 1988, reprinted in paperback 1989 (with an extensive bibliography).

DISCOGRAPHY

Gustav Leonhardt, *J.P. Sweelinck, Organ Works* (DHM 05472 774342).
Netherlands Chamber Choir (various conductors), *J.P. Sweelinck. Choral Works*, 3 vols (NM Classics 92003; 92010 and 92015)
Trinity College Chapel Choir (conducted by R. Marlow), *J.P. Sweelinck, Cantiones Sacrae*, 2 vols (Hyperion CDA 67103-104).

hronicle

Architecture

Autonomous Building Architecture according to Erick van Egeraat

Early in 2000 the Hague newspaper *Haagse Post* published a personal 'top 15' selected by the architecture critics Ids Haagsma and Hilde de Haan. Surprisingly, top of the list was the architect Erick van Egeraat. In fact it was a double surprise. Rem Koolhaas is generally regarded as the most important Dutch architect working today, but the idiosyncratic Haagsma and De Haan rated him no higher than tenth place and a dismissive description as an '*ex-filmmaker and ex-journalist turned architect*'. Just as surprising was the fact that the list was not headed by an architect from the structuralist tradition to whom these two critics have pledged their souls. Although the most likely candidate of that school, Herman Hertzberger, did make it to the top ten, he was beaten to first place by Van Egeraat, who was praised for his all-round ability.

Erick van Egeraat, who has had his own firm of architects since the mid-nineties, began his career as one of the founders of Mecanoo. Even before he had completed his studies he and his fellow-students in Delft – Francine Houben, Chris de Weijer, Henk Döll and Roelf Steenhuis – won a competition to design housing for young people at Kruisplein in Rotterdam. The assignment which resulted from this led directly to the foundation of Mecanoo in 1984, getting it off to a flying start. During the eighties Mecanoo developed into one of the leading centres of the neomodernism which dominated Dutch architecture at a time when postmodernism was ruling the roost elsewhere in the world.

Van Egeraat left Mecanoo in 1995, shortly after his divorce from Francine Houben, and set up his own firm, (EEA) Erick van Egeraat associated architects. During the last five years he has made a start on devel-

oping his own oeuvre. He appropriated the ownership of several works from his Mecanoo days and took a number of assignments from Mecanoo with him. The most unusual of these was the conversion of a neo-renaissance building in Budapest into offices for the Dutch ING Bank (1992-1997). The high point of the conversion is the whale-shaped conference room on the top floor, a baroque room which partly protrudes above the glass roof of the building.

The conference room is an example of what Erick van Egeraat himself has described as new baroque – just one of the registers in which he plays. This is typical of Van Egeraat, who has sometimes claimed that architecture must be fashionable. His work at Mecanoo was itself not free of contemporary trends, but since he set up his own firm these have become even more marked. He is constantly looking for the new and different, and as a result the oeuvre of EEA has not developed in a straight line, but as a range of approaches juxtaposed alongside each other. Apart from the baroque-style 'blobs', which are also to be found in a design for television and radio studios for the Dutch television and radio broadcasting service NOS, and a planned pop music hall in Breda, he has also designed several other works which are exceptionally linear in shape and which betray a radical minimalism.

He himself explains the differences on the basis of the context: each situation demands a different approach. But that is only part of the story. Just as important is his attitude towards the architectural design, in which he is not interested in one thing or another, but one thing *and* another. Yet his sensitivity to context is an essential factor which also explains his success in building in such widely differing settings as Prague, Tilburg (NL), Budapest, Groningen (NL), Cork, Rotterdam, London and Stratford upon Avon, where Erick van Egeraat is to build the new complex for The Royal Shakespeare Theatre, the plan for which has not yet been made public. He combines his capacity to open himself up to the influences of the setting with a high-

Tilburg a row of homes and a small block of flats have been built which are characterised by their minimalist design and use of materials: they are plain, rectangular boxes of concrete and glass, with heavy timber door and window frames made from Western red cedar and gables of polished slate, lending this solid architecture a soft-as-silk air. In all these buildings the visual and tactile impression is at least as important as the spatial impression.

When it comes to EEA's international projects, things are progressing more slowly for the moment. Apart from the offices completed for the Dutch ING Bank in Budapest and Prague, most international commissions have yet to be carried out. This is the case with the Photographer's Gallery in London and the Cork Arts Centre in Cork, and also the Royal Shakespeare Theatre. EEA is to remodel the Shakespeare Theatre itself and its second theatre, The Other Place, and will also add a third theatre. The firm is also designing all manner of ancillary facilities for the theatres. The main difficulty with this project is raising the estimated cost of almost 95 million pounds; an application is to be made for National Lottery funding to meet roughly half the cost, but it is likely to be 2003 before that money is available.

HANS IBELINGS
Translated by Julian Ross.

ly developed sense of individuality. Because however important the context may be, Erick van Egeraat is the opposite of a contextualist who adapts to the appearance and structure of a given location. All his buildings are highly autonomous objects, a striking presence in the urban landscape.

In the Netherlands he has produced a stream of completed projects over the last few years, including the extension to the Natural History Museum in Rotterdam, a concrete box surrounded by a glass box; a physics laboratory for the University of Leiden whose most striking feature is its tilting, forward-leaning facade; the Vaktechnische Lyceum pre-university school in Utrecht; housing developments in Groningen and Tilburg; and the recently completed blue glass box at the Ichthus College in Rotterdam. In the Vaktechnisch Lyceum Van Egeraat has created facades which make the principle of the insulated cavity wall extremely transparent; insulation material has been applied to the concrete inner leaf of the cavity wall, and is clearly visible through the glass outer wall. The bottom of this glass outer wall consists of a grille, and the cavity is open at the top to provide the necessary ventilation. The glass wool insulation blanket behind the glass gives the reflective building a remarkable yellow glow.

The housing development in Groningen consists of identical dwellings, but the fact that the facade of each home is divided up in a different pattern prevents the development from looking like a repetitive terrace. In

Cultural Policy

Building Collections The Low Countries in the British Library

The British Library is justifiably renowned for its holdings of early printed (pre-1850) material from the Low Countries. The collection is an excellent reflection of the rich history of printing and publishing in that time and geographic area. As to the extent of this collection, the BL can compete with any of the major libraries in the Netherlands or Belgium. In fact, the BL's participation in the STCN-project (Short Title Catalogue Netherlands, Royal Library / PICA – this concerns the Netherlands only) underlines and reinforces the wealth of the collection. At present, with the work in full progress, some 65% of the BL's seventeenth-century holdings (1622-1700) have been entered on the PICA file.

The level of acquisition is no longer what it used to be and curators have to work with substantially reduced budgets. We are, nevertheless, still trying hard to expand the collection and make additions where necessary and / or possible. Let me give a recent example, and show the motivation for acquiring a particular book.

As trading nations, it is understandable that dictionaries appeared at an early date in the Low Countries. The merchant community needed their phrase books, grammars and dictionaries. The earlier examples combine Dutch / Flemish and French; Dutch and English came somewhat later. The BL holds an excellent range of early dictionaries. Recently, however, I was able to acquire an important extension to this collection. It concerns the first dictionary of mathematics published in the Low Countries which most certainly heralded a new era in specialist lexicography in the Northern Netherlands in particular. The editor of this *Volkoomen wiskundig woordenboek, daar in alle kunstwoorden en zaaken, welke in de beschouwende, en oeffende wiskunst voorkoomen, duydelyk verklaart worden* (Leiden, Coenraad en Georg Jacob Wishoff, 1740) was Willem la Bordus. Little is known about this figure, but his encyclopedic treatment of both Dutch and foreign mathematical terms and his use of a system of refined cross-referencing makes this dictionary an outstanding example of its kind. Moreover, it underlines that, despite the general economic decline of the Netherlands, printing had maintained its very high level of skill and sophistication during the first half of the eighteenth century.

It is remarkable that in the field of dictionary and encyclopedia the Dutch – Elzevier in particular – have continued that strong tradition to this very day. It is this awareness of continuity that helps us, the curators, to build truly coherent collections. It is in that sense somewhat unfortunate that many historians or librarians tend to focus almost exclusively on early collections. The quality of a library is judged by the number of Elzeviers or Plantins the collection can boast. This is an understandable, but not entirely fair attitude.

Over the last century and a half, BL curators have built a substantial modern (post-1850) collection of imprints from the Low Countries. All major authors, be it in fiction, drama or poetry, are represented, and their work is almost without exception available in complete or near-complete form. The majority of relevant studies in the humanities and social sciences, irrespective of the language in which these works are written, have been and still are being acquired by the responsible curator. In spite of decreasing budgets, substantial numbers of books are bought on a regular basis. The aim remains to offer the readers in the BL a highly representative selection of materials published in the Netherlands and Belgium. The website of the BL modern collections will be put on line shortly, and will be accompanied by a substantial, subject-based *Catalogue of Reference Works* concerning the Low Countries. This catalogue will give a good insight into the scope of the modern collections.

However, the *uniqueness* of a library can only be measured by the special collections its holds. Within our holdings of modern Low Countries imprints, I would like to single out a couple of such collections, one formed by a predecessor of mine, Mrs Anna Simoni (who, incidently, also published the substantial catalogue of our 1600-1621 Low Countries holdings), and one that I myself am in the process of establishing.

In a website for our Newspaper Library, I have highlighted a massive collection we hold of underground material published during the Second World War in the Netherlands. That material consists mainly of newspapers, leaflets, brochures, etc. Very much of parallel interest is the outstanding collection (as a collection only matched by the one in Amsterdam University Library) of clandestinely printed books from the time of the Nazi occupation. Anna Simoni crowned her activities with a catalogue entitled *Publish and be free. A catalogue of clandestine books printed in the Netherlands, 1940-1945, in the British Library* (Nijhoff, 1975). Successors to the compiler have continued her work and in 1995 a supplement to the catalogue was published in Amsterdam (AD&L Foundation).

Over a period of time, different curators bring their own expertise and interest to the job. What they share is an interest in continuity, a desire to build collections that will supply readers and researchers with the widest possible range of materials at their disposal. A collection is like a jigsaw (albeit a forever expanding jigsaw): over a period of time missing pieces will be found and added to the overall image. It is the search for those missing pieces which is an essential part of our curatorial activities.

The British Library. Photo by Irene Rhoden.

As far as the Netherlands are concerned, the years 1940-1950 have been without any doubt the most traumatic of this century. The German occupation was followed by the conflict with Indonesia and the loss of status as a colonial power. The occupation was in many ways a 'shared' experience for the Dutch, the Indonesian years on the contrary were very much a time of internal division and strife. Whilst the BL could present the readers with an excellent collection of materials concerning the situation in the Low Countries during the war, until recently documents on the Indonesian conflict were barely available (the early history of Dutch colonialism, on the other hand, was / is extremely well represented).

The past five years I have actively collected primary material – published during the years 1945-1950 – dealing with the Japanese occupation of the Netherlands East Indies and the Dutch-Indonesian conflict which followed. The collection is restricted to Western languages and is intended to give a complete spectrum of argument and counter-argument on Indonesian independence, of the legal and political discussion that accompanied the developments, the military involvement, the economic consequences, etc. Only the Koninklijk Instituut voor Taal-, Land- en Volkenkunde (Leiden University) can claim to have a bigger collection than the one in the British Library. An annotated catalogue is planned for next year. This catalogue will show that the BL collection is not a mere repetition of the holdings in Leiden, but very much an extension and a complement.

Let me dwell for a moment on this particular collection. The idea that the relentless progress of the means of communication heralds the end of the printed book has become a platitude amongst senior library managers. Collection building is an activity of the past and budgets are cut accordingly. This discussion reminds me very much of the scare stories that circulated amongst painters in the mid- and later nineteenth century. The emergence of photography would mean the death of painting. Not long after this discussion had lost some of its impact, painting flourished in new and exciting ways. Even portrait painting did not die. Similarly, the printed book will survive and thrive. Collections of printed materials will remain the basis for research (in the humanities in particular): the Indonesia collection in the BL – even before publication of the catalogue – has already attracted the attention of an MA student at University College London and her dissertation will concern a related subject.

In this case the examples given concern the Netherlands. A future curator may want to focus in more detail on Belgian affairs. He or she may concentrate on the works of a single author; one can think of Pol de Mont for example. Thanks to an substantial donation by the De Mont family to the library, the BL holds an excellent collection of works by this particular author. Maybe, on the other hand, this future curator will want to look at wider politico-cultural developments. Again, there is plenty of scope for activity. The BL has, for example, an outstanding collection of materials on the Flemish Movement, from its very beginnings in the late eighteenth century up to more recent times. It would be a worthy undertaking to compile a catalogue of our holdings on this particular subject. It is not until one actually starts using the collections that one becomes aware of the extraordinary riches the BL holds. It happened to me, some twenty-five years ago …

JAAP HARSKAMP

For the BL websites, see: http://www.bl.uk

The Dutch / Flemish Early Collections contribution is available on this site, the one for Modern Collections is under construction at the time of writing and should be accessible upon publication of this article.

The 'Best of Flanders and the Netherlands' BVN-TV

On 1 July 1997, Radio Netherlands (the Dutch international broadcaster), together with the NOS (the Dutch domestic radio and TV station), began broadcasting satellite TV programmes for Dutch-speakers in Europe on a daily basis. Right from the start, Radio Netherlands felt that that programmes of the Flemish public broadcaster (VRT) should be included in the programming.

The idea behind the venture was that the medium of television offers an excellent opportunity to present, promote and strengthen the Dutch language and Dutch and Flemish culture within and beyond Europe. Conserving and furthering the Dutch language and culture of the Low Countries can, after all, be achieved more effectively, more cheaply and efficiently, by 21 million Dutch-speakers together than by 15 million inhabitants of the Netherlands and 6 million Flemings separately.

The joint Flemish / Dutch satellite TV-station BVN-TV seeks to provide viewers abroad with information about Flanders and the Netherlands. Although many Dutch and Flemish people live or spend time abroad, they almost always feel a bond with the homeland. Likewise, they often feel a need to keep up to date and enjoy the familiar feeling of 'home'. BVN-TV ('Beste van Vlaanderen en Nederland'; 'Best of Flanders and the Netherlands') provides that connection, the latest news and the culture of home.

Close cooperation between the public broadcasters of the two countries and between the Flemish and Dutch governments is vital to the success of this venture. During the course of 1999 this collaboration was developed further. BVN and the Flemish Community signed a management agreement covering programming, management, and administrative and financial aspects. In addition to the two founding members (Radio Netherlands and NOS), the Flemish VRT is now also represented on the BVN Board, and thus plays a full part in the BVN organisation.

BVN is funded entirely from Dutch broadcasting budgets, supplemented by contributions from Radio

Netherlands and NOS. The Flemish Community is bearing most of the costs of the satellite link to North and South America. The Dutch Ministry of Education, Culture and Science and the Ministry of the Interior and Kingdom Relations are also making a substantial contribution.

BVN-TV can be compared to TV-stations like the French-language TV5 (with which the French-language Belgian broadcasting service RTBF works closely), the German Deutsche Welle, RTP Internacional of Portugal, DUNA TV (Hungary), TRT (Turkey), TV Polonia, and TVE (Spain). All these broadcasting services have in common that they use satellites to target viewers abroad who speak the same language and share the same country of origin.

Since the launch of BVN, the broadcasts have been compiled from programmes made by the Dutch public broadcasting organisations, the VRT, Radio Netherlands itself and from regional broadcasters. From this total package BVN selects programmes which are of interest to fellow Dutch-speakers abroad to form a block of six hours a day (6 pm - 12 pm CET), and then repeated in a carousel-formula. The programmes include the daily NOS and VRT news and current affairs bulletins, but also sport, documentaries, series, talk shows, entertainment and children's programmes. The broadcasters supply their programmes free of charge.

Between 7 pm and 8 pm CET only Flemish programmes are broadcast, including the children's programme TikTak and the VRT-Journaal news programme at 7 pm.

BVN can be received free-to-air and unencrypted via the ASTRA satellite throughout Europe and North Africa as well as the Middle East.

On 1 September 1999 the reception area of BVN-TV was extended substantially. BVN can now also be received in North and South America. In Aruba and the five islands making up the Netherlands Antilles BVN is transmitted free by all cable systems, and some of the programmes are also carried by local tv stations. The

BVN satellite link to the Netherlands Antilles and Aruba was officially opened on Curaçao on 15 November 1999 by Queen Beatrix of the Netherlands. In order to receive BVN in the USA and Canada, however, viewers must have a satellite TV decoder and must subscribe to BVN (at nominal rates).

Programmes are transmitted to South America via the Orion-II satellite, which provides a sufficiently strong signal for reception on the South American continent.

From a technical point of view, making BVN available in regions such as South Africa and Australasia presents no (major) problems. The financial feasibility of broadcasting and reception in these regions is currently being examined.

ARMAND SLIEPEN
Translated by Julian Ross.

BVN-TV
P.O. Box 222 / 1200 JG Hilversum / The Netherlands
Tel.: +31 35 6724 333 / +31 35 6724 343 / e-mail: bvn@rnw.nl
http://www.bvn.nl

Film and Theatre

An Ode to Transience Terschellings Oerol

Theatre is an ephemeral art. It is there, the audience experiences it, and it has gone again. All that remains is a memory. The individual spectator's unique perception of that moment never returns. Thus it is in nature too: the sun sets as often as it rises, no tree keeps its leaves forever, and every footstep in the sand is erased. Nowhere does one experience the transience of nature more acutely than on an island, where the all pervasive sea is as generous in what it gives as it is ruthless in what it takes.

As soon as an island and a theatre make a pact with each other a special harmony, an ode to transience, is the inevitable result. In this case the island is Terschelling – the second largest of the Frisian islands in the Dutch Wadden Sea, two hours by boat from the mainland, with a surface area of about ninety square kilometres and a population of some five thousand – and the theatre is Oerol – a ten-day, international summer festival of theatre which includes music and dance, and also a wide variety of visual arts.

Location is all-important here: the whole island is a stage which inspires and stimulates theatre producers and visual artists alike. In 1999, to name one example, Tryater from Leeuwarden (Friesland) presented an adaptation in the Frisian language of Henrik Ibsen's famous classic *Peer Gynt* on a sand drift on the east side of the island. The Norwegian saga on which Ibsen drew and the story-telling tradition of the islanders; the adventurous voyage of Peer Gynt and the indefinable 'island feeling' of the visitors to Terschelling; the

Henrik Ibsen's *Peer Gynt* by Tryater during the 1999 Oerol festival. Photo by E. Coblijn.

primitive staging and the vastness of the landscape; all this gave rise to a unique chemical reaction from which sprang a genuine theatrical experience.

The natural settings of beach, dunes and woodland are not the only backdrops for the festival productions; performances are also given in the streets of the villages of West-Terschelling and Midsland, performances of the kind one would hope to encounter there: circus acts, colourful and expressive, with dressed-up street musicians, acrobats, jugglers and other strolling players. As the United Kingdom is traditionally the major source of supply of such entertainers, it is only natural that it should be strongly represented at the Oerol festival. The festival visitor on the way from one performance to the other is frequently taken by surprise by a spontaneous clowns' act, short and nameless and unlisted in the programme guide.

Together with the picturesque villages and the wide variety of places of natural beauty, the character of the Frisian islands is determined by the numerous barns and sheds scattered about the landscape. Some years ago the festival organisers discovered that these barns, boathouses and beachcombers' sheds were ideal small 'indoor-theatres'. They even proved so successful as locations that the so-called Oerol 'barn theatre' became a category all on its own. Just as in other venues, new productions are sometimes created on the spot, or existing productions are adapted to the surroundings.

Dogtroep, probably Dutch theatre's finest export, is an Amsterdam company that deliberately chooses to work within the possibilities and limitations of changing environments. On the occasion of Oerol's tenth season in 1991, Dogtroep turned the traditional closing feature of the festival into a superb show entitled *Fraternal Strife* (Broederstrijd). A rapidly swelling number of spectators joined a Dogtroep procession which began in Midsland and ended on the beach, almost three kilometres away. There the struggle between two men for the favours of a woman reached its apotheosis. The woman, grown sick and tired of the wrangling, disappeared in the direction of the sea and drifted coolly towards the horizon, leaving the men behind in dismay. The air was filled with the plaintive sound of the fog-horn.

The history of Terschellings Oerol is the history of Joop Mulder, better known to insiders as Captain Oerol. Mulder has lived on Terschelling since 1978 and is landlord of Kroeg De Stoep in Midsland, a café that has been the life and soul of the festival for almost twenty years. At the beginning of the Eighties Mulder, who wanted to do more on Terschelling than '*pull beer and fill his pockets*' got together with a handful of kindred spirits and made concrete plans to realise their dream of holding a cultural festival on the island. The first festival, in the summer of 1982, did little more than blaze the trail, with few performers, small audiences, not much media attention and above all very little money.

Time and time again over the years money has been the factor that has threatened the continued existence of the festival. In the early days neither regional nor governmental authorities could be convinced of the cultural and economic value of Oerol. Only when the festival had achieved success by its own efforts did structural grants from the municipality, the government and local businesses start to flow. Now, however, the organisers, with Mulder at their head, face a new problem: how to deal with their success. From the initial two to three thousand visitors in 1982 numbers have risen to more than forty thousand. The serious question now is: how to regulate this growth? One of the ways being tried is a general upgrading of the contents of the programme: no more big pop concerts on the beach or other big crowd pleasers; instead the selection of programme items aimed at specific target groups and simultaneous programming of a variety of acts. To avoid burdening the island with even greater numbers of visitors, the organisers of the 2000 festival, entitled *If the Tide Turns* (Als het tij keert), looked for ways of serving a mass audience by live broadcasts on the Internet. With creative solutions of this kind there is – for the time being at least – no need to fear for the continued existence of Terschellings Oerol despite the frequency and emphasis with which both the theatre and nature have demonstrated their ephemeral character.

JOS NIJHOF
Translated by Elizabeth Mollison.

Terschellings Oerol
P.O. Box 327 / 8890 AA Midsland (Terschelling) / The Netherlands
Tel.: + 31 562 448 448 / fax: +31 562 449 087
e-mail: oerol@frieslandnet.nl

Making Films for Mao and Stalin?
Joris Ivens and the Documentary Context

Two years ago the hundredth anniversary of the birth of the Dutch documentary filmmaker Joris Ivens (1898-1989)was commemorated with a three-day conference in the Dutch town of Nijmegen. The organiser of *Joris Ivens and The Documentary Context* was the European Joris Ivens Foundation. The proceedings of that conference have now been published under the editorship of Kees Bakker: a handful of articles which sketch various aspects of the oeuvre of this world citizen from Nijmegen, followed by five original texts by the master himself, dating mainly from the early years of his career.

Ivens was born in 1898: the same year as Bertolt Brecht and Hans Eisler, as André Stufkens notes in his article. And there are a number of striking parallels in their development. All three began their careers in the front line of the avant-garde movement. Their concerns were initially formal-artistic. Not long after, they embraced the communist doctrine and with great conviction produced work in accordance with the party ideology.

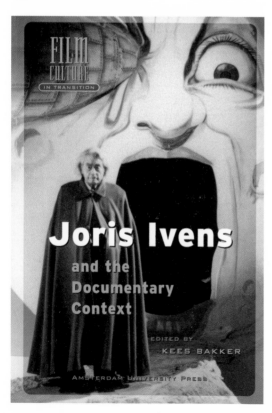

Ivens produced his first important work, *The Bridge* (De brug), in 1928. The theme was the new 'De Hef' railway bridge in Rotterdam. It was an abstract exercise in graphic and rhythmic design, a constructivist composition which ended with a true Malevich finale: a black square in a white field. The film immediately drew praise from his friends at the cinematophile Film League. The way in which Ivens and his kindred spirits reacted against contemporary mainstream cinema at the end of the 1920s sounds strikingly modern: according to them, Hollywood placed too much emphasis on *'the sentimental angle of cheap stories, as well as the sex angle'*. In a previously unpublished lecture from 1939, delivered at the Museum of Modern Art in New York ('Documentary: Subjectivity and Montage'), Ivens traces the origins of the documentary to that dissatisfaction with 'Hollywood': *'We thought they were too distant from reality. There was a very strong and logical reaction from students, artists and young people in Europe who thought we should fight against this sort of thing and base our work on reality. That was the beginning of the documentary film.'* Reality versus the Hollywood dream factory.

For Ivens, the documentary was not one genre among others; it represented a higher form of cinema: *'The documentary film expresses reality as it is, whereas the film industry usually expresses itself through bad taste that competes for the favour of the audience by adjusting to the bad taste of that audience – yes even drawing inspiration from it – without trying to generate any reaction or stimulating any activity.'* In these 'Notes on the Avant-garde Documentary Film' from 1931 we see the balance tilting towards a more activist approach to reality. Film not only has to represent reality; the filmmaker must actually change reality.

At first sight it would appear that history has found against Ivens' militant commitment. Bert Hogenkamp opens his lucid piece on the tumultuous relationship between Ivens and the Netherlands with a fragment of an interview from *Nieuwe Revue* (28 June 1995) in which the Dutch politician (now European Commissioner) Frits Bolkestein described Joris Ivens as *'a pur sang communist'*, *'a propagandist of an inhuman system'*. *'For me he equals Leni Riefenstahl, the Nazi filmmaker'*. A little further on Michel Korzec and Hans Moll, in an article from the weekly *Intermediair* (4 October 1985) reinforce this view. In 1985 Ivens received the most important Dutch film prize, the Golden Calf. How is that possible, wondered Korzec and Moll, for a filmmaker who has served two mass murderers – Stalin and Mao? *'Leni Riefenstahl's contribution to Nazism was a myth, that of Ivens was a fact'*. In other areas too, the message proclaimed by Ivens in his work does not always go down too well: the glorification of technological progress in a film like *Komsomol* (also known as *Song of Heroes*) about the selfless dedication of young people working in the Magnitogorsk blast furnaces in 1933. Or the series from 1976 about the consequences for the lives of ordinary people of the Cultural Revolution in China: *How Yukong Moved the Mountains* (Comment Yukong deplaça les montagnes). Ideologically, these works are no longer digestible. The political gullibility, the romantic tone, the paternalist vision of the relationship between the ignorant masses and the visionary filmmaker, belongs irrevocably to a distant past.

At the same time, this is precisely what makes this oeuvre so fascinating: together with filmmakers such as Robert Flaherty, Dziga Vertov and the Belgian Henri Storck, Joris Ivens was indeed in at the birth of a genre. He helped to shape the language of the documentary. He regarded the arrival of sound films with suspicion, feeling they were bound to lead to a general 'dumbing down' of the medium. Ivens had to discover the relationship between image and sound experimentally. And later, when the 16 mm camera and synchronous sound became commonplace, Ivens' documentaries would evolve yet again. The filmmaker who rounded off his oeuvre in 1988 with *A Tale of the Wind* (Une histoire de vent) lived in a world which was completely different from that before the First World War. Ivens was a privileged witness to the twentieth century. In the thirties he made films in the Netherlands, but also in Russia. Together with Ernest Hemingway he presented a view of the Spanish Civil War (*The Spanish Earth*; Terre d'Espagne, 1937), delivered a sharp commentary on the colonial policy of his country (*Indonesia Calling*, 1946), worked in East Germany and in Poland, and in the meantime made a poetic evocation of Paris (*The Seine Meets Paris*; La Seine a rencontrée Paris, 1957), for which he won the Palme d'Or award in Cannes. From the end of the 1950s onwards he popped up in Italy, Mali, Cuba, Chile, Vietnam and regularly in China too. His films not only recorded history, but also his own engagement with the events. A great many of his statements tend to jar somewhat on our ears today, but in turning things round like this we are doing the work of Ivens – and history itself – an injustice. We must not forget that a whole generation of intellectuals and artists shared Ivens' sympathies to a greater or lesser extent.

Anyone wishing to get to know this fascinating maker of documentaries will find, in addition to the films, something to his liking in a whole bookcase-full of biographies and works of reference. Ivens himself wrote two autobiographies (*The Camera and I*, 1969, and *Joris Ivens ou la mémoire d'un regard*, 1982), which are available in several languages.

This new collection of essays does not immediately go to the top of the list of required reading. The many different angles of approach, which merge anything but seamlessly, combine to form a very cubist portrait. After briefly making the acquaintance of Ivens' first wife, the reader suddenly ends up with his third wife. The thread of Stufkens' fine account of Ivens' youth and avant-garde years breaks off abruptly. At first, we by-pass Spain, but Ivens himself returns to it later in his own texts – albeit in a very plastic way. In the essay referred to by Bert Hogenkamp on Ivens' relationship with his mother country, we switch to widescreen; a series of other texts are in extreme close-up. In some articles we wade through sentences in which reality is buried under high-brow language. But this theoretical approach, too, was part of the mental world of Joris Ivens. His own texts demonstrate that he was occupied by fundamental themes: What is a documentary? Is it permissible to stage reality in a documentary? What does objectivity mean? Ivens' answer to this latter question – in *The Camera and I* – was in fact highly original: '*Do we demand objectivity in the evidence presented at a trial? No, the only demand is that each piece of evidence be as full a subjective, truthful, honest representation of the witness's attitude as an oath on the Bible can produce from him*'

ERIK MARTENS
Translated by Julian Ross.

Kees Bakker (ed.), *Joris Ivens and the Documentary Context*. Amsterdam: Amsterdam University Press, 1999; 320 pp. ISBN 90-5356-389-X.

The Taboos of the Documentary Film
The Work of Henri Storck

The eldest son of the owner of a shoe shop in the fashionable seaside resort of Ostend, Henri Storck (1907-1999) had a sheltered childhood. His father died when Henri was just sixteen years old. Storck's 'second father' Dr De Knop introduced him to a number of artists in Ostend, including James Ensor. It was the twenties and the young Henri Storck was captivated by the new medium of film; Robert Flaherty's *Moana* made a particularly deep impression on him. The young man from Ostend promptly founded a film club, which was a resounding success. No fewer than a thousand members joined up, including Ensor. Storck began making his own films, though he had to learn the tricks of the trade for himself, for there were no film schools in those days and film handbooks were few and far between. He had two yardsticks: painting, namely the 'Ostend School', and the films of like-minded young directors.

Films had one major advantage over painting and that was movement. With the film camera Storck observed what were for him everyday things like the sea and the dunes. Loyal to the avant-garde traditions of those years, he was less concerned about *what* the camera showed than *how* it showed it. Visual compositions and the associations that could be created using montage, producing a composite whole by combining several different shots, played an important role in this. The screening of one of Storck's films at an international congress in Brussels nevertheless proved a little too much for his young French counterpart Jean Vigo: '*So much water, so much water!*' he sighed aloud. But after the screening the two became firm friends, and in 1932 Storck helped Jean Vigo produce his provocative film about rebellious public schoolboys, *Zéro de conduite*.

Within the space of a few years Henri Storck had gained the necessary practical experience. He was 'official film director for the city of Ostend' for a while,

Two frame-enlargements from
Borinage (1934)

ran his own film laboratory, was correspondent for a newsreel, wrote surrealistic film scripts and worked in several French film studios. Yet when in 1933 the Brussels Club de l'Ecran invited him to make a film about the misery and suffering in the Borinage, the infamous Belgian mining region, he did not feel he was experienced enough. So he asked his Dutch counterpart and friend Joris Ivens to work on the Borinage film with him. In fact, Ivens had much the same background as Storck (son of a tradesman, founder of a film club, maker of avant-garde films), but because of his long stay in the Soviet Union Ivens was more politically aware. The Dutchman had no hesitation in accepting the proposal.

Thanks to doctor Paul Hennebert, Joris Ivens and Henri Storck were soon familiar with the problems in the Borinage and the terrible poverty that was rife among large groups of miners following the unsuccessful strike of 1932. The film-makers were forced to distance themselves from their avant-gardist principles: it was no longer a question of capturing the 'beauty' of poverty with the film camera, the images had to be a condemnation of that poverty. They decided to 'reconstruct' a number of the events told to them by the mineworkers. Thus the demonstration in Wasmes to

mark the fiftieth anniversary of Karl Marx's death was re-enacted by the parties concerned, complete with Marx's portrait in oils. Unaware of what was actually going on, the bystanders thought it was a real demonstration and raised their fists. What better proof of the success of the reconstruction technique that was so contentious among documentary makers!

Borinage became a turning-point in Ivens' career, the film that put him on the road to '*the hotbed of world history*', just as Vincent van Gogh went '*in search of the sun and himself*' after his stay in the Borinage. Storck remained in Belgium and made several more films about social issues. For *Houses of Misery* (Huizen der ellende, 1937), a poignant plea for the construction of cheap housing for the workers, he decided to use actors: '*In the Borinage the workers understood why we were making the film, but that was not the case in the slums. So there was no point in reconstructing. That's why I took actors.*' When making his *Peasants' Symphony* (Boerensymfonie, 1943), a film about a year in the life of a peasant family, with a peasant wedding as the epilogue, Storck was confronted with the harsh reality of war. He was twice forced to find another family, after the Gestapo had arrested the head of the household because of his involvement in the resistance. *Peasants' Symphony* is a marvellous film in which Storck observes man and nature, life and death in a highly creative manner.

According to Storck, two taboos distinguish the documentary from the feature film. A true documentary maker will never violate human suffering, grief and death, nor the intimate act of lovemaking, whereas there is scarcely a feature film made without an often very explicit reference to love and death. Hence, too, Storck's aversion to the 'close-up' which, he believed, is intended for actors and so for the feature film. Having said that, Henri Storck did make use of the 'close-up' to expose the intimate details of the work of painters like Rubens, Delvaux, Labisse and Permeke. These films are characterised by a sophisticated orchestration of camera movement, cutting and visual transitions and a fitting commentary. Another genre in which he excelled was Belgian folklore. Between 1969 and 1975 he produced *Festivals of Belgium* (Feesten van België), a series about national festivals with a bizarre, usually ritual character. The films show Storck at his best: intimately involved with the events, without ever indulging in voyeurism.

Besides being the maker of seventy films, Henri Storck also sat on an infinite number of committees. He was involved in every international initiative in the field of documentaries. In his own country, too, he initiated scores of important projects, from the Royal Belgian Film Archive in the thirties to the Centre Bruxellois de l'Audiovisuel in the seventies. A chair at the Free University of Brussels was named after him. Storck left his legacy of films and archive material to the Henri Storck Foundation in Brussels.

BERT HOGENKAMP
Translated by Alison Mouthaan-Gwillim.

Theatre on the Edge Jan Lauwers' Needcompany

Few makers of theatre in the Low Countries today explore the limits of their medium as intensively as the Fleming Jan Lauwers (1957-). Perhaps this is not surprising; he trained as a visual artist, and so still regards the medium with a mixture of critical awareness and admiration. What he tries to achieve in his productions is to make speech, text, movement and form rub up against and merge into each other until the image freezes time. Lauwers gives our eyes an erotic charge. What they see then, he calls 'borderline images': your attention is drawn to a single element. You dive into your memory, constructing a web of associations, but without forgetting the image you saw on the stage. Quite the reverse, in fact: charged with memory, the image becomes even more alive. That is the strength of Jan Lauwers' theatrical work: despite its complexity (while the text is the driving force of his productions, it is often obstructed by the actors' strange way of speaking, by movement or music, so that it does not always provide a firm reference-point) there are always those 'borderline images' which stick in your memory. With the result that for all their complexity Lauwers' productions are crystal clear. Joe Melillo, artistic director of New York's prestigious Brooklyn Academy of Music which hosted an extensive programme by Needcompany in 1999, says of them: 'The acting is often very direct, clear and physical. A style of direction very different to what we are used to here'. The production Melillo is referring to is Morning Song, a 1999 piece which harks back strongly to Lauwers' early days, when his work still had a marked 'performance' character. In 1979 he established the Epigonenensemble, soon rechristened Epigonentheater ZLV. The company was set up by people from all manner of artistic disciplines, who consequently had an uninhibited approach to theatre. The language of movement it developed was extremely energetic. Images bombarded the audience in unusually rapid succession; but like a musical score they also varied in intensity, with moments of repetition and tranquillity tempering the torrent of images.

The name Epigonentheater ZLV ('Zonder Leiding Van' – 'Not Directed By') refers to the way in which Jan Lauwers created his productions at the time: collectively, with no one individual definitively in charge. The personality of the actors played a significant part, so that elements in productions such as Wounded Already, And It's Not Even Wartime (Reeds gewond, en het is niet eens oorlog, 1981), The Demonstration (De demonstratie, 1983), The Ostrich-Bullet (De struiskogel, 1983) and Incident (Incident, 1985) gained an indirect social relevance through the input of the actors' own emotions and experiences. But the grotesque effects in these productions provided a kind of advance notice of what would become a constant in Lauwers' work: even then, simply by the rapid succession of images, he was making mincemeat of the traditional rules of theatre.

Morning Song has several features of that performance period – for instance, cooking is done on stage and there is a decided soap-element to the story – but at the same time this production engages with the themes which have occupied Lauwers in the last ten years. The story is set at a wedding-party, at which a good many fateful twists in the characters' lives come up in conversation. Life and death seem to be relative, certainly in art. In the production it is said that dying is a pleasure, but that does not spoil the enjoyment of the festive meal. Morning Song forms a diptych with Caligula (1998), under the title No beauty for me there where human life is rare. In Caligula the main character says: 'People die and are not happy'. But another character retorts: 'True, but that doesn't stop people enjoying a good meal'.

In Jan Lauwers' work you always have opposites which complement each other: his intention is to show beauty, but he never forgets to reveal the painful aspects as well. He even mixes the two. His whole oeuvre is built on bipolarity: individual performance as op-

Needcompany's King Lear, 2000. Photo by Maarten Vanden Abeele.

posed to that of the group, empathic acting contrasted with detachment, beauty set against decay, passion and violence, *eros* and *thanatos*. All these elements are absorbed into a constant battle between on one side the '*security of form*', as Lauwers describes conventional theatre, and on the other a fragmentation of the story by the way it is told, often in a confrontation between 'conscious' acting and non-acting. In short, everything is constantly being put at risk. And it is in that space between the two poles that Jan Lauwers' dramas are played out: for instance, when speech becomes a cacophony of voices or a mixture of Dutch and foreign tongues, or when an actress suddenly stops talking and begins to move, so that we almost seem to be watching a *tableau vivant* rather than a theatrical production. Normally the purpose of the acting, the props on stage and the timing of any part of the action is to make a story 'realistic', but that is not the case here. Lauwers thus reveals the absurd, unnatural way theatre works, for the theatre's reality is of course of a different order to actual reality. In his *Snakesong Trilogy*, in particular, which he reworked as a full-length production in 1998, Lauwers developed this idea in an intriguing way. In 1993 he had written the libretto for a musical, *Orfeo*. In it he laid the foundations for the trilogy, for in the oracle's English-language monologue he defines the lines of force that govern the role of art relative to society: '*(...) What more can I do than just watch, standing on the sideline, without even trying to understand, looking on without laughing or crying, when necessity, together with desire, is destroyed.*' This quotation is at the heart of the first part of the *Snakesong* trilogy, *Le voyeur* (1994), for which Lauwers drew on works by Alberto Moravia. The individual observes, is curious, but takes no part in the action: that is the message. As a spectator, you observe a glamour-show in which the actresses duly 'freak out'. Typical of Lauwers is the combination of detachment and emotionality he achieves in this scene by having the actresses speak parts of the text simultaneously. The spectator catches himself behaving like a voyeur, for he just sits there blithely watching and listening to the goings-on on stage. This leads the spectator to wonder: when watching Jan Lauwers' productions, which should he rely on most - his reason or his emotions?

In *Le pouvoir* (1995) this conflict between reason and feeling is developed further. Lauwers found the inspiration for this second part of the trilogy in *The Tears of Eros* by the French philosopher Georges Bataille, in which he writes about a rock-painting in the caves at Lascaux. It depicts a wounded bison with its entrails spilling out; in front of the animal lies a man with an erection. There is yet another phallic symbol in the painting: a bird on a stick. From this Lauwers concludes that sex and violence have evidently always been vitally important, and still are, but in a repressed way because our society appears to be governed by reason. This is precisely the subject of *Leda*, a piece by Lauwers himself which he reworked in *Le pouvoir*. It focuses strongly on the issue of guilt. Leda and the Greek god Zeus appear before the Supreme Court,

where they have to respond to the question whether or not they enjoyed the sexual act. No answer is possible, of course, for an extreme physical experience can never be completely expressed in words.

In Lauwers' trilogy the individual has to justify himself each time in rational terms. In *Le voyeur* that happens in a sort of television show, in *Le pouvoir* we get a complex court hearing. The Queen (synonymous with feeling) sees her realm being destroyed by excessive thinking, aided and abetted especially by her counsellor Professor Fight, synonym for reason. Strikingly, the Professor plays a far more active part here than in *Le voyeur*. This is not the case in the trilogy's irresistibly ironic final part, *Le désir* (1996), in which he appears on stage semi-paralysed. It turns out that he has murdered the Queen Mother: reason has destroyed feeling, but has to pay the price. To the Professor the women represent pleasure, and he makes clear that he is above all that; but it is precisely the women who take charge of his moribund existence. He has constantly to allow them to help him.

In the *Snakesong Trilogy*, then, not only reason and feeling but also sex, violence and death – what Jan Lauwers calls his Holy Trinity – are constantly in the foreground. That he should be so fascinated by these three phenomena is not surprising, for if there is anything that cannot be portrayed explicitly on stage without looking ridiculous or sentimental, it is these three.

Jan Lauwers has put his trademark also on Shakespeare's plays; he always comes back to them, in between the productions in which he mixes his own texts with those of others. He says of this: '*The reason I always end up back with Shakespeare is simple: I hardly know any other repertoire. Besides, Shakespeare's texts are so difficult that you can never understand them completely. You can follow the play, and feel what is going on. You can sense intuitively what it's about at a first reading or performance, but then when you start to read every sentence separately, suddenly you don't understand anything any more.*' This idea ties up with his own work, in which exploring '*borderline images*' is more important than analysing what happens. Sex, violence and death are of course key elements in Shakespeare's plays, but they are particularly involved with power - something which holds an equal fascination for Lauwers, to judge by his choice of plays: *Julius Caesar* (1990), *Antony and Cleopatra* (Antonius en Cleopatra, 1992), *Needcompany's Macbeth* (1996) and *Needcompany's King Lear* (2000). Often the power is in the hands of a ruler, whose seemingly unassailable position is undermined by irrational thoughts and motivations – not uncommonly planted in his mind by a woman. It is no accident, then, that in Lauwers' version much of the role of Macbeth is played by the actress Viviane de Muynck. She is supported in this by another actress, but there are also two male actors who each play part of the role: a metaphor for the polarity of reason and feeling common to both sexes. While in *Macbeth* the violence is still detached, in *King Lear* Lauwers really brings out the dark side of humanity. But again he makes effective use of antitheses, bringing light into the darkness by incorporating fragments of dance. And the lines themselves have an almost physical quality: throughout the play they are projected above the actors' heads like some supervisory power, so that one alternately reads and listens to them. Rarely has Jan Lauwers formulated the beauty of pain so acutely as in *King Lear*. He will undoubtedly take that fundamentally human story further still.

PAUL DEMETS
Translated by Tanis Guest.

History

Truth or Legend? Thomas Becket in Flanders

When, in 1164, Archbishop Thomas Becket opposed the arrogations the English King, Henry II of the Plantagenets, placed on the English church, he incurred the wrath of both the royal court and the English clergy. Who did he think he was? Despite his modest origins, as the chancellor and friend of the King he possessed incredible power and luxury. Having been catapulted to the position of Primate of All England in the space of a few days, in the view of the bishops and abbots he had earned hardly any credit as the defender of their interests.

Thomas Becket fled England to plead his case with Pope Alexander III and the French King, Louis VII. Only after six years of laborious negotiations was he able to effect a return to Canterbury. One month later, on 29 December 1170, four of Henry II's knights struck him dead in the cathedral. The grave of this new martyr drew thousands of pilgrims to Canterbury for centuries.

Was Thomas Becket also known in Flanders during his lifetime? His first significant visit to the county dates from 1163, when, in full regalia, he was welcomed by Count Philip of Alsace as he proceeded to the Council of Tours. He had certainly maintained good relations with Chancellor Robrecht van Aire since the Treaty of Dover.

In November 1164 he landed as a refugee, tired and spent, on the beach at Oye. He found accommodation at the nearby town of Gravelines, and then went to the abbey of Clairmarais. After three days of lying low in the marshes, he was warmly received at St Bertin's Abbey in the town of St Omer. He quickly travelled on to France in the company of Godescalc, Abbot of St Bertin, and Milo II, Bishop of Terwaan (now Thérouanne). Count Philip, who had promised to help him in time of need, did not intercede.

During his exile in Pontigny and Sens, Count Philip of Alsace made several attempts to bring about a reconciliation with the English King. It was mainly his chancellor who pressed for this; in 1168 Becket called him '*his only friend in time of adversity*'. The diplomatic negotiations took place at a very high level and

Anonymous Flemish Master,
Portrait of St Thomas of Canterbury. 17th century.
St Trudo's Abbey, Male. Photo
Stedelijke Musea, Kortrijk.

often in secrecy. When the agreement had finally been signed and Becket was able to return to Canterbury, he bade his Flemish friends farewell in the castle at Guines. He embarked for England from Wissant at the end of November 1170.

After Becket's death and canonisation (1173), pilgrims soon began to make their way to Canterbury, not only from England but also from the Continent. For example, in 1179 Philip of Alsace visited the grave of the English saint in the company of King Louis VII of France, who begged for a cure for his ailing son Philip August. On a broader European scale superb works of art were made in honour of this popular saint, and his relics became widely distributed. For example, the monastery of Dommartin got its hands on one of Becket's surplices, still stained with his blood. Pilgrims who could not afford the crossing to Canterbury went to this monastery to beg for his assistance.

Geoffrey Chaucer, who died in 1400, included various Flemish elements in his *Canterbury Tales*. 'The Pardoner's Tale' is set in an inn '*in Flaunders*', and one of the tales' most colourful figures is Sir Thopas, born in Poperinge.

Medieval pilgrims' badges with pictures of Thomas Becket have been found in Flanders and the Netherlands. In Ypres a splendid ampulla was found on which the saint's burial is depicted. Flemish miniaturists have illustrated Becket's murder in numerous books of hours, often destined for English customers. Ghent and Bruges were the leading centres of production of what are now world-renowned miniatures.

We know nothing of the origins of the veneration of a twelfth-century chasuble, maniple and stola in Groeninge Abbey in Kortrijk. Intensive examination of the fabric has been able to establish its date, but these relics are only mentioned in writings from the seventeenth century on. Is there a possible connection with the medieval Chapel of St Thomas which was once part of the fortress at Kortrijk, and which was demolished at the end of the fourteenth century? Chasubles of St Thomas were also venerated at the Abbey of St Nicolas des Prés near Tournai, in the Abbey of the Dunes and in the beguinage in Diksmuide. Their origins are unclear. The legend telling of St Thomas' dedication of the chapel at the count's castle in Male is attributed to Jan van Ieper or Iperius, a fourteenth- century chronicler at St Bertin's Abbey.

In the sixteenth century Henry VIII established Anglicanism in England and forbade the veneration of St Thomas of Canterbury. By contrast, Catholics who had fled from England brought their saint to the attention of the Flemish, supported in this by the Counter-Reformation. Several fine seventeenth-century portrayals of St Thomas of Canterbury are still preserved, one in St Trudo's Abbey in Male. He is depicted in a bishop's robes and usually with a sword across his skull. At the abbey in Hemiksem his portrait was included in a gallery of Cistercian saints.

The veneration of the saint flared up for a third time in the nineteenth century, when there was a marked revival in Christianity after the anticlimax of the French Revolution. The foundation of countless monasteries, and new churches and church ornamentation brought new popularity to several saints, such as St Rock, who was invoked against the plague and infectious diseases. The cult of St Thomas of Canterbury persisted in several places, including La Motte-au-Bois, Diksmuide and Male. His veneration at La Motte-au-Bois also had its roots in the Middle Ages, when a castle of the counts of Flanders was established there. And as far as Kortrijk is concerned, in the nineteenth century it was discovered that the Goethals family possessed a few fragments of a thirteenth-century illustrated life of St Thomas. The manuscript is attributed on stylistic grounds to the English monk Matthew Paris and was quoted by Thomas Stapleton, a sixteenth-century Catholic scholar who had fled England and worked in Douai and Leuven. It was only recently that the present owner lent these extremely valuable parchments to the British Library, where they form part of Loan no. 88.

GREET VERSCHATSE
Translated by Gregory Ball.

Thomas Becket in Flanders: Truth or Legend? was the title of an exhibition held in the chapel of Groeninge Abbey in Kortrijk in Spring 2000. A scholarly catalogue was also published (Project leader: I. de Jaegere). St Thomas' medieval chasuble is on permanent display in the dormitory at Groeninge Abbey. Information: Stedelijke Musea / Broelkaai 4 / 8500 Kortrijk / Belgium / Tel.: +32 56 240 870 / Fax: +32 56 240 871 / e-mail: musea.stadkortrijk@kortrijk.be

FURTHER READING
BACKHOUSE, J. and C. DE HAMEL, *The Becket Leaves*. London, 1988.
BARLOW, F., *Thomas Becket*. London, 1986.
URRY, W., *Thomas Becket. His Last Days*. Phoenix Mill, Stroud, Gloucs., 1999.

From Boer War to South African War

A century ago, the whole world was following events in South Africa with intense interest. Two small Afrikaner Boer republics were fighting there for freedom and justice against the British Empire. They refused to bow to imperialism, to the arrogance and tyranny of a world power. The Boers displayed great courage, achieving unexpected victories against their much more powerful enemy. They were heroes, who were ultimately brought to their knees only by concentration camps and the threat of genocide.

The image of South Africa has been determined for generations by such memories of the Boer War. Until, that is, apartheid undermined the credibility of the Afrikaners and a new image of their past emerged. How does the new South Africa of today remember the war of 1899-1902?

For Afrikaners of the time and for a long time afterwards, the Boer War was their second war of liberation in the unequal struggle against Great Britain. The British Empire was accused of a century of injustice. The British had arrived at the Cape as protectors in 1795, but this was quickly forgotten, and after the Napoleonic era the Cape remained in British hands. A process of forced Anglicisation of administration and education, of the Church and the judiciary followed. The colonial masters also turned the social order on its head, by placing the servant above the master. As a result, from 1834 onwards thousands of Boer families, their meagre possessions piled on ox-carts, set off with their sheep and oxen into the untamed wilderness of Africa. Their Great Trek was the exodus of a people in search of freedom and independence. The Voortrekkers endured all manner of dangers in the vast interior, facing attack by wild animals, unknown diseases and fearful natural phenomena. They also encountered resistance from native tribes: place names such as Blood River and Winburg speak volumes. No sooner had they acquired some space, freedom and security for themselves, however, than jealous Britain annexed their Republic of Natalia.

Once again the Voortrekkers took to their ox-carts. They carried all their worldly possessions over the steep Drakensberg mountains and established the Orange Free State and Transvaal Republic on the endless High Veldt. But yet again they were forced to take up their rifles and defend this territory against the British. And when diamonds were found in 1867, the Free State was only able to retain its independence by giving up Kimberley and the surrounding area. The Transvaal was annexed without ceremony in 1877, but regained its independence in 1880 at Paardekraal under the leadership of Paul Kruger. This independence was gloriously confirmed in the battles of Laingsnek and Majuba. But when gold was found at Witwatersrand in 1886 and within a few years Johannesburg became the focal point of southern Africa, there was growing talk in London of the grievances of the Outlanders and how they were being oppressed in that backward Boer Republic under the old Kruger. The Jameson Raid of Christmas 1895, an outrageous incursion, soon proved to be merely a rehearsal for the definitive attack. And now Britain was busy taking away the last rights of the Afrikaners, their freedom and independence. Despite their unimaginable deeds of heroism, the stubborn resistance and privations of the '*bitter-enders*' among the hills and plains of the immense South African veldt during an apparently endless war, they were finally forced to give up the struggle. By now their farms were destroyed, their livestock slaughtered, their lands ravaged. The worst thing of all to bear, however, was the fate of their women and children, who were herded together in concentration camps. More than 26,000 of them had already died in these camps. Continuation of that struggle would have led to the demise of the whole Afrikaner people.

After 1902 memories of the War were exalted to mythical heights and played a fundamental role in the nationalism and ethnic mobilisation of the defeated Afrikaner people. Being a conflict between England and the Boers, it was moreover generally seen as a 'White Men's War', from which the black population was excluded. There was no reason, therefore, to commemorate the Anglo-Boer war in the new South Africa which emerged in 1994: '*to celebrate a colonial war is an affront to the new democratic dispensation*', declared an ANC politician a few years ago; '*they (the British and Afrikaners) were fighting for spoils, for the domination of the oppressed (black) community*'. And yet President Thabo Mbeki officially opened the commemoration ceremonies in October 1999 – and not (just) as a gesture to the Afrikaner minority. His action was a formal recognition of a new and functional vision of what is now termed the South African War. Because the war of 1899-1902 was not an exclusively white affair: all South Africans were involved in it, black and white. And it embodied fundamental human rights, primarily freedom and resistance to oppression, colonialism and racism. This new vision, which accords a role to the black population, is not just a matter of political pragmatism, but has solid historical roots. It has long been recognised that South Africa in the nineteenth century was characterised, to quote the title of a study by W.M. Macmillan in 1929, by a triangular relationship between '*Bantu, Boer and Brit*'. Even though there are reasons for claiming that the Anglo-

The battle at Paardeberg (1900) during the Boer War, now known as the South African War, as portrayed on a tile in the Rotterdam Transvaal Theatre. Nederland-Zuid-Afrika Vereniging, Amsterdam.

Boer War was caused primarily by the conflict between imperialism and nationalism on the issue of political hegemony and decolonialisation, and between British and Afrikaner culture, it is equally clear that the black population was fundamentally affected. The surrender by the Boer Generals in 1902 was inspired less by the destruction of their land and the deaths of their women and children in the concentration camps, than by fears of the black peril; the exclusion of the black population from citizenship in the Union of 1910 confirmed this. But black South Africa was not involved in the Anglo-Boer War only as a passive victim; tens of thousands of black South Africans were actually involved on both sides of the struggle – as guides, helpers and personal servants ('*agterryers*' in Afrikaans), but also in semi- and actual combat functions. As a result, they also had their victims: prisoners of war, exiles, people dying on the battlefield and in front of firing squads, people dying in reprisals and counter-terrorist activities and thousands who died in the British concentration camps.

This 'discovery' of the participation of black South Africa in the War by South African historiography dates from the early 1980s, although a series of diaries of people who had taken part in the War which began appearing in the 1970s had made this clear earlier. In the present wave of commemoration it is this discovery that is receiving the most attention. Of course, this reflects the current political and social revolution in South Africa, but it does more that that. Academic historiography in South Africa, including that of Afrikaans-speaking historians, has since the 1970s adopted a critical approach to the traditional view of history. In this context it is not only the Great Trek which is removed from the realms of mythology, but also the Boer War. The War is now no longer an epic, a textbook example of heroic courage and patriotism, but a 'dirty war' which only produced victims. Victors and vanquished, 'bitter-enders' and 'hensoppers', perpetrators of violence and those who suffered injustice, whites and blacks: they are all losers, and the loss extends through many generations; the whole of South Africa is a 'Verliesfontein' ('fountain of loss'). A few well-known examples of this new approach are *Kommandolewe* by Fransjohan Pretorius, *Die 'hensoppers' en 'joiners'* by A.M. Grundlingh, and *Abraham Esau's War* by Bill Nasson.

The present commemoration is therefore marked by all manner of paradoxes. The historians, who have long since abandoned the old image of the Anglo-Boer War, are seeking to give a post-modern meaning to the everyday human events of a hundred years ago. And they are raising the question of human shortcomings, both personal and collective, in a war which was no more than a phase in the South African tragedy of history.

It is in fact the men of letters who have put this problem to the masses in the most penetrating way, in impressive novels such as *Verliesfontein* by Karel Schoeman (1998) and *Op soek na Generaal Mannetjies Mentz* by Christoffel Coetzee (1998). But the commemoration is not only the property of historians and writers. Politicians are also involving themselves in it. Their speeches show no trace of unease at a demonstration of human failures, and also pose no pregnant questions. They are supplying the building blocks for a new patriotism. Their South African War is an example of resistance to colonialism, racism and discrimination. They are demanding a confession of guilt from England and lay wreaths at the Afrikaner Women's Monument, but also at the recently rediscovered graves of black victims. They praise the Afrikaners who defended freedom so heroically, and they express their respect for their wives and children, examples of victims of discrimination and oppression. They have transformed the Anglo-Boer War into a South African war, the Afrikaner struggle for freedom and justice to a lesson in democratic freedom and human rights, a contribution to the renaissance of the new South African nation. Who would deny the existence of the irony of history?

G.J. SCHUTTE
Translated by Julian Ross.

A recent publication about this subject is David Smurthwaite's *Boer War 1899-1902* (Octopus Publishing).

Belgium as a Symbol in First World War Propaganda

For all the years of flag-waving and military service, the shock of war in the summer of 1914 caught European populations unawares. Military plans might be at the ready; civilians' mentalities, however, were, in the main, less so. On the very threshold of war, European public opinion still refuted the necessity of involvement: '*Why should I follow your fighting line / For a matter that's no concern of mine?*' asked London's *Punch*.

Why indeed? Within days, the question would answer itself, all doubts momentarily dwarfed by the urgency of war. Swept up in a wave of national solidarity, young men volunteered to serve in droves; in the process, the conflict took on the colours of a Cause. The undifferentiated melee of belligerents was transformed into a set of two clear-cut camps: Good vs. Evil.

No act of war was more portentous, in those early days of the conflict, than Germany's invasion of neutral Belgium (following the Belgian government's decision to stand by the country's neutrality and reject the German ultimatum demanding unhindered passage for the imperial troops). Instantly decried as an unforgivable breach of international law, the invasion transformed the war into a crusade, at least as far as Entente populations, and specifically the British, were concerned. A crusade for – as the phrase went – Right against Might: '*We must fight Prussia,*' declared a group of Oxford history professors, '*in the noblest cause for which men can fight. That cause is the public law of Europe, as a sure shield and buckler of all nations, great and small, and especially the small.*' Belgium, which due to Leopold II's Congo legacy had not had a particularly good international press before the war, now found itself suddenly elevated into a symbol of the conflict's higher meaning. The country's plight at the hands of the invader – the exodus of refugees from the burning towns, the civilian massacres – put Belgium on an even more exalted pedestal, as a martyr for the higher cause defended by the Entente. '*Only that nation can be called cultured,*' stated the chief rabbi of the British Empire, '*which by its living, and if need be, by its dying, vindicates the eternal values of life – conscience, honour, liberty. Judged by this test, two of the littlest of peoples, Judaea in ancient times and Belgium to-day, and not their mighty and ruthless oppressors, are among the chief defenders of culture, champions of the sacred heritage of man*' ...

Rabbi Hertz' repeated references to 'culture' were meant as a sneer at the German rhetoric of *Kultur*. *Kultur* denoted a unique German quality, presented as perpetually threatened by outside forces and needing the buttress of that 'German Militarism' so vehemently condemned by Germany's enemies. Thus the October 11 manifesto *Aufruf an die Kulturwelt*, signed by 93 prominent German intellectuals. The *Aufruf* sought to defend Germany against accusations of 'barbarism' following the destruction of the venerable

The Civil Guard preparing to defend Brussels in 1914. Koninklijk Legermuseum, Brussels.

University Library at Leuven. In this, it backfired spectacularly, and ended up providing Entente propaganda with a lasting trope of 'German hypocrisy'. (Years later, a US recruitment poster depicted Germany as a rampaging gorilla, brandishing a blood-spattered cudgel bearing the inscription '*Kultur*'.) Similarly, the German Chancellor's earlier shrugging off of Belgium's neutrality treaty as a mere '*scrap of paper*' ('*Ein Fetzen Papier*') had swiftly found its way into anti-German rhetoric. The vexed matter of Belgium, then, significantly tarnished Germany's reputation abroad.

Hence the ferocity of the German propaganda campaign against Belgium. This campaign both sought to represent Germany as the attacked party and downplay the significance of Belgium as a nation and as a culture – all of it in response to the Entente discourse which pinpointed Germany as the aggressor and elevated the aggressee, Belgium, to near-transcendental status. The massacres of August 1914 were thus presented as 'punishment' of the Belgian civilian population for the fierce guerrilla war it allegedly waged on the invading troops. A new rhetoric emerged, based on the figure of the Belgian *franc-tireur* (civilian sniper), who could be a woman, even a child, treacherously assailing the troops in often appalling ways – pouring boiling oil over passing regiments, blinding sleeping soldiers, even castrating wounded ones. The mass executions, then, were necessary to keep the population from engaging in further murderous mayhem. Kaiser Wilhelm informed President Wilson that '*his heart had bled*' at the news of how his soldiers had *had* to chastise the '*bloodthirsty population*'.

Before long, the *franc-tireur* trope found itself embedded in a larger discourse outlining Belgians' essential malice and unruliness. The Belgian mentality, as observed through the prism of *franc-tireur* hyperbole, was revealed as a striking foil to the Germans', the lat-

ter's way of fighting – open, orderly – a stark contrast to the Belgians' stealthy wreaking of havoc. Those contrasting ways of fighting corresponded to contrasts in national culture – or, to be precise, the lack thereof, in the Belgian case. The Belgian population had never been educated into national subjecthood, for the simple reason that its state ultimately lacked a *raison-d'être*. Far from being the exalted nation-with-a-mission of Entente lore, Belgium was but '*a still-born product of European diplomacy*,' as the economist Werner Sombart famously wrote. It was a makeshift country possessing neither national traditions, nor strong governments, nor a collective will. Belgium was only a state, and a ramshackle one at that; it certainly was no nation. An uneasy amalgam between those two vastly different 'races' that were the Flemings and Walloons, in which the former were helplessly subject to 'gallicisation', Belgium was yet another example of the stealthy suffocation of Germanic 'life-force' by foreign elements which obtained all over Europe. A new German Flemish discourse shed a gratifying light on Germany's actions vis-à-vis Belgium: far from having attacked a nation, the Empire, champion of authenticity against hypocrisy, was in effect saving a *nation* from the clutches of a *state*. The new *Flamenromantik* (as one critic put it) served to underscore the notion of Belgium's artificiality; an accident of European politics, there was no reason why its boundaries could not presently be redrawn along lines of greater authenticity.

All in all, German Belgian propaganda bolstered Germany's self-image as a beleaguered country fighting a just and civilised war in its own defence, much as British Belgian propaganda, with its crusader-for-murdered-innocence overtones, offered a flattering image of Britain at war. (As the Oxford historians had it: '*We are a people in whose blood the cause of law is the vital element. It is no new thing in our history that we should fight for that cause.*')

The two 'Belgian rhetorics' had different life-spans. The Entente's Belgian propaganda grew more and more hollow as the war wore on. Indifference was fanned, paradoxically, by the cynical exploitation of the August 1914 events for mobilisation propaganda, with the actual tragedy drowning in gory atrocity tales (from hacked-off children's hands via blinded peasants to bayoneted nuns). By war's end, the 'Brave or Gallant Little Belgium' trope had worn thin and Belgian international prestige was on the wane. Interwar pacifist discourse, in its effort to discredit the Entente's atrocity propaganda, obliquely endorsed the German franc-tireurs line – a line to which Weimar Germany, in the main, held fast. All in all, the 'Heroic Belgium' cant, used as it was in the context of a war increasingly seen as senseless, eventually turned against Belgium – whereas, conversely, the notion of Belgium's impossibility, so vigorously endorsed by German propaganda, was to cast a rather longer shadow.

SOPHIE DE SCHAEPDRIJVER

Language

A Secret Language Traces of Dutch in the United States

The sound of Dutch has been heard in the Hudson Valley ever since 1609, when Henry Hudson sailed up the river that was to take his name. Seventeenth-century Dutch and its dialects survived there for about three hundred and fifty years. It was certainly still spoken by a few people in the fifties, and almost certainly in the sixties too. So thirty to forty years ago, on a Sunday afternoon along the Hudson River, you might still have bumped into someone speaking a strange-sounding Dutch dialect. Since no tape-recordings were ever made, and because it was not a written language, we no longer know what it sounded like.

What we do know is that in about 1920 the historian Jacob van Hinte came across a little old man who spoke some Dutch, but he could hardly understand him. Others have told similar stories. This dialect, whose origins lay in seventeenth-century Dutch, had diverged too far from present-day Dutch.

By way of distinction, 'old' Dutch was called 'Laeg Duits', a defective translation of 'Low Dutch'. To make it more complicated, there were also several dialects of Laeg Duits or Low Dutch. For example, the Low Dutch spoken by many black people will have sounded quite different from that of the whites in the Hudson Valley, the Mohawk Valley and parts of New Jersey. As already mentioned, there are no reliable sources to tell us what the differences were or how Low Dutch sounded. We can only guess.

In 1872 a reporter from *Appleton's Journal* heard several blacks talking to each other in a dialect that he thought sounded devilish. 'A patois of a simple nature has evolved amongst them', he wrote, 'and the ear is so offended by these unsavoury sounds that one soon believes one has come among lunatics. They make hardly any gestures. When a man speaks he bows his head and blends his words with a laryngal intonation and speaks his sentences with such a strange vocabulary that one can only guess at its meaning and be satisfied with that. One does not hear separate syllables. Their speech is a succession of improvised links'. This is undoubtedly a comment on a foreign language (Dutch) but equally on the colour of the speakers' black skin.

Over the centuries, thousands of blacks must have known Dutch as their first or second language. Many slaves and free blacks had no common language. Because Dutch was prevalent in the countryside and many big landowners were of Dutch origin, this was the language their black slaves learned. Sojourner Truth, whose *Narrative* is one of the oldest autobiographies of a black American woman, was born a slave called Isabella near Kingston, New York in 1797. She spoke Dutch and that was the only language her mother knew. Initially it was the only language she spoke too. When she was sold to an English family she was frequently beaten because she did not understand her new masters! Sojourner Truth's autobiography occasionally mentions her Dutch mother tongue but it is clear that English was gaining the upper hand among blacks too. Even so, her story illustrates how widespread the use of Dutch must have been among the blacks.

In 1785 a Dutch minister, Herman Boelen, was called to the Dutch Reformed Church in Queens County, but the American believers already found his Dutch incomprehensible. Harm Jan Huidekoper, a traveller from the eastern Netherlands, heard Dutch

Stanley Arthurs, *Landing of the DeVries Colony at Swaanendaal, Lewes, Delaware, 1631.* 19th century.

being spoken when he arrived in Long Island in about 1790 and he wrote to his parents that it sounded like the dialect of the farmers in Drente. In any event, he was still able to understand these Low Dutch speakers! Dutch immigrants arriving in America around 1850 said in their letters home that to their surprise they had come across Americans who spoke an old sort of Dutch.

The presence of Dutch speakers along the Hudson River in the seventeenth century ensured that speakers of Low Dutch were to be found in many places for several centuries. Low Dutch disappeared first from New York City but certainly persisted for a long time on Long Island, in the Albany area, Schenectady and further up the Mohawk River. In addition, Dutch speakers were present for many years in several villages along the Hudson, including Saugerties, Kingston and Hurley. Low Dutch also held out a long time in Fishkill and Tarrytown. In Bergen County, New Jersey, and particularly in Paterson, many inhabitants were still speaking it relatively recently. In 1910, J. Dyneley Prince, a professor from Columbia University, wrote down some Low Dutch on the west bank of the Hudson on the border between New York and New Jersey. His interviewee was a black man who lived in a rather isolated community in the Ramapo Mountains.

There must have been many such communities, and they would be typical of the places where a little Low Dutch is preserved. It would be marvellous if, somewhere in the Catskill Mountains, there were hiding some Rip Van Winkle who has slept for fifty years and turns out still to speak Low Dutch. It would be sensational if someone like this were to turn up, especially if we could understand him too.

But this does not mean that Dutch is already a dead language in the United States. The Dutch immigrant to America is an exceptionally stubborn weed, whose identity is closely linked to his native tongue. In the nineteenth century large groups of emigrants left the Netherlands for the American Midwest, often led by ministers of the church. Language and church were the foundations of dozens of communities in such states as Iowa, Michigan and Wisconsin. It appears that now, about a hundred and fifty years later, there are still numerous Dutch speakers. Note that these are fourth or fifth generation native speakers who have never been educated in Dutch and have never set foot in the Netherlands. The language has been passed down from one generation to the next. By contrast, the wave of post-war twentieth-century immigrants very quickly switched to English.

Caroline Smits and Jaap van Marle, academic researchers from the Free University of Amsterdam, have already traced dozens of Dutch speakers of the fourth and fifth generation. The hard cores live in the countryside and it is striking that in their communities Dutch is often the language of the elite. It is handed down from father to son. Anyone who has learnt Dutch as a boy of twelve, thirteen or fourteen is admitted into the circle of men.

So Dutch is by no means dead in the United States, but its existence is somewhat akin to freemasonry. One has to know where to find its practitioners and approach them in the right way. In the meantime, the majority of Americans carry on using words from this 'secret language' that have become fully integrated into their own language. A sentence like '*He's loitering on the stoop hoping to get a cookie from his boss*' is almost correct Dutch. '*Cookie*', '*to loiter*', '*boss*' and '*stoop*' are just a few of the countless words American English has borrowed from Dutch.

LUCAS LIGTENBERG
Translated by Gregory Ball.

Literature

Siting the Singer Gezelle in Translation and Translating Gezelle

The Flemish poet Guido Gezelle (1830-1899) has become, a century after his death, something of a national institution in Belgium. It was natural that his centenary should be widely commemorated there, but it did not go unmarked in England either. On that date, the Centre for Dutch & Flemish Culture hosted an all-day event at University College, London, centred on the publication of *That Limpid Singer*, the widest selection of his poetry yet published in English.

Gezelle's work was disparaged for much of his life and only came into favour during the 1890s. It was, therefore, not until the beginning of the twentieth century that translations began to appear in English. There are still only thirty-five items in the bibliography of these (with three more soon to be added), and the lion's share have either appeared in Belgian publications or in those supported by Belgian embassies abroad. The most significant of them is Christine D'haen's selection of 25 poems, whose fourth edition was augmented and revised with the help of Paul Claes in 1989 (see also p. 307). There is, then, still much work to be done to make this major poet as well known outside Belgium as his European contemporaries.

Poems by Gezelle did turn up in English and American anthologies of Dutch or Belgian poetry and there were two interesting if obscure selections as well. The earliest appeared in G.L. Roosbroeck's study of the poet, *Guido Gezelle – The Mystic Poet of Flanders* (1919), published by a small press in Iowa. In addition, a more general study of Gezelle's work was published in America by H.J. van Nuis in 1986. Maude Swepstone's English translation of 36 poems, which also carried a short account of his life, was published by a similarly small press in Bristol in 1937. Until the recent appearance of *That Limpid Singer*, hers was the largest selection from his work ever to appear.

That Limpid Singer is bilingual and contains 82 of Gezelle's poems, as well as six that he wrote in English. The Flemish poems range from the epigram-

Guido Gezelle (1830-1899).

ve a spirited rendering of Gezelle's originals, while English actor Jeremy Spriggs read some of the translations. Francis Jones read his Yorkshire version of ''t er viel ne keer' while Edwin Morgan's Scots version of 'Het Schrijverke' was read on his behalf; these poems only appear in the anthology in Standard English, unfortunately. One enthusiast said afterwards that Scots was the closest thing to West Flemish dialect he had ever heard!

The Dutch Department at London University is a stronghold of Translation Studies belonging to the so-called Tel Aviv-Leuven axis, sometimes known as the Polysystems approach and a variety of other names as well. Rather than prescriptively concentrating upon the source text, it foregrounds, among other things, the importance of investigating the working practice of the translator. In keeping with this, the anthology kicks off with ten translations of the same poem by nine translators, together with personal comments on their approach and difficulties. Fittingly, too, the morning and afternoon sessions preceding the launch were given to a translators' conference devoted to the problems Gezelle's work presents. Several contributors to the anthology attended, as well as various academics, recent graduates from the Cambridge Dutch Department and MA students from London who had themselves been working on Gezelle as part of their course in literary translation. Four poems by Gezelle had previously been set as homework in preparation for the day and discussion ranged outwards from these to wider issues.

The main problem with translating Gezelle is the question of register. Pretoria University's Renee Marais commented of the Afrikaans into which she translates that where it differs most from its parent Dutch, let alone Flemish dialect, is at the idiomatic level. In staying faithful to the spirit of Gezelle's use of language, the paradox arises that her versions sound nothing like the original.

If the host language is a second cousin like English the problems are compounded. When Gezelle is at his most radical in his use of Flemish dialect, how is this to be conveyed? Is Standard English even acceptable? Hugh McDiarmid has commented of his own use of Scots that he resorted to it when the standard language was inadequate to carry his meaning, when what he had to say could only be said in his own tongue. Belgian poets using the Latin-derived dialects known as Walloon make much the same point: with them as with Gezelle, it is not so much in what you say as how you say it that the poem's significance lies; in its divergence from a standard speech imposed by officialdom but foreign to popular usage.

Inevitably the objection was raised that not everyone has access to dialect as a translation resource; a readership able to understand it will also be limited. Even in Belgium something like a quarter of what Gezelle wrote is incomprehensible without a dictionary and this has contributed to his not being better known outside his own country. Certainly one can fall back on vernacular usage in interpreting him, but here yet another problem arises. Gezelle was a nineteenth-

matic to one that is seven and a half pages long; from devotional lyric to drinking song; from playful nursery-rhyme and sound-poem to mournful evocation and even something very like a curse. The poet's variety is matched by variety of style among his translators. Some twenty are involved, ranging from Jethro Bithell (whose versions appeared in his anthology *Contemporary Flemish Poetry* in 1917) through Roosbroeck and Swepstone to the present.

At the anthology's inception, a core of translators were invited to make their own selection of six poems each and submit them to the editor, Paul Vincent, a former lecturer in Dutch at London University. Quite by chance, Albert van Eyken sent a booklength manuscript of translations to the Dutch Department at this time and thirty-two of these were also included. Resident in England for over fifty years, he speaks with a heavy Devon burr and one can only regret that he did not choose to make use of that dialect for some of his versions. Two contributors, however, did supply translations into Scots and Yorkshire dialect, thus underlining Gezelle's own programmatic use of dialect and archaic forms.

The anthology was launched on the evening of Thursday, 25 November – strictly speaking two days before that on which Gezelle died. Professor Piet Couttenier was there to preface the launch with an account of the present state of Gezelle studies. His essay on the poet's contacts with the English world, first published in the initial volume of *The Low Countries*, also prefaces *That Limpid Singer*. Another visitor from Belgium was the actress Tine Ruysschaert, who ga-

century poet and shared the sensibility of that century. Modern speech has not only moved on since then but has built into itself a virtual denial of that past sensibility.

Another paradox arises, therefore. To make Gezelle's emotionalism acceptable to English readers, one is tempted to employ as a distancing device the nineteenth-century literary idiom with all its anachronistic inversions and archaisms. This is noticeable to some degree in many of the versions in *That Limpid Singer*. It certainly reflects one side of Gezelle's use of language, but not its most important aspect. He turned to his own dialect precisely because he was in revolt against the Dutch literary usage of his day. His translators risk losing what is most experimental and vital in Gezelle, the appeal of the popular spoken language as against the authoritarian and alienating written idiom. The dilemma is virtually unresolvable.

A different problem arises when it comes to which poems of Gezelle's to translate. He was a Catholic priest much given to devotion. The sensibility of most English-speakers has been formed by Protestantism and England enters the twenty-first century to all intents and purposes an irreligious society. In this case, Gezelle's religious poetry is hardly likely to find a receptive readership, nor even sympathetic mediation, yet to ignore it altogether is to misrepresent the core of his work and his mission. At this point in the discussion, hard words like 'cowardly' and 'unprofessional' were uttered and the conference beat a hasty retreat in the direction of the tea tray.

No final solutions were reached that day, nor is it possible to do so. If it were, translators of the future would be out of a job! The best that can be done is to keep returning to the task and, like the translator who did two versions of the same poem for *That Limpid Singer* and professed himself satisfied with neither, clarify one's understanding through such failures. Discussion of the problems he poses not only keeps Gezelle's name alive, it points up what is still to be done and is an enticement to go on trying.

YANN LOVELOCK

That Limpid Singer: a bilingual anthology of the poems of Guido Gezelle (ed. Paul Vincent). Hull: Association for Low Countries Studies, Crossways Vol. 4; 238 pp. ISBN 0-9517293-4-9.
The Centre for Dutch & Flemish Culture: Dept. of Dutch / University College / Gower Street / London WC1E 6BT / United Kingdom.
Tel.: + 44-207-504 2116 / fax: + 44-207-916 6985.

Survivals and Escapes on a Grander Scale
Anna Enquist's The Masterpiece

Anna Enquist (Christa Widlund, 1945-), an Amsterdam psychoanalyst, classically trained pianist and award-winning and best-selling Dutch poet and novelist, is the author of four volumes of poetry and two novels. She was first published as a poet, writing poems for the review *Maatstaf* in the late 1980s, and soon after won the C. Buddingh' Prize for her first volume of poetry, *Soldiers' Songs* (Soldatenliederen, 1991). The late Flemish poet Herman de Coninck commented admiringly that her poems create a roar not heard in Dutch literature since Willem Bilderdijk, a late eighteenth / early-nineteenth-century poet. Manfred Wolf, who has published articles on and translations of her poetry, describes her first two volumes as yielding a rhetorical poetry of '*arresting phrases, shiny aphorisms, flamboyant metaphors*' and being evocative of '*a force and an agitation that will not be denied*'. Her subsequent volumes – *A New Goodbye* (Een nieuw afscheid, 1994) and *Broad Daylight* (Klaarlichte dag, 1996) – have, more quietly, explored poetry and language itself.

Enquist's novels have been equally successful in the Netherlands, and even internationally. *The Masterpiece* (Het meesterstuk, 1994), now available in English, has already appeared in German (1995), Swedish (1997), French (1998) and other languages. This English translation is rendered into a very readable and effectively balanced British and American English by translator Jeannette K. Ringold, who has also translated *Nightfather* (Tralievader, 1991) and other works by Dutch writer Carl Friedman. Ringold recently completed a translation of Enquist's second novel, *The Secret* (Het geheim, 1997), which like *The Masterpiece* is filled with musical allusions, themes, and characters.

The *Masterpiece* follows closely the rich and tempestuous 'opera buffa' range of tragic-comic tones and themes of Mozart's and Lorenzo Da Ponte's libretto for *Don Giovanni*. The novel's epigrams come from Mozart's opera and the central characters have associations with characters in the opera. The novel's protagonist Johan, the painter of the masterpiece, is a womaniser like Mozart's Don Giovanni. The interactions of other characters and even their names resonate to the opera as well. Johan's rival and brother Oscar, a museum administrator and art critic (a match to Don Ottavio) is envious of Johan's success with women and his favoured status with Alma, their mother. Alma seeks revenge (as did Donna Anna of the opera) upon her unfaithful husband, who ran away with an opera singer. Johan's wife Ellen, his mistress Zina and friend Lisa (counterparts to the opera's Donna Elvira, Zerlina, and Leporello) are interesting revisionist portrayals of Mozart's characters. Their lives recapture the vibrancy of the characters in *Don Giovanni*, and yet are distinctive and original creations within Enquist's fictional recounting of Johan Steenkamer's iconic role and fate as a contemporary Amsterdam painter and middle-aged womaniser.

Lisa (the 'Leporello' of the novel), is best friend to Ellen, Johan's ex-wife, and a family friend of all the Steenkamers. Her perceptions as a friend and a professional psychiatrist provide the observing eye in this novel and its reliable narrative centre, and some of its most psychologically astute drama. Lisa also serves as antagonist to Johan. She wants to be Johan, as the following excerpt shows: '*Lisa blushes. She is ashamed* when she realises that she is jealous of Johan because of his paintings. *He creates. . . . And what do I make? Children, jam, improved patients. Years of work, no public, no applause, nothing new. . . . She lacks something which Johan does have. The missing part is not a penis, not virility but something vague like creative power. Let's say: power. She has remained a slave to helpfulness, she would rather please than fight. Not because she's a woman but because she's cowardly.'*

Johan not only has power, he can make life brutal for others as well. A narcissist, he does not 'feel' angst like his mother Alma, or sorrow like Oscar and Ellen. He is detached as he observes and makes things out of experience. Johan is not compassionate as a son, brother, husband, lover, friend, or parent. He turns to one of his students, a younger woman, Zina, after the death of his and Ellen's ten-year-old daughter. Johan's response to the loss of his child and wife is desertion, although he later reveals great feeling in his painting called *The Pietà* that is a brilliantly disturbing portrait of Ellen screaming and crying, while being comforted in her grief by Lisa. Parents devouring their children and children trying to escape are themes carried throughout the novel. The opening line of the novel is *'The goldfish have eaten their young.'* Fish are symbolic in the painting that Johan refers to as his masterpiece; it is called *The Woman with the Fish* and has a shocking origin that Oscar reveals to Johan at the close of the novel. Secrets and shocks occur and reverberate dramatically through the lives of Johan, Oscar, Alma, Ellen, and Lisa, as their stories of love, marriages, families and failed relationships progress. The fish eat their own kind, but as the novel is nearing the

Anna Enquist (1945-). Photo by Bert Nienhuis.

end, we discover, along with Lisa, that the new-born fish were not all eaten and had survived being devoured by their parents. *'They were able to hide . . . until they were no longer considered as prey. Survivors. Conquerors!'*

The Masterpiece is about survivals and escapes on a grander scale. Few do survive as they would wish to, but they are vibrant even in their failures because of their phenomenal spirit. Alma's treatment of her sons rebounds upon her ultimately; both mother and sons are alternately sustained and destroyed by their interactions and contests of wills. Balanced against the tragic and disturbing elements in the lives of Enquist's fictionalised Steenkamers and friends, there remains a powerful excitement about being human, loving, creating, and enjoying art, music, and food. Lisa makes jam for Ellen as a gift of solace and warm feelings. Alma provides an elaborate buffet for Johan's exhibit opening at the museum. Oscar presents a CD of Stravinsky's *Sympathy of Psalms* to Ellen to show his sympathy. Enquist's iconic characters struggle within the full range of human toil, pain, and glory. Some seek to detach and create; others to grieve and love again; to respond and help others; to seek revenge and destroy themselves and others. The question always remains whether they can learn to skate *'over black ice with here and there a silver / fish caught in it, pushed quickly on / to never again, to nowhere'* (Enquist's poem, 'River' ('Rivier') in *The Low Countries* 1996-97: 20). Enquist challenges readers to look down at the dark ice rapidly speeding by them as they race on their mental skates across the beautiful, haunting world she creates. It is a world in which the choices are most often about combat or defence. In her work, even music which can bring calm repose is diffused with violent images of force and violence, where Mozart is a surgeon who opens up the patient.

RITA INGRAM GIVENS

Anna Enquist, *The Masterpiece* (Tr. Jeannette K. Ringold). London: The Toby Press, 1999; 230 pp. ISBN 1-902881-05-2.

At the time of writing a translation of *Het Geheim* is due to appear in 2000 (http://www.tobypress.com).

FURTHER READING

WOLF, MANFRED, 'Anna Enquist and the contemporary style in poetry'. In: *The Berkeley Conference on Dutch literature 1995* (eds. Johan P. Snapper and Thomas F. Shannon), Lanham, MD: University Press of America, 1997, pp. 63-73.

See also *The Low Countries*, 1993-94: 35 and 1996-97: 20

The English Reynard

In the Middle Ages, in the borderland where Romance and Germanic languages meet – Picardy, Flanders and Alsace – a new literary genre emerged: beast epic. From the Romance tradition it took elements of the fable and its non-moralising counterpart, monastic satire;

the 'world turned upside down', for instance, and the wolf as monk, abbot or bishop. The Germanic ancestry is harder to trace, since it is rooted in an oral tradition of animal tales; at any event, explanations of animal characteristics and the personal names of the fox, wolf and bear come from here.

Remarkably, in England where the arrival of William the Conqueror brought Anglo-Saxon and French together in a British context, no comparable literary tradition of fox and wolf developed. The fox texts were imported into England at a later date. However, certain iconographic material might tend to indicate that a popular oral tradition existed in England before Chaucer wrote *The Nun's Priest's Tale*. Kenneth Varty has devoted quite some time to tracking down medieval depictions of the English fox, interpreting them and tracing their origins. His much-admired study *Reynard the Fox* (Leicester University Press, 1967) and various smaller publications are proof of that. His handsomely produced *Reynard, Renart, Reinaert and Other Foxes in Medieval England* appeared in 1999 (Amsterdam University Press). In this he reproduces newly discovered representations of the fox in medieval English art, supplemented by interpretations and arguments. The approach, hypotheses and structure are virtually the same as in the – also illustrated – work of 1967, albeit with additional proofs.

Beast epic's first major achievement was the *Ysengrimus*, a Latin work written in Ghent around 1148. Motifs from animal stories from the Carolingian period on, fables and popular elements, dialogues imitating classical writers, all these the author weaves into a single entity: the reckless escapades, which eventually cost him his life, of the rapacious wolf Isengrim. Time and again he falls victim to fate, but also to his own greed and short-sighted rhetoric. The antagonist who gets the better of this tragi-comic hero is Reynardus.

Then, about 1175, in Northern France, Pierre de Saint-Cloud wrote the first stories of the *Roman de Renart* with Reynard as his protagonist. Contrary to what the name would suggest, the 'roman' is not a rounded whole but a cluster of separate adventures (known as *branches*). Pierre took most of his storylines from the Ysengrimus, but he wrote in the vernacular. He initiated the ironic-humorous tradition with Branche II, which opens with the tale of the fox and the cockerel. The most famous branche, which is usually placed first in the manuscripts (hence branche i), is 'The Trial' (Le Plaid, c.1180). Various (anonymous) versions of Branche I were produced on both sides of the Dutch-French language frontier, the acknowledged masterpiece among them being the Flemish *Vanden Vos Reynaerde* of c.1200.

After an excellent survey of Reynard's previous literary history Varty concerns himself with the confrontation between fox and cockerel. This first tale in Branche II was demonstrably known to the francophone Anglo-Normans; carvings in English cathedrals made between 1190 and 1390 must therefore derive from a familiarity with the French text. But still there

The fox at the gallows ladder.
From the Bell 1656 edition.

is no literary English fox. Attributes like a mallet or a ball, which are mentioned in Branche II, are evidence of the carvings' literary origins. The common motif of a distaff used to threaten a woman, however, is non-French and pre-Chaucerian. This leads Varty to hypothesise an English oral tradition, from which the English carvers and Chaucer took the distaff motif.

Varty then discusses the literary and (from 1330) visual representations of the fox preaching to geese or chickens. Here his regular attributes are a gown, a cowl, and a crosier or book. In this case the literary reminiscence is of the hermit-pilgrim in *Reynaerde* and *Renart*. While it is true that themes connected with the 'trial' stem from Branche I and *Reynaerde*, Varty merely records separate visual material in English buildings and the lack of it in French- or Dutch-speaking territory. There are only French miniatures and Dutch incunabula. Yet Varty offers no more than the – justly famed – misericords from Bristol Cathedral (c.1520) depicting the trapped bear and the tomcat castrating the priest.

Varty had already reconstructed the English cycle of 43 woodcuts in the Caxton translation and convincingly ascribed them to the London printer Wynkyn de Worde (c.1495). Wynkyn based his woodcuts on those by the Haarlem Master in a Dutch rhymed version with the continuation of *Vanden Vos Reynaerde*, printed by Gerard Leeu in Gouda in 1487. These first Dutch illustrations have left a trail that can be followed down to modern times, in their homeland and beyond, through a string of Reynard chapbooks.

As his argument proceeds, Varty's views of the literary tradition as a source for relief and representation, and of the oral tradition, quickly develop from hypothesis into fact.

Which Reynaert story carried the tradition? Secondary motifs rule out the *Ysengrimus* as a source. But the oldest themes depicted – the predator carrying his prey, the fox as preacher, as captive, as physician, and so on – seem to have no direct link with the *Roman de Renart* or with *Reynarde*. Most of these themes are connected: the fox who preaches and outwits his victims, snatches poultry, and – the world turned upside down – is himself caught. This last probably ties up with the theme of the fox playing dead.

What these themes contain is rather a spur to alertness (not unusual for misericords) than a literary allusion. Only the men playing ball must certainly come from Branche II. But chickens and distaffs are such stereotypical female attributes that one cannot build a native oral tradition on them alone. Moreover, these attributes feature in the tomcat scene in both *Renart* and *Reynaerde*. The moralising and the sleeping matrons are more suggestive of the saying 'beware your geese'. As well as proverbs, the bestiaries popular at the time, with their Christian symbolism, also require investigation. There is a mosaic in Murano which depicts a fox trussed to a pole, being carried off by two cockerels; it dates from 1141, well before the earliest Renart branches. The court session and the fox-physician will have been more familiar to medieval man from fables than from beast epic.

War, iconoclasm and papal prohibitions mean that more non-religious representations have been lost on the Continent than in England. But there too one can see foxes preaching and carrying off their prey. The centre for carved figures in wood or stone was Flanders. Flemish artists have left their mark in the Rhineland, and in France and Spain. But Varty's meticulous gathering of material does show that England almost certainly had a tradition of its own. So it was not the craftsmen who brought these themes across the Channel.

The significant data assembled by Kenneth Varty allow us to put forward another and more convincing argument. In the high Middle Ages, the fox-images in England can be traced back to the Anglo-Norman elite's literary preference for fables, bestiaries and the light-hearted Roman de Renart. The bogus monk, originally the Benedictine Isengrim, was transmuted in the visual arts into the preaching, confession-hearing friar of the contemporary mendicant orders. With Geoffrey Chaucer, one of those foreign tales gains an English voice.

A new, wider-reaching impetus came from William Caxton's late-medieval retelling. The popular chapbooks and their famous illustrations assured the more definitive Dutch-language Reynaert tradition of its own place in English fox-lore.

JAN FRANKEN
Translated by Tanis Guest.

Kenneth Varty, *Reynard, Renart, Reinaert and Other Foxes in* *Medieval England. The Iconographic Evidence.* Amsterdam: Amsterdam University Press, 1999; 355 pp. ISBN 90-5356-375-X.

How Can You Capture an Elusive Reality?
The Poetry of Eva Gerlach

In the speech of thanks she gave in late 1995 on being awarded the Jan Campert Prize for her collection *What Is Lost* (Wat zoekraakt, 1994), the poet Eva Gerlach (1948-) told her audience about the ambition she had had as a girl of ten: '*I wanted to describe the whole of reality in order to arrive at an overall picture of creation. Once I had achieved such a mirror image, which must be completely clear, I would understand the whole, since the inner connectedness of everything would then be revealed to me.*'

From her debut *No More Hurt* (Verder geen leed, 1979) to her most recently published collection *Nothing More Constant* (Niets bestendiger, 1998), her poetry clearly sets out to give an adequate description of reality, as represented in the mind. That sounds more simple than it is. Such a project requires not only exceptional powers of observation and thought, but also a versatile linguistic armoury. Gerlach possesses all these in full measure. The account of her search for the best way of representing that reality in words can be found in all the poetry she has published so far. In her poems she has experimented with all kinds of possibilities for recording in poetry a number of significant relationships that play a part in the perception of reality, such as those between present and past, life and death, motion and stasis, the visible and the invisible. The constant changes in form and content prompted by this endeavour are so striking that Eva Gerlach can rightly be characterised as one of the most innovative and self-renewing of contemporary Dutch poets.

Although the fascination with describing reality is a factor that causes constant modifications in her work, her oeuvre can be divided into two distinct periods. This division relates mainly to a difference in form. The first period extends from 1979 to 1990. *Temporary Abode* (Voorlopig verblijf, 1999), a selection from the six collections published during that time, confirms the validity of that periodisation. And the volume also provides non-initiates with a perfect introduction to Gerlach's early work.

This first period is dominated by the attempt to find a more or less fixed form for the representation of a chaotic reality. In her first collection the starting point is a sometimes oppressive situation from the distant past, often with a child or parent in the main role. The fact that description of situations from the past leads to distortion and falsification emerges in the second collection, *An Inverted Image* (Een kopstaand beeld, 1983). Almost all the poems in these collections are eight lines long. The greatest unity of form is found in *Daughter* (Dochter, 1984), her third collection, inspired by the fear of losing her prematurely born child. Here all the poems consist of eight lines with one line blank after the fifth line. This golden section proportion refers to the mother-child relationship as a division within the unity of the poem. In this way Gerlach establishes order in the face of a threatening reality. Other ordering principles appear for the first time in *Domicile* (Domicilie, 1987), which includes longer poems, among them a few in italics. The blurb tells us that '*How do death and life co-exist?*' is an essential question. Any attempt to describe, to fix what is constantly in motion is pursuing an elusive goal. Fixing kills what is alive. In poems that mirror each other, Gerlach investigates how a suitable form can be found. Italicisation turns out to be one possibility.

The title poem of *The Power of Paralysis* (De kracht van verlamming, 1988), which opens the collection, immediately reveals a new procedure. To resurrect the paralysing moment of a fatal collision she makes liberal use of uneven lines, enjambment, ellipses, a snatch of a children's song and colloquial language. Other poems from this collection and from *In a Bend of the Sea* (In een bocht van de zee, 1990) are less striking formally, but exhibit more shifts in content, which are connected with the problems of the transience of memory. Anyone who like Gerlach has set themselves the task of making poetry an abode of remembered reality, irrevocably encounters such problems. Of the vast quantity of impressions that a human being receives, little can really endure. By putting abstractions like memory and desire in a concrete context Gerlach tries to express this: '*again memory climbs with me off the train / and loses me ...*' Such metaphors give these poems a less realistic feel, besides adding a certain ponderousness to the problem.

A radical transformation is apparent in *What Is Lost*, which heralds a new phase in Gerlach's work. She indicates her indebtedness in this regard to the sixteenth-century magician of memory Giordano Bruno, who provides the motto for the following poem from *What is Lost*:

Which All Things

'*Sol qui illustras omnia solus*' (Bruno, Cantus Circaeus)

What was it that you said, something about pike
early in the winter morning when the dark
cloaked you and your father each separate
on the moped, each cut their ice-hole
and you cast the what's-it rod,
such-and-such a hook, tiddly
bait from the bucket: never caught
1 pike. Wasn't there a lamp,
didn't we have it later, a standing one ,
blotchy metal, it could hang up too.

Keeping everything in mind,
all things, time and place, substance, quantity and quality. Being
a god that moves it.

Sometimes you saw one

Eva Gerlach (1948-). Photo by Bert Nienhuis.

stop in the depths, with a pointed
snout like they have, grey patches.

The most striking feature here is that certain formal changes which occurred incidentally in earlier collections have now definitely established themselves. Ellipses, especially omission of the second part of a sentence, occur frequently, but so do casual questions, colloquialisms and quotations. All these forms are used in the description of the many moving images, but also serve to represent the complexity of perceiving a single moment of reality. A looseness and lightness previously absent from Gerlach's work break through.

Gerlach's interest in photography, which has played a part in her poetry from the start because it too is involved in representing reality, provides the most recent innovations. In *Everything is Really Here* (Alles is werkelijk hier, 1997), an exquisitely produced collection with poems by Eva Gerlach accompanying work by the Czech photographer Vojta Dukát, surprising shifts in perspective have been introduced between photographer, viewer and characters depicted. In addition Gerlach achieves a comic effect by describing some photographs in a superficial way. These procedures add many layers to the experience of reality, and poetry turns out to have greater potential than photography for accommodating all kinds of aspects of that experience. (In May 2000 *Solstice* (Solstitium), a collection of poems with paintings by M. Aartsen, was published.)

The fact that our perception of reality is of a fragmented whole becomes a theme of *Nothing More Constant*. The following poem prefaces the collection, which is divided into series, as a kind of point of departure:

Crumb

What is whole, we cannot see, it is
too big, doesn't befit us nor fit

inside our heads
but what's chopped up, minced, ground fine,
crumb, pureed, atomised, decayed –

all that's divided is in us for good.

The value of Gerlach's art is her ability to give form to that fragmented reality, creating a momentary coherence. Within the limited scope of each poem a kaleidoscopic image of a fragment of reality unfolds. This brings her very close to the ideal that she cherished as a ten-year-old. The P.C. Hooft Prize, which she received in 2000, after a poetic career spanning twenty years, confirms the esteem in which her work is held.

HANNEKE KLINKERT-KOOPMANS
Translated by Paul Vincent.

Music

Folk-Songs: Long before the EU

'*Daar was laatst een meisje loos / Hoera my boy! Hoera, my boy! / Die wou gaan varen als lichtmatroos / Hoera, hoera, my boy!*' These are the opening lines of the only real shanty in the Dutch folk-song tradition: '*There once was an artful lass / Hurrah my boy! Hurrah, my boy! / Who wanted to sail before the mast / Hurrah, hurrah, my boy!*'. To this day the song itself is often sung as a narrative song. The alternating line in English, '*Hoera my boy*', was added by Dutch-speaking sailors to turn it into a shanty. A shanty is a simple song that accompanied work on the ships or in the harbour during loading and unloading. The word 'accompanied', however, should not be given too cheerful an interpretation, for the purpose of the songs was to force the pace of the work. Shipowners engaged special people to strike up shanties and lead the singing. The songs told simple stories usually set against the background of the sea, but the refrain, in which all the working sailors joined, was the most important part of the shanty. The verse, which often made no sense whatsoever, determined the rhythm of the shanty and thus set the working pace. Shanties came into existence from the fifteenth century on and because Britannia ruled the waves for much of the time, the British provided the model for the working songs at sea. That model was so compelling that even a thoroughgoing seafaring nation like the Netherlands produced next to no shanties of its own. All of which suggests that Dutch and Flemish sailors simply sang the English shanties.

The story of the shanty is not unique in the history of the European folk-song. National and linguistic borders counted for little when it came to a song becoming known abroad. Songs originated within a specific group of people and spread with apparent ease to other regions and linguistic communities. The Flemish Jesuit Albert Boone has devoted a voluminous book to the subject. In *The Flemish Folk-Song in Europe* (Het Vlaamse volkslied in Europa) he covers the most important themes from the European folk-song tradition and examines the extent to which Flemish / Dutch folk-songs treat the same themes as songs in other European languages. The result is impressive, not only because of its encyclopaedic dimensions: over two thousand pages, more than twelve hundred songs in their original versions with a prose translation in Dutch, of which more than a quarter are provided with musical notation. Equally impressive is the conclusion Boone draws from his in-depth study: '*The European fund of folk-songs actually constitutes one large family whose themes and subjects are sung from Scandinavia to Sicily and from the Ural Mountains to the Atlantic Ocean. And the Dutch-language song is an important member of that family.*'

But let us return to the artful young woman in 'The Scruffy Girl' ('Het haveloos meisje') quoted at the beginning of this article. Apart from the fact that the sailors made it into a rather stilted shanty, its subject matter has close links with a frequently recurring theme in traditional sea-songs. Even those not particularly interested in folk music will certainly have heard the song 'The Handsome Cabin-Boy': '*It's of a pretty female as you will understand / Her mind was set on rambling into a foreign land / She dressed herself in man's attire and boldly did appear / And she engaged with a captain to serve him for a year.*' During the early years of the folk revival in the 1960s and 1970s, it was sung by various Irish groups, both in Europe and in America. The Sweeney's Men (with Andy Irvine, later co-founder of Planxty) topped the charts with it.

In both the Dutch and the Irish song the female sailor becomes pregnant by the captain. In the Low Counties this results in a happy marriage, in Ireland we know less about the fate of the handsome cabin-boy, because the captain is already married. What is more, the captain's wife is herself in love with the handsome boy.

Another frequently recurring theme is lovers separated by a job at sea. The singer quite often sings of the woman being unfaithful while he is away at sea for long periods. Hardly surprising perhaps, given that the Flemish fishermen who fished off Iceland, for example, were at sea continuously from the end of February to the beginning of August…. The Icelandic voyages inspired some of the most beautiful Flemish songs ever written. In particular the songbook of French-Fleming Edmond de Coussemaker contains a few real gems. These Arctic fishermen fished for cod (using a line!) but the most frequently praised marine animal is surely the herring. Whereas cod fishing and whaling entailed long and hazardous sea voyages, herrings were caught in relative safety in coastal waters close to home. So the herring is not cursed but idolised. As an Irish song would have it: '*Of all the fish that roam the sea / The herring alone our king shall be.*' Scotland, too, is awash with herring songs. Even Ewan MacColl, brother-in-law of the great Pete Seeger, and himself one of the most important figures in the British folk revival, wrote an ode to the herring, despite an awareness of the hardships and poor pay: '*O the work was hard and the hours long / And the treatment, sure it took some bearing / There was little kindness and the kicks were many / As we hunted for the shoals of herring.*'

Albert Boone's book reveals the same parallels between English-language and Dutch-language sea-songs in all the other major themes of folk music. His book opens with 'The Ballad of the Poisoned Daughter' ('De Ballade van de vergiftigde dochter'), a European ballad he tells us, and, indeed, he refers to 59 Italian versions, 103 in English and 32 in German. In England the song is much better known with a son as the victim, namely the unfortunate Lord Randal: '*O where have you been, Lord Randall, my son, / (...) mother, make my bed soon, / For I'm sick at the heart, and I fain would lie down*'. Interestingly, there are no male victims in the Dutch and German songs. In every version throughout Europe the offender is a woman, usually the stepmother but also the lover, the grandmother or an aunt. Poison is traditionally a female weapon in our folk literature. That weapon varies somewhat from version to version. For instance, Randal eats eels while the Flemish Isabelle is served '*a fish with yellow stripes*'.

Scores of songs take Boone on a journey through Europe in search of similarities and variants. In 'The Young Prince and Princess' ('De Twee Koningskin-

Pieter de Bloot, *Duet at an Inn.*
17th century.
Panel, 29.5 x 22.5 cm. Private collection.

deren'), the most famous medieval ballad in the Dutch language, the lovers cannot meet because '*the water is much too deep*'. Those familiar with Ireland will immediately think of 'Carrickfergus': '*But the sea is wide and I cannot swim over / And neither have I the wings to fly.*' Or we may be reminded of a song still sung on both sides of the Atlantic Ocean: '*The water is wide and I can't swim over.*' In a variant from the North of England, it is the River Tyne that is too wide and too deep. The examples are endless.

Mindful of the sometimes difficult process of European unification, Boone is perceptive in his observations: '*This book, then, shows just how old and how deep the spiritual unity of Europe is among ordinary folk and how lavishly it was fecunated, long before political ideals discovered it.*'

WIM CHIELENS
Translated by Alison Mouthaan-Gwillim.

Albert Boone, *Het Vlaamse volkslied in Europa* (2 vols.). Tielt: Lannoo, 1999; 2120 pp. ISBN 90-209-3666-2.

Beyond the Cluttered Years *The Dutch Jazz Archives*

Once, it was one great dust trap. After one afternoon amongst all these yellowing books and magazines your nose would be full of dust for days. The furniture looked as if it had come from the Salvation Army. One floor down was the BIMhuis, where noisy orchestras were always rehearsing. The floor vibrated.

It was a place where you would find a few men of pensionable age, including Herman Openneer, who answered every question at great length and invariably prolonged his account with information on all manner of related topics. He knew everything there was to know about pre-war jazz. When you asked what day a 78 rpm record by the Almelo Jazz Rascals was recorded, he answered without a blink: '*23 December 1923, from 2.30 to 7.30, at 38 Station Street, third floor back, top bell.*'

Openneer was often involved in lively discussions with Pim Gras, a radio worker and fellow jazz freak who was also not short on jazz knowledge. They occasionally referred to the whisky bottle, which was always ready in case of emergencies. Another permanent member of staff was Peter Kok, a specialist in jazz films. Once when I was doing research for books on Chet Baker and Ben Webster, Kok provided me with forgotten magazines full of forgotten information.

Those cluttered years are now in the past. The National Jazz Archives are now the Dutch Jazz Archives (Nederlands Jazz Archief; NJA) and have long since moved from Oude Schans, above the Amsterdam BIMhuis. Nearly three years ago, in January 1998, they moved to a clean basement on Prins Hendrikkade, a couple of hundred metres away. The NJA now has at least twice the space, new furniture, a group of industrious volunteers and three paid staff:

The Dutch Jazz Archives. Photo by Pieter Boersma.

Openneer has been joined by Tanya Wijngaarde and a cleaner. Every year they have at least five hundred visitors, mostly journalists, musicians and students researching for their theses, who rummage around in the ever-expanding collection. At the present time it comprises 10,000 LPs, 1380 video tapes, 2000 books, 13,520 magazines, 100,000 cuttings, 5000 photos and 5000 books of sheet-music. In addition to this the NJA publishes the *Nederlands Jazz Archief Bulletin* four times a year, an equally professional-looking magazine full of historical photos, with a circulation of about 1500.

Tanya Wijngaarde arrived on work placement several years ago and was then accepted into full-time employment. She is currently writing a 'policy plan' for the subsidising bodies. The Minister of Culture, Rick van der Ploeg, wants the various collections in the Netherlands to be 'opened up', and she agrees absolutely: '*I would like to welcome more visitors here. And I would like to provide many more people with information. We must have a good Website, so that all the data are easier to access. For that reason everything also has to be thoroughly catalogued.*'

She would also like to see more attention devoted to modern music. At the moment the emphasis is mainly on the pre-war period. The bulletin contains long, somewhat list-like articles about obscure musicians from a very dim past. Wijngaarde says: '*But for the time being we shall continue in the same way. Look, next year Herman will be retiring, and before he goes we want to profit as much as possible from his expert knowledge. There is no one else who knows so much about old jazz in the Netherlands.*'

Who will succeed Openneer? If it's up to Wijngaarde, it won't necessarily be a jazz freak who spends a lot of time on minute details: '*The new member of staff should be good at archive work and understand computer matters.*' Openneer, who was born in 1935 and had a long career as a washboard player in count-

less old-style groups, is in the meantime thumbing through a discography that has just arrived in the post, with an irritated look on his face. He has seen that the book is full of mistakes: '*You can tell them the ins and outs of things a hundred times, but if you are Dutch they don't take you seriously. The books by English-language authors like Brian Rust and Leonard Feather are taken as gospel, but they make mistakes too.*'

Can we have an example? '*You always read that Duke Ellington's first performance on the European continent was in Paris, but that's not true; he played in Scheveningen first. That was in 1933. But the trouble is, all those chauvinistic English and French can't read Dutch writing. And so you read everywhere that Ellington flew straight from London to Paris. If you phone them up to tell them what really happened, they say "You can tell me anything you like, but I have never heard of you."*' But the NJA does cooperate harmoniously with the German jazz archives: '*The German jazz experts are very modest people. They are open to any piece of information.*' Openneer was one of the founders of the archives twenty years ago. '*It all started with the death of Klaas van Beeck, a Dutch jazz pioneer, in 1979. His estate was to be auctioned off and we wanted to prevent his possessions being scattered all over the world. So Harry Coster, Wim van Eyle and I, with some other people set up a foundation. In the beginning Wim took a lot of the organisational work on himself. Originally we kept all the material in our houses, but a few years later we found the accommodation above the BIMhuis. It was thanks to Willem Breuker that we received a subsidy. He is a forceful negotiator and is still on the board.*'

JEROEN DE VALK
Translated by Gregory Ball.

Dutch Jazz Archives
Prins Hendrikkade 142 / 1011 AT Amsterdam / The Netherlands

Tel. +31 20 627 17 08 / fax: +31 20 428 84 25 /
e-mail: nja@worldonline.nl

Aspiring to Universality The Music of
Dirk Brossé

Dirk Brossé (1960-) is a Flemish all-round musician who over the last ten years has acquired international renown as a conductor and composer. As a composer, too, he is very versatile: he writes film music and concert music for various types of ensemble. His most personal pieces are those he calls *'ethno-classical symphonies'*. In 1999 he made a CD of his concert music with the London Philharmonic Orchestra, which he naturally conducted himself. His concert music is characterised by great expressiveness and direct appeal, achieved by a particular emphasis on melody. Brossé has not abandoned the tonal idiom, but is able to make the best use of this so-called 'outdated' medium by means of his excellent orchestration. This is apparent in such pieces as *Elegy* for cello and orchestra, *Black, White and In Between* for violin and orchestra, and *Meditation* for oboe and orchestra. His film music is conceived in the same way and, what is more, possesses the characteristics of the best film music: it is highly functional in relation to the film, but is also worthwhile in itself and can therefore be performed in concert. In recent years Brossé has been able to work with several of the best Flemish film directors: he wrote the music for Stijn Coninx' *Daens* and *When the Light Comes* (Licht) and, in a completely different genre but also for Coninx, for the comedy *Koko Flanel*, starring the singer and comedian Urbanus. He wrote his first film music for Roland Verhavert's *Farmers' Psalm* (*Boerenpsalm*). And for the quincentenary of the birth of Charles V in 2000, he wrote an *Emperor Charles Oratorio*.

Dirk Brossé aspires to universality in his music, something he achieves on the one hand by selecting subjects from outside Europe and on the other by using elements from world music. As far as themes are concerned, humanity is always the focus, though sometimes in extreme situations. *El Golpe fatal* describes a Latin-American bullfight: man against bull, with the bull in fact much stronger than the man. One of the two will die, and the man is defying death. *La Soledad de América* is based on a piece written by Gabriel García Marquez. This sheds light on an entirely different aspect of humanity: that of oppression under South American dictators. The last section is 'La Esperanza', in which Garcia Marquez' text starts: *'Our answer to oppression, plunder and neglect is life. No flood or plague, no starvation or disasters, not even eternal wars, nothing has ever been able to diminish the obstinate power of life over death.'*

The same sensitivity to man and life is the thread that runs through Dirk Brossé's two ethno-classical symphonies: *Artesia* and *The Birth of Music*. *Artesia* begins with 'Birth' and 'Life' and continues with 'Strife' and 'Hope', reaching 'Harmony' by way of 'Artesia'. In this way the sections encompass the aspirations of every human being everywhere in the world. The title assumes a whole range of meanings: art, objects from the past, artistically fashioned or not (artefact), a well (artesian well), and the musical terms *arsis* and *thesis*. In the third section, man, in the shape of a child, comes into contact with other cultures, symbolised by ethnic instruments. After a prayer the children try to create a new world (in a Bolero), which leads to an apotheosis in 'Harmony'.

The Birth of Music has several features in common with *Artesia*. The starting point here is not the birth of man, but the Big Bang. That was the first sound, and it is there that all musical languages were born. In 'Hunting', man is depicted both as a hunter and as the hunted or the prey (comparable to *El Golpe fatal*). The themes of myth and the elusive mystery of the cosmos are also used. Man also finds himself faced with others: he learns to handle feelings of love and hate, trust and pain. Here too there is a section in which man comes into contact with foreign cultures, as in *Artesia*. Through his evolution towards the hectic contemporary life of the city, man will realise that things have to change: in one way or another he has to transcend himself and arrive at a form of spirituality, which is possible in religion and astrology, and of course in music. This is the significance of *The Birth of Music*.

In *Artesia*, and even more so in *The Birth of Music*, Dirk Brossé writes for a combination of classical instruments (his own L'Arco Musicale ensemble) and ethnic instruments, such as a lithophone from the Paleolithic period and a Pre-Columbian flute from the tenth century. He has become acquainted with the latter during his travels throughout the world. But he does not have the ethnic instruments play separate passages, alternating with the classical instruments. Nor does he simply have the ethnic instruments improvise at set moments. He actually composes the music for them

Dirk Brossé (1960-). Photo by Heirman-Graphics.

Martinus Veltman (1931-).
Photo Belga.

Gerard 't Hooft (1946-).
Photo Belga.

and integrates it into the whole. Into both the range of instruments and into the course of the music. And this makes it genuinely 'ethno-classical', creating a powerful musical impression.

YVES KNOCKAERT
Translated by Gregory Ball.

INFORMATION

Maestro Music Productions
Leeuwerikstraat 20 / 3680 Maaseik / Belgium
Tel.: +32 89 56 75 57 / Fax: +32 89 56 11 17 /
URL: http://www.maestro-brosse.be

Philosophy and Science

Last Nobel Prize for Physics of the 1900s to Dutchmen Veltman and 't Hooft

At the close of the twentieth century, the Nobel Prize for Physics again went to the Netherlands, to Martinus Veltman and his former student Gerard 't Hooft. The award provides a welcome boost for physics in the Netherlands at a time when the sciences are failing to attract students, and fundamental, high-risk research is forced to compete more and more with short-term, contract-based applied science that offers little challenge. Looking back over the century, the Dutch have no reason to complain. Since the Nobel Prize was introduced in 1901, no fewer than eight Dutch physicists have received science's highest accolade. No other country in the world can match this record in terms of the ratio of winners to inhabitants. This is largely due

to the close cooperation between teaching and research in Dutch universities.

Veltman and 't Hooft received the prize for theoretical work carried out around 1970 in the field of (electro)weak interaction, one of nature's basic forces. In the 1960s scientists were busily searching for a mathematical model for weak interaction, which is responsible among other things for radioactive beta-decay. Veltman doggedly pursued the path that his fellow scientists had abandoned one by one after years of fruitless effort. Although it did not lead him to the ultimate theory, his work paved the way for his brilliant Ph.D. student Gerard 't Hooft, for whom the breakthrough came in 1970 during a summer school on Corsica. Shortly afterwards the completed 'mathematical machinery', in the form of a tool which physicists could actually use, was available in Utrecht. Weak interaction had been conquered.

As soon as the Veltman and 't Hooft prize had been announced, the media began to question whether their work had any social relevance – often concluding in the same breath that it did not. This is clearly a short-sighted reaction. While it is true that the ideas of Veltman and 't Hooft will not lead to better vacuum cleaners, those who employ a broader definition of 'relevance' know that scientific research *is* important to society. The talented young researchers working at the chalk face of fundamental science are acquiring the motivation, determination and powers of reasoning that will equip them to carry out applied research for companies in the future. A modern, knowledge-based economy simply cannot afford to be without sufficient numbers of well-qualified researchers.

The cultural aspect is equally important. We have all gazed up at the night sky and wondered how the universe began. Mankind is driven by curiosity. That same desire to know lies behind our journey to the very essence of matter. At present the last stop on that journey is the world of elementary particles. Far too small, even for the most powerful microscopes, these particles are to be found beyond the boundaries of the atom, inside protons and neutrons. They cannot be fragmented any further and are therefore known as the smallest building blocks of matter. They have exotic names (w particle; top quark; neutrino; Higgs boson particle) and the laws they obey defy common understanding. It is this bizarre quantum world – full of particles that appear out of nothing and disappear again – that Veltman and 't Hooft have elucidated with their theory.

The precise nature of Veltman and 't Hooft's work is difficult to explain in layman's terms. Field theory and the language of mathematics in which physicists communicate with each other are, to the man in the street, as incomprehensible as Chinese. The media therefore focussed on the uneasy relationship that has existed between the professor and his former student for more than a quarter of a century. There is clearly a personality clash involved. Veltman, the son of a teacher from Waalwijk, was a late developer. He says what he thinks, wants nothing to do with theoretical fantasies, and is led by the findings of his experiments. 't Hooft, by contrast, comes from a family of prominent physicists (his great-uncle Frits Zernike won the Nobel Prize in 1953 for his invention of the phase-contrast microscope) and quickly worked his way to the top of his field. 't Hooft is more distant, more reserved and much more inclined than Veltman to pursue mathematical vistas far removed from the results of experiments with particle accelerators. 't Hooft explores the essence of minuscule black holes and firmly believes, with Einstein, that God does not play dice. His search is for a theory of quantum mechanics that leaves no room for chance.

In focussing on the difficulties between Veltman and 't Hooft, the media has neglected the positive effect that such personal tensions can bring about. Top scientists are only human. Like us, they want to be top of the class, first past the post. They want to take the wind out of other people's sails, and not be dictated to by their colleagues. With luck, a 'positive' tension will develop between teacher and student. That tension will prove to be a constructive irritation that ultimately brings out the best in the researcher. This is what happened with Veltman and 't Hooft. The result: thirty years on, they were both invited to Sweden to receive the Nobel Prize.

DIRK VAN DELFT
Translated by Yvette Mead.

'Leuven Valley' IMEC, Latest Technology in Flanders

A high-tech valley is growing up more and more round the Catholic University of Leuven, on the analogy of the famous Silicon Valley to the south of San Francisco, the Mecca of the computer industry. The showpiece of the 'Leuven valley' is IMEC: the Interuniversity Micro-Electronics Centre. IMEC is a world-renowned centre for research into chips. The pick of

Flemish high-tech brains are assembled there; and to cash in on all this knowledge IMEC is supporting the creation of dozens of businesses in the neighbourhood. The driving force behind this scientific cluster policy was Professor Roger van Overstraeten, who died in April 1999. At the beginning of the year 2000 a Foundation named after him was set up to support and promote new scientific research.

Roger van Overstraeten had a brilliant academic career. In 1960 he graduated from Leuven as a civil engineer in electronics and mechanics, and three years later got his doctorate at Stanford University. In 1968 he was appointed to a full professorship in Leuven. He also taught in Florida, at Stanford University and at the Pilani University in India. But Van Overstraeten's strength was more than just academic: he combined an extensive and thorough knowledge of one of the newest domains in science, micro-electronics, with a vision of the future.

The greatest achievement of Van Overstraeten is perhaps that he managed to interest the Flemish government in the centralisation of all knowledge and scientific research with regard to micro-electronics in one place. This meant the immediate establishment of IMEC in 1984. Since then the Flemish government has already put more than 10 billion Belgian francs into IMEC. In return it wants technological know-how and high-level jobs. And it has been getting them.

Today there are more than 800 engineers, scientists and technologists working at IMEC. Now the largest independent research centre in Europe, they study what industry will need in the next three to ten years in terms of micro-electronics (chips, solar cells, sensors etc.). IMEC has established a world reputation in this area. It co-operates with other (Flemish) universities and with multinationals such as Philips, Siemens, Intel and Motorola, but it also carries out contract research for more than 65 Flemish firms. They often put into production technology developed by IMEC, as soon as it is ready for the market.

However, IMEC's role does not stop at research; development is also encouraged. In other words: IMEC helps its employees to take the step from scientist and researcher to business leader or entrepreneur. Because not all the results of brilliant research find their way into already existing businesses. For this reason IMEC has striven to be in at the birth of the so-called 'spin-offs', new companies which have grown up out of its lap.

It goes without saying that the IMEC spin-offs are high-tech companies, and it is not always so easy for the uninitiated to understand precisely what such firms get up to and what their place is at the international level. For instance there is CoWare, established in October 1996, which according to those in the know has the potential to become a world leader in its own sector. CoWare designs programmes to make the computer-controlled design of chips faster and simpler, which they are hawking to chip designers around the world. Not surprisingly a large portion of CoWare's market is in the USA, where a subsidiary company has

The IMEC clean-room facility, where integrated circuits are being produced.

been set up. Thus, as a young concern, CoWare is clearly aiming at the world market. Naturally that requires money – a lot of money. However, that has not seemed to be much of a problem: although the company only started with eight people, before very long it had found 175 million Belgian francs of venture capital. IMEC's reputation was largely to thank for this. CoWare's shareholders are the Flemish investment company GIMV, the private investor Leo Billion, the American venture capital fund Greylock, CoWare management and the IT-Partners fund. This last fund was set up by IMEC itself. IT-Partners has 2.5 billion Belgian francs in the kitty to invest in new high-tech companies. Meanwhile CoWare is operating with forty people. Among those who have already purchased CoWare technology are Alcatel, Sony, ST Micro Electronics and Motorola.

IMEC now has twenty or so spin-offs in addition to CoWare. For instance, there is Matrix, which develops etching equipment, and Basics, an enterprise that designs VLSI-ASICS – a sort of chip. Then Destin has brought out yet another measuring instrument for quality control of electrical and electronic components. And Sirius Communications is active in the field of specialised telecom chips.

The common characteristic of all the spin-offs is that they were set up close to IMEC, so that a Leuven valley is developing, where every company is concerned with chip design. Not surprisingly, IMEC likes to refer to the DSP-Valley (Digital Signal Processing), an allusion to Silicon Valley, where success stories like Hewlett-Packard, Silicon Graphics, Yahoo! and Cisco were created as spin-offs of Stanford University.

In the Leuven valley no world-famous concerns like these are to be found as yet, even though as a research centre, IMEC is certainly the equal of Stanford. However, in Flanders there is still a crippling fear of failure, so that steps which are very risky, but nonetheless essential to becoming really great are often not taken. Moreover, the American concerns have a better eye for marketing, whereas for many Flemish researchers and company heads that is still a dirty word.

But, no marketing, no international company. On the other hand, IMEC is still quite young, and its spin-offs barely out of the cradle. So it may very well be that in a few years' time an IMEC sprig will be a big name at international level.

EWALD PIRONET
Translated by Sheila M. Dale.

http://www.imec.be.

Two Spinoza Biographies

It is arguable that Spinoza, second only to Rembrandt, is today the most famous of all Dutchmen. His only real rival for this accolade – William the Silent – is assuredly far more emphasised and honoured within Dutch education and national culture but it is doubtful whether, at least in recent times, he has enjoyed a comparable status to Spinoza in the wider world. In any case, while there were other great, and perhaps even more innovative, philosophers in early modern times – Descartes, Locke, Hume and Kant, for example – no-one else before Marx, not even Rousseau, can truly be said to have the same sort of continuing relevance in the world today. This is especially obvious in areas such as the status of revealed religion and the Bible, the fundamentals of ethics, the origins of modern toleration and permissiveness, the existence or otherwise of the supernatural, and freedom of thought, speech and the press. When, therefore, the century's greatest scientist, Albert Einstein, replied in 1929, when asked whether he believed in God, that he '*believed in Spinoza's God who reveals himself in the harmony of all that exists, not a God who concerns himself with the fate and actions of men*', there is little reason to consider this an eccentric or surprising twentieth-century response.

During the last quarter of a century an immense amount of scholarly research into Spinoza's life and ideas has taken place and enormously extended and refined our picture of his place in human thought and indeed history more generally. Rigorous analysis of his system by academic philosophers such as Edwin Curley, Alexandre Matheron, Jonathan Bennett, Herman de Dijn, and Don Garrett have clarified the categories and terms of his thought, while a still larger phalanx of historians of philosophy, including Richard Popkin, Wim Klever, Manfred Walther, Pierre-François Moreau, Marc Bedjaï, Wiep van Bunge , and Winfried Schröder have even more dramatically transformed our awareness of Spinoza's intellectual context and impact; and yet a third impressive cohort, such as Filippo Mignini, Fokke Akkerman and Piet Steenbakkers, through philological techniques and meticulous scrutiny of Spinoza's texts, have appreciably enhanced understanding of the genesis, editing and early translations of his writings.

Yet most of this new research has remained tucked away in relatively obscure research monographs and scholarly journals, largely veiled from the eyes of the wider reading public so that its significance is yet to sink in more generally. It is therefore a thoroughly welcome event, as well as a remarkable coincidence, that after many years in which the reading public has lacked an up-to-date general account of Spinoza's life and thought, two admirably readable, indeed in their different ways fascinating, full-length biographies of Spinoza, both of around 400 pages, should appear almost simultaneously and, moreover, soon after the publication of the generally excellent *Cambridge Companion to Spinoza* edited by Don Garrett and published in 1996. Suddenly, Spinoza is beginning to receive the mainstream coverage he so amply deserves.

Steven Nadler's *Spinoza* is a generally reliable, judicious and well-balanced piece of work both when explaining ideas and on the strictly biographical side, written by an expert on seventeenth-century philosophy (he has previously written books on Arnauld and Malebranche). He has carefully studied all the diverse elements and factors moulding Spinoza's complex development and, in particular, handles his Sephardic Jewish origins and upbringing, and expulsion from the Jewish community in Amsterdam in 1656, more fully and with greater sensitivity than one finds in most works on the philosopher. His account of Spinoza's philosophical masterpiece, the *Ethics*, first published in 1677, by no means an easy work to grasp, is splendidly clear and helpful. Above all, he rightly stresses, more than most commentators, that the *Ethics* is a work *'bold to the point of audacity...a systematic and unforgiving critique of the traditional philosophical conceptions of God, the human being, and the universe, and, above all, of the religions and the theological and moral beliefs grounded thereon'*.

What is so remarkable about the system is that it coherently integrates within the fabric of the material universe around us the whole of reality – the spiritual and physical, Man and God, Nature and poetry, reason and emotion, science and religion, connecting all the parts in a logical fashion so that, whether one likes or loathes it, or even if one has enough mastery of logical categories to pick holes in it, at the end of the day it still makes obstinate, relentless sense to those who sample it even if they have no training in philosophy. It reduces the totality of our existence and universe, in a way that provoked the utmost outrage in his own time, to a rational unity, or what Einstein called *'trust in the rational nature of reality'*, in a way Descartes, Locke, or Hegel can hardly be said to have done. His system equates God with Nature, subsumes mind into matter, eliminates the possibility of miracles and the supernatural, renders Man part of Nature, and all occurrence inherent in the 'unalterable laws of Nature' definable in terms of mathematically expressed cause and effect, and welds all this into an organic whole. But while it is, says Nadler, *'one of the most radically original treatises in the history of philosophy'*, and makes little explicit reference to past thinkers, it is nevertheless, he points out, *'also hugely erudite, based on a wide knowledge of earlier classical, medieval, Renaissance and early modern thought, including Plato, Aristotle, the Stoics, Maimonides, Bacon, Descartes and Hobbes'*.

Nadler has carefully examined all the recent research, findings and differences of view, weighed them and sensibly arrived at his own conclusions. Thus, the recent flurry of interest in the influence of Spinoza's Latin master, Franciscus van den Enden, an atheistic ex-Jesuit from Antwerp, who has been shown to have been an extremely interesting radical writer in his own right, is deftly handled. Some current experts, notably Wim Klever and Marc Bedjaï, hold Van den Enden to have been crucially influential, a kind of 'proto-Spinoza' who provided the conceptual foundations on which much of Spinoza's subsequent greatness as a thinker was based. Others, including Herman de Dijn, grant that Van den Enden was a key figure in the radical intellectual circles linked to Spinoza but see him as following rather than leading, a skilful publicist rather than a major original thinker. Nadler gives Van den Enden all due prominence, stressing his remarkable talents as teacher and publicist, and the hitherto overlooked significance of his intellectual contribution, but also gently distances himself, on this topic, from Klever – who, however, as he observes, has generally has been one of the most innovative, creative and productive of the scholars contributing to the emergence of the 'new Spinoza' – concluding that *'it can hardly be doubted that Spinoza was an original and independent thinker at a relatively early age'*, and that it is *'an exaggeration to say that [Van den Enden] played the role of Socrates to Spinoza's Plato'*, but also noting that when he came to the ex-Jesuit's door *'he had much to learn, and would have been exposed to an impressive range of important texts, ideas, and personalities'*.

By contrast it would be easy to convey a rather negative view of Margaret Gullan-Whur's biography. Her book contains a relatively large number of factual inaccuracies and moments of confusion which betray some careless reading and a superficial grasp of the Dutch historical context. Prince Maurice is styled someone who was *'refused the title of Prince of*

Orange'. She says that in 1632 Spain did not want to '*lose the Dutch-speaking principality of Liège*', Rotterdam in 1627 was, according to her, '*a country village*', she repeatedly uses the term 'marranos' wholly incorrectly, she calls Petrus Serrarius '*a maverick elderly Englishman*', she says the Amsterdam Portuguese Jews spoke '*Judaeo-Spanish Ladino*' (in fact, they spoke Portuguese), and so on. Her explanation of Spinoza's expulsion from the Portuguese Jewish community of Amsterdam is odd: she says the community elders felt justified in acting as they did because of his '*discoursing with non-Jews on religious matters, disobeying the elders, fraternising and litigating outside the Jewish community and – probably possessing banned "writings", such as Descartes'* . In my opinion none of these relatively trivial points was of much, if any, relevance. What mattered, as Nadler correctly stresses, and as all the evidence, including the exceptionally severe form of excommunication employed in Spinoza's case, indicates, was his denial of the '*divine origin and Mosaic authorship of the Torah*'.

Ms Gullan-Whur is bound to provoke criticism with some of her remarks about the Jews. '*The Dutch*', she says, '*winked at the duplicity of Jewish merchant venturers at sea, but resented their lack of scruples in Amsterdam*'. She refers to '*Jewish insularity*', the '*marrano disputes of Bento's childhood [being] a Jewish affliction*', to Spinoza before his expulsion having '*deployed tricks of marrano dissimulation*', '*the common Jewish tendency to live on credit*', the '*mahamad's punitive fury*'. This is all the more unfortunate since when she comes, towards the end of her book, to discuss Spinoza's only outright attack on the Catholic Church, found in one of his longest letters, to a former disciple named Albert Burgh who had converted to Catholicism in Italy and now threatened him with '*eternal damnation*', summoning him to acknowledge the truth of Christianity and the greatness of the Church, she dismisses his answer out of hand as '*evidence of his sour view of Christ's sacraments and supernaturalism*'. She calls it '*abusive*', one of Spinoza's '*undignified lapses into invective*', and wonders whether Burgh bothered '*to read on after its sarcastic opening*' . Yet, in fact, this is one of Spinoza's most important letters which admittedly appalled, but also made a deep impression on, key readers, including Henry More and Leibniz, in various countries. Certainly it is hard-hitting but its comments about Christianity, the churches' teaching on the Devil and eternal damnation, and the financial corruption of the Church, together with its argument that there is nothing to distinguish the saints and holy men of Catholicism from the martyrs and holy men of other faiths, that the Jewish church is older, more persevering and reports more miracles than the Catholic, and that Islam is more powerful, unified and splendid than Christianity, while the Pope gained the leadership of the Christian world using forged documents, manipulation and clever 'artifice', far from being 'abuse' are not easy to refute. Evidently shaken, the Vicar-Apostolic of the Dutch Catholic Church in Utrecht, writing to the papal nuncio

Portrait of Spinoza. Dutch school, after 1650. Canvas. Historisch Museum, The Hague.

in Brussels, in September 1678, confided that '*scarcely anything more fatal for the Christian and Catholic religion can be thought of than this letter*' .

But if the defects of Ms Gullan-Whur's book are many and considerable, it also has one or two notable strengths. In the first place, she has grave reservations about Spinoza's personality and attitudes, blaming him in particular for his arrogance and '*misogyny*'. There is no reason why biographers of great men should necessarily be admirers and she is quite right to point out that there has been too much wishful thinking and uncritical eulogising of Spinoza's conduct and character. There undoubtedly was a measure of arrogance and ambition in him which has been systematically overlooked or de-emphasised by earlier biographers, a criticism which arguably applies in some measure to Nadler too. When she asserts, however, that '*throughout Spinoza's life his opinion of the capacity of anyone but himself to reason properly on any matter was low*', she is surely being less than entirely fair. In fact Spinoza never made any secret of his profound debt to Descartes or considerable respect for Machiavelli, Hobbes, and Pieter de la Court. But it is above all in her preoccupation with Spinoza's emotions and attitude to women and to sexual issues, that she has performed a novel and most useful service. For this is undoubtedly a key area both for assessing Spinoza's life and work and in appraising his philosophy and political thought, and one about which other biographers have said all too little.

The analysis of the emotions, of happiness and unhappiness, and of pleasure, forms a major part of the *Ethics* and, clearly, Spinoza regarded himself as something of an expert in this sphere. Whether or not Gullan-Whur is right to speculate at some length, as she does, about the only reported romantic attachment in Spinoza's life (Nadler barely pauses to discuss it and generally says little about Spinoza and sexuality) claiming Spinoza was fixated on Van den Enden's clever and erudite daughter Clara Maria van den Enden and suffered over many years deep pangs of jealousy because she bestowed her affections instead on the physician Dirk Kerckring, she is right to stress Spinoza's obvious preoccupation with the subject of sexual jealousy. But her real contribution here is to focus at considerable length on Spinoza's theoretical appraisal of women and their place in society. She repeatedly complains of his '*misogyny*', alleging that there is in Spinoza's mind a deep-seated contradiction, of which he himself was unaware, between his assuming '*women were radically and inevitably disadvantaged*' compared to men and his theory, expounded in the *Ethics*, '*that agreement between human beings is possible only if reason is used*' and that '*when he claimed that common notions were notions common to all men, he meant by men people, not males*'. The last part is correct but it is highly doubtful whether the contradiction she points to is really there. Unquestionably, Spinoza did believe women to be, in practice, more prey to 'superstition', and less susceptible to reason, than men and may well have been strengthened in this belief by the fact the most renowned blue-stocking of his time, Anna Maria van Schurman ended up a religious fundamentalist while Clara Maria, clever, witty and learned though she was adhered firmly (and increasingly) to her Catholic faith.

Undoubtedly, also, Spinoza did place women in an inferior position in his last work, the *Tractatus Politicus*, expressly excluding from voting for the supreme council in his proposed ideal democratic republic '*women and servants, who are subject to their husbands and masters, and also children and wards, as long as they are under the control of their parents and guardians*'. Also he answers the question are women '*under men's authority by nature or institution ?*' by concluding they are subordinate '*by nature*'. But it is important to recognise that he does this in accordance with his admonition that any meaningful political theory must begin with a realistic view of human nature. He is not saying (as most people then thought) that women are mentally inferior to men, or excluding women on 'conventional grounds'. His point is that he can find no historical instance where women have been able to throw off '*men's authority*' and assumes accordingly that women are by nature invariably too weak to resist control by their fathers and husbands. The very fact he classifies them together with servants who would be free were they not under masters, and youths who become independent when they are no longer under the supervision of parents, carries the theoretical implication that women would be independent, and therefore worthy to vote, if they could break free of domination by men.

The true irony of Gullan-Whur's strictures concerning Spinoza's '*misogyny*', however, lies in the fact that it was precisely the 'Spinozists' and radical deists of the late seventeenth and early eighteenth century, beginning with Van den Enden, who believed in giving girls and women the same educational opportunities as men (as Gullan-Whur correctly remarks), who first overturned the prevailing notion that women are intellectually inferior to men and first maintained that institutionalised subordination of women to fathers and husbands is not God-ordained and therefore has no legitimate basis. It is therefore nothing other than tyranny. The modern emancipation of woman could indeed not begin until this 'philosophical' step, or mental leap, was taken. Furthermore, the intellectual emancipation of the female libido began at exactly the same point, and for the same reason, as we see from the writings of such Spinozists and radicals as Beverland, Radicati and the Marquis d'Argens. For if the '*enslaving*', as one Dutch radical called it, of women to fathers and husbands is not 'God-ordained', neither is any sexual code which imprisons woman in a socially imposed chastity, and exclusive participation of sex within marriage, which does not apply equally, or in the same way, to men.

JONATHAN ISRAEL

Steven Nadler, *Spinoza. A Life*. Cambridge: Cambridge University Press, 1999; 350 pp. ISBN 05-21552-10-9.
Margaret Gullan-Whur, *Within Reason. A Life of Spinoza*. New York, NY: Saint Martin's Press, 1998; 416 pp. ISBN 03-12253-58-3.

The Pliny of the Indies Georg Rumphius and his *Ambonese Curiosity Cabinet*

In the 1620s, as the historian Giles Milton has recently recounted in his bestselling *Nathaniel's Nutmeg* (1999), the Moluccas – the original Spice Islands in the Eastern Seas (present-day Indonesia) – were ruthlessly brought under the control of the Dutch East India Company (VOC). From then on, the VOC held the monopoly over the production of spices and their transport to Amsterdam. In addition to its military and commercial exploits the VOC also engaged in exploration and discovery, and Amsterdam became a market not only for spices, but also for information and knowledge about the East. Many wealthy merchants in Amsterdam began to collect exotic objects, and established curiosity cabinets full of rare birds, insects, shells, precious stones, corals, prints, maps and books. The art of describing flourished, in the paintings of the Old Masters no less than in the atlases that were published in the Dutch Republic, and in the many books on travel, tropical medicine and astronomy, on the peoples of Asia and Africa, their religions and their languages.

Among the most illustrious contributions in this respect are the two books by Georg Rumphius in which he described the natural world of the East Indies. For almost fifty years, from 1653 till his death, Rumphius

EFFIGIES
GEORGII EVERHARDI RUMPHII, HANOVIENSIS ÆTAT' LXVIII.

Casus rubens oculos tam gnava mente acutos,
Et nemo mitius, ditisqat aut vidiat.
Attis oculis, mic critis est Germanus, origini, tint,
Absqe pale et scenni serene fuit opus.

Georg Everhard Rumphius
(?1628-1702). Photo
Letterkundig Museum,
The Hague.

(1628-1702) lived on the island of Amboyna in the Moluccas, where he served as VOC-merchant, administrator, soldier and judge. Rumphius was an accomplished mathematician and engineer, draughtsman and historian. Blind since about 1670, he was as multilingual as the *Hobson-Jobson* dictionary of 1886, which includes amongst its sources his 7-volume *Herbarium Amboinense* of 1741.

The other book of this Pliny of the Indies, *The Ambonese Curiosity Cabinet*, originally published in 1705, has now been translated into English and published in a beautiful scholarly edition by E.M. Beekman. It is a book about the shells of the Moluccas, in three parts: first the Soft shellfish, in 44 chapters, with 16 plates; then the Hard shellfish, in 39 chapters, with 33 plates; and finally the Minerals, Stones and Other Rare Things such as gold, amber, precious stones, snakes and whales, in 87 chapters with 11 plates. The book is published with all the original engravings, though not the frontispiece of 1705. Beekman has added a solid 70-page introduction on Rumphius' life and work, and some 160 pages of annotations and references which bear witness to his extraordinary erudition and scholarship.

Rumphius' book was inspired by a religious desire to read and understand God's book of nature. At the same time it reflects the interest in discovery, description and classification that is characteristic of early modern natural science. His descriptions offer careful and precise accounts of the shapes and colours of the shells of the East Indies, where and when they can be found, what they are used for and what medicinal properties they have, how to clean them and keep them or eat them. The book resounds with the delights of language and naming, in Dutch, English, Latin, French, Italian, Greek, Portuguese, Malay, Ambonese and at times also in Chinese and Arabic. It is full of local lore and legend, such as the tale of the Coral Woman hauled from the sea in Ambon Bay in 1681. Of the Marble Whelks, Rumphius tells us that they *'are eagerly sought after for making rings, which are worn on the fingers not only by the Native women, but by our women as well'*, and then proceeds to explain how these rings were made.

Later, the Moluccas' incredible riches in shells were mentioned by Darwin's friend, the explorer Alfred Russell Wallace, in his book *The Malay Archipelago* (1869). He recounts how in January 1858 he had gone *'by invitation, to see a collection of shells and fish made by a gentleman of Amboyna'*, containing – at a rough estimate – *'nearly a thousand different kinds of shells, and perhaps ten thousand specimens'*. But Wallace and Darwin did not know the works of Rumphius. It was their American contemporary, the naturalist A.S. Bickmore, who in 1868 travelled to the Moluccas with a copy of *The Ambonese Curiosity Cabinet*, and found the shells and stones there almost exactly as Rumphius had described them two centuries before. A scientific expedition in the early 1990s again confirmed the accuracy of Rumphius' descriptions.

For this English translation, Beekman has used the *English and Low-Dutch Dictionary* by William Sewell, published in Amsterdam in 1691. While he has retained the original Malay names and the Latin names of modern scientific terminology, Beekman has largely discarded the Dutch ones which Rumphius gave – thus losing the poetic quality and the Adamic force of names such as *'Droomhorentje'* (Little Dream Horn), *'Prinsenbegrafenis'* (Prince's Funeral), or *'Wilde Boerenmuziek'* (Peasant Music). The few that have been retained, such as *'Kinkhooren'* (Whelk) on p. 134, are not included in the index.

Published two hundred years after the demise of the VOC in 1799, this majestic English edition by Beekman testifies to the continuing fascination of Rumphius' work. Here it is worth noting a remarkable tradition of women's knowledge of the secrets of nature. This is hinted at in Beekman's dedication of the book, *'For Faith: my Susanna'*, which refers to Rumphius' first wife, the native woman Susanna, who knew and shared with him her knowledge of tropical nature and the local lore and legend pertaining to it. In Beekman's earlier anthology of Rumphius' nature writings, *The Poison Tree* (1981), there is an illustrated description of the orchid which Rumphius named *Flos Susannae* after her, 'who, when alive, was my prime Companion and Helpmate in the gathering of herbs and plants, and who was also the first ever to show me this flower'.

Then there is the artist Maria Sybilla Merian (1647-1717), who after her return from Surinam to Holland coloured in – 'most deliciously' – the plates of a special copy of The Ambonese Curiosity Cabinet. This copy, from the cabinet of the Amsterdam merchant and member of the Royal Society, Levinus Vincent (1658-1727), and now held in the Amsterdam University Library, inspired the enchanting novella on Rumphius, God's Magicians (God's Goochelaartjes, 1932) by the early twentieth-century Dutch novelist Augusta de Wit. And this in turn inspired Maria Dermoût to write her great novel of the Moluccas, The Ten Thousand Things (De tienduizend dingen,1956; English translation 1958), in which the names of 'shells and horns and snails and jellyfish and other such little fellows' given by Rumphius are a pervasive and evocative presence.

What these women artists share with Rumphius and his Susanna is their deep and intimate knowledge of tropical nature, and the loving descriptions they have left us of its wonders.

REINIER SALVERDA

Georgius Everhardus Rumphius, The Ambonese Curiosity Cabinet (Translated, edited, annotated, and with an introduction by E.M. Beekman. New Haven / London: Yale University Press, 1999; 567 pp. ISBN 0-300-07534-0.
E.M. Beekman (ed.), The Poison Tree. Selected Writings of Rumphius on the Natural History of the Indies. Amherst: The University of Massachusetts Press, 1981; 260 pp. ISBN 0-87023-329-7.

Society

From Saint Arnold to Burp Castle
Beer in Flanders

Beer drinking in Flanders goes back a long way. The patron saint of brewers, an eleventh-century Flemish monk called Arnold, is said to have eradicated plague in the villages around Oudenburg Abbey by persuading the locals to drink a concoction of fermented malts, hops and yeast rather than risk the polluted water. His initiative led to the establishment of breweries in monasteries throughout the Low Countries. The industry was later taken over by private brewers, but the monkish tradition of brewing is still kept alive in Flanders by Trappist monks who work the breweries at Westvleteren, near Poperinge, and Westmalle, near Antwerp.

The monastic origins of many brews may explain why beer drinking is almost a religious ritual in Flanders. Jan de Bruyne, who runs a specialist beer café in Bruges, has dedicated his life to teaching the art of beer drinking. He holds occasional seminars on beer culture in a back room and lays down the law on the type of glass to use and the amount of sediment to leave in the bottom.

Several organisations have been set up to ensure that a good beer is taken as seriously as a French grand cru, including the Belgian Office for Promoting the Art of Serving Beer (BSB). Its director, Johan Blervacq, has an office in the gilt-encrusted Brouwershuis on the Grote Markt in Brussels. 'The quality of Belgian beer is unquestionably high, but the problems begin the moment the beer is served in the café', he says.

The BSB was set up by the country's main breweries to maintain standards in café service. Since 1995, it has run professional beer-serving courses for café owners and waiters; graduates receive a diploma and a BSB-approved metal plaque to display outside their café. Around 3,500 Belgian cafés have received the coveted award, and inspectors carry out annual checks to ensure that pouring remains up to scratch.

The BSB is also a prime mover behind the creation of the world's first Academy of Beer and Gastronomy, which opened in September 1999 at the Ter Hercke Hotel School in Herk-De-Stad, in Limburg province.

The Beer Academy is a joint initiative of the BSB, the Confederation of Belgian Breweries (CBB) and the Belgian branch of the Association of European Hotel and Tourism Schools. Graduates are awarded a 'Master of Beer' diploma, similar to the Master of Wine certificate awarded by the Bordeaux Wine School.

The first 16 students are now immersed in a syllabus that will teach them the art of tasting beer, the role of aromas, the typology of beer and the theory and practice of fermentation. They also learn the increasingly important art of combining different beers with different food. The courses are mainly aimed at people in the catering trade, but are open to anyone with an interest in beer.

Sadly, the days when Duke Jean I of Brabant quaffed 144 mugs of beer in one night are long past. The country's beer drinkers now sip their way through a modest 101 litres a year, which puts them sixth in the world league table, well behind the Germans (131 litres a head), the Irish (123) and the British (103).

The country's beer industry has shrunk dramatically this century, from about 3,000 breweries in 1900 to about 100 today. Many of the smaller breweries have been taken over by the Interbrew group based in the university town of Leuven, which is now the world's fourth largest brewer. Its main brand, Stella Artois, comes fifth in the league table of export beers, after Heineken, Carlsberg, Budweiser and Guinness. In May 2000 Interbrew also took over Whitbread.

The sobering news is that Europeans are drinking less beer. Despite the best efforts of the Germans and the Irish, breweries in the EU have seen sales drop by 0.5 percent every year since 1992. The Belgians are contributing to the malaise by downing two million litres less, equivalent to the output of several small breweries.

There are a few bright spots among the gloom. The popularity of Trappist beers has rocketed, with 68.7

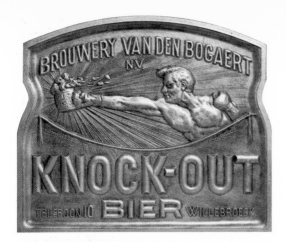

A Flemish brewery with punch,
but it still went out of business
years ago.

million litres drunk in 1997 compared with 66.2 million in 1996.

Brewers are now pinning their hopes on export markets, such as the United States and Japan. The most recent figures gathered by the American Beer Institution show that the amount of Belgian beer imports to the United States in 1998 was double the 1996 figure, though at 2.5 million litres it is still small beer compared to Heineken's 435 million litres.

CBB export director Jan de Brabanter shares St Arnold's conviction that beer is good for you. '*Beer has beneficial properties that protect against heart disease,*' he claims. '*We want to try to convince people that they can prolong their life by drinking a healthy amount of beer a day.*'

Back home, the CBB is trying to boost business with events like the annual Beer Weekend on the Grote Markt in Brussels and the opening in April 1999 of a Belgian Beer Information Centre in Japan.

The rich heritage of Flemish beer used to be a well-kept secret, but the efforts of café owners such as Jan de Bruyne and of writers such as Michael Jackson and Peter Crombecq have helped to promote the image of Flemish ales. Connoisseurs can now track down rare Flemish brews in beer taverns such as De Brakke Grond in Amsterdam, the Comptoir des Belges in La Rochelle, and Burp Castle in Manhattan. As word gets around, the names of Flemish brewing villages such as Hoegaarden and Zottegem are gradually becoming as well known as the great wine-producing vineyards of France. We'll drink to that.

DEREK BLYTH

The Beer Museum, Grote Markt 10, Brussels, is open every day from 10 to 5 pm. Entry costs 100 BF and includes a glass of dark or light beer, poured by one of the best barmen in the country. Information on +32 2511 4987. The CBB's Website can be found at http://www.beer-paradise.be

On the day of the Queen's speech, the third Tuesday in September, the Dutch government presents its policy for the coming year in the Speech from the Throne. Queen Beatrix reads the text which the ministers have been responsible for preparing. In 1999 – most unusually – she began with a quip. She addressed the members of Parliament as '*Gentlemen ...*', although women too have been members of parliament in the Netherlands for a long time. After all, this was the opening of the Speech from the Throne spoken by her grandmother, Wilhelmina, exactly a hundred years earlier. It was a more or less subtle indication that the Netherlands have had female rulers for a whole century – a royal matriarchy which will come to an end as soon as Beatrix makes way for her eldest son, Willem-Alexander.

Meanwhile, the opening '*Gentlemen*' also calls attention to the composition of the Dutch parliament around the turn of the century: men only. Not surprisingly it was men who, at the beginning of this century, introduced the ban on brothels, a fine example of hypocritical legislation. Hypocritical in that neither the prostitute nor her client were liable to punishment, but only the person who '*provided the facilities*', the keeper of the brothel. Although brothel-keeping was a punishable offence, police action has never amounted to much. The ban on brothels incorporated into the 1911

Hendrick ter Brugghen, *Brothel Scene*. 17th century. Canvas, 105.5 x 86.4 cm. Galerie Bruno Meissner, Zürich.

Penal Code sprang from a surge of left-over Victorian prudery. With a ban on paper Government could congratulate itself: it had done monogamous marriage a favour. Government closed its eyes to reality: sexual intercourse between men and women who were not married to each other simply continued on the quiet. In The Hague, the seat of government, quite a lot of brothels were established in the course of the century, within walking distance of the parliamentary buildings. Moreover, the still unsolved murder of the prostitute Blonde Dolly in the fifties has always been associated with visiting gentlemen from government circles – without proof of course.

Actually, the ban on brothels had been a dead letter for a long time. It came as no surprise when in the police budget in September 1999 the government announced that the legislation on public decency is being 'modernised' by lifting the ban on brothels. This will apply from 1 October 2000. It is noticeable that 'providers of facilities' are really not at all jubilant at the lifting of the ban. The reason is that the authorities are about to make drastic changes in their attitude to prostitution. After turning a blind eye for a long time (if you can't see it, it doesn't exist) the authorities are now advocating an active policy. They could not take action against sex houses which 'actually' were not supposed to exist. Now that brothels are to be legalised, as it were, by the lifting of the ban, the government can impose conditions. In the seat of government, The Hague, this active policy on the part of government is already tangible. There are a few streets which, like the embankments in Amsterdam, are full of window prostitutes. Those who control the windows can feel the change in the wind now that the mayor of The Hague has already ordained that the curtains must be closed after one o' clock at night (and half-past one at weekends). The measure, taken with the agreement of the municipal council, is intended to reduce the level of nuisance in the residential streets around those where the prostitutes operate. The sex bosses of The Hague are disturbed that the municipality is getting more and more strict with them and 'their' girls. Spokesman Arie de Jong, who over the years has become a well-known sex boss in the capital, says, outraged, in the newspaper *Haagsche Courant*: '*They let those junkies and dealers, the people who cause all the trouble, carry on unmolested.*' Another window prostitution operator informs us: '*The ban on brothels is to be lifted soon. We'll be getting all sorts of rules about room sizes, safety, working conditions. It's nothing less than a clearance operation in fact.*' And in an interview in *De Groene Amsterdammer* the artist Petra Urban, president of the *Rode Draad* interest group for prostitutes, doubts that the lifting of the ban will do away with illegal networks. She also expresses her concern for the establishment of a proper prostitutes' union.

The brothel as a closed house where the client can select a girl and retire with her, and then pay the 'madam', no longer exists in its classic form in Holland. In the seventies a large number of sex clubs of

various sorts shot up like mushrooms. In the eighties there were considerable population changes among the prostitutes because of the high percentage of (illegal) immigrants. The problem of drug addiction among prostitutes has also increased enormously. Young women especially have fallen into prostitution through an addiction. Government has been obliged to open its eyes, and has taken all sorts of measures to get young prostitutes to kick the habit, through social work for instance. The abolition of the ban on brothels is to be seen, then, as the final move in a series of activities aimed at combating the consequences for society of prostitution as effectively as possible. Prostitution itself is impossible to get rid of. The Dutch government has now finally recognised this with its proposal to lift the ban on brothels.

PETER RIEMERSMA
Translated by Sheila M. Dale.

A Good Rembrandt Year

Each year numerous new publications about Rembrandt come onto the market and 1999 was no exception. It was a good Rembrandt year, particularly since two Rembrandt exhibitions were mounted in the Netherlands: one at the Mauritshuis in The Hague, where the exhibition of self-portraits (previously on show at the National Gallery in London) attracted

Left: Rembrandt H. van Rijn, *Self-Portrait with Gorget.* c.1629. Panel, 38.2 x 31 cm. Germanisches National-museum, Nuremberg. Right: Anonymous artist, *Portrait of* *Rembrandt with Gorget.* 17th century. Panel, 37.9 x 28.9 cm. Mauritshuis, The Hague. Until 1991 the latter was regarded as one of the high points of Rembrandt's oeuvre.

200,000 visitors, and another at the Rembrandthuis in Amsterdam about Rembrandt's art collection, which more than 50,000 people came to see. Research into Rembrandt and his work continues, and so the books keep on coming.

Every fifteen to twenty years someone comes along who sifts through all that information again and adds his own opinions. In 1968 it was Bob Haak with his *Rembrandt. His Life, his Work, his Age* (Rembrandt. Zijn leven, zijn werk, zijn tijd), a matter-of-fact study written with great authority. In 1984 along came Gary Schwartz with *Rembrandt. His Life, his Paintings* (Rembrandt. Zijn leven, zijn schilderijen), which puts the emphasis on Rembrandt's patrons. Three years ago Ernst van de Wetering published his *Rembrandt. The Painter at Work*, which concentrates on Rembrandt's painting technique. In 1999 a sort of companion piece to that book appeared, about Rembrandt's etchings: the second edition of *Rembrandt as an Etcher*, by Christopher White. In this fine book White takes a de-tailed look at the practical aspects of etching and espe-cially at the creative process during which the work takes shape.

Now the historian Simon Schama has also had a shot at the subject with his *Rembrandt's Eyes*, a lavish and voluminous book, written with pace and consider-able imaginative power, about Rembrandt, his imme-diate environment and his wider historical and art-his-torical context. Schama is a storyteller *par excellence*. He describes what he sees or what he thinks he would have seen had he lived three-and-a-half centuries earli-er, and that is a great deal. The writer focuses on the first thirty or forty years of Rembrandt's life, possibly because Schama originally had a rather different book in mind: a book in which he wanted to describe Rembrandt's envy of Rubens. Rubens as a 'father-fig-ure' for Rembrandt, Rubens as a role model and *dop-pelgänger*. Hence the lengthy prehistory of Rubens and his Antwerp background. But Schama seems to have abandoned that plan half-way through.

There is no doubt that Rubens was important to Rembrandt, but the same applies to every seventeenth-century painter. Schama is looking for emulation at all costs, ambitious rivalry and a desire to surpass, with Rubens as the rival and example. However, Schama is not altogether convincing. Rembrandt was indeed a so-cial climber, and even in his early twenties he received commissions from the stadtholder and his circle and from the regents of Amsterdam. So, in a Dutch context, he was indeed a sort of Rubens – albeit for a limited pe-riod. But however handsomely he may have rigged himself out in his self-portraits, in his lifestyle Rembrandt, unlike Rubens, never ranked as upper class.

In fact Rembrandt was a different kettle of fish alto-gether. In his self-portraits he compared himself im-plicitly with illustrious, much older predecessors. Recent research into Rembrandt's clothes reveals that he usually portrayed himself in what was even then old-fashioned – mainly sixteenth-century – dress. He did this not as amusing fancy dress but to show that he placed himself in the tradition of the predecessors he so admired. Dürer, Lucas van Leyden and Titian, painters whose work he owned in print form and whose paint-ings he had seen. He must have been trying to say something like: I admire them, they are my great role models; I am part of that tradition. For Rembrandt, who came from Leiden, that must have applied to Lucas van Leyden in particular.

Rembrandt had several thousand prints by or after the old masters, and innumerable details in his work show that he borrowed from them. This is confirmed in the book *Rembrandt's Treasures* produced for the exhibition of the same name organised at the Rembrandthuis, the house where Rembrandt lived from 1639 to 1658, which is currently undergoing restoration. The old interior by the architect De Bazel has been removed and the whole of the inside is being restored to the way it must have been in the mid-sev-enteenth century. The public were given a foretaste with this exhibition about Rembrandt's famous art and curiosities collection. When Rembrandt was bankrupt-ed in 1656, an inventory of his effects was drawn up. On the basis of that source and by comparison with items in the possession of other Amsterdam collectors, it was possible to establish with reasonable accuracy what must have been in Rembrandt's '*kunstkamer*' or 'art room' and elsewhere in his house. That '*kunst-kamer*' has now been reconstructed in its entirety, including the stuffed animals, shells, curiosities from the East Indies and the volumes containing prints and drawings. It was the latter – there must have been some 7,000 – that were so valuable financially and artistically. In addition, objects, drawings, prints and documents were exhibited all over the house and on the two exhibition floors. The accompanying book contains essays about the art and curiosities Rembrandt amassed in his '*kunstkamer*' and about the use he made of them in his teaching and in his own work. In contrast to what had previously been claimed, this collection played no role in Rembrandt's alleged aspiration to become a 'gentleman virtuoso'. Quite the reverse, in fact: analysis of the sources reveals the extent to which he did his own thing and his complete disregard for social convention.

Schama calls Rembrandt a '*metaphysician*' as regards his self-portraits. In so doing he adopts a position that runs counter to the latest views. The catalogue for the exhibition at the Mauritshuis, *Rembrandt by Himself*, takes a sober, unromantic approach to the subject: no introspection, no self-conscious psychology or artistic philosophy about the transience of human life. A face was a subject like any other, with the advantage that it was always to hand. A self-portrait is nothing more than a portrait, except that it is a portrait in mirror image.

But then: why oh why *so many* self-portraits? Ernst van de Wetering suggests in the catalogue that these self-portraits served as a sort of marketing tool. They were 'samples' showing what Rembrandt was capable of. They may have hung in the place of honour in art collections alongside works by the great master. Such collections certainly existed, but we know of none that contained self-portraits specially commissioned for the purpose during Rembrandt's life-time. The Sicilian patrician Antonio Ruffo, who ordered no fewer than three paintings by Rembrandt from distant Messina, apparently had no desire for a self-portrait. Ruffo and his huge collection of 516 paintings are the subject of Jeroen Giltaij's dissertation. It is as if he holds a magnifying glass to a detail from Rembrandt's life, thereby suddenly illuminating an aspect – in this case the purchase and the identification of those three paintings. Michiel Roscam Abbing's dissertation is another such example. His five articles provide a cautious interpretation of details from Rembrandt's life. For instance, he tests the credibility of the anecdote that Rembrandt painted a portrait of a maidservant and placed it in a window of his house to confuse passers-by. It tells us a good deal about the human *trompe l'oeil*, but the author has to conclude that there is probably no truth in the story. He does however manage to identify a number of paintings by Rembrandt in eighteenth-century French collections, which tells us something about the appreciation of Rembrandt's work and about the confusion that existed even then about correct attributions.

Finally, it was not only the interested layman and the specialist who were well served in this Rembrandt year; children were also given a taste of the great mas-

ter. The writer / artist Jan Wolkers, like Rembrandt born in Leiden, was the obvious person for the job. In his charmingly illustrated book he takes a personal approach to Rembrandt's life and work.

ROELOF VAN GELDER
Translated by Alison Mouthaan-Gwillim.

Simon Schama, *Rembrandt's Eyes*. Harmondsworth: Allen Lane / The Penguin Press, 1999; 750 pp. ISBN 0-713-99384-7.

Christopher White and Quentin Buvelot (ed.), *Rembrandt by Himself*. Zwolle: Waanders; 272 pp. ISBN 90-400-93-15-6.

Bob van den Boogert (ed.): *Rembrandt's Treasures*. Zwolle: Waanders, 1999; 159 pp. ISBN 90-400-9381-4.

Christopher White, *Rembrandt as an Etcher. A Study of the Artist at Work*. New Haven: Yale University Press, 1999; 284 pp. ISBN 0-300-07953-2.

Jeroen Giltaij, *Ruffo en Rembrandt. Over een Sicilaanse verzamelaar in de zeventiende eeuw die drie schilderijen bij Rembrandt bestelde*. Zutphen: Walburg Press, 1999; 192 pp. ISBN 90-5730-083-4.

Michiel Roscam Abbing, *Rembrandt toont sijn const. Bijdragen over Rembrandt-documenten uit de periode 1648-1756*. Primavera Pers, 1999; 270 pp.

Jan Wolkers, *De spiegel van Rembrandt*. Zwolle: Waanders, 1999; 32 pp. ISBN 90-400-9378-4.

Between Emotion, Devotion and Polemic
The Art of Rogier van der Weyden

Little is known about the majority of Flemish Primitives. Although the names of so many painters have been preserved in archives, there are few works which can be attributed with certainty. But no one painter gives rise to more discussion than Rogier van der Weyden. In 1435 he became official painter to the city of Brussels, where he died in 1464. But there is endless debate about the period before that, the period when Rogier was in Tournai, where he was born in 1399 as Rogier de le Pasture. The thirty-odd years of Rogier's 'youth' have become the most controversial period in our art history.

Van der Weyden – De la Pasture has been an internal Belgian problem for a long time. When it began to be established that the Brussels official city painter with a Flemish name might well have originated from Tournai, and been given a French name there, this was the signal for a francophone frontal attack on the 'Flemish' Primitives. However, that aggression now seems to have receded. The creation of a school of Walloon Primitives – which remains, moreover, a difficult undertaking – is no longer a priority. And on the Flemish side people have understood for a long time that the arrival of artists 'from abroad' can only enhance their prestige.

The authors who are active at present are scarcely concerned at all with that internal Belgian aspect, but that does not prevent them from defending widely differing points of view with great conviction. The point at issue is the relatively long period that Van der Weyden spent in Tournai, where, according to the records, there were a few things that do not quite tie up, such as the late date (for someone with his skill) at which he was formally recognised as a Master (1432), although he had already been accepted as a Master by the city authorities in 1426! During this period he was working in the atelier of Robert Campin, until the latter was convicted of adultery and had to disband his atelier.

One sometimes has the impression that the entire literature on Van der Weyden has turned into an academic battle over footnotes – and that is true in part, but fortunately not entirely so. This is not just a matter of references to one source or another, but of works of art which awaken interest and continue to fascinate even though they bear no name-plate. Some authors sometimes forget that.

But not Dirk de Vos. In his substantial book, published on the occasion of the six-hundredth anniversary of the painter's birth, one discovers Van der Weyden, not through an initial classic biography, followed by a commentary on the works, but in the manner in which his contemporaries discovered those same works. In the prologue De Vos quotes two travel accounts from the early sixteenth century, in which a German and a Spaniard describe famous works without a single word to show any interest in their author. When the German scholar, Hieronymus Münzer, saw the *Adoration of the Lamb* in Ghent in 1495, he described it as the '*illustrious altarpiece at St John's, which, as I believe, has no equal in all the world*'. And when in 1549 the future Philip II visited the castle of his aunt, Mary of Hungary, in Binche, one of his retinue, a certain Vincente Alvarez, noted: '*There was a painting in the chapel showing the Descent from the Cross; it was the best painting in the entire castle and even I believe, in*

the world, for I have seen many fine paintings in this country, but not a single one that could match its verisimilitude or piety. This opinion is shared by all who have seen it. I am told that the painting is more than 150 years old. It appears that it was once in Louvain and that Queen Mary had it brought from there, replacing it with a copy that was very nearly as good as the original.' Admiration for the work, consideration for the age, the origin and the reputation of the work, but not a word about the painter. And that in Spanish court circles in the middle of the sixteenth century! The offer of a sum of money and a copy to get hold of a masterwork was, so it would seem, a frequently employed 'trick' of the rulers of the time. Philip II also obtained Van der Weyden's *Crucifixion* from the monastery in Scheut in the same way (a work that the painter had presented to the monastery a century earlier!).

Thus the reader approaches the *Descent from the Cross* (now in the Prado), which will prove to be a central work in the oeuvre, in the same way as in earlier times, when it was the quality of the work and not the name that made an impression. And the painting most certainly did make an impression, in the first place by reason of the almost sculptural nature of the figures who occupy all the available space – a painted retable surround. In addition there is the expressive depiction of grief, unique in that period. The book contains interesting pages full of close-ups in which all sorts of comparisons can be made.

De Vos succeeds in seasoning his analysis with all kinds of caustic observations, which sometimes have a topical ring. Of the foreign merchants and bankers around the Burgundian court in Brussels who ordered altarpieces he writes: '*The ne plus ultra was to own a costly altarpiece by the Brussels master, who was a much more prestigious artist than they could find in their native Germany, Italy or Spain, even if they failed to notice that he did not always finish the paintings himself. The pairing of financial acumen and artistic blind spots was evidently a common one in those days, too.*'

Rogier van der Weyden,
The Descent from the Cross.
c.1430-1435.
Panel, 220.5 x 259.5 cm.
Musea del Prado, Madrid.

Today one can read suggestive complaints here and there with regard to the supposed influence of the charismatic movement in Belgian court circles. De Vos observes, without referring to the present, that something similar was going on then. He states that the dukes of Burgundy exhibited a definite preference for the Carthusians, for instance by locating their family mausoleum in a Carthusian monastery specially founded for the purpose near Dijon (Champmol). The Carthusians emphasised '*the suffering of Christ, Mary's acceptance of it, and the believer's identification with it*'. They played an important part in the development of the Devotion Moderna, which focuses on personal sympathy with the Passion. It is a fact that Van der Weyden's son, Cornelis, who had a university Master's degree, became a Carthusian, and indeed the painter bestowed gifts on the Carthusian monasteries of Herne and Scheut. De Vos analyses the works of Van der Weyden further in this sense, and that leads to a number of telling observations with regard to the value which can be attached to the symbolism in these works.

De Vos describes in detail the manner in which Van der Weyden painted, and the extent to which this differed from the traditional technique (with as example Jacques Daret of the Tournai school) and that of Van Eyck. He also goes into the relationship between the modello – a careful concept drawing for the patron – and the under-drawing, the first sketch on the prepared panel. Van der Weyden proves to be a highly-strung draughtsman who can evoke attitudes and movements with absolute accuracy, though without equalling Van Eyck's tactile qualities. How these drawings were scaled up (sometimes to monumental format) is not entirely clear. Here De Vos points out that chemical analyses can tell us nothing about the manner of painting itself.

In the epilogue De Vos breaks a lance for a change of name for the Flemish Primitives, who at present hover awkwardly between terms which are not wholly appropriate such as Late-Gothic and Northern-Renaissance. He proposes the introduction of the term 'Ars Nova'. Back in 1953 Erwin Panofsky applied that concept (borrowed from music) to the innovative painting of the Burgundian regions in the fifteenth century. This can only contribute to a fairer positioning of Van der Weyden and other painters within the development of western art. The international impact of the style of Van der Weyden (and Van Eyck) has already been studied; what is still lacking is the fitting context in which to set it.

JOOST DE GEEST
Translated by Sheila M. Dale.

Dirk de Vos, *Rogier van der Weyden* (Tr. Ted Alkins). Antwerp: Mercatorfonds. 1999; 445 pp. ISBN 90-6153-429-1.

Short takes

In 2000 Brussels is one of the nine European Cities of Culture. The plan of Robert Palmer, the Scottish manager in charge of the project, and his team is first and foremost to show what is going on in the Belgian capital. No eye-catching parade of big names from the international art circuit, then, but an approach which puts the spotlight on the city itself and its cultural potential: Brussels' liveability, culture as an agent binding together different population groups, and so on. As manager of *Glasgow, Cultural Capital 1990*, Palmer had already highlighted municipal themes. At the opening weekend in February 2000 the focus on the city was apparent: fanfares rang across the rooftops, there was a procession in the working-class district of the Marollen, and on the Kunstberg, a spot in urgent need of some new life, films were scheduled. Another striking initiative was 'Bloom in Brussels': following the example of James Joyce's Leopold Bloom, who wanders round Dublin for a day in *Ulysses*, writers from the French and Dutch language communities trod a course around Brussels. They not only produced a number of texts about it, but also held discussions along the way with residents of a wide variety of districts.

In 2001 it will be Rotterdam's turn to be a European City of Culture. Here too the accent will be on the city itself. The organisers said in a press release: '*The principal aim is to show everyone who lives in the city, in the Netherlands, in Europe and the rest of the world that Rotterdam is an inexhaustible, enterprising and unique city as regards culture in the broadest sense of the word*'. In the preparatory stages people talked about 'Cities in Scaffolding': some twenty 'cities' will be set up in Rotterdam. Each 'city' will have its own face and its own story, embracing a number of artistic disciplines. Some examples: 'Rotterdam Pleasure City' (major circus projects, summer performances in the renovated Luxor Theatre, stand-up comedians in the old Calypso cinema), 'City of Erasmus' (a 'city' made up of an international network of seven cities where Erasmus lived and worked, the central theme being communication with the foreigner) and 'Forest of Sin and Folly' (with the Boymans - van Beuningen Museum's exhibition of Hieronymus Bosch forming the centrepiece of a city in which the world is turned upside down, as in Bosch's hallucinatory paintings).

Brussels 2000: tel. +32 2 214 20 00 - http://www.brussels2000.org
Rotterdam 2001: tel. +31 10 402 20 01 - http://www.rotterdam01.nl

In 1800 the National Gallery of Art in Amsterdam opened its doors for the first time. In 1808 it became the Royal Museum, established by Louis Napoleon, brother of Emperor Napoleon Bonaparte and first King of the Netherlands. This Royal Museum was housed in part of the Town Hall on Dam Square, which the King was using as his palace. Following a further change of

dence. It was a fitting part of this exhibition, celebrating as it did the birthday of a museum the basis of whose collection consists of items from that same Huis ten Bosch.

Judikje Kiers and Fieke Tissink, *The Glory of the Golden Age. Painting, Sculpture and Applied Arts.* Amsterdam / Zwolle: Rijksmuseum / Waanders Uitgevers, 2000; 352 pp. ISBN 90-400-9437-3.
Jan Piet Filedt Kok, Ger Luijten and Peter Schatborn, *The Glory of the Golden Age. Prints and Drawings.* Amsterdam / Zwolle: Rijksmuseum / Waanders Uitgevers, 2000; 128 pp. ISBN 90-400-9441-1.

History of the Low Countries is a translation, adapted for an international readership, of J.C.H. Blom and E. Lamberts' *Geschiedenis van de Nederlanden*. The book outlines the history of the Low Countries – the present-day Netherlands and Belgium – as a single area. The editors acknowledge that the borders took shape only after 1500, and that the Low Countries were a political entity only for very brief periods. But they stress the common features and comparable developments that distinguished the region from the countries around it: flourishing trade, urbanisation, political system, language etc. And in the second half of the twentieth century the Netherlands and Belgium were in at the start of the march of European integration – in which they still steer parallel courses today.

   History of the Low Countries offers a comprehensive overview, beginning with the Celts, Romans and Germanic tribes. The book concentrates on political developments. In defence of this approach the editors quote the great Dutch historian Johan Huizinga: '*I often sigh: Doesn't the wider public actually learn the history of civilisation best through a well-structured political history?*'. This book, then, gives a positive answer to Huizinga's question. The editors and translator have succeeded in putting together a pleasantly readable and admirably lucid political history of the Low Countries. On top of this, the book contains a great many very well-chosen illustrations. Such as the splendid print which illustrates the final political partition of the Low Countries in 1830-1831: Dutch soldiers rushing headlong out of rebellious Belgium and taking cover in a gigantic Edam cheese.

J.C.H. Blom and E. Lamberts (ed.), *History of the Low Countries* (Tr. James C. Kennedy). New York / Oxford: Berghahn Books, 1999. 503 pp. ISBN 1-57181-085-4.

In 1993 the Scarecrow Press started the series of 'European Historical Dictionaries', which has since grown to over thirty titles. In 1998 Arend H. Huussen produced the volume on the Netherlands, and in 1999 Scarecrow Press brought out Robert Stallaert's *Historical Dictionary of Belgium*. Series Editor Jon Woronoff describes Belgium in his foreword as '*a land that has been rocked by conflict*', '*a complex country, a paradoxical place at once both insular and cos-*

Johannes Vermeer, *The Milkmaid.* c.1658-1660. Canvas, 45.5 x 41 cm. Rijksmuseum, Amsterdam.

address, in 1885 the Rijksmuseum, as it was by then called, moved to its present home, designed in neo-renaissance style by P.J.H. Cuypers.

   In the Spring of 2000, then, the Rijksmuseum was 200 years old. A series of exhibitions celebrated the anniversary, the focal event being the *The Glory of the Golden Age* exhibition. Threehundred master pieces of the Dutch seventeenth century, from paintings, drawings and sculpture to colourful tulip vases and imposing furniture, were brought together in one of the most expensive and extensive exhibitions ever organised by the Rijksmuseum. Alongside its own treasures, such as Rembrandt's *Night Watch* and Vermeer's *Milkmaid*, there were also a number of superb pieces from other Dutch collections and from abroad. From Berlin came Vermeer's *Glass of Wine*, restored especially for the occasion. Other works of art were making their first trip away from their original homes: the statues from William the Silent's tomb in the Nieuwe Kerk in Delft, a great candelabra from the temple complex in Nikko (Japan), once a gift to the Shogun from the young Dutch Republic, and the gigantic canvas *Allegory on the Birth of Frederick Henry* (373 x 243 cm) by Caesar van Everdingen. This last work comes from the Orange Hall of the palace of Huis ten Bosch, the Queen's resi-

mopolitan', but also *'a leading participant in the drive toward European integration and close transatlantic cooperation'.*

The book opens with a series of 'Abbreviations and Acronyms', intended to familiarise the reader with such disparate concepts as PSC (Parti Social Chrétien – Social Christian Party, the francophone counterpart of the Flemish CVP), VTM (Vlaamse Televisie Maatschappij – Flemish Television Society, the commercial competitor of the public service broadcaster VRT) and ABVV (Algemeen Belgisch Vakverbond – General Federation of Belgian Trade Unions). This is followed by a 'Chronology' running from 58-51 BC ('*Julius Caesar subjects the Gallic Tribes; among them are the Belgae*') to 25 May 1998 ('*Philippe Maystadt accepts the presidency of the PSC*'). The dictionary section proper is an alphabetical listing of the most important individuals, parties and organisations. It describes political and social institutions and also provides information on the Belgian economy and culture. The book ends with a bibliography, arranged by topic, by means of which the interested foreign reader can extend his knowledge of Belgian history.

Robert Stallaerts, *Historical Dictionary of Belgium.* Lanham, MD / London : The Scarecrow Press, Inc., 1999; 368 pp. ISBN 0-8108-3603-3.

CODART 3 took place in March 2000, its theme being 'The Spanish Habsburgs and the Netherlands'. CODART is an initiative of the Netherlands Institute for Cultural Heritage: it stands for 'International Council for Curators of Flemish and Dutch Art' and the aim is '*to further cooperation in the study and display of art from the Low Countries*'.

In his circular letter about CODART 3, director Gary Schwartz pointed out that for the last two years the association had been supported by money from HGIS-Cultuur, a joint programme of the Netherlands Ministries of Foreign Affairs and of Education, Culture and Science. An initial interim evaluation had taken a favourable view of CODART's activities. The comment was made, however, that international networking such as CODART was involved in should be supported financially by other countries as well. The association is therefore appealing for funds to the Flemish government. In future more than mere passive participation will be expected of members, and this was a major item on CODART 3's agenda. The gathering, which began in Maastricht and Antwerp and ended in Toledo, was in any case already assured of support from Flemish, Dutch and Spanish museums and institutions.

CODART also has its own Website, with '*high-quality links to museum home pages*'. These are all museums with Flemish or Dutch art in their collections. There are links to obvious Websites such as those of the Amsterdam Rijksmuseum, the Antwerp Royal Museum of Fine Arts, the Hermitage in St Petersburg, the Metropolitan Museum in New York and London's National Gallery. But there are also less familiar names, such as the Bob Jones University Museum and Gallery (Greenville, SC), the Musée des Beaux-Arts in Valenciennes and the Kaiser Wilhelm Museum in Krefeld. And also one finds great museums whose rich collections of Low Countries art are relatively unknown, such as the Pushkin Museum of Fine Arts in Moscow. In Eastern Europe and Cuba there are still many paintings from Flanders and the Netherlands waiting to be 'discovered'.

http://www.codart.nl

In May 1999 Andrew Motion became Great Britain's nineteenth Poet Laureate, continuing a tradition that began with John Dryden in 1668. Nothing much has really changed since then, for the 'court poet', whose appointment must be approved by the Queen, still receives a cask of white port and a nominal salary. The chosen one gets to open festivals and bookshops, shed lustre on literary gatherings and, last but not least, write poems for all manner of royal occasions.

At the start of 2000 the Netherlands too acquired its own poet laureate (the Dutch term is '*dichter des Vaderlands*' – 'the Nation's Poet'). No royal approval here, but a democratic election: more than 3000 Dutch poetry-lovers voted by e-mail or snail mail for their choice out of two hundred candidates for the new post. Eventually Gerrit Komrij emerged the winner. Komrij is not only an established poet and prose writer, he is also a leading anthologist of Dutch and South African poetry. For the next five years he will be the Dutch ambassador of poetry. At least four times a year he will publish a poem on an international event of his choice in the newspaper *NRC Handelsblad*. In return he will receive a work of art chosen by himself and – the equivalent of the British cask of port – a bunch of flowers every month. As a start, in 2000 he wrote 9 sonnets about Queen Beatrix on the occasion of her official birthday – a critical homage to a '*professional queen*'.

1999 saw the publication, shortly after its author's death, of an exhaustive work on Flemish miniatures by Maurits Smeyers (1937-1999). Smeyers was a specialist in the field, with countless articles and books on the subject to his name. But this *Flemish Miniatures* exceeds them all in its comprehensiveness and above all its accessibility. It is a splendidly produced work, in which the impressive legacy of several generations of miniaturists is presented to a broad readership. Over 600 colour plates and 500 lucidly written pages tell the story of miniature-production in Flanders from the preromanesque period (eighth century) to its late-gothic final flowering in the sixteenth century.

And Smeyers goes even further. Right at the end of *Flemish Miniatures* he also brings in miniatures from the nineteenth and twentieth centuries. Nineteenth-century neo-gothic brought a revival of 'all things medieval', and thus also of the art of manual book illumination. A striking document in this respect is a pastoral

Ministry of the Flemish Community and the British Society of Authors.

Although it is still hard for translated literature from the Netherlands and Flanders – or indeed any translated literature – to break into the Anglo-Saxon market, publishers and translators are not giving up the struggle. And they do not confine their efforts to great names like Mulisch, Claus and Nooteboom. In the past year, for example, there have appeared translations of young Dutch writers such as Hafid Bouazza (*Abdullah's Feet* – De voeten van Abdullah, 1996, again translated by Ina Rilke) and Nanne Tepper (*The Happy Hunting Grounds* – De eeuwige jachtvelden, 1995). Of the latter, a novel about a young Dutch author working in Paris on a book about Jack Kerouac, *The Daily Telegraph wrote: 'The novel is dense, learned, oblique and allusive (...). Tepper binds his material together with admirable artistry. He is a writer of real talent'.*

It is a pity that in the present modest stream of translations the 'classic' authors are rather lagging behind. The British translator Paul Vincent has already written several times in this yearbook about the risks and problems involved (see his article on Willem Elsschot in this issue). In 1999 Vincent published an anthology of translations of poems by the Fleming Guido Gezelle (for more on this, see pp. 280-282 of this issue) for which he drew among other things on *The Evening and the Rose*, a series of Gezelle translations by Christine D'haen and Paul Claes. A fifth, revised version of this also appeared in 1999.

Margriet de Moor, *The Virtuoso* (Tr. Ina Rilke). London: Picador, 1996 / Cees Nooteboom, *Roads to Santiago* (Tr. Ina Rilke). New York: Harcourt Brace, 1996; London: Harvill, 1997 / Hafid Bouazza, *Abdullah's Feet* (Tr. Ina Rilke). London: Headline Book Publishing, 2000 / Nanne Tepper, *The Happy Hunting Grounds* (Tr. Sam Garrett). London: Flamingo, 1999 / Guido Gezelle, *The Evening and the Rose* (Tr. Christine D'haen & Paul Claes). Antwerp: Guido Gezellegenootschap & Pelckmans, 1999.

Carol Fehringer's *A Reference Grammar of Dutch* is aimed at English-speaking students of Dutch at '*beginner / intermediate level*'. It is expressly designed to be user-friendly: the grammatical information is presented in alphabetically arranged short entries (beginning with 'Accents' and ending with a brief chapter on the verb form 'Zou'). Each grammatical rule of thumb is illustrated with simple examples from everyday language, with the inevitable exceptions to the rule at the end of each entry. The entries are also linked to a number of exercises of different levels of difficulty.

Because Fehringer wrote her book for practical use, its structure is more like a dictionary than a traditional grammar. Specialised terminology is shunned like the plague, and the essential linguistic terms are given in a glossary. At the back of the book is an excellent index, making it even easier to resolve specific problems.

Carol Fehringer, *A Reference Grammar of Dutch*. Cambridge: Cambridge University Press, 1999; 185 pp. ISBN 0-521-64521-2.

German soldiers set fire to the Leuven University Library and drive away the population. Illustration from Joseph-Désiré Cardinal Mercier, *Patriotisme et Endurance. Lettre pastorale*, 1914 (fol. 5v, 2.6 x 15.5 cm).

letter from the Belgian Cardinal Mercier about the German invasion of 1914; it was copied and illuminated by Benedictine nuns.

Maurits Smeyers, *Flemish Miniatures* (Tr. Karen Bowen *et al.*). Leuven: Davidsfonds, 1999; 528 pp. ISBN 90-5826-024-0.

The Vondel Translation Prize for 1999 went to Ina Rilke for her translations of *The Virtuoso* (De virtuoos, 1993) by Margriet de Moor and *Roads to Santiago* (De omweg naar Santiago, 1992) by Cees Nooteboom. The prize is awarded biennially for the best English translation of a significant work of literature or cultural history and is an initiative of the Foundation for the Production and Translation of Dutch Literature, the

A great many people in the Netherlands and Flanders are becoming concerned at the large number of English words making their way into Dutch. What many people fail to realise is that the converse also applies. Dutch is craftily fighting back, and when Dutch-speakers use English according to Dutch rules the result is 'Dunglish'. Joyce Burrough-Boenisch, a British translator who lives and works in the Netherlands, used this term for the first time in her article *When is an Editor a Corrector?* Dunglish is perfectly intelligible to Dutch-speakers, but gives rise to some confusion in native speakers of English.

But it is not only the Flemings and the Dutch who dutchify their English. English-speakers resident in the Dutch-speaking area are far from immune to 'infection' by Dutch. Burrough-Boenisch herself started writing a column entitled *Don't Go Dutch* when she began to feel that daily contact with Dutch and Dutch-speakers was making her lose her grasp on her mother tongue.

These columns, with a couple of new pieces, were published in book form as *Righting English that's Gone Dutch*. An index allows the reader to track down specific topics in the various pieces. The author tells us that over the years she has collected examples of written Dunglish in the same way as others collect stamps or beer-mats. Among the subjects discussed are 'false friends' (words wrongly assumed to mean the same in Dutch and English), incorrect use of abbreviations and muddling of spelling rules. And at the end of the book the Anglophone living in the Netherlands can play doctor and diagnose the health of his / her mother tongue by doing the short quiz 'How Dutch have you gone?'.

Joy Burrough-Boenisch, *Righting English that's Gone Dutch*. The Hague / Antwerp: Sdu Uitgevers / Standaard Uitgeverij, 1998; 94 pp. ISBN 90-57-97008-2.

In 1986 Jan Hoet, then still Director of a Museum of Contemporary Art with no home of its own, came up with a remarkable exhibition. *Chambres d'amis* was an exhibition without a gallery, in which a whole string of artists magicked the interiors of Ghent houses into works of art. And just when Hoet and his SMAK (Stedelijk Museum voor Actuele Kunst – Municipal Museum of Current Art, as it is now called) had finally got a roof over their heads in 1999, he again opted to move outside the building, the 'institute'. Again he marched into Ghent with an international troop of artists. Not to private homes this time but to the streets and squares, the corners, the hinges of the town, to its beating heart.

Over the Edges ran from 1 April to 30 June 2000 and offered not only established names but also up-and-coming talent from the contemporary art scene. Jan Fabre caused some controversy in Ghent by covering the columns of the University's assembly hall with slices of ham, but most of the thousands of tourists strolling round the city centre had smiles on their faces. Provided, that is, they didn't get hit by the plates being hurled out of an open window to an accompaniment of quarrelling voices. The title of this installation? *Scène de ménage au coin de la rue.*

Jan Hoet & Giacinto di Pietrantonio, *Over the Edges* (Catalogue). Leuven: Exhibitions International, 2000; 312 pp.

When the Antwerp collector Walter Couvreur died in 1996 he left behind a particularly rare and important collection of nineteenth-century photographs. In 1999 this collection provided the starting-point for an exhibition of the oldest photos of Antwerp at the Ronny van de Velde Gallery. It also forms the nucleus of the book *Photography and Realism in the 19th Century. Antwerp: The Oldest Photographs 1847-1880*. A large part of the photographs included were taken by the renowned Brussels photographer Edmond Fierlants in the 1860s. Along with work by other photographic masters the book also contains photographs by lesser-known and even anonymous devotees of the camera.

Photography and Realism in the 19th Century consists of three parts. The first of these looks at the earliest history of photography, and particularly the influence of the new medium on the artistic movement that came to the fore in Europe around 1850: realism. The second part, occupying the largest number of pages, is a feast for the eye: old photos of Antwerp (catalogued and dated in the third part), interspersed with texts from the period 1847-1880. During those years the city underwent a number of facelifts: its Spanish ramparts were demolished, its canals filled in, and new wharves were built along the banks of the Scheldt. The curtain finally came down on medieval Antwerp, and these splendid black-and-white images show that somewhat sleepy town suddenly coming to life and bursting out of its ancient walls.

Herman van Goethem, *Photography and Realism in the 19th Century. Antwerp: The Oldest Photographs 1847-1880* (Tr. Dorothy Norman). Antwerp: N.V. Petraco-Pandora / Ronny van de Velde N.V., 1999; 419 pp. ISBN 90-5325-2266.

The death took place on 27 April 2000 of the British historian Charles Boxer – '*the greatest historian of the Dutch expansion*', as Van Goor describes him in his standard work *Dutch Colonies* (De Nederlandse koloniën, 1994).

Boxer's versatility was particularly apparent in the range of his published works, which cover a truly enormous area of seventeenth-century colonial history and European expansion, especially of the Portuguese and the Dutch in Asia and South America. Among other honours, this brought him honorary doctorates from the universities of Utrecht, Lisbon and Bahia, as well as high Portuguese and Brazilian decorations.

In the field of Dutch history, of which he had an exceptional knowledge and understanding, he published a great many studies, including *The Journal of Maarten Harpertszoon Tromp, Anno 1639* (1930), *Jan*

Compagnie in Japan 1600-1850 (1936), *The Dutch in Brazil 1624-1654* (1957), *The Dutch Seaborne Empire 1600-1800* (1965), *The Anglo-Dutch Wars of the 17th Century* (1974), *Jan Compagnie in War and Peace 1602-1799* (1979) and *Dutch Merchants and Marines in Asia 1602-1795* (1988).

Boxer's approach was typified above all by the breadth of his syntheses. He concerned himself not only with economic and military history but with cultural, religious and social dimensions. Moreover, he also investigated the other side of the history of European expansion: the point of view of the colonised. In doing so he certainly broke new ground in colonial historiography. He was among the first historians to analyse the 'intellectual exploration' of the Dutch East India Company. For this reason his work continues to be an indispensable source for modern historiographers.

A selection of documents concerning the decolonisation of Indonesia has been published in *Official Documents Relating to Netherlands Indonesian Relations 1945-1950* (Officiële bescheiden betreffende de Nederlands-Indonesische betrekkingen 1945-1950; 20 vols, The Hague, 1971-1996). The majority of these documents come from Dutch archives. A supplementary series of documents on relations between 1950 and 1963 is in preparation.

Meanwhile, an English-language *Guide to the Archives on Relations between the Netherlands and Indonesia 1945-1963*, complementary to both projects, has been published. This guide, compiled by researchers from the Institute of Netherlands History in

The Hague and the Arsip Nasional Republik Indonesia, comprises seven chapters which examine the official and semi-official archives in the Netherlands, Indonesia, the United Kingdom, Australia, the US, Belgium and the United Nations in New York. Each chapter contains information on the role of the three parties to the conflict, on the institutions and persons concerned, their administrative and records systems, and a summary of the content of the relevant documents.

P.J. Drooglever, M.J.B. Schouten and Mona Lohanda, *Guide to the Archives on Relations between the Netherlands and Indonesia 1945-1963*. The Hague: Institute of Netherlands History, 1999; 477 pp. ISBN 90-5216-110-0.

'A work of real architectural brilliance (...). It stands out with the force of a skyscraper in the prairie (...). The whole thing has a jangling tension between the natural and the manmade, which is what Holland is all about.' The object of this high praise, which appeared in *The Observer* in May 2000, is the Dutch Pavilion at Expo 2000 in Hanover. The 40-metre-high structure, designed by the MVRDV firm of architects, consists of a number of open floors which are alternately built on and landscaped. This hamburger-like construction, open until 31 October 2000, is meant to illustrate how the Netherlands has made its way in the world through water, wind and will power.

FILIP MATTHIJS
Translated by Tanis Guest.

of Dutch-Language Publications translated
into English (traced in 1999)

Antwerp
Antwerp, shopping &
restaurant guide / [ed. Petra
de Hamer; directing ed.
René Bego ... et al.;
introductory texts Frits
Schetsken; translating ed.
Becky Broer,[transl. from
the Dutch]; photogr. Joost
Govers].
Tilburg: Mo'Media, cop.
1999. 223 p.
Transl. of: Antwerpen,
winkel & restaurantgids.
1998.

Arion, Frank Martinus
Double play: the story of an
amazing world record /
Frank Martinus Arion;
transl. from the Dutch by
Paul Vincent.
London: Faber and Faber,
1998. 371 p. (The Faber
Caribbean series)
Transl. of: Dubbelspel. 1973.

Baens, Ria
Wanda, the little Panda /
Ria Baens; [transl. from the
Dutch]. Mascot, NSW:
Koala Books, 1999.
Transl. of: Wanda, kleine
panda. 1998.

Bakas, Adjiedj
The balance of blue: love
and loss in Amsterdam /
[authors: Adjiedj Bakas and
Sjoerd Groenewold Dost;
transl. from the Dutch:
Vinco David ... et al.; ed.:
Vinco David]. Lelystad:
Stichting IVIO, cop. 1998.
Transl. of: Pluk de dag,
passeer de nacht: over afscheid nemen en verder lev-
en: met actuele wegwijzer
patiëntenrecht en al wat
geregeld moet worden bij
ziekte en dood. 1995.

Barend, Frits
Ajax, Barcelona, Cruyff:
the ABC of an obstinate
maestro / Frits Barend and
Henk van Dorp; transl.
[from the Dutch] by David
Winner and Lex van Dam.
[1st pr.].

London: Bloomsbury, 1999.
264 p.
First English ed.: 1998.
Transl. of: Ajax, Barcelona,
Cruijff: het abc van een
eigenzinnige maestro. 1997.

Bavinck, Herman
In the beginning: founda-
tions of creation theology /
Herman Bavinck; ed. by
John Bolt; transl. [from the
Dutch] by John Vriend.
Grand Rapids: Baker
Books, 1999.

Beeftink, Jonatan
My name is Philo Sopher...
/ Jonatan Beeftink; [transl.
from the Dutch]. Haarlem:
Teologies Uitgeverijtje
Miniboekjes, cop. 1997.
[32] p. (Minibook; 48E)
Transl. of: Mijn naam is
filo, soof.... 1997.
(Miniboekje; 48).

Beer, Hans de
Little Polar Bear and the
husky pup / written and
ill. by Hans de Beer;
transl. from the German by
Rosemary Lanning. New
York: North-South Books,
1999.
Transl. of: Kleiner Eisbär,
lass mich nicht allein!: eine
Geschichte mit Bildern.
1999.
Simultaneous publ. in
English, German and
Dutch.
Dutch ed. publ. as: Kleine
ijsbeer, laat me niet alleen!
1999.

Benali, Abdelkader
Wedding by the sea /
Abdelkader Benali; transl.
[from the Dutch] by Susan
Massotty. London: Phoenix
House, cop. 1999. 186 p.
Transl. of: Bruiloft aan zee.
1996.

Berg, Maaike van den
London, shopping &
restaurant guide / [author
Maaike van den Berg;

directing ed. Joyce
Enthoven ... et al.; photogr.
Monika Rehberger; transl.
from the Dutch].
Tilburg: Mo'Media, cop.
1999. 221 p.
Transl. of: Londen, winkel
& restaurantgids. 1999.

Beumer, Jurjen
Henri Nouwen: a restless
seeking for God / Jurjen
Beumer; transl. from the
Dutch by David E. Schlaver
and Nancy ForestFlier.
New York: Crossroad Publ,
1997. 190 p.
Transl. of: Onrustig zoeken
naar God: de spiritualiteit
van Henri Nouwen. 1996.

Bie, Ceciel de
Rembrandt: see and do chil-
dren's book / Ceciel de Bie,
Martijn Leenen; [transl.
from the Dutch: Baxter
Associates]. Blaricum:
V+K Publishing, cop. 1999.
64 p.
Publ. in cooperation with
Museum Het Rembrandthuis.
Transl. of: Rembrandt: doe-
boek voor kinderen. 1999.

Binneveld, Hans
From shell shock to combat
stress: a comparative histo-
ry of military psychiatry /
Hans Binneveld; transl.
from the Dutch by John
O'Kane. Amsterdam:
Amsterdam University
Press, cop. 1997. XI, 220 p.
Transl. of: Om de geest van
Jan Soldaat: beknopte
geschiedenis van de mili-
taire psychiatrie. 1995.
(Pantaleon reeks; no. 21).

Blockmans, Wim
The promised lands: the
Low Countries under
Burgundian rule, 1369-
1530 / Wim Blockmans and
Walter Prevenier;
transl. [from the Dutch] by
Elizabeth Fackelman;
transl. rev. and ed. by
Edward Peters.
Philadelphia: University of
Pennsylvania Press, cop.
1999. XIII, 285 p.
(The Middle Ages series)
Transl. of: In de ban van
Bourgondië. 1988.

Bodde, Albert
Reincarnation & karma /
Albert Bodde; transl. from
the Dutch by Jill Penton; index. comp. by Lyn
Greenwood.
Saffron Walden: Daniel,
cop 1999. XII, 116 p.
Transl. of: Karma en reïn-
carnatie: een zoektocht naar
liefde en logica in de schepping. 1997.

Boer, Esther de
Mary Magdalene, beyond
the myth / Esther de Boer;
[transl. from the Dutch by
John Bowden]. London:
SCM Press, 1997. 147 p.
Transl. of: Maria
Magdalena: de mythe voor-
bij: op zoek naar wie zij
werkelijk is. 1996.

Botanic
Botanic adventure: a guide
to the purchase, care and
use of exclusive plants,
vegetables and herbs for the
house, conservatory and
garden / XOTUS; with
a pref. by Elisabeth de
Lestrieux; [photos and ill.
Herman Boonstra ... et al.;
text and composition Gert
Jan Jansen ... et al.; transl.
from the Dutch Jaap Guijt
... et al.].
Nootdorp: Tinro, cop. 1998.
256 p.
Transl. of: Botanisch avon-
tuur. 1998.

Bovens, Mark
The quest for responsibility:
accountability and citizen-
ship in complex organisa-
tions / Mark Bovens.
Cambridge [etc.]:
Cambridge University
Press, 1998. XII, 252 p.
(Theories of institutional
design) Adapt. of:
Verantwoordelijkheid en
organisatie. 1990.

Bremmer, R.H.
Johannes C. Sikkel: a pioneer in social reform / by
R.H. Bremmer; [transl.
from the Dutch]. Pella,
Iowa: Inheritance Publications, 1998.
Transl. of: Ds. J. C. Sikkel
als sociaal profeet en
pionier. 1976.

Bruggen, Jakob van:
Christ on earth: the Gospel narratives as history / Jakob van Bruggen; transl. [from the Dutch] by Nancy ForestFlier. Grand Rapids, Mich: Baker Books, cop. 1998. 320 p.
Transl. of: Christus op aarde: zijn levensbeschrijving door leerlingen en tijdgenoten. 1987.

Bruna, Dick
Aunt Alice's party / Dick Bruna; [transl. from the Dutch by Patricia Crampton]. Handforth, Cheshire: World International, 1998. [44] p. (Miffy's library)
Transl. of: Het feest van tante Trijn. 1992.

Bruna, Dick
Playtime / Dick Bruna; [transl. from the Dutch]. [1st pr.] London: Methuen Children's Books, 1998. [14] p.
Originally publ. in several books of "Nijntje" 1953-1998.

Century
A century of statistics: counting, accounting and recounting in the Netherlands / J.G.S.J. van Maarseveen and M.B.G. Gircour [English editor in chief] (eds.); [transl. from the Dutch]. Voorburg [etc.]: Statistics Netherlands; Amsterdam: Stichting beheer IISG, 1999. 558 p.
Publ. on the occasion of 100 years Central Bureau of Statistics in the Netherlands
Transl. of: Een eeuw statistieken: historisch-methodologische schetsen van de Nederlandse officiële statistieken in de twintigste eeuw / B. Erwich and J.G.S.J. van Maarseveen (ed.). 1999.

Century
A century rounded up: reflections on the history of the Central Bureau of Statistics in the Netherlands / J.G.S.J. van Maarseveen, M.B.G. Gircour, and R. Schreijnders (eds.);

[transl. from the Dutch by Elizabeth Daverman]. Voorburg [etc.]: Statistics Netherlands; Amsterdam: Stichting beheer IISG, 1999. 207 p.
Publ. on the occasion of 100 years Statistics Netherlands Transl. of: Welgeteld een eeuw. 1999.

Child
Child labour worldwide / [ed.: Marijke Stegeman ... et al.; transl. from the Dutch]. The Hague: Directie Voorlichting Ontwikkelingssamenwerking, 1998. 41 p.
Child labour policy memorandum.
Transl. of: Kinderarbeid wereldwijd. 1998.

Chong, Alan
Still-life paintings from the Netherlands, 1550-1720 / Alan Chong & Wouter Kloek; with Celeste Brusati ... [et al.; transl. from the Dutch Ruth Koenig]. Amsterdam: Rijksmuseum; Cleveland, OH: Cleveland Museum of Art; Zwolle: Waanders, cop. 1999. 319 p.
Publ. on occasion of the exhibition "Het Nederlandse stilleven, 1550-1720" in the Rijksmuseum at Amsterdam, June 19, 1999 - September 1999, and "Still life paintings from the Netherlands, 1550-1720" in The Cleveland Museum of Art, October 31, 1999 - January 9, 2000.
Transl. of: Het Nederlandse stilleven, 1550-1720. 1999.

Contemporary
Contemporary chic / [ed.] Rozemarijn de Witte; photography by Hotze Eisma.; [transl. from the Dutch]. London: Conran Octopus, 1997. 191 p.
Simultaneous publ. in the United States as: Modern essentials. San Francisco: SOMA Books, 1997.
Transl. of: Persoonlijk wonen. 1996

Damisch, Hubert
Moves: schaken en kaarten

met het museum = playing chess and cards with the museum / Hubert Damisch; met een essay van / with an essay by Ernst van Alphen; [vert. uit het Nederlands door / transl. from the Dutch by Ernst van Alphen ... et al.]. Rotterdam: Museum Boymans van Beuningen, 1997. 133 p.
With selected bibliography of H. Damisch
Publ. on occasion of the exhibition "Moves: playing chess and cards with the museum" in Museum Boijmans van Beuningen, June 14, 1997 - August 17, 1997.
Text in English and Dutch.

David
David Salle / [transl. from the Dutch: Beth O'Brien; red.: Ida Boelema]. Ghent; Amsterdam: Ludion, cop. 1999. 127 p.
Publ. on occasion of the exhibition "David Salle, 20 years of painting" in the Stedelijk Museum, Amsterdam, April 24, 1999 - June 14, 1999.
Transl. of: David Salle. 1999.

De Bode, Ann
Grandad, I'll always remember you / Ann de Bode [ill.] and Rien Broere [story; English text transl. by Su Swallow].
London: Evans Brothers Ltd, 1999. 33 p. (Helping hands)
First English ed.: 1997.
Transl. of: Opa duurt ontelbaar lang. 1996. (Hartenboeken).

De Bode, Ann
Tomorrow I will feel better / Ann De Bode [ill.] and Rien Broere [story; English text transl. by Su Swallow].
London: Evans Brothers Ltd, 1999. 33 p. (Helping hands)
First English ed.: 1997.
Transl. of: Morgen ben ik weer beter! 1996. (Hartenboeken).

De Bode Ann
You will always be my dad

/ Ann de Bode [ill.] and Rien Broere [story; English text transl. by Su Swallow].
London: Evans Brothers Ltd, 1999. 33 p. (Helping hands)
First English ed.: 1997.
Transl. of: Maar jij blijft mijn papa. 1996. (Hartenboeken).

Development
Development and poverty in the Netherands Antilles: a policy evaluation of Sede Antia (1987-1996) / [Dirk Kruijt (coordinator) ... et al.]. Amsterdam: Thela Publishers, 1998. 102 p.
Publ. by the direction of the Kabinet van Nederlands Antilliaanse en Arubaanse Zaken (KabNA) en het Departement voor Ontwikkelingssamenwerking van de Nederlandse Antillen (DepOS). Transl. of: Ontwikkeling en armoede op de Nederlandse Antillen: een beleidsevaluatie van Sede Antia (1987-1996). 1997.

Dictionary
A dictionary of medieval heroes: characters in medieval narrative traditions and their afterlife in literature, theatre and the visual arts / ed. by Willem P. Gerritsen and Anthony G. van Melle; transl. from the Dutch by Tanis Guest; [adapt. for English readers by Richard Barber]. Woodbridge: Boydell Press, 1998. VII, 336 p.
Transl. of: Van Aiol tot de Zwaanridder. 1993.

Dijk, Hans van
Twentieth-century architecture in the Netherlands / Hans van Dijk; [transl. from the Dutch John Kirkpatrick; photogr. Piet Rook ... et al.]. Rotterdam: 010 Publishers, 1999. 189 p.
Transl. of: Architectuur in Nederland in de twintigste eeuw. 1999.

Dijkzeul, Lieneke
A tiger under my bed! / Lieneke Dijkzeul; ill. by Dinie Akkerman; series ed.:

David P. Weikart; [English version from the Dutch by Eric van Deventer]. Ypsilanti, Michigan: High / Scope Press, cop. 1997. 25 p.
Transl. of: Een tijger onder mijn bed! 1995.

Droogenbroodt, Germain
The road: poems / Germain Droogenbroodt; drawings Satish Gupta; [English version from the Dutch: Germain Droogenbroodt & Martin Culverwell = De weg: gedichten / [Germain Droogenbroodt]; tekeningen [Satish Gupta]. Ninove [etc.]: POINT [etc.], [1999]. 69 p.
(Point Editions; E3)
Text in English and Dutch.

Duijker, Hubrecht
The Rhone / Hubrecht Duijker; [transl. from the Dutch].
London: Mitchell Beazly, 1998. 152 p. (Touring in wine country)
Transl. of: Rhône: een reisgids voor wijn en fijnproevers.
1998. (Reisgidsen voor wijn en fijnproevers).

Dutch
Dutch and Flemish plays / sel. by Della Couling.
London: Hern, 1997. XVIII, 295 p.
In association with Theater Instituut Nederland.
Contains: The Buddha of Ceylon / Lodewijk de Boer; transl. [from the Dutch] by Della Couling. Transl. of: De Buddha van Ceylon. 1991,
The wedding party / Judith Herzberg; rev. by Rhea Gaisner and Rina Vergano. Transl. of: Leedvermaak. 1982. (Publikatie / Baal; 12), Drummers / Arne Sierens; transl. [from the Dutch] by Nadine Malfait. Transl. of: De drumleraar. 1994, Burying the dog / Karst Woudstra; transl. [from the Dutch] by Della Couling. Transl. of: Een hond begraven. 1989. (Toneelteksten / Het Nationale Toneel; 7), and:

The Stendhal syndrome / Frans Strijards; transl. [from the Dutch] by Della Couling. Transl. of: Het syndroom van Stendhal, in: Vier toneelstukken. 1991.

Endenburg, Gerard
Sociocracy: the organization of decision-making: "no objection" as the principle of sociocracy / Gerard Endenburg; [ed. by Jasper Lindenhovius; transl. from the Dutch by Clive Bowden]. Delft: Eburon, 1998. 264 p.
Transl. of: Sociocratie: het organiseren van de besluitvorming: een waarborg voor ieders gelijkwaardigheid. 1981.

Enquist. Anna
The masterpiece / Anna Enquist; transl. [from the Dutch] by Jeannette K. Ringold. London: Toby, 1999. 230 p.
Transl. of: Het meesterstuk: roman. 1994.

European
European woman's thesaurus: a structured list of descriptors for indexing and retrieving information in the field of the position of women and women's studies / [Gusta Drenthe, Maria van der Sommen; ed. by Marianne Boere; transl. from the Dutch: Jean Vaughan].
Amsterdam: International Information Centre and Archives for the Women's Movement (IIAV), cop. 1998. XII, 209 p.
First version.
Transl. and adapt. of: Vrouwenthesaurus: lijst van gecontroleerde termen voor het ontsluiten van informatie over de positie van vrouwen en vrouwenstudies. 1992.

Forests
Forests and forestry: projects in the development cooperation of the Netherlands, 1996 / [red. Ton van der Zon en Jeannette van Rijsoort; English text [transl. from the Dutch]:

English text Company].
The Hague: Ministry of Foreign Affairs, Information Department; The Hague: Ministry of Housing, Spatial Planning and Environment, 1997. 193 p. (Focus on development; 5)
Under the authority of Environment and Development Department, Biodiversity and Forest Division.
Transl. of: Bossen en bosbouw: projecten van Ontwikkelingssamenwerking, 1996, 1997. (Focus op ontwikkeling; 5).

Gemeentemuseum
Gemeentemuseum The Hague: H.P. Berlage / [ed.: Gerrit Jan de Rook ... et al.; photogr. Fas Keuzenkamp ... et al.; cartogr. Rik van Schagen; transl. from the Dutch Janey Tucker ... et al.]. Zwolle: Waanders; Den Haag: Gemeentemuseum Den Haag, cop. 1999. 63 p.
Contains: H.P. Berlage's Gemeentemuseum / Pieter Singelenberg, Objects in the applied arts collection of the Gemeentemuseum The Hague based on designs by H.P. Berlage / Titus M. Eliëns, and: Walking route: Berlage in The Hague.
Transl. of: Gemeentemuseum Den Haag: H.P. Berlage. 1999.

Ginneken, Jaap van.
Understanding global news: a critical introduction / Jaap van Ginneken; [transl. from the Dutch]. London [etc.]: SAGE, 1998. VIII, 239 p.
Transl. of: De schepping van de wereld in het nieuws: de 101 vertekeningen die elk 1 procent verschil maken. 1996.

Golden
The Golden Age of Dutch painting in historical perspective / ed. by Frans Grijzenhout, Henk van Veen.
New York: Cambridge University Press, 1999.
Transl. of: De Gouden Eeuw in perspectief: het beeld van de Nederlandse

zeventiendeeeuwse schilderkunst in later tijd. 1992.

Grift, F.U.
The ABC of IPW: implementation of a process-oriented workflow / F.U. Grift, M. de Vreeze; [transl. from the Dutch].
Den Haag: Ten Hagen & Stam, 1998. 52 p. (ICT management pocket guides)
Transl. of: Het ABC tot IPW: implementatie van een procesgerichte werkwijze. 1998.

Groeneboer, Kees
Gateway to the West: the Dutch language in colonial Indonesia 1600-1950: a history of language policy / Kees Groeneboer; transl. [from the Dutch] by Myra Scholz.
Amsterdam: Amsterdam University Press, cop. 1998. XIV, 400 p.
Transl. of: Weg tot het Westen: het Nederlands voor Indië, 1600-1950: een taalpolitieke geschiedenis. 1993.
(Verhandelingen van het Koninklijk Instituut voor Taal, Land en Volkenkunde; 158).
Originally publ. as thesis Leiden, 1992.

Groothof, Frank
Vincent & Theo: brothers in art / Frank Groothof; design Stang Gubbels; [ed.-in-chief and idea: Wim Pijbes; transl. from the Dutch: Sue Baker]. Zwolle: Waanders; Amsterdam: Van Gogh Museum; Rotterdam: Kunsthal Rotterdam, cop. 1999. [48] p.
Transl. of: Vincent & Theo: broeders in de kunst. 1999.

Grunberg, Arnon
Blue mondays / Arnon Grunberg; transl. [from the Dutch] by Arnold and Erica Pomerans. London [etc.]: Vintage, 1997.
First English ed.: New York: Farrar, Straus and Giroux, 1997.
Transl. of: Blauwe maandagen. 1994.

Grunberg, Arnon
Lechaim; Grill Room /
Arnon Grunberg; transl.
[from the Dutch by] Arnold
& Erica Pomerans;
[photogr.: Peter Daalderop].
Amsterdam: International
Theatre & Film Books,
1996. 120 p. (Theatre in
translation)
Transl. of: Rattewit, and:
Grillroom, in: Rattewit.
1994.

Haaften, Eleonore van
A refuge for my heart:
trusting God even when
things go wrong / Eleonore
Van Haaften; [transl. from
the original Dutch by
Mariette Woods ... et al.].
London: Hodder &
Stoughton, 1997. XV, 271 p.
Transl. of: Een woning voor
mijn hart. 1995.

Haeringen, Annemarie van
Heron's lucky break / [text
and ill. by] Annemarie
van Haeringen; transl.
[from the Dutch] by
Marianne Serfontein.
Durbanville: Garamond,
1997. [25] p.
Transl. of: Op hoge poten.
1994.

Haeringen, Annemarie van
Malmok / [ill.:] Annemarie
van Haeringen; [text:]
Sjoerd Kuijer: transl. from
the Dutch by: Jan Michael.
Amsterdam: Stichting
Culturele Manifestaties
NANA, 1998.
Transl. of: Malmok. 1998.

Hagen, Monique
The tidy-up spider /
Monique Hagen & Hans
Hagen; ill. by Sandra
Klaassen; series ed.: David
P. Weikart;
[English version transl.
from the Dutch by Eric van
Deventer]. Ypsilanti,
Michigan: High / Scope
Press, cop. 1997. 25 p.
Transl. of: De opruimspin.
1994.

HamakerZondag, Karen
Tarot as a way of life:
a Jungian approach to
the tarot / Karen
HamakerZondag; [transl.
from the Dutch].

York Beach, Maine:
Weiser, 1997. 271 p.
Transl. of: De tarot als lev-
ensweg: een Jungiaanse
benadering van de tarot.
1995.

HamakerZondag, Karen
The way of the tarot:
a Jungian approach for
working more deeply with
the tarot / Karen
HamakerZondag; [transl.
from the Dutch]. London:
Piatkus, 1998. XIV, 271 p.
First English ed.: Tarot as
a way of life: a Jungian
approach to the tarot. York
Beach, Maine: Weiser,
1997.
Transl. of: De tarot als lev-
ensweg: een Jungiaanse
benadering van de tarot.
1995.

Hammink, Ruud J.
The perfins of Greece and
Crete / Ruud J. Hammink;
[transl. from the Dutch].
Tilburg: Perfin Club
Nederland, 1997. 51 p.
([PCN-reeks; nr. 11])
Transl. of: Perfins van
Griekenland en Kreta.
1997.
(PCN-reeks; nr. 10).

History
History of the Low
Countries / ed. by J.C.H.
Blom, E. Lamberts; transl.
[from the Dutch] by James
C. Kennedy.
New York [etc.]: Berghahn
Books, 1999.XIII, 503 p.
Transl. and rev. ed. of:
Geschiedenis van de
Nederlanden. 1993.

Holwijk, Ineke
Asphalt angels / Ineke
Holtwijk; transl. [from the
Dutch] by Wanda Boeke.
Ashville, NC: Front Street
[etc.], 1998. 184 p.; 22 cm.
Publ. in cooperation with:
NOVIB.
Transl. of: Engelen van het
asfalt. 1995.

Huizinga, J
The waning of the Middle
Ages / J. Huizinga; [transl.
from the Dutch]. Mineoloa
N.Y: Dover Publ, 1998.
First English ed.: London:

Arnold, 1924.
Transl. of: Herfsttij der
middeleeuwen: studie over
levens en gedachtenvormen
der veertiende en vijftiende
eeuw in Frankrijk en de
Nederlanden. 1919.

Iens
Iens independent index:
Amsterdam restaurants /
[ed. by: Iens Boswijk ... et
al.; transl. from the Dutch:
Liz Waters]. Ed. 2000.
Amsterdam: Forum, 1999.
160 p.
Transl. of: Iens independent
index: restaurants van
Amsterdam. Ed. 2000.
1999.

Jacobs, Els M.
In pursuit of pepper and tea:
the story of the Dutch East
India Company / Els M.
Jacobs; [transl. from the
Dutch: Kist Kilian
Communications; photogr.:
Frans Hemelrijk ...
et al.].
3rd ed. Amsterdam:
Netherlands Maritime
Museum; Zutphen:
Walburg Pers, [1999]. 96 p.
First English ed.: 1991.
Transl. of: Varen om peper
en thee: korte geschiedenis
van de Verenigde Oostin-
dische Compagnie. 1991.

Kapteyn, P.J.G.
Introduction to the law of
the European Communities:
from Maastricht to Amster-
dam / P.J.G. Kapteyn &
P. VerLoren van Themaat.
3rd ed. / ed. and further rev.
by Laurence W. Gormley;
in cooperation with the ed.
of the fifth Dutch edition:
P.J.G. Kapteyn ... [et al.].
London; The Hague [etc.]:
Kluwer Law International,
1998. CXLVI, 1447 p.
First English ed. publ. as:
Introduction to the law of
the European communities:
after the accession of new
member states. London:
Sweet and Maxwell;
Deventer: Kluwer;
Alphen aan den Rijn:
Samsom, 1989.
Transl. and rev. ed. of:
Inleiding tot het recht van
de Europese Gemeenschap-

pen: na Maastricht. 5th rev.
ed. 1995. (Handboek voor
de Europese gemeenschap-
pen; 1A).
1st Dutch publ.: 1970.

Kat, Lian de
Crocodile tears / Lian de
Kat; ill. by Maarten
Wolterink; series ed.: David
P. Weikart; [English ver-
sion from the Dutch by Eric
van Deventer]. Ypsilanti,
Michigan: High / Scope
Press, cop. 1997. 25 p.
Transl. of: Krokodilletra-
nen. 1994.

Kemenade, Willem van
China, Hong Kong, Taiwan,
inc.: the dynamics of a new
empire / Willem van
Kemenade; transl. from the
Dutch by Diane Webb.
London: Abacus, 1999.
First English ed.: New
York: Knopf, 1997.
Transl. and rev. ed. of:
China, Hongkong, Taiwan
BV: superstaat op zoek naar
een nieuw systeem. 1996.

Kerkhofs, Jan
A horizon of kindly light:
a spirituality for those with
questions / Jan Kerkhofs;
[transl. from the Dutch].
London: SCM, 1999.
224 p.; 22 cm.
Transl. of: Een horizon van
teder licht. 1997.

Kind, Richard E.L.B. de
Houses in Herculaneum:
a new view on the town
planning and the building of
insulae III and IV / Richard
E.L.B. de Kind; [transl.
from the Dutch by Brigitte
Planken ... et al.].
Amsterdam: Gieben, 1998.
332 p., [27] p.
(Circumvesuviana; vol. 1)
Transl. of: Huizen in
Herculaneum: een analyse
van de stedebouw en de
maatvoering in de huizen-
blokken III en IV. Nijmegen:
[s.n.], 1992. (Indagationes
Noviomagenses ad res anti-
quas spectantes; 7). Thesis
Katholieke Universiteit
Nijmegen.

Kings
Kings. Leuven: Peeters,

cop. 1998. XXIX, 604 p.
(Historical commentary on
the Old Testament)
Vol. 1: 1 Kings 1-11 / by
Martin J. Mulder; [transl.
from the Dutch by John
Vriend] Transl. of.: Koningen. Dl. 1: 1 Koningen 17.
1987. (Commentaar op het
Oude Testament), and of
the manuscript of 1 Kings,
8-11, finished in 1994.

Klerck, Bram de
The brothers Campi: im-
ages and devotion: religious
painting in sixteenth-centu-
ry Lombardy / Bram de
Klerck; transl. [from the
Dutch] by Andrew
McCormick. Amsterdam:
Amsterdam University
Press, cop. 1999. 240 p.
Transl. of.: Giulio, Antonio
& Vincenzo Campi:
schilderkunst en devotie in
het zestiende-eeuwse
Lombardije, 1565-1591.
1997. (Nijmeegse kunsthis-
torische studies; dl. 4).
Thesis Katholieke
Universiteit Nijmegen,
1997.

Knijpenga, Siegwart
Stories of the saints / retold
by Siegwart Knijpenga;
[transl. from the Dutch by
Tony Lanham ... et al.].
Edinburgh: Floris Books,
1997. 221 p.
Transl. of.: Heiligenlegen-
den. 1993.

Knippels, P.J.M.
Growing bulbs indoors /
P.J.M. Knippels; [transl.
from the Dutch by Marja
Smolenaars]. Rotterdam
[etc.]: Balkema, cop. 1999.
XI, 101 p., [16] p. pl.
Transl. of.: Kweken van bol-
len in kamer of kas. 1999.

Koelman, Kamiel J.
Copyright aspects of the
preservation of electronic
publications / [Kamiel J.
Koelman, Babiche N.
Westenbrink; transl. from
the Dutch]. Amsterdam:
Instituut voor Informatie-
recht, 1998. 43 p. (IViR reports; 7)
Research commissioned by
the Koninklijke Bibliotheek

Transl. of.: Auteursrechte-
lijke aspecten van pre-
servering van elektronische
publikaties. 1998.

Korteweg, Hans
Each year of life: its sym-
bolism and meaning = Nog
vele jaren / by Hans
Korteweg; ill. by Erica
Duvekot; [transl. from the
Dutch by Mark DeSorgher].
Center City, Minnesota:
Hazelden, cop. 1997. IX,
155 p.
Transl. of.: Nog vele jaren:
de symboliek van elk
levensjaar: een boek voor
het leven. 1992.

Korteweg, Hans
The great leap: face-to-face
with initiation and change /
Hans Korteweg, Hanneke
Korteweg and Jaap Voigt;
[transl. from the Dutch].
Center City, Minn:
Hazelden, 1998.
Transl. of.: De grote sprong.
1990.

Kraaijpoel, Diederik
Diederik Kraaijpoel / with
contributions by Ernst van
de Wetering, Toine
Moerbeek, Laurens
Balkema; [transl. from
the Dutch: JoAnn van
Seventer-Keltie ... et al.;
dia's: Henk Vos ... et al.].
Aduard: Art Revisited,
1998. 107 p.
Transl. of.: Diederik
Kraaijpoel. 1998.

Kraan, Hanna
The wicked witch is at it
again / Hanna Kraan; ill. by
Annemarie van Haeringen;
transl. [from the Dutch] by
Wanda Boeke. 1st ed. New
York: Puffin Books, 1998.
122 p.
First English ed.: Arden,
North Carolina: Front Street
Lemniscaat, 1997.
Transl. of.: De boze heks is
weer bezig. 1992.

Kranendonk, Anke
A grandpa cookie for
grandpa / Anke
Kranendonk; ill. by Saskia
Halfmouw; series ed.:
David P. Weikart; [English
version transl. from the

Dutch by Eric van
Deventer].
Ypsilanti, Michigan: High /
Scope Press, cop. 1997.
17 p.
Transl. of.: Een opa voor
opa. 1994.

Kroon, Coen van der
The golden fountain: the
complete guide to urine the-
rapy / Coen van der Kroon;
transl. [from the Dutch] by
Merilee Dranow. Bath:
Gateway Books, 1998. XIII,
138 p.
First English ed.: Banbury:
Amethyst, 1996.
Transl. of.: De gouden
fontein. 1993.

Kuiper, Nannie
What are you planning to
do? / Nannie Kuiper; ill. by
Dagmar Stam; series ed.:
David P. Weikart; [English
version transl. from the
Dutch by Eric van
Deventer].
Ypsilanti, Michigan: High /
Scope Press, cop. 1997.
25 p.
Transl. of.: Wat ga jij doen?
1993.

Landscapes
Landscapes of Rembrandt:
his favourite walks /
Boudewijn Bakker ... [et al.;
ed. Boudewijn Bakker ... et
al.; final ed. Johan Giskes ...
et al.; transl. from the
Dutch Wendie Shaffer ... et
al.]. Bussum: Thoth;
Amsterdam: Gemeente-
archief; Paris: Fondation
Custodia, cop. 1998. 391 p.
Publ. on the occasion of the
exhibition "Rembrandt aan
de Amstel: wandelingen in
en om Amsterdam" in the
Gemeentearchief Amster-
dam, September 30, 1998 -
November 29, 1998, and in
the Insitut Néerlandais in
Paris, December 17, 1998 -
February 14, 1999.
Transl. of.: Het landschap
van Rembrandt: wandelin-
gen in en om Amsterdam.
1998.

Lange, Frits de
Waiting for the word:
Dietrich Bonhoeffer on
speaking about God / Frits

de Lange; transl. [from the
Dutch] by Martin N.
Walton. Grand Rapids,
Mich: W.B. Eerdmans,
1999.
Transl. of.: Wachten op het
verlossende woord: Dietrich
Bonhoeffer en het spreken
over God. 1995.

Lemmens, Frans
Visions of the Netherlands /
Frans Lemmens [photogr.];
text Martijn de Rooi;
[transl. from the Dutch:
Tony Burrett]. 2nd pr.
Alphen aan den Rijn: Dutch
Publishers, cop. 1997.
128 p.
Transl. of.: Dromen van
Nederland. 1997.

Linden, Nico ter
The story goes... / Nico ter
Linden. London: SCM Press,
1999. 296 p.
1: The stories of the Torah /
[transl. from the Dutch by
John Bowden]
Transl. of.: Het verhaal
gaat... . 1: De thora. 1996.

Linden, Nico ter
The story goes... / Nico ter
Linden. London: SCM Press,
1999. 291 p.
2: Mark's story and
Matthew's story / [transl.
from the Dutch by John
Bowden]
Transl. of.: Het verhaal
gaat... 2. Het verhaal van
Marcus en het verhaal van
Mattheüs. 1998.

Louf, André
Mercy in weakness: medita-
tions on the Word / André
Louf; translator: John
Vriend, [transl. from the
Dutch].
London: Darton, Longman
and Todd, 1998. IX, 148 p.
Transl. of.: Genade in
zwakheid: woorden van een
abt ter meditatie. 1992.

Lubbe, Jan C.A. van der
Basic methods of cryptog-
raphy / Jan C.A. van der
Lubbe; transl. [from the
Dutch] by Steve Gee.
New York: Cambridge
University Press, 1998. XIV,
229 p.
Transl. of.: Basismethoden

cryptografie. 1994.

Martens, Ronny
Making sense of astrology / by Ronny Martens and Tim Trachet; [transl. of the Dutch]. Amherst, NY: Prometheus Books, 1998. Transl. of: Astrologie, zin of onzin? 1995. (De "witte" reeks).

Matti, Anni
The flood wave / Anni Matti & Wim Spekking; [ed.: E. Zuinigh; transl. from the Dutch: David Henebury; ill.: Fred Marschall]. Groningen: Wolters-Noordhoff, 1999. 23 p. (My first blackbirds; 1999/2) Transl. of: Toen de lucht bewoog.

Melet, Ed
Sustainable architecture: towards a diverse built environment / Ed Melet; [copy ed.: Solange de Boer ... et al.; transl. from Dutch: Victor Joseph]. Rotterdam: NAi, cop. 1999. 192 p. Research commissioned by the Netherlands Architecture Fund. Transl. of: Duurzame architectuur: streven naar een contrastrijke omgeving. 1999.

Micha
Micha Klein / [red. Han Steenbruggen & Hanneke Huls; red. vert. uit het Nederlands: Froukje Hoekstra ... et al.]. Groningen: Groninger Museum, 1998. 118 p. + CDROM Catalogue, publ. on the occasion of the exhibition "Micha Klein" in the Groninger Museum, September 20, 1998 - November 29, 1998, to mark 100 years Rabobank Transl. of: Micha Klein. 1998.

Mijksenaar, Paul
Visual function: an introduction to information design / Paul Mijksenaar; [transl. from the Dutch]. Rotterdam: 010 Publishers, 1997. 56 p. (Delftse cahiers;

1) Transl. of: ...De vorm zal u toegeworpen worden: over vormgeven van visuele informatie. 1996.

Modern
Modern essentials / [ed.:] Rozemarijn de Witte; photography by Hotze Eisma. San Francisco: SOMA Books, 1997. Simultaneous publ. in the United Kingdom as: Contemporary chic. London: Conran Octopus, 1997. Transl. of: Persoonlijk wonen. 1996.

Möring, Marcel
In Babylon / Marcel Möring; transl. from the Dutch by Stacey Knecht. [1st pr.]. London: Flamingo, 1999. 417 p. Transl. of: In Babylon. 1997.

Mols, Stephan T.A.M.
Wooden furniture in Herculaneum: form, technique and function / Stephan T.A.M. Mols; [transl. from the Dutch by Rob Bland]. Amsterdam: Gieben, 1999. 321 p., [122] p. pl. (Circumvesuviana; vol. 2) Transl. of: Houten meubels in Herculaneum: vorm, techniek en functie. 1994. (Indagationes Noviomagensis ad res spectantes; 10). Thesis Katholieke Universiteit Nijmegen

Netherlands'
The Netherlands' national manual on decision-making in crises / [National Coordination Centre]. The Hague: Ministry of the Interior and Kingdom Relations, National Coordination Centre, cop. 1998. 43 p. Transl. of: Nationaal handboek crisisbesluitvorming. 1998.

Nooteboom, Cees
The captain of the butterflies / Cees Nooteboom; transl. from the Dutch by Leonard Nathan and Herlinde Spahr; with an introd. by Herlinde Spahr and an author's note.

Los Angeles: Sun & Moon Press, 1997. 117 p. (Sun & Moon classics; 97) Transl. of a choice from: Vuurtijd, ijstijd. 1984, en: Het gezicht van het oog. 1989

On
On country roads and fields: the depiction of the 18th- and 19th-century landscape / [ed.:] Wiepke Loos, RobertJan te Rijdt, Marjan van Heteren; with an introduction by Ronald de Leeuw; and contributions from Alexander Bakker ... [et al.; photogr.: Department of Photography, Rijksmuseum ... et al.; transl. from the Dutch by Barbara Fasting ... et al.]. Blaricum: V+K Publishing/Inmerc; Amsterdam: Rijksmuseum, cop. 1997. 384 p. Publ. on occasion of the exhibition "On country roads and fields" in the Rijksmuseum at Amsterdam, November 28, 1997 - March 3, 1998. Transl. of: Langs velden en wegen: de verbeelding van het landschap in de 18de en 19de eeuw. 1997.

Ospina, Martha
Pergamano: parchment craft basic techniques / Martha Ospina; [transl. from the Dutch]. 4th ed. Baarn: La Rivière, creatieve uitgevers, 1998. 64 p. Transl. of: Pergamano: basisboek voor perkamentkunst. 1997.

Pagan
The pagan Middle Ages / ed. by Ludo J.R. Milis; transl. [from the Dutch] into English by Tanis Guest. Woodbridge: Boydell Press, 1998. 160 p. Transl. of: De heidense Middeleeuwen. 1991.

Peter
Peter Blokhuis: schilderijen en tekeningen / introd. of John Sillevis; [transl. of the Dutch by Andrew McCormick]. Den Haag: [s.n.], 1998.

118 p.
Text in English and Dutch.

Poels, Frans
How to set up and run an effective job evaluation and remuneration system: strategies, methods and techniques / Frans Poels; [transl. from the Dutch]. London: Kogan Page, 1997. 256 p. Transl. of: Functiewaardering en belonen: techniek, procedures, methoden. 1994. (Monografieën personeel & organisatie).

Pol, Martin
Structured testing of information systems: an introduction to TMap / Martin Pol, Erik van Veenendaal; [transl. from the Dutch]. Deventer: Kluwer BedrijfsInformatie, cop. 1998. 154 p. Based on: Testen volgens TMap. 1995.

Polak, Chaja
Summer sonata / Chaja Polak; transl. [from the Dutch] by Susan Massotty. Edinburgh: Canongate, cop. 1999. 96 p. Transl. of: Zomersonate. 1997.

Posthumus Meyjes, G.H.M.
Jean Gerson, apostle of unity: his church politics and ecclesiology / by G.H.M. Posthumus Meyjes; transl. [from the Dutch] by J.C. Grayson. Leiden [etc.]: Brill, 1999. XIII, 435 p., [7] p. pl. (Studies in the history of Christian thought; vol. 94) Transl. of: Jean Gerson, zijn kerkpolitiek en ecclesiologie. 's Gravenhage: Nijhoff, 1963.

Quintana, Anton
The baboon king / Anton Quintana; transl. [from the Dutch] by John Nieuwenhuizen. New York: Walker and Company, 1999. 183 p. First English ed.: St. Leonards, NSW: Allen & Unwin, 1998. (Ark fiction). Transl. of: De bavianenkoning. 1982.

Renkema, Johan
Lamentations / by Johan Renkema; [transl. from the Dutch by Brian Doyle]. Leuven: Peeters, cop. 1998. 641 p.
(Historical commentary on the Old Testament)
Transl. of: Klaagliederen. 1993. (Commentaar op het Oude Testament).

Roermund, Bert van
Law, narrative and reality: an essay in intercepting politics / Bert van Roermund. Dordrecht [etc.]: Kluwer Academic Publishers, cop. 1997. VII, 236 p. (Law and philosophy library; vol. 30)
Partial transl. and adapt. of: Recht, verhaal en werkelijkheid. 1993.

Roukema, Riemer
Gnosis and faith in early Christianity: an introduction to Gnosticism; [transl. from the Dutch]. London: SCM, 1999. 224 p.
Transl. of: Gnosis en geloof in het vroege christendom: een inleiding tot de gnostiek. 1998.

Rumphius, G.E.
Waerachtigh verhael, van de schrickelijcke aerdbevinge/ nu onlanghs eenigen tyd herwaerts, ende voornaementlijck op den 17. February des Jaers 1674 voorgevallen, in/en ontrent de Eylanden van Amboina, ... / G.E. Rumphius; facsimile, Dutch transcription and edition W. Buijze; (with an English [by E.M. Beekman ... et al.] and Indonesian [oleh Theresia Slamet] transl.). [2nd rev. ed.]. [S.l.]: Buijze, 1998. 79 p.
First impression of this edition: 1997.
Photomechanical repr. of the ed.: Batavia, 1675.
Contains the English translation, entitled: True history of the terrible earthquake, and the Indonesian translation, entitled: Kisah nyata tentang gempa bumi yang dahsyat.

Rumphius, G.E.
The Ambonese curiosity cabinet / Georgius Everhardus Rumphius; transl. [from the Dutch], ed., annot. and with an introd. by E.M. Beekman. [1st pr.]. New Haven, CT [etc.]: Yale University Press, cop. 1999. CXII, 567 p.
Transl. of: D'Amboinsche rariteitkamer, behelzende eene beschryvinge van allerhande zoo weeke als harde schaalvisschen, te weeten raare krabben, kreeften, en diergelijke zeedieren, als mede allerhande hoorntjes en schulpen, ... die men in d'Amboinsche zee vindt: daar beneven zommige mineraalen, gesteenten, en soorten van aarde, die in d'Amboinsche, en zommige omleggende eilanden gevonden worden. 1705.

Scheers, Rob van
Paul Verhoeven / Rob van Scheers; transl. [from the Dutch] by Aletta Stevens. London [etc.]: Faber and Faber, 1997. XIX, 300 p.
Transl. of: Paul Verhoeven: de geautoriseerde biografie. 1996.

Schreuder, D.A.
Road lighting for safety / D.A. Schreuder; transl. [from the Dutch] by Adriana Morris; ill. J. Kosterman. London: Thomas Telford, 1998. XIII, 294 p.
Transl. of: Openbare verlichting voor verkeer en veiligheid. 1996.

Schubert, Ingrid
There's a hole in my bucket / Ingrid and Dieter Schubert; [transl. from the Dutch]. Asheville, North Carolina: Front Street Lemniscaat, cop. 1998. [28] p.
Other ed.: London: Andersen, 1998.
Transl. of: Een gat in mijn emmer. 1998.

Schuman, Hans
Gardening within arm's reach: gardening and experiencing nature for the visually handicapped: how to set up a garden with this in mind / Hans Schuman; [transl. from the Dutch: Graham Broadribb]. Zeist: Bartiméus, 1998. 104 p.
Transl. of: De tuin te lijf. 1998.

Selderhuis, Herman J.
Marriage and divorce in the thought of Martin Bucer / Herman J. Selderhuis; translated by John Vriend and Lyle D. Bierma. Kirksville, Mo: Thomas Jefferson University Press, 1998. (Sixteenth century essays & studies; vol. 48)
Transl. of: Huwelijk en echtscheiding bij Martin Bucer. 1994.
Thesis Theologische Universiteit der Christelijke Gereformeerde Kerken, Apeldoorn

Smit, Jos
Walks through the Jordaan past and present / Jos Smit; [red. Paul Spies; transl. from the Dutch: Michèle Hendricks; route maps: Carto Studio; ill.: Annemieke van Oordde Pee ... et al.]. Amsterdam: Island Publishers/D'ARTS, cop. 1997. 45 p.
Publ. on the occasion of the manifestation: "25 Jaar stadsvernieuwing Jordaan".
Transl. of: Wandelen langs oud en nieuw in de Jordaan. 1997.

Spetter, Jung-Hee
Lily and Trooper's fall / Jung-Hee Spetter; [transl. from the Dutch]. 1st ed. Asheville, NC: Front Street Lemniscaat, [1999]. Transl. of: Natte voeten. 1998.

Spetter, Jung-Hee
Lily and Trooper's spring / Jung-Hee Spetter; [transl. from the Dutch]. 1st ed. Asheville, NC: Front Street Lemniscaat, [1999]. [28] p. Transl. of: Lentekriebels. 1998.

Spetter, Jung-Hee
Lily and Trooper's summer / Jung-Hee Spetter; [transl. from the Dutch]. 1st ed. Asheville, NC: Front Street Lemniscaat, [1999]. Transl. of: Zonnebrand. 1998.

Spetter, Jung-Hee
Lily and Trooper's winter / Jung-Hee Spetter; [transl. from the Dutch]. 1st ed. Asheville, NC: Front Street Lemniscaat, [1999]. Transl. of: Koude neuzen. 1998.

Stam, Dagmar
What is Sinan going to do? / Dagmar Stam; ill. by Dagmar Stam; series ed.: David P. Weikart; [English version from the Dutch by Eric van Deventer]. Ypsilanti, Michigan: High / Scope Press, cop. 1997. 12 p.
Transl. of: Wat gaat Sinan doen?: een voorleesboekje voor het Opstapje programma. 1993.

Stevens, Henrik
The institutional position of seaports: an international comparison / by Henrik Stevens; [transl. from the Dutch by Kathy Owen]. Dordrecht [etc.]: Kluwer Academic Publishers, cop. 1999. XIII, 353 p. (The GeoJournal library; vol. 51)
Transl. of: De institutionele positie van zeehavens: een internationale vergelijking. 1997. Thesis Technische Universiteit Delft.

Strauven, Francis
Aldo van Eyck: the shape of relativity / Francis Strauven; [transl. from the Dutch Victor J. Joseph]. Amsterdam: Architectura & Natura, 1998. 680 p.
Adapt. and rev. transl. of: Aldo van Eyck: relativiteit en verbeelding. 1994.

Teng, Tais (pseud. of: Thijs van Ebbenhorst Tengbergen)
Life on Mars / Tais Teng; [adapt.: E. Zuinigh; transl. from the Dutch:

David Henebury; ill.: Jos Thomassen].
Groningen: WoltersNoordhoff, 1999. 23 p. (My first blackbirds; 1999/1)
Transl. of: De koepelbewoners.

Tepper, Nanne
The happy hunting grounds / Nanne Tepper; transl. from the Dutch by Sam Garrett. London: Flamingo, 1999. 247 p.
Transl. of: De eeuwige jachtvelden. 1995.

This
This time is our time: the messages of the Lady of all Nations: a summary / [Stichting Vrouwe van alle Volkeren; transl. from the Dutch]. 3th ed. Amsterdam: Stichting Vrouwe van alle Volkeren, cop. 1999.
First English ed.: 1997.
Transl. of: Deze tijd is onze tijd: de boodschappen van de Vrouwe van alle Volkeren: een samenvatting. 1997.

Tuyll, Sirdar van ("kloosternaam" van H.P. van Tuyll van Serooskerken)
Prayer, mediatation and silence / talks by Sirdar van Tuyll; [transl. from the Dutch: Anne R. Knulst]. London; The Hague: EastWest Publications Fonds, cop. 1999. 277 p.
Transl. of: Gebed, meditatie, stilte. 1978.

Van der Stock, Jan
Printing images in Antwerp: the introduction of printmaking in a city: fifteenth century to 1585 / Jan Van der Stock; transl. from the Dutch by Beverley Jackson. Rotterdam: Sound & Vision Interactive Rotterdam, 1998. 508 p., [16] p. pl. (Studies in prints and printmaking; vol. 2) Transl. of: Beeld in veelvoud te Antwerpen (15de eeuw - 1585): produktie - controle - consumptie: vijf perspectieven met speciale aandacht voor houtsnede en kopergravure. 1995. Thesis Katholieke Universiteit Leuven, 1995.

Velmans, Edith
Edith's book / Edith Velmans. London [etc.]: Viking, 1998. XIII, 240 p., [16] p. foto's.
Contains: transl. of diaries and letters from the period: February 6, 1939 - December 27, 1946.
Dutch ed.: Het verhaal van Edith. 1997.

Velmans, Edith
Edith's story / Edith Velmans. Thorndike, Me: Thorndike Press, 1999. 410 p.
First English ed.: Edith's book. - London [etc.]: Viking, 1998.
Contains: transl. of diaries and letters from the period: February 6, 1939 - December 27, 1946.
Dutch ed.: Het verhaal van Edith. 1997.
Large print book.

Velthuijs, Max
Frog and a very special day / Max Velthuijs; [transl. from the Dutch]. London: Andersen, cop. 1999.
Transl. of: Kikker en een heel bijzondere dag. 1999.

Velthuijs, Max
Frog and the wide world / Max Velthuijs; [transl. from the Dutch by Janice Thomson]. [1st pr.]. London: Andersen, 1998. [28] p.
Transl. of: Kikker en de horizon. 1998.

Velthuijs, Max
Frog is a hero / Max Velthuijs; [transl. from the Dutch]. [4th pr.]. London: Andersen, [1998]. [33] p.
First English ed.: 1995.
Transl. of: Kikker is een held. 1995.

Verhaeghe, Paul
Does the woman exist?: from Freud's hysteric to Lacan's feminine / Paul Verhaeghe; transl. [from the Dutch] by Marc du Ry. Rev. ed. London: Rebus Press, cop. 1999. 290 p.
First English ed.: 1997.
Other ed.: New York: Other Press, 1999.

Transl. of: Tussen hysterie en vrouw. 1987.

Vincent
Vincent van Gogh / Van Gogh Museum. Amsterdam: Van Gogh Museum; London: Lund Humphries Publishers, 1996. 259 p.
Vol. 1: Drawings: the early years, 1880-1883 / Sjraar van Heugten; [ed.: Louis van Tilborgh ... et al.; transl. from the Dutch and English ed.: Michael Hoyle].

Vincent
Vincent van Gogh / Van Gogh Museum. Amsterdam: Van Gogh Museum; London: Lund Humphries Publishers, 1996. 284 p.
Vol. 2: Nuenen, 1883-1885 / Sjraar van Heugten; [ed.: Louis van Tilborgh ... et al.; transl. from the Dutch and English ed.: Michael Hoyle].

Visitors
The visitors and funshopping guide to Amsterdam 1998: the most fun, the happiest, the handiest / Merel Thomése ...
[et al.; transl. Babel; photogr. Suzanne Dorrestein ... et al.]. 1e pr. Amsterdam: Made on Earth, 1998. 154, [19] p. (Mike's guides)
Transl. of: De bezoekers & funshopping gids van Amsterdam. 1998.

Vugts, H.F.
Wonders of weather / H.F. Vugts and F. Beekman; [transl. from the Dutch]. London: New Holland, 1998. 80 p. (Natural phenomena) Transl. of: Weer fenomenen. 1997. (Natuur in beweging).

Waal, Frans de
Chimpanzee politics: power and sex among apes / Frans de Waal; with photogr. and drawings by the author. Rev. ed. Baltimore [etc.]: The Johns Hopkins University Press, 1998. xv, 235 p.

First English ed.: New York: Harper & Row, 1982.
Transl. of: Chimpanseepolitiek: macht en seks bij mensapen. 1982.

Weren, Wim
Windows on Jesus: methods in gospel exegesis / Wim Weren; [transl. from the Dutch] John Bowden. London: SCM, 1999. 300 p.
Transl. of: Vensters op Jezus: methoden in de uitleg van de evangeliën. 1998.

Westerink, H.
A sign of faithfulness: covenant & baptism / H. Westerink; transl. from the Dutch]. Neerlandia, Alta; Pella, Iowa: Inheritance Publications, 1997.
Transl. of: Een teken van trouw: over onze doop. 1987.

Wetering, Janwillem van de
A glimpse of nothingness: experiences in an American Zen community / Janwillem van de Wetering; [transl. from the Dutch]. 1st ed. New York: St. Martin's Griffin, 1999. 180 p.
Transl. of: Het dagende niets: beschrijving van een eerste bewustwording in Zen. 1974.

Wit, Han F. de
The spiritual path: an introduction to the psychology of the spiritual traditions / by Han F. de Wit; transl. by Henry Jansen & Lucia Hofland-Jansen. Pittsburgh, PA: Duquesne University Press, cop. 1999.
Transl. of: De verborgen bloei: over de psychologische achtergronden van spiritualiteit. 1993. (Interacties).

Wolde, Ellen van
Mr and Mrs Job / Ellen van Wolde; [transl. from the Dutch by John Bowden]. London: SCM Press, 1997. VIII, 152 p.
Transl. of: Meneer en mevrouw Job: Job in gesprek met zijn vrouw, zijn vrienden en God. 1991.

Wolde, Ellen van
Ruth and Naomi / Ellen van
Wolde; [transl. from the
Dutch by John Bowden].
London: SCM Press, 1997.
VIII, 149 p.
Transl. of: Ruth en Noömi,
twee vreemdgangers. 1993.

Women
Women and development:
policy and implementation
in Netherlands development
cooperation 1985-1996 /
Policy and Operations
Evaluation Department,
Ministry of Foreign
Affairs; [ill.: Heidi Lange;
transl. from the Dutch by
All-Round translations; fig.:
Geografiek]. The Hague:
Neda, Netherlands development assistance, 1998. XI,
263 p. Transl. of: Vrouwen
en ontwikkeling: beleid en
uitvoering in de Nederlandse ontwikkelingssamen-
werking 1985-1996, 1998.

Zanden, J.L. van
The economic history of the
Netherlands, 1914-1995:
a small open economy in
the "long" twentieth century / Jan L. van Zanden.
London [etc.]: Routledge,
1998 [i.e. 1997]. XIX, 200 p.
(Contemporary economic
history of Europe series)
Adapt. of: Economische
geschiedenis van Nederland
in de 20e eeuw / J.L. van
Zanden, R.T. Griffiths.
1989. (Aula paperback;
190).

Editor:
Dutch Book in Translation
Koninklijke Bibliotheek
The Hague
The Netherlands

Contributors

Lieven van den Abeele
(1957-)
Art critic
25 Rue des Grands-
Augustins,
75006 Paris, France

Fred G.H. Bachrach (1914-)
Emeritus Professor of
English Literature
(University of Leiden)
55 Cole Park Road,
Twickenham TW1 1HT,
United Kingdom

Saskia Bak (1964-)
Staff member of the Fries
Museum, Leeuwarden
Radesingel 14 B,
9711 EJ Groningen,
The Netherlands

Derek Blyth (1953-)
Staff writer *The Bulletin*
Lange Haagstraat 18,
1050 Brussels, Belgium

Frans Boenders (1942-)
Art critic
Spichtestraat 18,
9771 Nokere, Belgium

Ignace Bossuyt (1947-)
Professor of Musicology
(Catholic University of
Leuven)
Lostraat 40,
3212 Pellenberg, Belgium

Ton J. Broos (1947-)
Lecturer in Dutch
(University of Michigan,
Ann Arbor)
1405 Harbrooke Avenue,
Ann Arbor, MI 48103, USA

Wim Chielens (1960-)
Producer (VRT Radio)
Neerhofstraat A2,
8970 Reningelst, Belgium

Jozef Deleu (1937-)
Chief editor / Managing di-
rector
'Stichting Ons Erfdeel'
Murissonstraat 260,
8930 Rekkem, Belgium

Dirk van Delft
Journalist *NRC Handels-
blad*
Kalvermarkt 5,
2312 LL Leiden,
The Netherlands

Paul Demets (1966-)
Theatre critic / Teacher
Kasteelstraat 56,

9870 Olsene, Belgium

Gita Deneckere (1964-)
Professor of History
(University of Ghent)
Martelaarslaan 327,
9000 Ghent, Belgium

Luc Devoldere (1956-)
Deputy editor
'Stichting Ons Erfdeel'
Murissonstraat 260,
8930 Rekkem, Belgium

Ed van Eeden (1957-)
Writer / Journalist /
Translator
Amsterdamsestraatweg 489,
3553 ED Utrecht,
The Netherlands

Herman Franke (1948-)
Writer
Van Breestraat 149 II,
1071 ZL Amsterdam,
The Netherlands

Jan Franken (1938-)
Literary critic / Teacher
Torenakker 97,
5056 LM Berkel-Enschot,
The Netherlands

Cees van der Geer (1931-)
Art critic *Haagsche Courant*
Vlaardingerdijk 306,
3117 ZV Schiedam,
The Netherlands

Joost de Geest (1942-)
Cultural attaché
(Dexia)
Erf de Keyzer 23,
1652 Alsemberg, Belgium

Roelof van Gelder
Editor *NRC Handelsblad*
Weesperzijde 133 II,
1091 ES Amsterdam,
The Netherlands

Rita Ingram Givens
Writer / Teacher
1396 18th Avenue,
San Francisco, CA 94122,
USA

Peter Greenaway (1942-)
Film director
c / o The Vue,
387B King Street,
London W6 9NH, United
Kingdom

J.P. Guépin (1929-)
Writer

Stadionweg 114',
1077 SV Amsterdam,
The Netherlands

Jaap Harskamp (1946-)
Curator Dutch Section,
British Library
251 Ramsay Road,
London E7 9EX,
United Kingdom

Stefan Hertmans (1951-)
Writer / Lecturer
Dikkemeerweg 91,
1653 Dworp, Belgium

Bert Hogenkamp (1951-)
Head of the Research
Department (Netherlands
Audiovisual Archive) /
Professor of the History of
Film, Radio and Television
in the Netherlands
(University of Utrecht)
Hendrik Jacobszstraat 28,
1075 PE Amsterdam,
The Netherlands

Marc Hooghe (1964-)
FWO Researcher
(Free University of
Brussels)
Breendonkstraat 24,
9000 Ghent, Belgium

Hans Ibelings (1963-)
Architecture critic
Korte Keizerstraat 13 / 3,
1011 GG Amsterdam, The
Netherlands

Jonathan Israel (1946-)
Professor of Dutch History
(University of London)
University College London,
Gower Street,
London WC1E 6 BT,
United Kingdom

*Hanneke Klinkert-
Koopmans (1948-)*
Literary critic / Teacher
Vondelstraat 35,
1901 HT Castricum,
The Netherlands

Yves Knockaert (1954-)
Lecturer in the History and
Aesthetics of Musicology
(Lemmens Institute,
Leuven)
Vaarstraat 51 A / 14,
3000 Leuven, Belgium

John Leighton (1959-)
Director of the Van Gogh

Museum, Amsterdam
P.O. Box 75366,
1070 AJ Amsterdam,
The Netherlands

Ron Lesthaeghe (1945-)
Professor of Demography
(Free University of
Brussels)
Pleinlaan 2,
1050 Brussels, Belgium

Lucas Ligtenberg
Writer
72 Lawton Avenue,
Hartsdale, NY 10530, USA

Yann Lovelock (1939-)
Writer / Translator
80 Doris Road,
Birmingham B11 4NF,
United Kingdom

Erik Martens (1962-)
Film critic
Mellinetplein 1,
2600 Berchem, Belgium

Filip Matthijs (1966-)
Editorial secretary *The Low
Countries*
Murissonstraat 260,
8930 Rekkem, Belgium

*Anne Marie Musschoot
(1944-)*
Professor of
Dutch Literature
(University of Ghent)
Nieuwkolegemlaan 44,
9030 Ghent, Belgium

Jos Nijhof (1952-)
Theatre critic / Teacher
Berkenkade 14,
2351 NB Leiderdorp,
The Netherlands

Ewald Pironet (1961-)
Journalist *Financieel-
Economische Tijd*
Sint-Hubertusdreef 11,
3250 Wakkerzeel-Haacht,
Belgium

Herman Pleij (1943-)
Professor of Medieval
Dutch Literature
(University of Amsterdam)
Nieuwe Hilversumseweg 36,
1406 TG Bussum,
The Netherlands

G.F.H. Raat (1946-)
Lecturer in Modern Dutch
Literature

(University of Amsterdam)
Mariënstein 113,
1852 SJ Heiloo,
The Netherlands

Peter Riemersma (1942-)
Editor *Haagsche Courant*
Prins Hendrikplein 4,
2518 JA The Hague,
The Netherlands

Carla Rosseels (1966-)
Writer
Pol de Montstraat 2,
2020 Antwerp, Belgium

Reinier Salverda (1948-)
Professor of Dutch
Language and Literature
(University of London)
University College London,
Gower Street,
London WC1E 6BT,
United Kingdom

*Sophie de Schaepdrijver
(1961-)*
Visiting Associate
Professor of Modern
European History
(New York University)
c/o Ninovesteenweg 32,
9320 Erembodegem,
Belgium

G. J. Schutte (1940-)
Professor of the History of
Dutch Protestantism
(Free University of
Amsterdam)
Roeltjesweg 10,
1217 TD Hilversum,
The Netherlands

Armand Sliepen (1942-)
Project manager BVN /
Executive secretary
Wereldomroep Nederland
Ereprijs 12,
1273 XK Huizen,
The Netherlands

Johan de Smet (1970-)
Art critic
Zeswegenstraat 46,
8970 Waregem, Belgium

A.L. Sötemann (1920-)
Emeritus Professor of
Modern Dutch Literature
(University of Utrecht)
P. Saenredamstraat 5,
3583 TA Utrecht,
The Netherlands

Marian Unger (1946-)
Head of the Free Design
Department
(Sandberg Institute,
Amsterdam)
Parklaan 29 A,
1405 GN Bussum,
The Netherlands

Jeroen de Valk (1958-)
Journalist
De Vlijtstraat 24,
3816 VT Amersfoort,
The Netherlands

Daniël Vanacker (1951-)
Editor *De Gentenaar*
Bagattenstraat 60,
9000 Ghent, Belgium

Harry van Velthoven (1944-)
Professor at the
'Hogeschool Gent'
Kloosterstraat 1,
1930 Zaventem, Belgium

Greet Verschatse (1958-)
Staff member of Kortrijk
Municipal Museums
Jan Breydellaan 109,
8500 Kortrijk, Belgium

Paul Vincent (1942-)
Translator
3 Lancaster Gardens,
London W13 9JY,
United Kingdom

Translators

Gregory Ball (B)

Wanda Boeke (USA)

James Brockway (NL)

Peter Brodie (UK)

Sheila M. Dale (UK)

Lindsay Edwards (UK)

Roy Edwards [+]

Jane Fenoulhet (UK)

Nancy Forest-Flier (NL)

Tanis Guest (UK)

Lloyd Haft (NL)

Yvette Mead (NL)

Elizabeth Mollison (NL)

*Alison Mouthaan-Gwillim
(B)*

Sonja Prescod (UK)

Julian Ross (UK)

John Rudge (NL)

Paul Vincent (UK)

Diane L. Webb (NL)

Judith Wilkinson (UK)

ADVISOR ON ENGLISH
USAGE

Tanis Guest (UK)

As well as the yearbook *The Low Countries*, the Flemish
Netherlands foundation 'Stichting Ons Erfdeel' publishes
a number of books covering various aspects of the culture
of Flanders and the Netherlands.

O. Vandeputte / P. Vincent /
T. Hermans
*Dutch. The Language of
Twenty Million Dutch and
Flemish People.*
Illustrated; 64 pp.

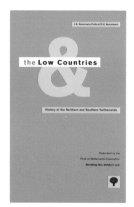

J.A. Kossmann-Putto &
E.H. Kossmann
*The Low Countries.
History of the Northern and
Southern Netherlands.*
Illustrated; 64 pp.

Jaap Goedegebuure &
Anne Marie Musschoot
*Contemporary Fiction of
the Low Countries.*
Illustrated and with
translated extracts from
15 novels; 128 pp.

Hugo Brems &
Ad Zuiderent
*Contemporary Poetry of the
Low Countries.*
With 52 translated poems;
112 pp.

Ludo Bekkers &
Elly Stegeman
*Contemporary Painting of
the Low Countries.*
Illustrated in four colour
printing; 128 pp.

Elly Stegeman &
Marc Ruyters
*Contemporary Sculptors of
the Low Countries.*
Illustrated in four colour
printing; 128 pp.

Hans Ibelings &
Francis Strauven
*Contemporary Architects of
the Low Countries.*
Illustrated in four colour
printing; 128 pp.

Between 1993 and 1999
the first seven issues
of the yearbook *The Low
Countries* were published.